Transformations in Legal Education in the Age of AI

Sam Rany
https://orcid.org/0000-0003-3266-5974
National University of Battambang, Cambodia

IGI Global
Scientific Publishing
Publishing Tomorrow's Research Today

Vice President of Editorial Melissa Wagner
Director of Acquisitions Mikaela Felty
Director of Book Development Jocelynn Hessler
Production Manager Mike Brehm
Cover Design Jose Rosado

Published in the United States of America by
IGI Global Scientific Publishing
701 East Chocolate Avenue
Hershey, PA, 17033, USA
Tel: 717-533-8845 | Fax: 717-533-7115
Website: https://www.igi-global.com E-mail: cust@igi-global.com

Library of Congress Cataloging-in-Publication Data

Names: Rany, Sam, 1982- editor
Title: Transformations in legal education in the age of AI / Sam Rany.
Description: Hershey : IGI Global Scientific Publishing, 2026. | Includes bibliographical references and index. | Summary: "This book aims to critically examine and identify transformative strategies for legal education in response to the growing influence of artificial intelligence, addressing gaps in current scholarship by focusing specifically on practical pedagogical innovation and ethical considerations"-- Provided by publisher.
Identifiers: LCCN 2025020692 | ISBN 9798337334516 hardcover | ISBN 9798337334523 paperback | ISBN 9798337334530 ebook
Subjects: LCSH: Law--Study and teaching | Law--Study and teaching--Automation | Law--Computer-assisted instruction | Technological innovations--Law and legislation | Artificial intelligence--Law and legislation | Law--Study and teaching--Moral and ethical aspects
Classification: LCC K103.L44 T73 2026
LC record available at https://lccn.loc.gov/2025020692

British Cataloguing in Publication Data
A Cataloguing in Publication record for this book is available from the British Library.

Table of Contents

Detailed Table of Contents

Legal practice has existed in some form since the dawn of civilization. It stood for protecting the interests and claims of people against the violators. The existence of lawyers can be traced back to the ancient Greek, Roman, and Indian cultures. The present form of the legal profession has its prototype in the British Empire. Thereafter, it is considered a prestigious social position, which has attracted many to legal education and practice. Toward the end of the 20th century, technological advancements initiated digitalization, promoting Artificial Intelligence (AI) systems to accelerate human flourishing. AI tools enhanced the productivity and efficiency of human activities, forcing them to incorporate AI technologies in almost all fields of social relations, including law. Lawyers must be empowered with AI-supported legal education to utilize AI tools, without disregarding the ethical concerns. From this perspective, this chapter critically examines the ethical considerations of AI integration in legal education and practice.

Integrating artificial intelligence (AI) into legal education in Cambodian higher education presents both transformative opportunities and significant challenges. AI has the potential to enhance legal research, streamline administrative processes, and enrich pedagogical approaches. However, its adoption is hindered by several barriers, including inadequate technological infrastructure, limited faculty preparedness, ethical concerns, and misalignment with existing curricula. This study investigates these challenges while identifying practical pathways for effective AI integration, such as policy reforms, capacity-building initiatives, and strategic collaborations with technology providers. The chapter discusses global best practices and considers Cambodia's distinctive educational context. It offers actionable recommendations to bridge the gap between traditional legal training and AI-driven innovation. The findings aim to guide educators, policymakers, and stakeholders in developing a legal education system that is both future-ready and contextually grounded.

This chapter explores the pedagogical and ethical implications of integrating artificial intelligence (AI) into legal education. Drawing upon the Adaptive Legal Intelligence Framework (ALIF) and the AIDLP model, the authors propose a dialogic and reflective approach that prioritizes critical thinking, ethical awareness, and mostly personalized learning. The chapter examines how AI systems can support or undermine legal reasoning and professional identity, and highlights the need for legal educators to engage with AI not merely as a tool, but as a co-thinker in the learning process. Through theoretical analysis and practical examples, the chapter

legal profession now undergoes a transformation because AI integrates with compliance practices while requiring legal practitioners to develop new skills along with ethical understanding and knowledge acquisition. This section details how AI technology affects compliance structures by using automated tools together with predictive algorithms to track regulations intricate technical barriers to governance. The educational realm requires immediate modification which involves integrating AI competencies alongside data management disciplines and automated system transparency throughout educational programs. The chapter performs a current modifications and anticipated developments to educational methods that help professionals prepare for changing compliance requirements. text proposes both ethical and multidisciplinary training to enable lawyers to understand AI systems properly while evaluating how these technologies affect laws and social justice systems. The development of future professionals today ensures proper ethical and effective compliance standards for an AI-driven era.

Rapid advancements in artificial intelligence have created new opportunities in legal education. Large language models (LLMs) such as ChatGPT, ChatGPT-4o, and DeepSeek V3 are increasingly used by students; however, concerns about their accuracy, reliability, and cultural sensitivity—particularly in areas such as family law—remain significant. This study evaluates these LLMs within the framework of Saudi Arabia's family law, which is rooted in Islamic Shari'a. By assessing their responses to 100 questions across four key categories—foundational knowledge, direct questions, legal advice, and textual analysis—the research offers insights into their accuracy in relation to codified law, culture, and religion. Results show that ChatGPT-4o outperformed the other models, yet all exhibited significant shortcomings in applying statutory provisions and accounting for cultural and religious factors. These findings underscore that while LLMs can enhance legal education, their use must be guided by expert oversight to ensure nuanced understanding within complex legal systems.

This chapter addresses the regulatory challenges and prospects of digital technologies related to human rights and risk control. Laws are sometimes out of date or insufficient to tackle emerging threats such as algorithmic bias, surveillance capitalism, data exploitation and digital poverty in a world where people's everyday activities can be fundamentally shaped by their interactions with digital technologies. The chapter maps the historical development of digital law and regulation, global governance trends and argues for a human rights-based approach based on transparency, accountability and equality. It stresses the importance of such frameworks being inclusive, adaptive and risk-based to safeguard core freedoms while stimulating innovation. From the perspective of digital justice, it advocates for a multi-stakeholder collaboration to ensure that the digital transformation fosters rather than detracts from human dignity and democratic interests.

This chapter critically explores the integration of artificial intelligence (AI) into legal education through the lenses of critical pedagogy, experiential learning theory, and human-computer interaction. It argues that AI must not be treated as a neutral tool for enhancing efficiency but instead aligned with values of justice, equity, and democratic participation. Drawing on Freire's critical pedagogy and Kolb's experiential learning cycle, this chapter examines how AI can support interactive and student-centered legal education through simulations, intelligent tutoring systems, and adaptive assessment. It also highlights risks, such as algorithmic bias, epistemic injustice, and over-reliance on opaque systems developed without educator oversight. This chapter advocates participatory design, algorithmic transparency, and inclusive implementation strategies. It concludes by advancing practical recommendations for

Foreword

With great pleasure, I introduce *Transformations in Legal Education in the Age of AI*, a timely and critical volume edited by Dr. Sam Rany. The legal profession stands at a pivotal crossroads in an era of rapid technological disruption. Artificial Intelligence is no longer a futuristic concept but a present-day reality, reshaping the very foundations of legal theory, practice, and pedagogy. This book arrives at a crucial moment, offering a comprehensive and multidisciplinary examination of how legal education must evolve to prepare the next generation of legal professionals.

The scope of this work is both impressive and necessary. Spanning diverse jurisdictions—from Cambodia and India to Saudi Arabia and beyond, the contributions collectively address a universal challenge: how to harness the power of AI to enhance legal training while safeguarding the core principles of justice, equity, and ethical practice. The chapters move beyond theoretical discourse to provide actionable insights, exploring everything from AI-integrated learning platforms like Moodle and dialogic pedagogical models to the practicalities of AI in legal research, compliance, and judicial decision-making. What makes this collection particularly valuable is its balanced approach; it celebrates the potential of AI to democratize access, personalize learning, and streamline legal services, while confronting head-on the profound ethical dilemmas concerning bias, accountability, and the erosion of human oversight.

This book serves as an essential guide for educators, policymakers, and practitioners. It successfully bridges the gap between technological possibility and pedagogical responsibility, arguing convincingly for developing a "technological jurisprudence." The contributors do not merely advocate for adopting new tools but call for a foundational rethinking of legal education, one that is interdisciplinary, experientially grounded, and critically engaged. The emphasis on cultivating a hybrid skill set in future lawyers, combining digital literacy with ethical reasoning, empathy, and complex problem-solving, is a recurring and vital theme.

Transformations in Legal Education in the Age of AI is more than just an academic compilation; it is a call to action. It compellingly argues that integrating AI into legal education is not a mere technical upgrade but a profound opportunity to build more inclusive, efficient, and just legal systems. Sam Rany and the contributors have produced a work that is both intellectually rigorous and deeply practical. It deserves to be read by anyone committed to the future of law and legal learning.

Seng Bunthoeun
National University of Management, Phnom Penh, Cambodia

Preface

The twenty-first century has witnessed the rapid advancement of Artificial Intelligence (AI), which is reshaping virtually every dimension of human endeavor, including the theory, pedagogy, and practice of law. Traditionally grounded in doctrinal reasoning and textual interpretation, legal education faces a paradigm shift driven by automation, data analytics, and machine intelligence. These developments are not merely technological; they signify a profound epistemological transformation that challenges how law is taught, learned, and practiced. The convergence of AI and legal education compels scholars, practitioners, and institutions to reimagine the formation of legal professionals who are both technologically adept and ethically grounded.

AI-assisted tools can increasingly perform complex legal research, predictive analytics, and document drafting with remarkable accuracy and speed. Their adoption across global legal systems enhances efficiency, accessibility, and consistency but raises critical concerns regarding accountability, transparency, and bias. As legal systems incorporate algorithmic reasoning, the central question emerges: how can legal education cultivate practitioners who harness AI effectively and safeguard the principles of justice, equity, and human dignity? Addressing this question requires comprehensively reconfiguring curricula, pedagogical methodologies, and institutional priorities.

Transformations in Legal Education in the Age of AI seeks to illuminate this transformative moment by bringing together multidisciplinary perspectives that interrogate the intersections of law, technology, and ethics. The contributions in this volume span diverse jurisdictions and contexts from Cambodia and India to Saudi Arabia and beyond reflecting both the universal and localized challenges of integrating AI into legal education. Collectively, the chapters explore the ethical dimensions of AI-assisted legal practice, the design of AI-enhanced pedagogical frameworks, and the policy imperatives necessary for responsible innovation in legal training.

CHAPTER OVERVIEW

Chapter 1: AI Integration in Legal Education and Practice: Ethical Considerations

Legal practice has existed in some form since the dawn of civilization. It stood for protecting the interests and claims of people against the violators. The existence of lawyers can be traced back to the ancient Greek, Roman, and Indian cultures. The present form of the legal profession has its prototype in the British Empire. Thereafter, it is considered a prestigious social position, which has attracted many to legal education and practice. Toward the end of the 20th century, technological advancements initiated digitalization, promoting Artificial Intelligence (AI) systems to accelerate human flourishing. AI tools enhanced the productivity and efficiency of human activities, forcing them to incorporate AI technologies in almost all fields of social relations, including law. Lawyers must be empowered with AI-supported legal education to utilize AI tools, without disregarding the ethical concerns. From this perspective, this chapter critically examines the ethical considerations of AI integration in legal education and practice.

Chapter 2: Integrating AI into Legal Education in Cambodian Higher Education: Barriers and Pathways for Effective Adoption

Integrating artificial intelligence (AI) into legal education in Cambodian higher education presents both transformative opportunities and significant challenges. AI has the potential to enhance legal research, streamline administrative processes, and enrich pedagogical approaches. However, its adoption is hindered by several barriers, including inadequate technological infrastructure, limited faculty preparedness, ethical concerns, and misalignment with existing curricula. This study investigates these challenges while identifying practical pathways for effective AI integration, such as policy reforms, capacity-building initiatives, and strategic collaborations with technology providers. The chapter discusses global best practices and considers Cambodia's distinctive educational context. It offers actionable recommendations to bridge the gap between traditional legal training and AI-driven innovation. The findings aim to guide educators, policymakers, and stakeholders in developing a legal education system that is both future-ready and contextually grounded.

Chapter 3: AI-Supported Dialogic Legal Pedagogy (AIDLP): A Theory of Complementary Intelligence for Legal Education

This chapter explores the pedagogical and ethical implications of integrating artificial intelligence (AI) into legal education. Drawing upon the Adaptive Legal Intelligence Framework (ALIF) and the AIDLP model, the authors propose a dialogic and reflective approach that prioritizes critical thinking, ethical awareness, and mostly personalized learning. The chapter examines how AI systems can support or undermine legal reasoning and professional identity, and highlights the need for legal educators to engage with AI not merely as a tool, but as a co-thinker in the learning process. Through theoretical analysis and practical examples, the chapter offers strategies for incorporating AI in ways that reinforce legal ethics, promote cognitive autonomy, and respect the relational nature of legal knowledge.

Chapter 4: AI-Integrated Moodle: Building Scalable, Interactive E-Learning Environments for Legal Education

The chapter demonstrates how Moodle integrates artificial intelligence to build interactive educational systems which accommodate the needs of contemporary legal educational environments. The article evaluates how AI systems including adaptive quizzes together with natural language processing (NLP) feedback systems as well as predictive analytics and chatbot simulations can advance teaching and learning in law schools. The paper focuses on ethical aspects as well as practical design frameworks together with actual case examples which show better student participation rates and higher levels of satisfaction. AI systems deployed responsibly add value to traditional teaching practices and teach legal professionals about working within the technologically advanced law profession.

Chapter 5: Breaking Barriers by Leveraging AI to Enhance Inclusivity and Access in Legal Education in India

Artificial Intelligence can transform legal education in India by tackling barriers to inclusivity and access, affiliating with the spirit of equitable education under Article 21 A of the Indian Constitution and the National Education Policy 2020. AI tools like adaptive learning platforms, simulated legal clinics, natural language translation, and assistive technologies can aid students with disabilities and address the digital divide pertinent especially in rural areas. These resolutions personalize education, enable applied training, and make education available across dialectal and geographic divides. For students with infirmities, AI offers accommodations like screen readers aligning with the Rights of Persons with Disabilities Act, 2016, though infrastructure and stigma pose challenges. With community engagement, AI can create an all-encompassing legal education system, empowering marginalized students and upholding equity and justice, if infrastructural and societal obstacles are addressed collectively

Chapter 6: Preparing Legal Professionals for New Realities: Integrating AI in Compliance

legal profession now undergoes a transformation because AI integrates with compliance practices while requiring legal practitioners to develop new skills along with ethical understanding and knowledge acquisition. This section details how AI technology affects compliance structures by using automated tools together with predictive algorithms to track regulations intricate technical barriers to governance. The educational realm requires immediate modification which involves integrating AI competencies alongside data management disciplines and automated system transparency throughout educational programs. The chapter performs a current modifications and anticipated developments to educational methods that help professionals prepare for changing compliance requirements. text proposes both ethical and multidisciplinary training to enable lawyers to understand AI systems properly while evaluating how these technologies affect laws and social justice systems. The development of future professionals today ensures proper ethical and effective compliance standards for an AI-driven era.

Chapter 7: Beyond Text: Evaluating Large Language Models Through Law, Culture, and Religion in Saudi Arabia

Rapid advancements in artificial intelligence have created new opportunities in legal education. Large language models (LLMs) such as ChatGPT, ChatGPT-4o, and DeepSeek V3 are increasingly used by students; however, concerns about their accuracy, reliability, and cultural sensitivity—particularly in areas such as family law—remain significant. This study evaluates these LLMs within the framework of Saudi Arabia's family law, which is rooted in Islamic Shari'a. By assessing their responses to 100 questions across four key categories—foundational knowledge, direct questions, legal advice, and textual analysis—the research offers insights into their accuracy in relation to codified law, culture, and religion. Results show that ChatGPT-4o outperformed the other models, yet all exhibited significant shortcomings in applying statutory provisions and accounting for cultural and religious factors. These findings underscore that while LLMs can enhance legal education, their use must be guided by expert oversight to ensure nuanced understanding within complex legal systems.

Chapter 8: Ethical Implications of AI Integration in Legal Practice and Education

This chapter addresses the regulatory challenges and prospects of digital technologies related to human rights and risk control. Laws are sometimes out of date or insufficient to tackle emerging threats such as algorithmic bias, surveillance capitalism, data exploitation and digital poverty in a world where people's everyday activities can be fundamentally shaped by their interactions with digital technologies. The chapter maps the historical development of digital law and regulation, global governance trends and argues for a human rights-based approach based on transparency, accountability and equality. It stresses the importance of such frameworks being inclusive, adaptive and risk-based to safeguard core freedoms while stimulating innovation. From the perspective of digital justice, it advocates for a multi-stakeholder collaboration to ensure that the digital transformation fosters rather than detracts from human dignity and democratic interests.

Chapter 9: Transforming Legal Education in the Age of AI: Towards a Critical and Experiential Pedagogy

This chapter critically explores the integration of artificial intelligence (AI) into legal education through the lenses of critical pedagogy, experiential learning theory, and human-computer interaction. It argues that AI must not be treated as a neutral tool for enhancing efficiency but instead aligned with values of justice, equity, and democratic participation. Drawing on Freire's critical pedagogy and Kolb's experiential learning cycle, this chapter examines how AI can support interactive and student-centered legal education through simulations, intelligent tutoring systems, and adaptive assessment. It also highlights risks, such as algorithmic bias, epistemic injustice, and over-reliance on opaque systems developed without educator oversight. This chapter advocates participatory design, algorithmic transparency, and inclusive implementation strategies. It concludes by advancing practical recommendations for educators, curriculum designers, and policymakers to ensure that AI is deployed in ways that foster experiential, equitable, and justice-oriented legal education.

Chapter 10: Redesigning Legal Pedagogy In Age Of Artificial Intelligence: Insights from Educational Psychology

Legal pedagogy is at a turning point in the 21st century, particularly with the rise of Artificial Intelligence (AI). In professional fields like law, pedagogy is central to shaping the institution of justice. Traditionally grounded in disciplines like political science, sociology, and law, legal pedagogy must now draw from educational psychology to meet evolving needs. As AI enters the law classroom both as content and as a tool it enhances learning while also posing cognitive and ethical challenges. This chapter offers a psychological and technological framework for redesigning legal pedagogy. It emphasizes the distinctive nature of legal education, the critical role of pedagogy in developing legal professionals, and the implications of AI in teaching and learning. The chapter also addresses concerns surrounding AI integration and proposes a model that balances its potential benefits and risks with foundational pedagogical goals.

Chapter 11: AI-Driven Legal Writing and Drafting: Skills for the Next Generation of Lawyers

The integration of artificial intelligence (AI) is transforming legal writing and drafting, redefining the skills required for contemporary legal practice. AI tools, including natural language processing and generative systems, enhance efficiency, accuracy, and consistency in document creation, while also supporting legal research, contract analysis, and quality control. These technological advancements present opportunities for improved client service, greater access to justice, and innovative practice models. However, they also raise challenges related to ethical responsibility, data privacy, algorithmic bias, and regulatory compliance. This chapter examines the evolution of legal drafting, highlights AI applications and their benefits, and identifies the hybrid skill set necessary for the next generation of lawyers, including digital literacy, critical oversight, and ethical judgment. Finally, it explores the implications for legal education, professional training, and future practice, emphasizing a collaborative model where human expertise complements AI capabilities.

This volume emphasizes that integrating AI into legal education is not a matter of mere technological adaptation but of cultivating a reflective, critical, and human-centered pedagogy. It argues for the development of what may be termed technological jurisprudence: a mode of legal thought that embraces the analytical capacities of AI while remaining anchored in the moral and social purposes of law. By engaging with issues such as digital inclusion, algorithmic bias, intellectual property, and the automation of legal reasoning, the book underscores the necessity of balancing innovation with accountability and efficiency with equity.

The chapters presented here chart a path toward re-envisioning legal education as interdisciplinary, globally conscious, and ethically attuned. They demonstrate that when responsibly integrated, AI can enhance the quality of legal education by fostering adaptive learning, improving access to justice, and promoting professional competencies aligned with the demands of the digital age. Yet, as these authors collectively remind us, the promise of AI must be tempered by an enduring commitment to human judgment, empathy, and social responsibility.

As editor, I express my profound gratitude to the contributors for their intellectual rigor and dedication and to the academic institutions and research partners whose continued support makes such scholarship possible. This book represents not only a reflection on the transformation of legal education but also a call to action to build systems of learning that are as just, transparent, and humane as the legal ideals they seek to uphold.

Sam Rany
National University of Battambang, Cambodia

Acknowledgment

The completion of this book, *Transformations in Legal Education in the Age of AI*, has been made possible through the collective efforts, intellectual engagement, and unwavering support of many individuals and institutions. I am sending my deepest appreciation to all who have contributed directly or indirectly to its realization.

First and foremost, I am profoundly grateful to all contributing authors for their exceptional scholarship, commitment, and collaboration. Their diverse perspectives and rigorous analyses have enriched this volume and provided valuable insights into the evolving intersection of artificial intelligence and legal education.

I sincerely thank the National University of Battambang, Cambodia, for its institutional support and encouragement in fostering academic research and interdisciplinary inquiry. My appreciation also goes to the colleagues, peer reviewers, and academic partners who offered constructive feedback and expert guidance throughout the preparation of this work.

Special acknowledgment is due to the educators, researchers, and professionals whose continued dedication to advancing technology-enhanced legal education has inspired this publication. Their contributions exemplify the global spirit of innovation, ethical awareness, and collaborative learning that this book seeks to promote.

Finally, I extend heartfelt thanks to my editorial collaborators and the publishing team at IGI Global for their professionalism, patience, and editorial expertise in guiding this work to completion.

Your efforts are sincerely appreciated by all who have contributed whether through research, review, dialogue, or encouragement. This book is a testament to the shared pursuit of knowledge, innovation, and excellence in legal education during an era of rapid technological transformation.

Chapter 1
AI Integration in Legal Education and Practice:
Ethical Considerations

Jipson Joseph
https://orcid.org/0009-0005-1795-5051
Christ University, India

ABSTRACT

Legal practice has existed in some form since the dawn of civilization. It stood for protecting the interests and claims of people against the violators. The existence of lawyers can be traced back to the ancient Greek, Roman, and Indian cultures. The present form of the legal profession has its prototype in the British Empire. Thereafter, it is considered a prestigious social position, which has attracted many to legal education and practice. Toward the end of the 20th century, technological advancements initiated digitalization, promoting Artificial Intelligence (AI) systems to accelerate human flourishing. AI tools enhanced the productivity and efficiency of human activities, forcing them to incorporate AI technologies in almost all fields of social relations, including law. Lawyers must be empowered with AI-supported legal education to utilize AI tools, without disregarding the ethical concerns. From this perspective, this chapter critically examines the ethical considerations of AI integration in legal education and practice.

1 INTRODUCTION

Artificial Intelligence (AI) is the latest technological advancement regarding computer systems' capacity and efficiency to perform tasks, which were conventionally considered a monopoly of human intelligence (Silviu, 2025). These include learning,

DOI: 10.4018/979-8-3373-3451-6.ch001

reasoning, understanding, problem-solving, and decision-making (Anderson et al., 2018). Since AI systems are equipped with strong and vibrant intelligent options, they have the potential to perform typical human functions at an unimaginable speed and perfection (Qamar et al., 2020). The influence of AI has entered almost all fields of human life, and people cannot even think of life without AI-supported systems. It guides people from day-to-day activities to complex industrial functions and high-potential research (Silviu, 2025). AI has advantages and drawbacks, but its capacity to analyze vast amounts of data and perform herculean tasks makes it a better option in today's society.

The legal profession is conventionally regarded as a skilled profession that can protect the clients' interests and influence judgments. However, the evolution of AI in the legal field shows that it can even outshine humans in the legal process (Alarie et al., 2018). The evolution of ROSS, "the robot lawyer," since 2016 has instigated a paradigm shift in the legal profession (Fornasier, 2021). This necessitates a positive approach that extends the horizon of the legal profession with the incorporation of AI technologies. However, legal education and practice were conventionally not receptive to technological progress (Brooks et al., 2020). The courtrooms of many countries followed conventional methods, unwilling to accept the latest technological changes. Professional behavior, customs, codes of conduct, and other elements of the legal profession have remained unchanged for many decades. To activate changes in the legal profession, emphasis should be placed on legal education and practice to align with the latest technological advancements. Legal education and practice are vital concerns for an ordered society. The latest trends in AI show that it can leverage legal education and practice with its problem-solving and decision-making capacities (Solanki, 2021). Globalization's interconnectedness, the COVID-19 pandemic, and the ever-growing nature of international law have complicated legal education and practice with new concepts, problems, and methods of solutions. Human intelligence finds it challenging to sort out and examine many case laws (precedents) and other related data for the legal field's meaningful functioning. The nature and quantity of litigations have changed as managing the clients, case files, and litigation process has become challenging. These complications can easily be addressed by incorporating AI as a suitable assistant (Ma & Hou, 2021).

AI has a key role in legal education, just as in any other field of education. It can provide students with more possibilities, engagement, and practical knowledge. The use of AI in the legal profession strengthens the capabilities of practitioners and provides options for online case hearings, fast document analysis, risk assessments, and predictions of case results. However, over-reliance on AI and algorithmic opacity may create confusion in the legal field, as legal practitioners may disregard their commitment and accountability toward their clients. This necessitates considering specific ethical considerations like data privacy, bias, justice, and accountability.

Incorporating machine intelligence (even when it mimics human intelligence) is not always trustworthy. Suppose the question of liability and accountability for the mistakes of the application of AI in the legal profession is not suitably addressed. In that case, it may endanger the lives of innocent people and harm the code of conduct of the legal profession. In this perspective, this chapter explores the ethical principles that should guide the process of AI integration in legal education and practice.

In line with the above, the chapter examines the possibilities of incorporating AI in legal education and practice, its benefits and drawbacks, and the recommendations of various Supreme Courts. The chapter also critically analyzes the required ethical concerns for the legal profession's smooth functioning with AI's support. The chapter's objective is to situate the incorporation of AI in the legal profession within a well-designed ethical framework.

2 CONCEPTUAL FRAMEWORK

The evolution of AI has significantly contributed to human progress and societal well-being. The educational and professional sectors widely employ the assistance of AI to enhance the capacity and potential of students, teachers, and professionals. The legal education and legal profession also utilize the advantages of technological progress through the adoption of AI. Many countries have incorporated AI and machine learning to effectively manage cases (Ministry of Law and Justice, 2025). It helps to streamline and optimize their traditional ways of functioning, updating their interaction capacities. They also substitute the professionals in these activities, reducing the expenses and increasing the capacities of the AI systems (Vučić, 2023). However, AI incorporation in the legal profession is recent compared to many other fields. Accordingly, the ethical concerns guiding the AI-supported legal profession are not explicitly spelled out. This section examines the core elements of the chapter: AI, the legal profession, legal education, and professional ethics, to provide a specific understanding of the interconnection between these four.

2.1 Artificial Intelligence

The 1956 Dartmouth conference is widely recognized as the birthplace of AI, wherein John McCarthy first used the term 'Artificial Intelligence.' Many diverse definitions of AI exist, but none are universally accepted (Glasser et al., 2025). But all of them converge on a basic understanding that it points to the machine's predesigned capacity to imitate intelligent human behavior. It points to the performance of complex tasks that generally require human intelligence, like learning, reasoning, and decision-making. They can even make choices and decisions based on the provided data. They imitate human intelligence through data inputs and training or trial and error (Donahue, 2018). The often quoted functions that AI systems imitate are visual perception, speech recognition, translation between languages, and decision-making (Solanki, 2021). AI is "a comprehensive discipline that studies and develops theories, methods, technologies, and application systems for simulating, extending, and expanding humans and other animals and developing various machine intelligence and intelligent machines" (Ma & Hou, 2021, p.44). Machine learning (ML) is an AI application that helps machines learn and improve without direct instruction. It reduces the role of human instructors. It learns from data, adapts with experience, and enriches AI's efforts to create intelligent machines. Compared to other machines that function based on their explicitly programmed capacity, ML learns and improves by using data or experience. Although AI has many benefits, it is not without any drawbacks. AI technologies are not neutral, but double-edged. However, its good vector is much stronger than the evil one (Mittelstadt et al., 2016; Floridi, 2023).

The Turing test, invented in the 1950s, to examine and measure the intelligence of a computer, can be considered the initial step for the evolution of AI. The last decade of the 20th century has seen tremendous progress in the evolution of AI. Machines have been helping humans automate routine tasks for a long time. However, AI helps automate non-routine and knowledge-based work, giving more opportunities (Armour & Sako, 2020). The US' National Artificial Intelligence Initiative Act of 2020 explains the core functions of AI systems: "a) perceive real and virtual environments; b) abstract such perceptions into models through analysis in an automated manner; and c) use model inference to formulate options for information or action" (Sec. 5002(3)). The technological world realized the immense possibilities and opportunities that AI can bring to all sections of society. It combines social and technical features in view of economic development (Ma & Hou, 2021). Such an increased realization resulted in massive investments from public and private actors, contributing to further growth and expansion. Accordingly, the present world underlines the active use of AI in all fields of societal interactions. It is highly beneficial to economic progress, but how far it aligns with ethical and legal concerns is not yet fully realized. Besides, clubbing AI with law faces limitations due to a significant lack of teachers who are experts in both law and AI technologies. The specialists of AI fail to apply it within the framework of law, and the specialists of law fail to explain the potential possibilities, challenges, risks, and ethical concerns about the application of AI in law (Ma & Hou, 2021). This necessitates the presence of interdisciplinary teachers who can ensure a systematic and ethical use of AI in legal education and the legal profession.

2.2 Legal Profession

The legal profession is understood based on an individual's expertise in law and its implications. The traces of this prestigious profession could be seen in the ancient Greek, Roman, and Indian cultures. Kings, priests, and wisemen were the holders of judicial powers in most of these ancient cultures. In Greek and Roman histories, law experts advised ordinary people in law matters, accepting a fee (Glendon & Alford, 2025). However, in its modern systematic nature, the legal profession evolved from the 11th or 12th century as a separate field governing societal interactions. The modern-day understanding of the legal profession has its prototype in the British Empire, consisting of two groups: serjeants and attorneys. The serjeants were the elites of the profession, who were only allowed to speak directly to the judges. They were not representatives of the clients but part of the court, whereas attorneys represented the clients (Brand, 1992). The serjeants represented and served the whole people of the king. In the modern-day understanding, we could say that they were advocates of the state or public prosecutors.

Throughout history, the legal profession has been respected as a noble profession. Lawyers were given an ambiguous social position. The medieval European history of crediting high status to lawyers continued in the coming centuries. At the same time, the early communist leaders in Russia and China had a negative perception of the legal profession, as they imagined that law and lawyers were instruments of the ruling class, causing problems to the meaningful lives of other sections of society. From the 19th century onwards, most countries started to control the legal profession by statutory provisions to ensure an effective legal service to the community. These provisions included the provisions that admission to practice automatically makes the lawyer a member of an association; these associations are given substantial powers concerning the education, admission to practice, and professional discipline, with an overriding effect of the decisions of the government and/or the courts; and the practice of law by those who are not admitted to the profession. Most Bar Associations evolved in this stage of history (Glendon & Alford, 2025). In the Imperial colonies, like India, lawyers were also the main protagonists of the independence movements (Both Gandhi and Nehru were lawyers by profession). Accordingly, they used their legal knowledge to transform society.

Until the 2008 economic recession, lawyers in most countries preferred hourly billing. The recession forced clients to demand cost-effective representation. Legal professionals tackled this situation by increasingly incorporating technological advancements that reduced human labor. It primarily helps them with the e-discovery of essential documents advantageous to the litigation process (Alarie et al., 2018). Incorporating AI in the legal profession allows lawyers to do the same amount of work with less time. This helps them concentrate on other areas of work, increasing their productivity. Since they can perform several tasks in less time, taking support from the AI tools, they are not worried about working in small firms. With the support of AI, they can augment their areas of expertise (Yoon, 2016). Legal professionals slowly realized they could become more efficient and effective by adopting technological advancements like AI and ML.

The legal profession is one of the largest sub-sectors of the professional services sector in many countries. The British legal profession has almost 13% of the GVA from the professional services sector (Brooks et al., 2020). However, many studies point to the widespread career dissatisfaction among lawyers (Shiltz, 1999; Sheldon & Krieger, 2004). The increased engagement of AI tools for generating legal documents, verifying legal validity, and predicting legal decisions complicates the routine activities of the courts, which challenge the core of the legal framework, causing severe adversities to people. Although these techniques can reduce costs and save time, they do not increase satisfaction (Vučić, 2023). One of the basic disadvantages of the legal profession is the lack of technological awareness. Since technological updates, like AI, were not part of legal teaching in most law schools, they do not have the proficiency to incorporate AI tools in the legal profession (Ma & Hou, 2021). Their horizon is limited due to a lack of technical know-how. Such a scenario demands more positivity from policymakers and law schools to revise their curriculum to prioritize the ethical use of AI for enhancing the legal field in the future with professionals who are qualified both in law and AI technologies. The quality and technological excellence of the legal profession depend on the legal education they receive. Many countries' legal education has not been updated to include the advancements of AI and ML, which restricts legal professionals from taking advantage of those advancements. This necessitates a refined and updated legal education system.

2.3 Legal Education

Legal education started in the medieval period to prepare students for the legal profession. During the 18th and 19th centuries, it began to evolve as a separate discipline in the universities. Most law schools try to trade off between theory and practice, but this results in the overemphasis of one side without due concern for the other. Both theoretical knowledge and practical experience are essential for substantially engaging in the legal profession. Legal education is primarily oriented to familiarize students with legal concepts and institutions and make them capable of legal reasoning. It aims to impart a specific understanding of law in the socio-economic, political, and scientific context. It also addresses the changing scenario of technological progress, which expands the scope of legal applications and the opportunities of legal professionals (Glendon & Alford, 2025a).

A well-designed legal education is essential to promote well-qualified legal professionals who are experts in law and qualified in the latest technological skills. Society cannot think of lawyers who practice without a basic awareness of technological advancements, such as AI. They should have a progressive social vision and a positive mental state to achieve these objectives. The legal profession should echo their psychological well-being and social commitment. However, the complicated issues in the legal profession show that their legal education is the source of many complexities. Scholars sort out several negative aspects of legal education that adversely affect realizing a meaningful legal profession, such as stress, excessive workloads, status-seeking placement competitions, loss of connections with values and principles, isolating and intimidating teaching practices, and suppression of moral reasoning (Sheldon & Krieger, 2004). When such complexities increase, it affects the productivity and performance of lawyers. Legal education should be legally grounded, ethically sound, and oriented toward personal well-being and societal welfare. The prime objective of legal education should be transformative: by transforming the students, it should aim to change the legal profession and society. In this transformative process, the legal professional ethics play a key role.

2.4 Professional Ethics

Regardless of the differences in profession, there is a fundamental requirement for a code of conduct, which is essential for the smooth functioning of the profession. Each profession evolved by incorporating some ethical principles and values from the dawn of civilization. The ancient cultures suggested specific moral values for teachers and doctors, affirming the importance of professional ethics. Realizing the importance of a code of conduct, every profession in the present era demands the practice of specific moral values and principles that promote its dignity. The same applies to the legal profession as well. Professional ethics revolves around a question: does "being able to do something" point to "being allowed to do it" (Nurata, 2022). All that we are capable of doing may not be ethically and legally permissible. Professional ethics of the legal profession insist that lawyers' behavior patterns reflect ethical values.

From the English legal system period, a specific code of conduct for the legal profession also evolved. It does not explicitly speak about the conduct of the serjeants in or outside the court. However, it precisely deals with how an attorney should behave. It addressed ethical issues like conflict of interest, overcharging, and cheating the clients (Rose, 1998). Since the attorneys were the clients' representatives in the court, it was necessary to regulate their professional conduct to protect the clients' interests and rights. The legal professional ethics were designed to safeguard the clients' valid claims against the attorneys' money-oriented and incompetent behaviors. The legal professional ethics also demand discipline in the profession. Until the last quarter of the 20th century, nobody thought of the need for a separate course on professional ethics in legal schools. Since the Clark report of 1970 described lawyer discipline as scandalous and identified 36 problems, some legal schools started to teach professional ethics as an optional subject. There were many disciplinary rules within the legal profession. However, most of these courses and disciplinary rules failed to establish an interconnection between the legal profession and ethics (Hazard Jr., 1998).

Advancements in technology have also caused changes in the legal profession. Professional ethics must be able to address the changed dynamics of the profession. The professional ethical behavior of lawyers has become a crucial concern during this techno-legal intricacy (Stagg-Taylor, 2011). The objective of professional ethics is to give guidelines on general morality but to affirm the relevance of a disciplined professional practice. It does not speak the truth and the good in general. It aims to underline what is right or wrong, permissible or non-permissible in the legal profession. The appropriateness, morality, and fairness are restricted to the four walls of the legal profession. This means that what is appropriate in the legal profession may not be suitable for the medical or teaching profession (Nurata, 2022).

3 LITERATURE REVIEW

Bostrom (2017) and Bostrom and Yudkowsky (2018) have systematically studied the ethical implications of AI with particular reference to safety and security. Alarie et al. (2018) have made a brilliant study on the impact of AI on legal practice. They argue that the legal field cannot stand aside from the influence of technology. The growing impact of technology presents both opportunities and challenges to the field of law. It can lead to greater legal transparency, efficient dispute resolution, and easy access to justice. Armour & Sako (2020) explore the impact of AI-enabled business models on traditional law firms. They state that the effects can be positive or negative. They underline that including AI tools will facilitate the efforts of law firms. However, it also needs to incorporate specific ethical concerns, which they primarily examine from the perspective of law firms. Brooks et al. (2020) make a thorough analysis, using qualitative methodology's interview method, on the pressures and challenges brought in by incorporating AI in the British legal system. They say that if AI is used to enhance the expertise and efficiency of legal practitioners, it is laudable. However, they do not delve into the ethical concerns of AI incorporation in the legal sector. Ma and Hou (2021) discuss the various challenges and responses to the application of AI in legal education. They state that AI has brought three perspective changes in legal education: introducing new technologies, establishing new models, and shaping new paradigms. Although these three changes are interrelated, they echo the progressive incorporation of AI in the legal field. However, the scope of this interconnected relationship between AI and law is not fully established. Many think that the challenges outweigh the advantages of incorporating AI in law. From this perspective, the authors examined the challenges and proposed specific crucial responses, affirming the need to incorporate AI in the legal field.

Nurata (2022) critically examines the significance of professional ethics in the legal field. The author analyzes the evolution of professional ethics and its core principles about the legal profession. The author also conducted a field study to understand the perceptions and expectations of lawyers regarding professional ethics. Although technological advancements are referred to, the article does not explicitly focus on the ethical concerns of the AI-supported legal profession. Vučić (2023) critically analyzes the changes in the legal profession in terms of the digital era advancements of AI. The author examines how AI has changed legal education and practice. Although AI has brought significant changes in the legal field, it also raises ethical concerns, like privacy, accountability, and transparency, demanding new perspectives in legal education and practice. Sadiku et al. (2025) state that though lawyers had a traditional resistance to technology, they are incorporating AI tools significantly into their profession to enhance compliance, boost efficiency, and improve client service and decision-making. Emejuo et al. (2025) affirm that AI is making crucial changes in the legal sector. With the support of AI technologies, legal services have become more accurate, efficient, and easily accessible. However, it has some drawbacks, like bias, lack of transparency, and misuse or abuse. Hence, the authors demand a fair and responsible functioning of the system.

The literature mentioned above affirms that some studies have focused on the ethical concerns of incorporating AI in the legal field. However, most studies focus on the benefits of incorporating AI in the legal profession. Except for a few studies, most have not given due space to discuss the required ethical principles that should guide the AI-supported legal profession.

4 SIGNIFICANCE OF THE STUDY

The application of AI in the legal field is praiseworthy, as it gives ample opportunities to law-making and law enforcement agencies. As defenders of law and justice, the judiciary and legal professionals are also progressively utilizing the possible incorporation of AI. It allows for minimizing human error, increasing efficiency, and strengthening decision-making (Glasser et al., 2025). However, when attempts are made to incorporate the amplified opportunities of AI into the legal profession, specific care should be given to ensure that it complies with lawyers' ethical and professional responsibilities. Some bar associations, such as the ABA (American Bar Association), have already stated that the model rules of ethical conduct for lawyers should adapt to the realities of modern law practice (Veasey, 2002). It affirms that on the one hand, there is a progressive demand to align with technological advancements, and on the other hand, there is an ongoing mandate that it should align with the values and principles of professional ethics. If established ethical standards exist that evolved along with technological progress, applying them to maintain an atmosphere of professional excellence without disregarding values and principles would have been easy. Precisely clarifying the nature and scope of AI adoption is essential to examine whether the existing ethical principles could address this paradigm shift. Since the application of AI into the legal profession enlarges its ambit, the field of lawyers' professional ethics should also rise to address the new complexities, challenges, and confusions in the profession. For instance, lawyers are supposed to ensure a competent representation of their clients. Instead, if they engage some AI systems, it would be a violation of trust and transparency (Yamane, 2020).

The importance and advantages of AI incorporation in the legal field have been proven positively. However, they are not without drawbacks, especially concerning the ethical dimensions like data privacy, accountability, bias, and justice. The AI and ML algorithms can provide inaccurate or biased results, fail to protect the personal information of clients and case details, challenge the safety of confidential information, and violate the standards of lawyers' professional ethics (Glasser et al., 2025). This requires that even when lawyers employ AI tools and ML algorithms, they should closely monitor them to ensure that they do not cause them to violate ethical principles and standards of the profession. Although the ethics of AI in general have received much attention across the globe (e.g., Holmes et al., 2022), it has not yet received adequate attention in the legal field. Although there are some studies, as we examined in the literature review section, the studies addressing the ethical concerns of legal education and legal practice are scarce. Besides, the evolving nature of AI tools demands more erudite attention to the essential moral values that should guide the AI-supported legal field.

5 AI AND LEGAL PROFESSION: AN ANALYSIS

The globe is making significant changes in its approaches, perspectives, and ways of interaction due to the increased adoption of AI, ML, and blockchain technologies. Each profession tries to adapt to the latest technological advancements, realizing these changes can bring more efficiency, perfection, and profit/growth. Incorporation of AI in various sectors, such as human resource management (Qamar et al., 2021), customer relationship management (Roba & Maric, 2023), supply chain management (Min, 2010), industrial management (Silviu, 2025), public sector management (Wirtz et al., 2018), and healthcare (Al Kuwaiti, 2023) is already well-established and well-studied. Although not so efficiently explored, the interaction between AI and the legal profession is evolving slowly. Some changes have already occurred, and the legal field is progressing toward a heavily technology-influenced field. Some areas traditionally occupied by lawyers are already being replaced by AI systems, like online lawsuit platforms (Yoon, 2016). Due to the highly competitive spirit in the profession, many lawyers and law firms are devising strategies for the increased adoption of AI (Armour & Sako, 2020). Compared to many other fields, the incorporation of AI in the legal field was modest. It is regarded as a unique sector that consistently disregards the value of technology utilization due to its overemphasis on traditional practice and risk aversion. However, the wider utilization of AI by almost all sectors forced the legal profession to take advantage of the benefits of technological progress. Besides, since AI-driven technologies have significantly influenced the whole business environment across the sectors, the legal profession is forced to update with technological changes (Brooks et al., 2020).

AI is not intended to substitute legal practitioners but to assist them in making their work easier and effective (Yamane, 2020). AI can augment the capacity of lawyers to make the initial drafting, handle their caseloads, and reduce their workload by assisting in managing administrative duties, like scheduling meetings and court appearances, handling monetary transactions, and transmitting written communications to the clients and opposing counsel. Identifying and analyzing associated case laws was a herculean task for the attorneys. The most important advantage of the AI system is that it reduces the amount of work needed for a thorough analysis of the existing laws and case laws. Several AI companies, like Spellbook, started to assist in drafting and reviewing legal documents to reduce the possibility of mistakes and errors (Glasser et al., 2025). "The development of legal big data analysis and the emergence of legal robots" have significantly changed the legal framework, providing vast possibilities for automation and machine intelligence in legislative, executive, and judicial functions to empower and enhance the justice delivery system (Ma & Hou, 2021).

The Supreme Court of India created a software called SUVAS (Supreme Court Vidhik Anuvaad Software) in 2019 to translate its judgments into ten regional languages to facilitate legal practitioners, students, and ordinary people. Since the adopted AI-powered software is proficient in language and translation, it becomes easy to convert the translation quickly (Ministry of Law and Justice, 2023). It helps to make the judicial proceedings simple and accessible to the public. Since the AI system can translate any number of documents without much time compared to human translators, it reduces the workload of the Supreme Court and guarantees speedy justice to the people through a clear understanding of the judgments and orders in their vernacular language.

Many legal research platforms have initiated people-centered programs to enhance their legal awareness by answering their queries concerning legal doubts and apprehensions. Some platforms also critically examine the facts of a case to provide the potential claims and defenses about the litigation matter (Glasser et al., 2025). It helps ordinary people to get free legal advice and access to justice without approaching lawyers. Since AI can reduce the percentage of human capital in legal firms, it can also effectively reduce legal expenses, which were unaffordable for many ordinary people (Herrington, 2019). Making a comparison between the evolution of the Justinian Code and the AI incorporation into law, Vučić (2023) states that the Code was a massive work that provided unimaginable information to students, teachers, and practitioners of law; similarly, AI empowers those who are involved in the legal field with large amount of data and its analysis. Such an analysis helps them to realize the new legal trends and risks. Just like the Code, AI also improves the fields of legal education with more sophisticated academic and professional expertise and the automation of daily legal tasks. While the Code presented specific challenges concerning information overload due to its broader scope, AI poses particular challenges regarding the consequences of its incorporation into the legal field that have detrimental effects on ethical values and principles.

5.1 AI in Legal Education

The impact of AI is also visible in the field of education (Forcier, 2016). Generative AI has the potential to generate practical tools that enhance the students' active involvement in education (Wu et al., 2023). Effective teaching methods, like situational teaching, can be made more useful through generative AI tools (Shi et al., 2023). The field of legal education should also grow along with technological advancements to incorporate the advantages of AI and ML technologies for solving complex problems, increasing efficiency, and improving accessibility. It strengthens them with the capacity for critical thinking and problem-solving skills (Vučić, 2023). When other fields of education increasingly incorporate AI tools into their curriculum to help students adapt to the changed circumstances, legal education cannot disregard its importance. They should be able to understand how AI influences law and society, what possible benefits and challenges can arise due to the application of AI in law, and how AI can be better utilized to amplify the performance level of lawyers. This necessitates that legal schools offer vibrant and specialized courses on legal innovation and technological updates, covering areas like AI, ML, natural language processing, and data analytics. They should also use the advantage of collaborative learning, taking support from legal tech companies or other organizations (Susskind & Susskind, 2015). Besides, continuous discussion and systematic study are required on the possible ethical implications of using AI tools in the legal field.

Law students should be able to learn the required skills essential for working in their profession, alongside technological improvements. Legal education should also incorporate into its curriculum the possible implications of autonomous AI systems on society, particularly concerning tort liability and criminal guilt. If an autonomous driverless car or pilotless aircraft causes an accident and kills someone, who will be liable? (Donahue, 2018). The field of legal application and reasoning is expanding along with the broader application of AI and ML algorithms. Besides understanding the benefits and challenges of using AI in the legal profession, they should also be taught the ethical values involved in this advanced use of AI in law. The already established intellectual property law examines their connection and demands an ethical framework concerning the use and promotion of intellectual properties (Vučić, 2023). However, AI has become a crucial concern in all vital areas of the discipline of law, such as public law, constitutional law, company law, center-state relations, local self-government, insurance law, e-commerce law, etc. Accordingly, law students should learn and understand the vast possibilities of AI applications in different sections of law rather than just being confined to intellectual property law. A systematic training of AI technologies is crucial for law students, as they are future legal practitioners who are supposed to represent their clients meaningfully and most effectively. They must be empowered with the ability of legal thinking and legal application to analyze and use the prospects of AI technology to adapt to the demands of the digital era (Ma & Hou, 2021). A thorough change in the curriculum to adjust to the changing landscape is essential for legal education. Otherwise, future law professionals will become incompetent in addressing the changes.

5.2 AI in Legal Practice

AI programs can increase the legal practitioners' productivity, efficiency, and accuracy. It helps lawyers review documents, perform legal research, analyze contracts, and predict case outcomes (Donahue, 2018). For instance, the search for related case laws and precedents has become easy with the support of AI algorithms. AI systems are more capable of doing this as their data analysis capacity is stronger than human intelligence. For instance, in a contract review contest between twenty experienced corporate lawyers and AI programs, it was affirmed that while the AI programs spotted the risks in the contract with a 94% accuracy level within 26 seconds, the experienced lawyers took almost 92 minutes to achieve an accuracy level of 85% (Herrington, 2019). AI systems can go through, analyze, and sort out relevant data from a large quantity of data within a fraction of the time. For the same activity, humans might require weeks. This shows that incorporating AI systems can reduce the lawyers' workload. The ABA (2009, Rule 1.1) mandates that lawyers should "maintain the requisite knowledge and skill, a lawyer should keep abreast of changes in the law and its practice, including the benefits and risks associated with relevant technology." It thus encourages lawyers to engage in continuous education and study, and get accustomed to the latest technological advancements (Yamane, 2020). The support of AI programs for legal practitioners is laudable, but it also has some drawbacks. Suppose we use Grammarly software to correct language and grammar. We cannot simply accept all the corrections it provides. Human authors should verify whether the provided correction suits the context. In the same manner, the other AI tools also have similar issues. They are prone to mistakes for many reasons. This shows that lawyers cannot wholly rely on AI tools without utilizing their intelligence and competence to ensure effective justice.

Critics of using AI in professional fields argue that it can adversely affect people's employment opportunities. It is intended to automate tasks, not reduce jobs (Armour & Sako, 2020). However, when AI systems efficiently do tasks, they can also affect job opportunities. It creates a complicated situation, which needs to be addressed prudently. The role of humans remains unchanged, as they still make most decisions. At the same time, it reduced the magnitude of the jobs that humans performed in a particular sector. The decreased amount of work in an industry due to the adoption of AI leads to less demand for human capital. Specific digital platforms provide people with legal advice and support. Accordingly, people may not be interested in approaching lawyers for simple legal matters. Even when AI tools have great possibilities to reduce the pressure and increase the efficiency of lawyers, they also adversely affect their job security. This may not be an issue for large law firms mainly dealing with multinational companies, institutions, and wealthy people. However, it troubles the smooth functioning of small law firms and individual practitioners.

5.3 International Law Perspective

The UN (n.d.) encourages states to utilize all available opportunities to ensure increased access to justice for all sections of society. Access to justice is a foundational principle of the Rule of Law. Without access to justice, no person can make their voice heard, exercise rights, challenge societal discrimination, or hold the decision-makers accountable for the wrong policies and decisions. Access to justice has become more efficient with the possibility of online case filing, virtual hearings, online verification of the posting date, interim orders, or final judgments of the cases. Since affordability is the main issue that most people face concerning access to justice, international institutions and national governments imagine that incorporating technological advancements like AI can reduce the expenses in the legal profession. The availability of many legal self-help platforms is a positive mechanism that enhances the possibilities for access to justice (Yamane, 2020).

AI tools are increasingly used in Alternative Dispute Resolution (ADR) and Online Dispute Resolution (ODR) in the International legal system. International adjudication will become more meaningful with the incorporation of AI (Dimitropoulos, 2023). It can be utilized to monitor international treaties and agreements concerning arms control, cybersecurity, environmental protection, and war against terrorism (Maas, 2019). AI can leverage the protection and promotion of international customs, which are an essential component of international law. Language barrier is a complicated issue in international law. The international treaties use English, and the translation from English to national languages sometimes causes confusion due to mistranslation. The AI tools can solve this complication through their powerful translation tools. AI can leverage and strengthen the international efforts toward human rights protection. For instance, the application JustBot has proven successful in providing individuals with opportunities to approach the European Court of Human Rights to avoid customary summary rejection (Dimitropoulos, 2023).

5.4 National Judicial Systems

Several countries have amplified their attempts for AI integration to ensure a meaningful justice delivery system. We do not make a detailed study of all those countries, but select two examples: the USA and India. The USA is chosen since it has the world's oldest written constitution, which is still in use. India is the largest democratic country in the world and one of the strongest representatives of the emerging economies.

USA

The American judicial system is supposed to uphold judicial integrity, impartiality, conscientiousness, and a sense of justice in its procedures and judgments. However, studies reveal that the blacks are still given longer sentences than whites. Such a biased approach forces the general public and lawmakers to believe that AI systems are less biased than humans (Kim, 2024). They feel a positive and more humane approach can be expected from AI tools rather than humans. The US has introduced AI at every step of client interaction. Both courtrooms and lawyers' offices are increasingly utilizing the advantages of AI for efficiency and productivity. A study conducted in Virginia claims that AI tools have helped or informed judges about the offenders' chances of re-offending in more than 50,000 convictions. It also states that AI tools will effectively reduce gender and racial discrimination in judgments. The New York State Parole Board uses an AI tool, COMPAS Risk and Needs Assessment, to support the parole decisions (Brunette, 2024). It shows that AI tools are widely employed in various areas of the legal system.

India

The Supreme Court of India, with the support of the Ministry of Electronics and Information Technology and various IITs (Indian Institute of Technology), attempts to incorporate both AI and ML technologies into the judicial system. The widespread attempts started during the COVID-19 pandemic. The virtual court proceedings during that time highly depended on the system's intelligence. The already examined SUVAS was a pioneer of AI adoption attempts. Although it began with translating judicial orders and judgments into nine regional languages, the system currently translates them into 18 languages. The AI and ML tools are used to transcribe oral arguments in the constitutional bench matters, which can be accessed from the official website of the Supreme Court. AI and ML tools are also employed to identify defects in electronic filing systems. It works with IIT Madras to design an integrated case management and information system (ICMIS) to strengthen the electronic filing module and the case management software. It has also developed an intelligent system called SUPACE (Supreme Court Portal Assistance in Court Efficiency) to support the judges in examining and analyzing the precedents and managing the cases effectively. However, the Supreme Court has not yet used AI support in decision-making (Ministry of Law and Justice, 2025).

6 ETHICAL CONCERNS

The technological advancements are advantageous to society in many ways. At the same time, it also raises specific ethical concerns. Complex AI systems and ML algorithms adversely affect the realization of citizens' fundamental rights (Kearns & Roth, 2020). The European Commission's Ethics Guidelines for Trustworthy AI (2019) demand that AI technologies and systems adhere to ethical principles, like accountability, transparency, and fairness, to make them more human-centric and ensure the common good. Besides, the General Data Protection Regulation (GDPR) insists on the importance of data protection for maintaining people's confidence and trust in AI systems. Although international and national legal systems use AI, many doubt its accuracy and the ability to understand and deal with complicated cases (Dimitropoulos, 2023). Society must not disregard technological advancements, like AI and ML, if there are drawbacks, but should situate them within an ethical horizon that ensures a morally right behavior pattern from such AI tools.

6.1 Data Privacy

The increased use of AI systems can cause data breaches, leading to the disclosure of confidential client information. Violation of data privacy complicates and challenges the claims of lawyer-client communication's confidentiality. Although some Bar Councils, like the ABA, have specifically instructed lawyers to obtain informed consent from the clients about the use of AI, many of the clients may not be fully aware of the complexities and issues involved in the potential data breach (Glasser et al., 2025). The AI technologies have brought new problems and challenges, like data privacy and cybersecurity, which lawyers must understand and be trained in (Vučić, 2023). Lawyers may know how AI should be used to increase efficiency and productivity. However, they may not know the AI tools' inner mechanisms and design. They may also not know how to design an AI tool for their legal firm. Accordingly, they may utilize the possibility of outsourcing. Sometimes, the clients' personal information can end up in the hands of the outsourcing service agencies. In certain rare cases, it can even happen that the same outsourcing agency may be providing technical support to both the petitioner's and defendant's law firms. Both the vendor of the AI systems and the outsourcing service agents should ensure confidentiality in their transactions (Jacobowitz, 2018). Otherwise, it can adversely affect the clients' privacy and security rights. Jacobowitz (2018) cautions lawyers that their continuous interactions with Apple's Siri, Google Assistant, Amazon's Alexa, and Samsung's Bixby can cause adverse insecurities to people's right to privacy. These may breach the system's security and cause confidential information to leak into the public domain. Therefore, using a single device for personal and professional assignments may cause privacy violations, constant worries, and professional insecurities. Besides, the increased use of AI systems can also cause data leakage. For instance, when the SUVAS system translates the Supreme Court of India's judgments to 18 regional languages, if proper care is not taken, it can cause data leakage and translation errors, leading to confusion and injustice.

6.2 Operational Risks

AI and ML are employed in various areas of law. Just like human interactions can result from bias and prejudice, AI tools can also cause a biased approach toward certain sections of people. They originate from the system's operational risks. For instance, Insurance law significantly employs AI mechanisms to examine an individual's credit score or zip code to determine insurance premiums. The insurance premiums are thus not equally applied but are based on some biased calculations. Most insurance companies use chatbots to interact with insured persons when they raise their insurance claims. Without a human reviewer, the chatbot may reject a valid claim based on the available data, causing enormous issues to the client. The same biased approach occurs in predictive analytics concerning certain medical conditions (Vučić, 2023).

Since AI technologies can reduce the time and workload of lawyers, there is a tendency to overdependence. Many legal practitioners think that AI and ML can do almost all activities. They can assist lawyers but cannot replace them. The technologies cannot replace lawyers' critical thinking and judicial assessment skills. Most notably, AI or ML algorithms are not infallible. They are prone to mistakes depending on the false data or the system's failure. Depending heavily on machine intelligence can lead to bias and the resulting insecurities (Vučić, 2023).

6.3 Accountability

Accountability demands commitment to the profession and responsibility to the clients. Lawyers should have a basic understanding of AI and ML and try to use them to facilitate the profession's demands. However, they should not allow the AI system to replace the lawyer's role, as they are responsible for showing their competence to respond to the clients' trust (Yamane, 2020). The prominent inclusion of AI technologies has increased the possibilities of digital discovery and e-document tracking, simplifying legal practitioners' tasks and judicial proceedings (Vučić, 2023). However, a lawyer cannot allow an AI system "to research, write, and file a pleading without the lawyer's review of the research and the pleading" (Jacobowitz, 2018, p. 420). The system might be efficient but the lawyer cannot wholly depend on the system, disregarding his/her accountability to the clients. Lawyers cannot take the excuse for the clients' insecurity because of the system's mistakes or drawbacks. Suppose the system is prone to making mistakes due to technical failures or data issues. In that case, lawyers should give more attention to ensure increased efficiency, as they are accountable to their clients. No legal professional can mindlessly rely on the legal work of an AI tool or a chatbot.

6.4 Justice

Many people affirm that AI helps people to be more productive, but others claim that it may challenge people's productivity and the use of free will (Anderson et al., 2018). Since AI tools mimic many human activities, ordinary people are forced to restrict their use of intelligence, which challenges their productivity. For instance, people used to remember many phone numbers, but with the evolution of mobile phones and innovative technologies, they rarely use their intelligence and memory to recollect and calculate numbers. The problem with the overdependency on AI tools is the failure of the intelligent application of people's free will. An act becomes a human act only when free will is engaged. The rightness or wrongness of an individual's action depends on evaluating their use of free will. When AI tools that are supposed to assist humans become highly influential in changing and dictating one's routine activities, it finally leads to 'AI colonization,' which may also challenge the justice delivery system. Justice demands fairness. Accordingly, incorporating AI in the legal profession should lead to fair decision-making advantageous to the people at large (Selbst et al., 2019).

Technologies like AI and ML benefit large law firms more than individual lawyers. Since large firms are involved in large-scale transactional or litigation matters, using AI tools helps them enhance their productivity. However, it has a detrimental effect on individual lawyers and small law firms, as they cannot provide adequate competence in the market. Furthermore, the increased availability and use of AI technologies in the legal field may challenge their work as the AI tools can easily perform some of their tasks, like preparing a Will or a contract, without the supervision of a trained lawyer. Since it challenges the profession of lawyers, it is a matter of injustice (Fornasier, 2021).

The former Chief Justice of India, Justice D.Y. Chandrachud, said AI is not human. It cannot be used to replace the role of judges, but it can support them in reevaluating the process and judgment. Since the ultimate objective of the judiciary is to ensure justice, AI can help judges deliver fair and just judgments (Solanki, 2021). The role of AI in the legal system is to be specifically established. It is not to substitute the role of a lawyer or a judge, but to assist them in making their activities more productive and competent. Utilization of AI should ultimately be oriented towards a well-designed delivery of justice. Besides, applying AI in the legal profession should contribute to the demands of global justice (Floridi & Cowls, 2019).

6.5 People-Centered Development

Technological developments are praiseworthy. The globe has made significant progress in technological innovation and implementation in the 21st century. These advancements should be people-centered, oriented towards their well-being and societal welfare. Incorporating AI in the legal field should affirm the well-being of the legal professionals, people, and society. However, it raises some concerns about the security of lawyers. The increased use of AI tools can lead to a situation where people prefer them over human lawyers (Jacobowitz, 2018). Since creative thinking and genuine ethical concerns are specific characteristics of humans, which are still miles away from the AI tools, many claim that it will not happen. However, a British teenager developed an automated system, DoNotPay, which has successfully represented its clients in almost 160,000 traffic ticket disputes, affirming that human lawyers should fear the security of their profession (Fornasier, 2021).

Lawyers' overdependency on AI tools can also risk the security of their clients, as most such lawyers disregard their creative thinking capacity and systematic study, entirely relying on AI-supplied data.

7 CONCLUSION

The story of AI started with Turing's (1950) famous question, "Can machines think?" The last decades of the 20th century saw the evolution of the thinking machines. The first two decades of the 21st century affirm the significant progress of AI technologies in almost all fields of societal relations. Although the legal profession initially showed its hostile attitude toward AI adoption, it now widely employs them, realizing its benefits for the legal system's progress. The intense competition in the legal profession during the last few decades has created a situation where lawyers across the globe are trying hard to find a place for themselves in socioeconomic relations (Nurata, 2022). Such a situation demands more productivity and efficiency from the lawyers, which can be achieved with the support of AI tools.

Many law firms and senior lawyers affirm that law schools should train students to adapt to the latest technological developments, like AI. However, they fail to specify the nature of these technologies. A specific study on the crucial AI systems in connection with the legal profession needs to be done for their increased adoption into the field. Although the advantages are manifold, many legal schools and legal professionals fail to adapt to technological changes. Their resistance to change, ethical concerns, and regulatory issues complicate things and challenge the full realization of the application of AI in the legal regime. Using AI tools responsibly, ethically, and effectively is essential for legal education and practice growth. Since several societal areas and professional sectors incorporate technological changes for better productivity and efficiency, the legal field must also be receptive and open-minded to improve the industry and social well-being. The legal field must actively collaborate with policymakers, industrialists, scientists, technology developers, ethicists, and regulatory experts to incorporate the latest technological tools in legal settings without undermining its ethical concerns.

REFERENCES

ABA. (2009). Rule 1.1 Competence — Comment. https://www.americanbar.org/groups/professional_responsibility/publications/model_rules_of_professional_conduct/rule_1_1_competence/comment_on_rule_1_1/

Al Kuwaiti, A., Nazer, L., Al-Reedy, A., Al Shehri, S., Al-Muhanna, A., Subbarayalu, A. V., Al Muhanna, D., & Al-Muhanna, F. A. (2023). A Review of the Role of Artificial Intelligence in Healthcare. *Journal of Personalized Medicine*, *13*(6), 951. https://www.mdpi.com/2075-4426/13/6/951. DOI: 10.3390/jpm13060951 PMID: 37373940

Alarie, B., Niblett, A., & Yoon, A. H. (2018). How Artificial Intelligence Will Affect the Practice of Law. *University of Toronto Law Journal*, *68*(1, supplement 1), 106–124. https://utppublishing.com/doi/10.3138/utlj.2017-0052. DOI: 10.3138/utlj.2017-0052

Anderson, J., Rainee, L., & Luchsinger, A. (2018). Artificial Intelligence and the Future of Humans. *Pew Research Center*, 10(12), 1. https://www.pewresearch.org/internet/wp-content/uploads/sites/9/2018/12/PI_2018.12.10_future-of-ai_FINAL1.pdf

Armour, J., & Sako, M. (2020). AI-Enabled Business Models in Legal Services: From Traditional Law Firms to Next-Generation Law Companies? *Journal of Professions and Organization*, *7*(1), 27–46. DOI: 10.1093/jpo/joaa001

Bostrom, N. (2017). Ethical Issues in Advanced Artificial Intelligence. In Wallach, W., & Asaro, P. (Eds.), *Machine Ethics and Robot Ethics*. Routledge., https://www.taylorfrancis.com/chapters/edit/10.4324/9781003074991-7/ethical-issues-advanced-artificial-intelligence-nick-bostrom

Bostrom, N., & Yudkowsky, E. (2018). The Ethics of Artificial Intelligence. In Yampolskiy, R. V. (Ed.), *Artificial Intelligence Safety and Security*. Routledge., https://www.taylorfrancis.com/chapters/edit/10.1201/9781351251389-4/ethics-artificial-intelligence-nick-bostrom-eliezer-yudkowsky DOI: 10.1201/9781351251389-4

Brand, P. (1992). *The Origins of the English Legal Profession*. Blackwell.

Brooks, C., Gherhes, C., & Voley, T. (2020). Artificial Intelligence in the Legal Sector: Pressures and Challenges of Transformation. *Cambridge Journal of Regions, Economy and Society*, *13*(1), 135–152. https://academic.oup.com/cjres/article/13/1/135/5716343. DOI: 10.1093/cjres/rsz026

Brunette, A. (2024). Humanizing Justice: The Transformational Impact of AI in Courts, From Filing to Sentencing. *Thomson Reuters*. https://www.thomsonreuters.com/en-us/posts/ai-in-courts/humanizing-justice/

Dimitropoulos, G. (2023). Artificial Intelligence and International Adjudication. Oxford Public International Law. https://opil.ouplaw.com/display/10.1093/law-mpeipro/e3888.013.3888/law-mpeipro-e3888?d=%

Donahue, J. (2018). A Primer on Using Artificial Intelligence in the Legal Profession. *JOLT Digest*, https://jolt.law.harvard.edu/digest/a-primer-on-using-artificial-intelligence-in-the-legal-profession

Emejuo, C. C., Joseph, O. C., Odeyemi, E., & Igwe, A. O. (2025). The Impact of Artificial Intelligence on Legal Practice: Enhancing Legal Research, Contract Analysis, and Predictive Justice. *International Journal of Science and Research Archive*, *14*(1), 603–611. https://journalijsra.com/node/336. DOI: 10.30574/ijsra.2025.14.1.0124

Floridi, L. (2023). On Good and Evil, the Mistaken Idea that Technology is Ever Neutral, and the Importance of the Double-Charge Thesis. *Philosophy & Technology*, 36(60). https://link.springer.com/article/10.1007/s13347-023-00661-4

Floridi, L., & Cowls, J. (2019). A Unified Framework of Five Principles for AI in Society. *Harvard Data Science Review*, *1*(1). https://hdsr.mitpress.mit.edu/pub/l0jsh9d1/release/8

Fornasier, M. O. (2021). The Impact of the Introduction of Artificial Intelligence in Advocacy: Skills and Professional Ethics Necessary for the Future Lawyer. *Revista Da Faculdade De Direito UFPR*, 66(2), 69-94. https://revistas.ufpr.br/direito/article/view/73458

Glasser, N. M., Green, F. M., Zumwalt, G., & Wold, I. (2025). AI and Ethics in the Legal Profession. *Epstein Becker Green*. https://www.ebglaw.com/assets/htmldocuments/eltw/eltw385/AI-and-Ethics-in-the-Legal-Profession-Epstein-Becker-Green.pdf

Glendon, M. A., & Alford, W. P. (2025). Legal Profession. *Britannica*. https://www.britannica.com/topic/legal-profession

Glendon, M. A., & Alford, W. P. (2025a). Legal Education. *Britannica*. https://www.britannica.com/topic/legal-education

Hazard, G. C.Jr. (1998). The Legal Profession: The Impact of Law and Legal Theory. *Fordham Law Review*, *67*, 239–248. https://ir.lawnet.fordham.edu/cgi/viewcontent.cgi?article=3503&context=flr

Herrington, A. (2019). How AI Can Make Legal Services More Affordable. *Smart-Lawyer*. https://nationaljurist.com/smartlawyer/how-ai-can-make-legal-services-more-affordable/

Holmes, W., Porayska-Pomsta, K., Holstein, K., Sutherland, E., Baker, T., Shum, S. B., Santos, O. C., Rodrigo, M. T., Cukurova, M., Bittencourt, I. I., & Koedinger, K. R. (2022). Ethics of AI in Education: Towards a Community-Wide Framework. *International Journal of Artificial Intelligence in Education*, *32*(3), 504–526. https://link.springer.com/article/10.1007/s40593-021-00239-1. DOI: 10.1007/s40593-021-00239-1

Jacobowitz, J. L. (2018). Happy Birthday, Siri! Dialing in Legal Ethics for Artificial Intelligence, Smart Phones, and Real Time Lawyers. *Texas A&M Journal of Property Law*, 4(5), 407-442. https://scholarship.law.tamu.edu/cgi/viewcontent.cgi?article=1078&context=journal-of-property-law

Kearns, M., & Roth, A. (2020). *The Ethical Algorithm: The Science of Socially Aware Algorithm Design*. Oxford University Press.

Kim, E. (2024). The Limited Potential for AI Implementation in US Courts. *Research Association for Interdisciplinary Studies: Conference Proceedings*, 65-74. https://rais.education/wp-content/uploads/2024/07/0394.pdf.

Ma, B., & Hou, Y. (2021). Artificial Intelligence Empowers the Integrated Development of Legal Education: Challenges and Responses. *Future Human Image*, 16, 43-54. https://www.fhijournal.org/16-4/

Maas, M. M. (2019). International Law Does Not Compute: Artificial Intelligence and the Development, Displacement, or Destruction of the Global Legal Order. *Melbourne Journal of International Law*, *20*(1). https://classic.austlii.edu.au/au/journals/MelbJIL/2019/3.html

Min, H. (2010). Artificial Intelligence in Supply Chain Management: Theory and Applications. *International Journal of Logistics*, *13*(1), 13–39. DOI: 10.1080/13675560902736537

Ministry of Law and Justice. (2023). Action Plan for Simple, Accessible, Affordable, and Speedy Justice. https://www.pib.gov.in/PressReleasePage.aspx?PRID=1947490

Ministry of Law and Justice. (2025). Use of AI in Supreme Court Case Management. https://www.pib.gov.in/PressReleasePage.aspx?PRID=2113224

Mittelstadt, B. D., Allo, P., Taddeo, M., Wachter, S., & Floridi, L. (2016). The Ethics of Algorithms: Mapping the Debate. *Big Data & Society*, *3*(2), 2053951716679679. https://journals.sagepub.com/doi/10.1177/2053951716679679. DOI: 10.1177/2053951716679679

Nurata, Z. C. (2022). The Concept of Professional Ethics and Debates on Professional Ethics in the Legal Profession: The Case of Ankara. *SİYASAL: Journal of Political Science*, 31(1), 173-193. https://dergipark.org.tr/en/download/article-file/2064936

Qamar, Y., Agarwal, R. K., & Samad, T. A. (2020). When Technology Meets People: The Interplay of Artificial Intelligence and Human Resource Management. *Journal of Enterprise Information Management*, *34*(5), 1339–1370. DOI: 10.1108/JEIM-11-2020-0436

Roba, G. B., & Maric, P. (2023). AI in Customer Relationship Management. In Kryvinska, N., Greguš, M., & Fedushko, S. (Eds.), *Developments in Information and Knowledge Management Systems for Business Applications*. Springer., https://link.springer.com/chapter/10.1007/978-3-031-25695-0_21 DOI: 10.1007/978-3-031-25695-0_21

Rose, J. (1998). The Legal Profession in Medieval England: A History of Regulation. *Syracus Law Review*, 48(1). https://papers.ssrn.com/sol3/papers.cfm?abstract_id=1422764

Rose, L., Holmes, W., Griffiths, M., & Forcier, L. B. (2016). Intelligence Unleashed: An Argument for AI in Education. https://oro.open.ac.uk/50104/

Sadiku, M. N. O., Ajayi, S. A., & Sadiku, J. O. (2025). Artificial Intelligence in Legal Practice: Opportunities, Challenges, and Future Directions. *Journal of Engineering Research and Reports*, *27*(4), 68–80. https://journaljerr.com/index.php/JERR/article/view/1456. DOI: 10.9734/jerr/2025/v27i41456

Selbst, A. D., Boyd, D., Friedler, S. A., Venkatasubramanian, S., & Vertesi, J. (2019). Fairness and Abstraction in Sociotechnical Systems. *Proceedings of the Conference on Fairness, Accountability, and Transparency*, 59-68. https://dl.acm.org/doi/10.1145/3287560.3287598

Sheldon, K. M., & Krieger, L. S. (2004). Does Legal Education Have Undermining Effects on Law Students? Evaluating Changes in Motivation, Values, and Well-being. *Behavioral Sciences & the Law*, *22*(2), 261–286. https://onlinelibrary.wiley.com/doi/epdf/10.1002/bsl.582. DOI: 10.1002/bsl.582 PMID: 15048864

Shi, S. J., Li, J. W., & Zhang, R. (2023). A Study of the Impact of Generative Artificial Intelligence-Supported Situational Interactive Teaching on Students' 'Flow' Experience and Learning Effectiveness — A Case Study of Legal Education in China. *Asia Pacific Journal of Education, 44*(1), 112–138. https://www.tandfonline.com/doi/full/10.1080/02188791.2024.2305161. DOI: 10.1080/02188791.2024.2305161

Silviu, G. A. (2025). The Use of Artificial Intelligence in Industrial Management. In Rackov, M., Miltenović, A., & Banić, M. (Eds.), *Machine and Industrial Design in Mechanical Engineering. KOD 2024. Mechanisms and Machine Science* (Vol. 174). Springer., DOI: 10.1007/978-3-031-80512-7_80

Solanki, S. C. (2021). Artificial Intelligence and Legal Profession. *International Journal of Law, 7*(5), 173–175. https://www.lawjournals.org/assets/archives/2021/vol7issue5/7-5-45-715.pdf

Stagg-Taylor, J. (2011). Lawyers' Business: Conflicts of Duties Arising from Lawyers' Business Models. *Legal Ethics (Oxford, England), 14*(2), 173–192. https://philpapers.org/rec/STALBC. DOI: 10.5235/146072811798828558

Susskind, R. E., & Susskind, D. (2015). *The Future of the Professions: How Technology Will Transform the Work of Human Experts*. Oxford University Press. DOI: 10.1093/oso/9780198713395.001.0001

The National Artificial Intelligence Initiative Act of 2020. https://aip.brightspotcdn.com/37/63/f3a3682c6afce34c0d28f3d8e37e/national-ai-initiative-act-final.pdf

Veasey, E. N. (2002). Ethics 2000 Chair's Introduction. *ABA*. https://www.americanbar.org/groups/professional_responsibility/publications/model_rules_of_professional_conduct/model_rules_of_professional_conduct_preface/ethics_2000_chair_introduction/

Vučić, F. (2023). Changes in Legal Education in the Digital Society of Artificial Intelligence. In Vasić, D., & Vasić, M. K. (Eds.), *Digital Transformation in Education and Artificial Intelligence Application* (pp. 159–176). Springer., https://link.springer.com/chapter/10.1007/978-3-031-36833-2_12

Wirtz, B. W., Weyerer, J. C., & Geyer, C. (2018). Artificial Intelligence and the Public Sector — Applications and Challenges. *International Journal of Public Administration, 42*(7), 596–615. DOI: 10.1080/01900692.2018.1498103

Wu, D., Li, H., & Chen, X. (2023). Analysis on the Influence of General Large Model of Artificial Intelligence on Education Application. *Open Education Research, 2*, 19–25.

Yamane, N. (2020). Artificial Intelligence in the Legal Field and the Indispensable Human Element: Legal Ethics Demands. *The Georgetown Journal of Legal Ethics, 33*, 877–890. https://www.law.georgetown.edu/legal-ethics-journal/wp-content/uploads/sites/24/2020/09/GT-GJLE200038.pdf

Yoon, A. H. (2016). The Post-Modern Lawyer: Technology and the Democratization of Legal Representation. *University of Toronto Law Journal, 66*(4), 456–471. https://utppublishing.com/doi/10.3138/UTLJ.4007. DOI: 10.3138/UTLJ.4007

KEY TERMS AND DEFINITIONS

Accountability: Accountability is a virtue that echoes one's commitment towards responsibilities and others. It is the willingness and openness to take responsibility for one's actions, whether right or wrong.

Digitalization: Digitalization refers to the process of using digital technologies to make significant transformative changes in the socioeconomic, cultural, civil, and political spheres of society. Various technologies, like AI and ML, are part of the digitalization process.

International Law: International law is not an entirely written or codified law. International law is the total of international treaties, agreements, conventions, customs, and general principles of law. It primarily guides the relationship between sovereign states and monitors the functioning of international institutions.

Legal Profession: Legal profession refers to a subset of professional services whose members are involved in the study and practice of law to make a living and ensure societal welfare.

Legal System: Legal system refers to a country's or community's specific framework of rules, procedures, institutions, and principles used to interpret the laws of the country/community.

Machine Learning: Machine learning (ML) evolves from Artificial Intelligence (AI), which can develop systems by learning from data and improving their performance capacity without specifically depending on previous programming.

Professional Ethics: Professional ethics refers to a set of values and principles guiding a particular function. It is the code of conduct specified for the protagonists of a specific sector of service. Accordingly, the professional ethics of lawyers are different from those of doctors.

Chapter 2

Integrating AI into Legal Education in Cambodian Higher Education:

Barriers and Pathways for Effective Adoption

Morin Tieng
https://orcid.org/0009-0000-1564-3381
National University of Battambang, Cambodia

Sovann Ly
https://orcid.org/0000-0003-3733-9975
National University of Battambang, Cambodia

Rany Sam
https://orcid.org/0000-0003-3266-5974
National University of Battambang, Cambodia

Sinath No
https://orcid.org/0009-0001-1644-8702
National University of Battambang, Cambodia

Ry Hour
https://orcid.org/0009-0002-6488-4370
National University of Battambang, Cambodia

Sarith Chiv
https://orcid.org/0009-0000-0239-5307
National Meanchey University, Cambodia

Chenda Soeurn
https://orcid.org/0009-0002-5992-565X
National University of Battambang, Cambodia

Mina Pich
https://orcid.org/0009-0007-3400-5159
National University of Battambang, Cambodia

Voithna Nhean
https://orcid.org/0009-0008-7235-8876
National University of Battambang, Cambodia

Vicheka Chhoeurm
https://orcid.org/0009-0003-8204-7733
National University of Battambang, Cambodia

DOI: 10.4018/979-8-3373-3451-6.ch002

ABSTRACT

Integrating artificial intelligence (AI) into legal education in Cambodian higher education presents both transformative opportunities and significant challenges. AI has the potential to enhance legal research, streamline administrative processes, and enrich pedagogical approaches. However, its adoption is hindered by several barriers, including inadequate technological infrastructure, limited faculty preparedness, ethical concerns, and misalignment with existing curricula. This study investigates these challenges while identifying practical pathways for effective AI integration, such as policy reforms, capacity-building initiatives, and strategic collaborations with technology providers. The chapter discusses global best practices and considers Cambodia's distinctive educational context. It offers actionable recommendations to bridge the gap between traditional legal training and AI-driven innovation. The findings aim to guide educators, policymakers, and stakeholders in developing a legal education system that is both future-ready and contextually grounded.

1. INTRODUCTION

1.1. Research background and rationale

The arrival of artificial intelligence (AI) has proven to be a very transformative force in world higher education, revolutionizing not only learning and teaching but also the principal skills required by current occupations. In the context of legal education, the introduction of AI-enabled tools—such as natural language processing (NLP) platforms to predictive analytics—has led to a reconfiguration of received truths about research, argument, and advocacy (Flynn, 2021; Prakash & Nair, 2024). Around the world, law faculties are receiving the call to adequately prepare students for a profession in which legal technology familiarity is becoming increasingly necessary. Legal practice is steadily incorporating AI-enabled legal databases, robotized contract examination systems, and programmatic litigation prediction tools as commonplace features (Migliorini & Moreira, 2025). As a consequence, educators as well as policymakers are reaching a watershed moment: how must legal education evolve to ensure that graduates retain their professional competence, ethics, and preparedness for the future in the world transformed and extended by AI?

In postsecondary learning, AI has also come to be used to personalize learning, computerize grading and other assessment procedures, and enhance administrative effectiveness (Zawacki-Richter et al., 2019). UNESCO (2021, 2025a) highlights the importance of embedding digital as well as AI literacy within curricula to prepare learners for the data- and algorithm-controlled worlds. There are nevertheless some grave perils in the use of AI in educational environments. Research scholars cite some of these issues as violations of academic integrity, overdependence on generative AI to fulfill assignments, bias within algorithms, and possible destruction of students' capacity to be creative and to form proper judgmental decisions (Holmes et al., 2022; Williamson & Eynon, 2020). Such issues hold specific relevance within the context of the state of legal instruction, one area wherein managed thinking, ethic discernment, and independence of the mind form the building blocks of professional competence.

Cambodia offers a uniquely compelling context within which to explore the integration of artificial intelligence with legal education. After a catastrophic loss of its educational apparatus during the Khmer Rouge years (1975–1979), Cambodia has worked hard to redevelop its higher education over the course of the last four decades. The higher education sector of legal education, as a whole, has had to be rebuilt almost from the ground up, with new waves of legal professionals being instructed at such faculties as the Royal University of Law and Economics (RULE), as well as at private faculties of law. There are now over 20 faculties of law operating within Cambodia, with over 18,000 undergraduate students of law; however, most of these programs still overwhelmingly use the methodologies of didactics and memorization (Keo et al., 2024). Such cross-cutting skills as digital literacy, the solving of problems, and the integration of technologies are still weakly developed, with strong concerns about the extent to which graduates are prepared to meet the challenges of professional legal practice within the twenty-first century.

At the policy level, Cambodia has expressed a growing interest in the application of artificial intelligence (AI) for national development. In 2025, the Ministry of Education, Youth and Sport, in collaboration with UNESCO, issued the AI Readiness Assessment Report, which identified infrastructure shortcomings, limited faculty capabilities, and ethical concerns as among the major challenges to adopting AI (UNESCO, 2025a). The report highlighted the urgent need for digital infrastructure investment and training projects to ensure that AI benefits are shared fairly. Legal education, which sits at the intersection of law, ethics, and governance, seems to be a strategic focus in which the incorporation of AI could have widespread impacts—both on the legal profession and throughout Cambodian civil society. Despite this advancement, AI incorporation in Cambodian legal education remains a fledging process and faces sheer challenges. First, universities still face challenges related to inadequate information technologies, including unstable internet connections, obsolete computer labs, and limited access to high-level AI tools (Keo et al., 2024). Second, many law faculty have little exposure to digital technologies, never mind AI uses, and thus have enormous capacity gaps (Iqbal et al., 2025). Third, budgetary constraints limit universities' ability to invest in costly software licensing, training workshops, and specialized IT staff (Sok et al., 2025). Finally, ethical issues are burdensome: Cambodian instructors are concerned that generative AI, among other things, may increase plagiarism, diminish critical thinking, and sullie the ethical standards of higher education (Chandarin, 2024).

The research question framed in this article is thus of a twin nature. First, the legal education framework of Cambodia needs to transform to remain relevant in a world where artificial intelligence is increasingly becoming integral to legal practice. Second, the country is faced with both structural and cultural challenges that delay the integration of AI within educational matrices as well as in educational processes. This dynamic raises crucial questions: What are the key challenges to the integration of AI within Cambodian legal education? What are the possible strategies that could be adopted to overcome such challenges in ways that are contextually appropriate, ethically mindful, and pedagogically beneficial? The purposes of this study are triadic. First, it aims to survey the challenges associated with the integration of AI with Cambodian legal education, with particular reference to areas such as infrastructure, faculty preparedness, funding issues, curriculum development, and ethics. It then looks to unearth possible strategies—such as the reform of policies, measures that facilitate capacity building, innovations within the field of curriculum design, and strategic partnerships—that might facilitate the integration of AI. Finally, it wishes to situate the Cambodian case within broader international phenomena, learning from international best practices even as it acknowledges the peculiar constraints of the Cambodian higher education context.

This article adopts a desk research approach based on close readings of the academic literature, policy briefs, and case studies from Cambodia as well as elsewhere. The depth of analysis is that it presumes that embracing artificial intelligence in learning spaces entails something beyond a technological imperative, including social, cultural, and ethical architectures (Selwyn, 2019). The article combines the world academic literature with grassroots realities to present pragmatic recommendations to policymakers, educators, and legal education stakeholders in Cambodia.

The value of this work is both in practice and in theory. It presents policy-makers and universities with a roadmap to incrementally and sustainably incorporating AI in legal studies. Theoretically, it adds to the growing body of scholarship on AI in education by accounting for a voice from the Global South that has been lacking in conventional accounts (Bond et al., 2024). The case of Cambodia demonstrates that resource-sparse yet reformally aspiring states can adapt to the possibilities as well as the challenges of adopting AI in higher studies. On the whole, this paper purports that, regardless of daunting challenges in integrating AI in legal studies, these challenges could be surmounted with policy alignment, the building of capacities, changes in the curriculum, and international cooperation. The research reiterates that AI literacy in the field of law is no longer a choice but rather a condition precedent to prepare a new generation of Cambodian jurists to practice law ethically as well as successfully in this AI-enabled world.

1.2. Research problem

There are both potential opportunities and daunting challenges with the integration of artificial intelligence (AI) into Cambodian studies of the law. On the positive side, AI technologies such as computerized systems of legal research, predictive systems, and generative platforms are rapidly changing the practices of lawyers around the world and require new skills among graduates. The faculties of laws in Cambodia, meanwhile, are beset with structural problems such as outdated computer systems, unprepared professors, costliness, lecture-focused orientation, and unresolved ethics challenges. The tension between the two camps has created a profound issue: Cambodia needs to increase legal studies to remain competitive around the world, but cultural and structural hurdles may set back the pace or direction of integrating AI. Without envisioned breakthroughs, the Cambodian graduands of the law will be poorly equipped to confront a legal practice that becomes increasingly reliant on AI.

1.3. Research Question

What are the main challenges that hamper the adoption of artificial intelligence in Cambodian legal studies, and what is the best approach to make it efficient, effective, and sustainable?

1.4. Research Objectives:

To achieve the general goal, the researchers set three specific goals as follows:

- To address the significant barriers to the adoption of AI among Cambodian law schools
- Determining effective ways to integrate AI adoption.
    -placing the Cambodian case in regional as well as international developments

1.5. Research Limitations

A number of limitations can be identified. First, the use of secondary sources implies that the study synthesizes but does not produce empirical data. Second, the Cambodian higher education environment is dynamic, and policies or measures enacted after 2025 will change the picture. Third, the desk review cannot document informal practices among universities. However, this study provides a helpful basis for future empirical studies by delineating existing barriers and opportunities.

2. LITERATURE REVIEW

2.1 Higher education and AI around the world

Artificial intelligence soon proved to be a transformational force in higher education across the world. Generative AI systems such as ChatGPT, Gemini, and Claude have provided new avenues for personalized learning, automated assessment, and enhanced access to information (Zawacki-Richter et al., 2019). Furthermore, universities are employing AI to develop learning platforms that can adapt to students, plagiarize assignments, aid-providing chatbots, and perform predictive analytics that can encourage students to stay in school and perform better (Holmes et al., 2022; Selwyn, 2019). Such tools will help to streamline things as well as personalize them, yet they contravene the conventional modes of learning. Higher education institutions (HEIs) across the world use AI in various manners. AI is extensively used in student services as well as learning management systems across the United States (Iqbal et al., 2025). The European Commission (2021) advocates the use of ethical AI standards across the European Union so that everybody is included and things are made clear. As part of national digital strategies, Singapore, China, and South Korea have invested many finances in AI-enabled learning systems (Ocen et al., 2025). UNESCO (2021, 2023) insists that AI literacy as well as ethics be incorporated across education policy and seeks frameworks that preserve human rights yet allow new things to be experimented with. Despite its promise, critical research signals peril. AI could reduce the gap between resource-rich and resource-scarce institutions, inject bias within the programmatic core of algos, and disempower students to generate decisions (Williamson & Eynon, 2020; Bond et al., 2024).

Thus, there is concern among faculty that too much use of generative AI reduces the ability to think critically and be truthful in school (Iqbal et al., 2025). To address this, most universities are experimenting with "AI literacy" courses so that students and faculty both understand how to use AI and the moral, legal, and social consequences of it (Sullivan et al., 2022). According to the international literature, three key things are learned: (1) AI literacy can no longer be optional but becomes a requirement in high education; (2) ethics and governance structures need to govern the use of AI; and (3) educator skills must be developed as much as the technological infrastructure (Wischmeyer & Rademacher, 2020; UNESCO, 2025a; OECD, 2021). This lays the groundwork for discussing legal education, where the dangers of utilizing AI are greatest.

2.2 AI in Legal Education

The introduction of AI in legal education is reflective of larger developments in the legal world. AI-enabled products such as Lexis+ with AI, Casetext CoCounsel, and Ross Intelligence revolutionized the way lawyers research and prepare cases by making it possible to locate and analyze precedents instantly (Flynn, 2021; Lampou, 2023; Prakash & Nair, 2024). Some law faculties use mock AI judges and litigation forecasting models to prepare students for learning about algorithmic decision-making and to prepare them for AI-led legal practice (Remus & Levy, 2017). Legal educators insist that AI must be viewed as one such tool to assist with conventional legal reasoning rather than replace it. AI is capable of assisting with routine research as well as draftings, but people still need to practice critical thinking, ethical reasoning, and advocacy (Migliorini & Moreira, 2021). Researchers state that overdependence on AI-enabled products will produce "AI-dependent" graduates incapable of thinking for themselves (Susskind, 2021).

Law schools around the world are beginning to react to the transformation that technology is causing in the practice of law. The American Bar Association (ABA) has driven this revolution in the United States. The Model Rules of Professional Conduct were officially altered to state that remaining competent as a lawyer requires knowing "the benefits and risks associated with relevant technology" (American Bar Association, 2020). The legal education rules were subsequently set out in writing as the moral code applicable to lawyers to the effect that law schools must educate students about the impact that technology has on practice (American Bar Association, 2023). This development does not happen in isolation in the United States. The 2023 global review revealed that Canadian, British, and Australian law schools are also rapidly incorporating legal technology into their curricula. The courses range from standalone classes in AI and data privacy to comprehensive legal technology clinics where students can put what they have learned into practice (Khoalenyane & Ajani, 2024). Barton and Rhode (2019) state that such developments are required because the integration of technology into core legal practice is no longer desirable but necessary.

More than 86% of Australian universities' juris doctor programs now integrate law-and-technology courses (Migliorini & Moreira, 2025). Increasingly diverse numbers of UK postgraduate studies, such as legal tech and AI ethics, are offered (Surden, 2019). Double degree schemes in law with AI have also been attempted in India as well as in China to allow graduates to find jobs both within legal practice and within the governance of technologies (Sam et al., 2025d; Ocen et al., 2025). Despite such improvements, adoption is still nonuniform. High-resource universities within developed states dominate the innovation agenda. However, developing state universities tend to lag due to scarce funds as well as the absence of infrastructural facilities to practice with the latest technological developments (Bond et al., 2024). Researchers opine that legal education reform initiatives ought to aim toward equitable access, contextual adaptation and overt education on the social and ethics of AI (Prakash & Nair, 2024).

2.3 Integration of Cambodian higher education with technology

Cambodia's higher education system has expanded significantly since the 1990s, but it continues to face persistent challenges. Internet access remains inconsistent, computer labs are often underequipped, and faculty digital literacy is limited (Sam et al., 2013; Keo et al., 2024). Legal education in Cambodian higher education is currently being implemented at both public and private universities. According to private education statistics and indicators from 2020--2021, the total number of 128 higher education institutions in Cambodia consists of 80 private higher education institutions (MoEYS, 2021). However, the statistics of the Cambodian Education Congress Report 2023--2024 revealed 194 higher education institutions nationwide, including 115 private and 79 public higher education institutions (MoEYS, 2025). Seventeen ministries and institutions supervise higher education institutions in Cambodia. The Ministry of Education, Youth and Sports supervises 21 public HEIs (17 Bases, 4 Branches) and 118 private HEIs (77 bases, 41 branches), for a total of 139. The statistics in the two tables below were written from a guidebook for Cambodian students to choose scholarship majors from both public and private universities. This table shows that 20 public universities provided scholarships for students in the 2025--2026 academic year. However, these are only 10 HEIs providing legal education services in Cambodia. Ten public higher education institutions do not offer legal education services.

Table 1. Public higher education institutions with legal education provisions in Cambodia

Name of Higher Education Institutions	Degree Offered
1. Royal Academy of Cambodia	Undergraduate/Graduate
2. National University of Management	Undergraduate/Graduate
3. National University of Battambang	Undergraduate
4. National Mean Chey University	Undergraduate
5. Royal University of Law and Economics	Undergraduate/Graduate
6. Chea Sim University of Kamchaymea	Undergraduate
7. Svay Rieng University	Undergraduate

continued on following page

Table 1. Continued

Name of Higher Education Institutions	Degree Offered
8. Heng Samrin Tbong Kmom University	Undergraduate
9. Preah Sihanouk Raja Buddhisht University	Undergraduate/Graduate
10. Preah Sihamoniraja Buddhist University	Undergraduate/Graduate
11. Samdech Akka Mohasenapadei Techo Hun Sen Buddhist University	Undergraduate/Graduate

In this table, 23 private higher education institutions provided scholarships for Cambodian students in the new academic year, 2025--2026. Eighteen HEIs provide law education and are available for scholarships, but 5 HEIs do not offer any scholarships or educational services for law education.

Table 2. Private higher education institutions with legal education provisions in Cambodia

Name of Higher Education Institutions	Degree Offered
1. Western University	Undergraduate/Graduate
2. Mekong University of Cambodia	Undergraduate/Graduate
3. Asia Europe University	Undergraduate/Graduate
4. Human Resources University	Undergraduate/Graduate
5. University of Management and Economics	Undergraduate/Graduate
6. University of Cambodia	Undergraduate/Graduate
7. Dewey International University	Undergraduate
8. University of Specialization of Cambodia	Undergraduate/Graduate
9. Pannasastra University of Cambodia	Undergraduate/Graduate
10. Life University	Undergraduate
11. Panna Cheat University	Undergraduate/Graduate
12. Phnom Penh International University	Undergraduate/Graduate
13. Samdech Preah Mahasangharajah Bour Kry University	Undergraduate/Graduate
14. University of Economics and Finance	Undergraduate/Graduate
15. IIC University of Technology	Undergraduate/Graduate
16. ACLEDA University of Business	Undergraduate
17. Digital University of Cambodia	Undergraduate
18. Angkor City Institute	Undergraduate/Graduate

A UNESCO study (2025b) revealed that the infrastructural basis of AI is weakly developed and that most universities do not have clear regulations to govern the use of technologies. Such systems problems are also prevalent in the context of legal education. There are several dozen law schools in Cambodia, such as the Royal University of Law and Economics (RULE), the University of Puthisastra, and Pannasastra University of Cambodia. They train thousands of students, but most of the programs are examination- and lecture-centric (Iqbal et al., 2025). Technologically based courses are the exception, with most legal research outdated (Sok et al., 2025; Sam et al., 2025a, 2025b, 2025c). Graduates in the discipline of law in Cambodia, therefore, are unable to use digital technologies that are playing an ever-greater role in neighboring states such as Singapore and Malaysia.

Institutional and cultural barriers also inhibited reform. Senior faculty mostly do not yet trust digital technologies, and the nature of the way that institutions run is reluctant to change over time. Additionally, universities cannot afford as much as they want to invest in AI platforms or professional development programs because they need to pay high tuition fees, and the government does not grant them enough funds (Heng et al., 2022; Keo et al., 2024). Similarly, the push toward change continues to gain momentum. The Ministry of Education has directed universities to integrate digital literacy into the curriculum. The University of Puthisastra has actually set out a policy regarding the use of AI as well as academic integrity (Chandarin, 2024). Donor-supported projects, such as UNESCO's toolkit on AI as well as international collaborations, present Cambodia with new opportunities to integrate legal education with what is going on in the world (UNESCO, 2025a).

2.4 Ethical and Pedagogic Issues

The use of AI in learning presents inevitable ethical issues. Researchers around the world point to the possibility of algorithmic bias, violations of data privacy, and surveillance (Holmes et al., 2022; Williamson & Eynon, 2020). Their worries are still greater in legal studies, where making the right moral decisions is very important. There is a need to analyze AI tools critically to be confident that they are fair, clear, and aligned with human rights values (UNESCO, 2021). In Cambodia, ethics are mostly related to academic integrity. The use of generative AI tools supports the potential of students to plagiarize others' work, making people worried that academic integrity will decrease (Chandarin, 2024). Teachers in Cambodia say that plagiarism harms both the learning and moral integrity of universities and colleges. Surveys among Cambodian students as well as among educators revealed that although many had observed the benefits of AI, they feared that it might make people less original as well as less self-sufficient (Sok et al., 2023).

To introduce AI to the classroom, teachers need extensive training. Chinese studies have shown that teachers who want to introduce generative AI to the classroom need specific training, new grading systems for students, and clear ethics policies (Iqbal et al., 2025). Global studies have mirrored the same results: to be effective, AI needs to be brought with teachers who are trained, with the curriculum redesigned to be project-oriented on the basis of critique rather than rote learning (Selwyn, 2019). This means that in Cambodia, introducing AI will necessitate teacher training, policies regulating proper ethics, and a shift away from rote learning to project-oriented learning on the basis of critique.

3. METHODOLOGY

The research applies a desk research approach, synthesizing and critically analyzing existing academic publications, policy reports, industry studies, and relevant case studies to investigate the challenges and opportunities for embedding artificial intelligence (AI) in Cambodian legal education. Desk research can be valuable where limited empirical data are found. This is the case because it applies a range of secondary materials to deliver the entire picture quickly and inexpensively, and it can also help to identify the pattern and gaps in the data (Formpl.us, 2023; Sisinternational, 2025). However, its weaknesses include possible biases, issues with the relevance and timeliness of the data, and a lack of in-depth qualitative understanding, which can be mitigated with careful selection of data sources as well as triangulation. Empirical research on the adoption of AI in higher education, especially legal education, in Cambodia remains rare. There is, however, growing policy momentum as represented by the efforts of the government as well as the institution to enhance digital skills, set up ethics standards, and prepare interdisciplinary curricula (Sok et al., 2025; UNESCO, 2025; Leng & Srun, 2025). This review synthesizes the findings of regional research in Southeast Asia to put the Cambodian experience into context as a way of enhancing the analysis (Lai, 2025).

4. FINDINGS AND DISCUSSION

The results of this study highlight the numerous opportunities and challenges associated with implementing artificial intelligence (AI) in Cambodia's law schools. As AI can be highly beneficial for improving learning practices, research activities, and professional development, it is limited by core systemic obstacles, including infrastructure, faculty preparedness, funding resources, and moral challenges. The results were inferred on the basis of three specific research objectives and explained on the basis of international as well as local developments, guided by applicable theoretical frameworks.

4.1 Findings

4.1.1 Conclusion Based on the First Objective: Determining the Key Obstacles to the Implementation of AI in Cambodian Legal Education

Research has shown that the use of AI in legal studies in Cambodia is limited by certain interrelated technological, institutional, pedagogic, economic, and cultural barriers. The barriers are due to both structural factors and human factors.

Improper utilization of technology and infrastructures

The structural limitations of the law schools of Cambodia also inhibit the efficient utilization of AI technologies. The computer labs in the majority of schools are obsolete, internet connectivity remains weak, and access to cloud centers or AI-focused software remains limited (UNESCO, 2025a). Owing to these factors, it becomes challenging to set up digital learning platforms, carry out AI-enhanced research, or expand equitable internet penetration among students beyond major urban centers. Most rural schools suffer from these technological ills, deepening the digital divide and restricting access to legal studies. Selwyn (2019) labels this "technological stratification of opportunity," where digital infrastructures are a new predictor of academic inequalities.

Teacher preparation and pedagogical limitations

Research has shown that most Cambodia law professors are unaware of AI or how to utilize digital learning modes. Teachers still use lecture-style, content-dominated strategies that promote memorization rather than learning through practice or analysis (Keo et al., 2024). The skill gap is caused by the lack of opportunities to professionally develop, excessive workload for the teacher, and insufficient motivation for the school to experiment. Rogers' (2003) diffusion of innovation states that people resist new technologies because they are apprehensive, poorly trained, or lack sufficient peer support. As a result, AI tools are insufficiently harnessed or harnessed inappropriately, which limits their potential to improve.

Policy and fiscal limitations

The other significant issue was the unavailability of funds. The majority of the universities and colleges in Cambodia use tuition fees to stay afloat, so they lack funds to buy AI software, professional development programs, or in-house IT specialists. Only the top universities can utilize AI in the absence of state funding or projects paid with funds from donors (Padilla Flores & Mean, 2024). There is also a lack of defined national policies as well as regulations with regard to what can be done with AI in school, so people are unsure about standards, how to handle data, and who should be in control of ethics (UNESCO, 2025a). The absence of policy makes institutions find it hard to collaborate with each other and makes them less inclined to undertake large innovations.

Questions about ethics and academic integrity

Cambodian educators are concerned about the moral implications of generative AI programs such as Gemini and ChatGPT because they are developing so exponentially. Everyone tends to be concerned about plagiarism, overreliance on AI-based composition, and the loss of the power to analyze critically (Chandarin, 2024; Sok et al., 2025). Without regulations governing the use of AI in educational venues, the situation becomes even more challenging for students and educators. In a discipline such as the law, where integrity and rational analysis matter most, the use of AI without restrictions may damage the credibility of the academic discipline as well as the moral core of legal studies itself.

Resistance to cultural change and institutional change

Cultural attitudes also render adoption more challenging. The old-guard faculty and administrators, trained within traditional legal education paradigms, typically view AI as unimportant or harmful to prevailing pedagogic pecking orders (Keo et al., 2024). Governance frameworks within the institution demonstrate similar inertia in accommodating change, with rigid bureaucracy and limited interdepartmental cooperation. These findings are in line with the Technology Acceptance Model (TAM) (Venkatesh et al., 2003), which purports that negative attitudes and perceived complexity are major impediments to adopting technologies. The integration of AI can remain superficial and cosmetic without cultural or leadership transformation.

In brief, the findings are that there are numerous varied reasons why AI has failed to be incorporated into the legal studies of Cambodia, and they all mutually contribute to making it harder. A lack of infrastructure hinders being able to reach things, traditional modes of teaching inhibit the development of new ideas, a lack of finances hinders investment, and moral reservations inhibit experimentation. To address these issues, cooperation on strategies that address both the technological environment and the human infrastructure, including faculty competence, the institutional culture, and governance policies, is needed.

4.1.2 Findings Based on Objective Two: Identifying Practical Pathways for AI Integration

The study revealed six interrelated pathways that can help ensure the long-term, principled use of AI in Khmer legal research, but the pathways are daunting. The pathways call for a step-by-step, capacity-driven, and policy-informed approach that matches aspiration with what can be done.

1. Policies and rules

A consistent national policy direction is needed to help guide the adoption of AI. The recommendations are that the Ministry of Education, Youth and Sport of Cambodia (MoEYS) and the Accreditation Committee of Cambodia (ACC) must incorporate AI literacy and digital skills as core elements of the national standards in legal studies (UNESCO, 2025a). Legal education should be reformed to be consistent with new data protection, privacy, and AI ethics legislation that the Ministry of Post and Telecommunications of Cambodia (MPTC) is preparing (MPTC, 2025). They simplify the rules and engender confidence across the board.

2. Improving the skills of faculty members and enhancing their professional development

A crucial element of successfully integrating AI is that of capable faculty. The research includes the significance of needs-based training programs, "train-the-trainer" programs, and international exchanges to enhance digital literacy and innovation in teaching (Iqbal et al., 2025). Capacity should be developed beyond the teaching of technical skills, such as the development of moral reasoning, assessment design, and utilization within the classroom. Collaborating with international bodies such as UNESCO, the ABA, and the ASEAN law networks could give you access to cheap training materials that meet your specifications.

3. New ideas regarding learning as well as teaching in the course

Incorporating the curriculum is one of the most significant ways to introduce AI to the field of legal studies. On the basis of these findings, electives or core courses could incorporate AI-related topics such as AI ethics, the law and the technologies of control, or lawyer programming. Experiential learning, such as AI-enabled moot courts, legal simulations, or online research exercises, can bridge the gap between practice and theory (Migliorini & Moreira, 2025). This aligns with what is emerging globally, with increased emphasis on interdisciplinary legal studies that encompass the study of law, ethics, and data literacy.

4. Academic Integrity Guidelines and Ethical Frameworks

To ensure academic integrity in an AI-powered learning environment, specific ethical parameters as well as regulations governing the institution should be defined. Universities should outline the allowable uses of AI in research as well as in academic assignments with the addition of educational programs for students on the proper use of AI (Chandarin, 2024). Redefine testing with a greater emphasis on oral examinations, project screening, and class writing can decrease the possibility of AI-aided plagiarism further (Sullivan et al., 2022). A clear integrity policy will cause individuals to be all the more secure in their degree of legal education.

5. Planning of collaborative activities and resource sharing

Collaboration has become a key to making strides. Khmer universities can collaborate with international groups, regional organizations, and tech firms to access AI technologies, expertise, and funds. UNESCO's AI and the Rule of Law Toolkit (2025b) and the ASEAN Digital Education Framework are two examples of blueprints for scalable collaborative innovation. The sharing of digital library access, research databases, and simulation programs can reduce costs and help balance the playing field between universities.

6. Gradual Adoption Pilot Projects

The findings demonstrate that pilots of small, evidence-based projects best represent the optimal method to begin integrating AI in a persistent manner. Some ideas to get pilots off the ground involve the use of AI-enabled chatbots to assist students, experimentation with predictive analytics during the admissions process, or establishing AI-powered legal research labs. Successful pilots can subsequently be applied to numerous institutions, making adoption gradual with limited risk, as learning and adaptation can occur within context (Padilla Flores & Mean, 2024). Incrementalism fosters institutional trust as well as the guarantee that they will be around for a long time to come. The six avenues, as a collective, demonstrate that integrating AI within Cambodian legal education is possible with planned gradual change. Using a top-down policy leadership-driven model with bottom-up innovation from universities can help ensure that ethics are maintained while still promoting institutional ownership.

4.1.3 Findings Based on Objective Three: Contextualizing Cambodia's Experience Within Global and Regional Trends

The third objective situates Cambodia's experience within international best practices and ASEAN regional developments, highlighting both the divergence and convergence of trends in AI-driven legal education.

Worldwide perspective

Law schools around the world are rapidly incorporating AI and digital technologies into their curricula to address the evolving needs of legal practice. The American Bar Association (2023) states that American lawyers have a moral obligation to be comfortable with technology. Similarly, universities across Canada, Australia, and the UK have incorporated AI, data ethics, and technological governance into their core curricula (Migliorini & Moreira, 2025; Surden, 2019). Universities educate students in the classroom with real-life applications, such as virtual mock courts, AI-powered legal clinics, and predictive models of litigation (Remus & Levy, 2017). The legal education in Cambodia remains founded on traditional teaching in old schools, with a focus on theory and memorization. This gap highlights what Susskind (2023) dubs the "innovation lag" in legal education, the consequence of which could be developing countries graduating students unprepared to compete in digitalized legal markets. However, the growing policy push in Cambodia combined with membership in UNESCO's AI projects signals that people are taking growing notice of and preparing to address this gap.

Loessia Regional

A few neighboring states within the ASEAN region can be cited as good examples of how to gradually introduce AI. Singapore law faculties, for example, set up legal tech incubators and introduced electives with regard to AI within the curricula. Digital standards of literacy are included within the accreditation framework of Malaysia (Ministry of Higher Education, 2022). The road to AI-enabled e-courts fully driven with AI was paved by Indonesia, enabling students of law to participate in virtual digital litigations in real time (Muhidin et al., 2023). Such efforts indicate that long-term development can be attained in emerging regions on the basis of clear policies, capacity building, and regional cooperation.

Unique Circumstances of Cambodia

Cambodia is different from these cases because of challenges with infrastructure, faculty capacity, and governing structures. However, given the smaller scale, new things can be easily experimented with. The UNESCO AI Readiness Maturity Tool (2025a) and the MPTC Artificial Intelligence Governance Framework (2025) demonstrate that nations are beginning to collaborate around AI ethics, data protection, and digital transformation. The developments permit experimenting with integrating AI with legal education.

Cambodia's population is young and is increasingly invested in technology. This puts it in a great position to nurture new ideas. Younger students and faculty, who are typically better resourced with tech, can initiate bottom-up reform with proper school-provided training. This demographic advantage can position Cambodia as a regional model for the use of AI in legal education in a people-centric, open, and ethical way. Cambodia is in the nascent but promising phase of adopting AI in higher education. By learning the best ideas globally and tailoring them to the needs of the nation, the nation can develop a blended model to leverage the best of what it can do and minimize the worst. This guarantee ensures that Khmer legal education uses imported technologies but also contributes to discussions about AI ethics, law, and education in the region and globally.

4.2. DISCUSSION

4.2.1 Interpreting Barriers as Being

This research reveals that the incorporation of artificial intelligence (AI) in the legal education of Cambodia represents a long-overdue step ahead as well as a multifaceted national dilemma. Reports have shown that although AI possesses transformative possibilities to expand education, research, and professionalization, effective implementation relies on overcoming numerous technological, institutional, pedagogic, ethical, and budgetary challenges. The research demonstrates that Cambodian legal studies continue to be grounded extensively in conventional, teacher-dominated instructional strategies, characterized by limited digital skills among the faculty as well as inadequate infrastructural provisions to facilitate learning environments enhanced with AI. These conditions have gradually suppressed innovation and exacerbated the digital divide between legal centers of learning in Cambodia and their international counterparts. The research revealed, however, a great deal of room to reframe on the basis of the alignment of policy, faculty skill improvement, curricular upgrading, and regional cooperation.

The review stresses that integrating AI is not easy but rather a systemic transformation—a need for coordinated answers across policymakers, university leaders, and international partners. To ensure that the adoption of AI complements but does not undermine legal education's intellectual and moral value, Cambodia needs to embrace a gradual, context-adaptive approach founded on human-centered, inclusive, and moral values. As long as it is fully implemented, the integration of AI can bring international benchmarks to Cambodian legal education, render graduates globally competitive, and promote the innovation of the justice sector. Ultimately, AI should usher in the creation of sharp, ethical, and tech-savvy jurists capable of managing the challenges of a probable AI-centric legal environment.

4.2.2 Faculty Capacity and Pedagogic Innovation

The preparation of faculties is a key shaper of the effective adoption of artificial intelligence in the learning field. The literature has shown that the majority of Cambodian legal educators possess professional experience in traditional, doctrinally focused systems that are highly reliant on lecture-style learning modes and rote memorization (Migliorini & Moreira, 2025). The evidence substantiates that educators are most likely to use digital materials in their practice if they are offered highly structured AI pedagogy professional development in workshops, cross-faculty networks, and reduced teaching burdens (Iqbal et al., 2025). The law faculties in Cambodia should make professionalizing their faculties their topmost agenda, possibly in unison with international networks such as UNESCO, the American Bar Association (ABA), and the ASEAN academic networks. The professional development of faculties offers the required competences to move the applications of AI from superficial to profound pedagogic transformation.

4.2.3 Ethical and Financial Issues

The question of ethical integrity remains a top one in the AI-enabled legal classroom. Cambodian educators reported growing academic dishonesty around AI-created essays and assignments (Sok et al., 2025). However, most universities still lack specific rules governing the use of AI, leaving both students and faculty unclear (Chandarin, 2024). In accordance with UNESCO's (2021) Guidance for Policy-Makers on AI and Education, universities and schools must establish clear ethics and transform assessment procedures to prevent students from cheating. They could, for example, incorporate oral presentations, reflective writing, or guided problem-resolution exercises. These issues are exacerbated by a shortage of funds. Most universities rely on tuition fees and lack access to donor funding as well as institutional grants, making it difficult to upgrade AI infrastructure, software, and professional development to utilize AI facilities (Keo et al., 2024). Collaborative efforts across the globe can help address such issues. For example, collaboration with international legal tech companies can ensure discounted AI platforms as well as professional development opportunities to ensure that all institutions have access to the same degree (UNESCO, 2025b).

4.2.4 Curriculum and Institutional Reform

The research also reveals that there remains a substantial gap between the legal education curriculum in Cambodia and the current technological skills necessary to practice law. Most programs remain doctrinal, with learning practices grounded in memorization as opposed to skill-based learning with hands-on practice (Pak, 2020). In contrast, an increasing number of international law schools cover AI and law, programming for lawyers, and artificial intelligence ethics (Migliorini & Moreira, 2025; Surden, 2019). Adding similar modules in Cambodia will be helpful in filling the gap between the legal education curriculum and the dynamic needs of the profession. Cambian universities can promote innovation further with the creation of AI legal research centers or virtual law clinics where students can practice with AI tools in simulated legal environments. The projects are sociotechnical since they accept that new technological adoption should go hand-in-hand with the evolution of policy governance, the organizational form, and the way educators teach (Selwyn, 2019). Such combined efforts would not only enhance learning but also allow

Cambodia law schools to be in a better position to participate in the regional debate about AI as well as legal ethics.

4.2.5 Contextual and Incremental Adoption

Cambodia's development should be guided by step-by-step, contextually relevant strategies rather than the broad-scale imitation of the West. AI-equipped legal research modules, virtual mock courts, and conversational bots that assist students are low-cost, high-impact pilot projects that can begin (Padilla Flores & Mean, 2024). Following sociotechnical systems theory, these projects are consistent with the notion that innovation that lasts needs to transform the human, organizational, and technological subsystems all at the same time (Venkatesh et al., 2003). Collaborating in the region still makes more things possible. Singapore, Malaysia, and Indonesia have established new regulations and curriculum changes that incorporate digital literacy and legal education as components of national accreditation standards (Ministry of Higher Education, Malaysia, 2022; Muhidin et al., 2023). Cambodia can reproduce these templates to address the needs of the kingdom with the help of ASEAN collaboration, cross-border degree offerings, and faculty exchanges. This regional convergence closes the gap between technologies that are coming to the kingdom and the adoption of AI, which is more cognizant of culture and ethics.

4.2.6 Recalibrating the role of AI: Efficiency to empowerment

A key discovery of this study is that the educational role of AI transcends herer efficiency; it can be an effective tool for empowerment and inclusion. AI-based classroom platforms can personalize learning to students with diverse abilities. Virtual classrooms can reach students in remote areas with little opportunity to study law as well (Lai, 2025). In this way, AI becomes a democratic force that opens up opportunities, engenders participation, and challenges law students to be critically and ethically mindful. The UNESCO (2025b) toolkit on AI and the rule of law share this ideal. The toolkit supports AI, which is people-oriented and ethics-centric and complements human judgmental skills rather than displaces them. For Cambodia, this means building AI systems that uphold the very values of legal studies, including justice, fairness, and human dignity, but yet endow students with the digital skills to keep pace with the fast development of the legal profession.

In summary, the findings and discussions demonstrate that the integration of AI with Cambodian legal studies is both necessary and challenging. To be successful, Cambodia needs to adopt a balanced strategy that involves investment in infrastructure, building human capacity, fair governance, and transformation of the way the instructors educate. The utilization of AI as a complement to the classical form of learning, as opposed to replacing it, will enable the school of law to graduate globally competitive, technologically educated, morally upright students. The people-centric balanced strategy guarantees that the use of AI enables Cambodia's evolving higher level of learning to be fairer as well as innovative.

4.2.7 Synthesis

The analysis demonstrates that the momentum toward AI-enabled legal education in Cambodia is nascent but promising. The agenda needs to be comprehensive with respect to building facilities, capacity building among faculty, ethics in governance, and new concepts in the curriculum. The findings demonstrate that the adoption of AI is not a technological initiative but rather a social transformation that needs an institutional vision, stakeholder collaboration, and continuous capacity development. Cambodia can construct a future-looking legal education framework that applies a step-by-step, human-centric roadmap based on international best practices customized to the needs of the nation. Such a system will equip graduates with the potential to lead a legal practice that leverages AI, as well as turn the nation into a new voice in regional as well as international debates on the frontiers between law, technology, and ethics.

5. CONCLUSIONS AND RECOMMENDATIONS

5.1. Conclusion

This research concludes that the integration of artificial intelligence (AI) in the legal education of Cambodia is a necessary development and a complex national task. Research has revealed that AI can transform the ways in which we teach, conduct research, and prepare for professional life. Only then will it be effective as long as we address the numerous obstacles within technologies, institutions, instructional strategies, ethics, and finances. The findings demonstrate that legal education in Cambodia depends on conventional, lecture-only modes of instruction. The faculty lacks the ability to utilize the technologies adequately, and the facilities are inadequate to facilitate AI-equipped learning environments. These factors have made new initiatives harder to accomplish and widened the digital gap between the schools of the Cambodian and world laws. The research revealed numerous opportunities to transform with the alignment of policies, the development of faculty capacity, the revision of the curriculum, and collaboration with other regions.

This study proves that AI adoption involves more than the purchase of new machinery; it involves the retooling of the entire apparatus, requiring collaborative efforts between policymakers, higher education administrators, and global partners. Cambodia needs to embrace a gradual, context-sensitive trajectory of adopting AI founded on human-centered, inclusive, and moral principles to ensure that it strengthens the moral and intellectual integrity of legal studies and does not undermine them. Specifically, the injection of AI into the Cambodian legal curriculum could bring it to international standards, prepare graduates to be job-ready, and help modernize the adjudicatory apparatus. Ideally, AI should never replace human judgment and rationality; instead, it should be a stimulus to produce critical, ethical, and technologically literate jurists equipped with the challenges of the AI-dominated legal world.

5.2. Recommendations

Consequently, this study recommends the following key constituents: the government and policymakers; universities and law faculties; and international partners and donors. The recommendations ensure that the integration of AI use within Cambodian legal education is systematic, long-term, and morally justifiable.

5.2.1 Suggestions for the government and decision-makers

– The Ministry of Education, Youth, and Sport (MoEYS), the Ministry of Post and Telecommunications (MPTC), and the Accreditation Committee of Cambodia (ACC) must develop a National AI in Education Policy Framework. The framework will be required to encompass standards, benchmarks, and ethics guidelines to utilize AI in higher education, including in law.

– In the program of law accreditation requirements, the ACC should require that students be digital and AI literacy. This will standardize all universities in Cambodia and put Cambodia in step with the ASEAN Digital Education Framework.

– The availability of broadband should be increased, IT systems in universities should be revamped, and AI learning centers should be installed across public law schools. Therefore, all individuals can have equitable access to AI-powered education, and the most important step is to bridge the technological gap between rural areas and cities.

– Initiate grants to innovation or competitive funding programs to support AI pilot projects, research partnerships, and faculty development programs at both public and private universities.

– To protect school districts and students from exploitation, data privacy, AI ethics, and algorithmic responsibility legislation must be crafted and enacted. Such policies must be aligned with international human rights as well as UNESCO's (2025b) recommendations on reliable, human-centered AI.

5.2.2 Suggestions for law schools and colleges

– The courses can include digital evidence and data law, governance and AI ethics, as well as law and technology.
– The AI materials should cover topics ranging from legal theory to computer science and ethics.
– Periodic professional development workshops on the use of AI tools, course development, and judging individuals morally should be held. Universities should set up “AI centers of pedagogic innovation” to allow instructors to try new things and to share resource materials.
– Institutions must embrace specific institutional policies that define permissible uses of generative AI technologies in learning, research, and assessment. The integration of AI-laden behavior in academic integrity policies enables the retention of the integrity of legal studies.
– Mini pilots, such as AI-powered moot courts, virtual legal clinics, or learning systems that adapt, are launched to build confidence in the system and gain localized insights into how effective they are before they can scale them to the whole nation.
– It will be helpful to encourage Khmer law faculties, computer science faculties, and provincial legal entities to collaborate to develop artificial intelligence-infused models of legal studies. Cambodia can catch up with regional concepts with research initiatives among ASEAN universities.

5.2.3 Suggestions for Donors and International Partners

– The Asian Development Bank, UNESCO, and the ASEAN University Network should help Cambodia law schools improve their ICT infrastructures, conduct capacity building workshops, and cooperate to prepare new curricula.
– Craft platforms that cross borders to help people share the best practices of teaching AI and the law. Local scholars can be strengthened with programs such as faculty exchanges, regional conferences, and online training to stimulate new ideas.
– Cambodian NGOs are in the process of localizing UNESCO's toolkit on AI and the rule of law (2025b) to align with Cambodian culture and schooling.
– Subscription-free digital legal databases as well as AI tools that are available to minimize costs should be encouraged. Donors can enable universities to use free or cheap AI platforms that are best suited to resource-constrained destinations.

– International partners should ensure that external services focus on capacity transfer to help Cambodian educators and learning institutes sustain AI initiatives autonomously after the donor-funded phases.

5.3 Prospects for Further Research

– The current study offers preliminary insight into the infusion of AI within the Cambodian legal curriculum; however, numerous factors necessitate further empirical studies:
– Such research should carry out extensive surveys or mixed-method studies to investigate students' and law educators' attitudes, preparedness, and moral consciousness at various universities.
– Prospective longitudinal evaluations of pilot AI projects (e.g., AI-enabled moot courts or online learning systems) can be performed to assess true learning outcomes, economic value, and ethics.
– Comparative regional studies between the ASEAN states, especially between Cambodia, Malaysia, and Indonesia, could perhaps address region-wide challenges as well as localized innovations to enhance regional policy coherence.
– Studies of the influence of AI skills on graduates' preparedness to practice as lawyers and their job marketability would aid the integration of curriculum reform with employment market needs.
– Additional research needs to investigate the interplay between new national AI policies and research freedom, data security, and the digital transformation of the judicial field.

Cambodia is on the verge of a significant change in education. Bringing AI into legal education is a great way to modernize the legal field, make learning more accessible to everyone, and train ethical and tech-savvy lawyers to shape the country's justice system in the digital age. However, this change must be planned, open to everyone, and based on values. The findings and discussion show that technology alone cannot guarantee progress. Success depends on people's skills, moral commitment, and policy alignment. Cambodia can create a legal education system that meets the needs of an AI-driven world and reflects the country's long-standing commitment to justice, fairness, and human dignity by taking an incremental, collaborative, and contextually based approach.

REFERENCES

American Bar Association. (2020). Model rules of professional conduct: Rule 1.1 competence. https://www.americanbar.org/groups/professional_responsibility/publications/model_rules_of_professional_conduct/rule_1_1_competence/comment_on_rule_1_1/

American Bar Association. (2023). 2023--2024 ABA standards and rules for the approval of law schools. Standard 303. https://www.americanbar.org/groups/legal_education/resources/standards/High Educ 21, 4 (2024). DOI: 10.1186/s41239-023-00436-z

Bond, M., Khosravi, H., De Laat, M., Bergdahl, N., Negrea, V., Oxley, E., Pham, P., Chong, S. W., & Siemens, G. (2024). A meta systematic review of artificial intelligence in higher education: A call for increased ethics, collaboration, and rigour. *International Journal of Educational Technology in Higher Education*, *21*(1), 4. DOI: 10.1186/s41239-023-00436-z

Chandarin, C. (2024, May 29). Ethical use of artificial intelligence in Cambodian education. Cambodianess. https://cambodianess.com/article/ethical-use-of-artificial-intelligence-in-cambodian-education

European Commission. (2021). Ethics guidelines for trustworthy AI. Publications Office of the EU. https://www.europarl.europa.eu/cmsdata/196377/AI%20HLEG_Ethics%20Guidelines%20for%20Trustworthy%20AI.pdf

Flynn, S. (2021, June 9). How natural language processing (NLP) AI is used in law. Law Technology Today. American Bar Association. https://www.americanbar.org/groups/law_practice/resources/law-technology-today/2021/how-natural-language-processing-nlp-ai-is-used-in-law/

Formpl.us. (2023, April 24). Desk research: Definition, types, application, pros & cons. https://www.formpl.us/blog/desk-research-definition-types-application-pros-cons

Heng, S., Tsilionis, K., Scharff, C., & Wautelet, Y. (2022). Understanding AI ecosystems in the Global South: The cases of Senegal and Cambodia. *International Journal of Information Management*, *64*, 1–15. DOI: 10.1016/j.ijinfomgt.2021.102454

Holmes, W., Bialik, M., & Fadel, C. (2022). *Artificial intelligence in education: Promises and implications for teaching and learning* (2nd ed.). Center for Curriculum Redesign., https://discovery.ucl.ac.uk/id/eprint/10139722/

Iqbal, J., Asgarova, V., Hashmi, Z. F., Ngajie, B. N., Asghar, M. Z., Arslan, M. M., Hassan, E., & Järvenoja, H. (2025). Exploring faculty experiences with generative AI tool integration in second language curricula in Chinese higher education. Discover Computing, 28(1), 1–29. https://link.springer.com/article/10.1007/s10791-025-09655-6

Keo, V., Sam, R., Lan, B., & Wen, R. (2024). Challenges and opportunities of educational technology integration in Cambodian higher education institutions: A literature review. International Journal of Education, Psychology and Counseling, 9(54). https://gaexcellence.com/ijepc/article/view/285

Khoalenyane, N. B., & Ajani, O. A. (2024). A systematic review of artificial intelligence in higher education-South Africa. *Social Sciences and Education Research Review*, *11*(1), 17–26. DOI: 10.5281/zenodo.15258127

Lai, M. K. (2025). AI-personalized learning in higher education: A study on learning outcomes and motivation among university students. *International Journal of Research and Innovation in Social Science*, *9*(6), 6075–6085. https://rsisinternational.org/journals/ijriss/articles/ai-personalised-learning-in-higher-education-a-study-on-learning-outcomes-and-motivation-among-university-students/

Lampou, R. (2023). The integration of artificial intelligence in education: Opportunities and challenges. *Review of Artificial Intelligence in Education*, *4*(00), e15. DOI: 10.37497/rev.artif.intell.educ.v4i00.15

Leng, P., & Srun, M. (2025). Liberal arts for ethical and critical AI adoption in Cambodia. Science Technology and Sustainability Review, STS002/25, 1–15. https://camtech.edu.kh/wp-content/uploads/2025/08/CC_001_25_Liberal-Arts-Education.pdf

Migliorini, S., & Moreira, J. I. (2025). The case for nurturing AI literacy in law schools. *Asian Journal of Legal Education*, *12*(1), 1–15. DOI: 10.1177/23220058241265613

Ministry of Higher Education. Malaysia. (2022). Standards and criteria for law programmes (2nd ed.). Malaysian Qualifications Agency. https://www.mqa.gov.my/new/mqf.cfm?utm_source=chatgpt.com#gsc.tab=0

Ministry of Post and Telecommunications (MPTC). Cambodia. (2025). Press release on process of artificial intelligence governance. https://mptc.gov.kh/en/2025/04/press-release-on-process-of-artificial-intelligence-governance/?utm_source=chatgpt.com

MoEYS. (2021). Private education statistics and indicators 2020-2021. https://moeys.gov.kh/index.php/en/emis/4205.html#.YSy6MtOA63I

MoEYS. (2025). Education Congress: The Education, Youth and Sport Performance in the Academic Year 2023-2024.

Muhidin, E., Suparman, E., Perwira, I., & Hamzah, M. G. (2023). Digital Acceleration During Covid-19 Pandemic: How the Indonesian Constitutional Court Brings the Citizens Justice. DOI: 10.36745/ijca.512

Ocen, S., Elasu, J., Aarakit, S. M., & Olupot, C. (2025). Artificial intelligence in higher education institutions: Review of innovations, opportunities and challenges. *Frontiers in Education*, *10*, 1530247. DOI: 10.3389/feduc.2025.1530247

Padilla Flores, E., & Mean, U. (2024). Digital Transformation in Cambodian Higher Education and Its Impact on Teaching and Learning Outcomes. *Journal of Accounting, Finance, Economics, and Social Sciences*, *9*(1), 23–34. DOI: 10.62458/jafess9(1)3

Prakash, G. A., & Nair, V. (2024). Integrating generative AI into legal education: From casebooks to code, opportunities and challenges. Law. *Technology and Humans*, *6*(3), 60–79. DOI: 10.5204/lthj.3640

Remus, D., & Levy, F. (2017). Can robots be lawyers? Computers, lawyers, and the practice of law. *The Georgetown Journal of Legal Ethics*, *30*(3), 501–558. https://www.iadclaw.org/assets/1/7/10.1-_Remus_Levy.pdf?utm_source=chatgpt.com

Rogers, E. M. (2003). *Diffusion of Innovations* (5th ed.). Free Press., https://www.simonandschuster.co.uk/books/Diffusion-of-Innovations-5th-Edition/Everett-M-Rogers/9780743222099?utm_source=chatgpt.com

Sam, R., Lan, B., Keo, V., Kheuy, S., & Em, S. (2025a). Emerging Trends in Educational Leadership Research: A Systematic Literature Review. In Musundire, A. (Ed.), *Research Methods for Educational Leadership and Management* (pp. 31–66). IGI Global Scientific Publishing., DOI: 10.4018/979-8-3693-9425-0.ch002

Sam, R., Li, X., Sok, K., Tieng, M., & Yoeng, H. (2025d). Effective Turnaround Leadership Practices in Cambodia: Perspectives from School Principals. In Liu, P., & Thien, L. M. (Eds.), *Turnaround Leadership in Southeast Asian Countries*. Springer., DOI: 10.1007/978-981-96-7894-5_5

Sam, R., Serey, M., Ry, H., Sarith, C., Tieng, M., & Yoeng, H. (2025c). Academic Accreditation and Evaluation in Cambodian Higher Education Institutions: Development, Challenges, and Opportunities. In Lytras, M., & erban, A. (Eds.), *Academic Accreditation and Evaluation in Higher Education: Practices, Experiences, and Quality Assurance* (pp. 241–262). IGI Global Scientific Publishing., DOI: 10.4018/979-8-3693-5608-1.ch010

Sam, R., Souriyavongsa, T., Md Zain, A. N., Jamil, H., Wu, X., & Sovath, S. (2013). Conceptualizing institutional policies for students' academic success in Cambodian universities: What matters for policy? *Asian Social Science*, *9*(10), 283–293. DOI: 10.5539/ass.v9n10p283

Sam, R., Tieng, M., Yoeng, H., Sarith, C., Serey, M., & Sam, S. (2025b). Enhancing Research for Academicians in Cambodian Higher Education Institutions: A Policy Perspective. In Mdikana, A. (Ed.), *Enhancing Research for Academicians in Higher Education* (pp. 225–248). IGI Global Scientific Publishing., DOI: 10.4018/979-8-3693-4496-5.ch012

Secretariat, A. S. E. A. N. (2023, December). Tech for Good Institute; ASEAN Digital Economy Framework Agreement (DEFA) Report. Tech for Good Institute. https://techforgoodinstitute.org/wp-content/uploads/2023/12/TFGI_DEFA-Report.pdf?utm_source=chatgpt.com#page=26.26

Selwyn, N. (2019). Should robots replace teachers? AI and the Future of Education. (1st ed.) Polity Press. https://www.wiley.com/en-gb/Should+Robots+Replace+Teachers%3F%3 A+AI+and +the+Future+of+Education-p-9781509528967

Sisinternational. (2025, August 27). Secondary desk research. https://www.sisinternational.com/solutions/qualitative-quantitative-research-solutions/desk-research/

Sok, S., Heng, K., & Pum, M. (2025). Investigating High School Students' Attitudes Toward the Use of AI in Education: Evidence from Cambodia. *SAGE Open*, *15*(3), 21582440251353575. Advance online publication. DOI: 10.1177/21582440251353575

Sullivan, M., Kelly, A., & McLaughlan, P. (2022). ChatGPT in higher education: Considerations for academic integrity and student learning. *Journal of Applied Learning & Teaching*, *6*(1), 12–25. DOI: 10.37074/jalt.2023.6.1.17

Surden, H. (2019). Artificial intelligence and law: An overview. Georgia State University Law Review, 35(4), 1305–1345. https://readingroom.law.gsu.edu/gsulr/vol35/iss4/8/?utm_ source=chatgpt.com

Susskind, R. (2023). *Tomorrow's lawyers: An introduction to your future* (3rd ed.). Oxford University Press., https://global.oup.com/academic/product/tomorrows-lawyers-9780192864727?utm_source=chatgpt.com DOI: 10.1093/9780192864727.001.0001

UNESCO. (2021). *AI and education: Guidance for policy-makers*. UNESCO Publishing., DOI: 10.54675/PCSP7350

UNESCO. (2025a). Artificial intelligence readiness assessment: Cambodia. United Nations Educational, Scientific and Cultural Organization. https://www.unesco.org/en/articles/cambodia-artificial-intelligence-readiness-assessment-report

UNESCO. (2025b, July 29). UNESCO's AI and the rule of law toolkit transforming legal education. https://www.unesco.org/en/articles/unescos-ai-and-rule-law-toolkit-transforming-legal-education

Venkatesh, V., Morris, M. G., Davis, G. B., & Davis, F. D. (2003). User acceptance of information technology: Toward a unified view. *Management Information Systems Quarterly*, *27*(3), 425–478. DOI: 10.2307/30036540

Williamson, B., & Eynon, R. (2020). Historical threads, missing links, and future directions in AI in education. *Learning, Media and Technology*, *45*(3), 223–235. DOI: 10.1080/17439884.2020.1798995

Wischmeyer, T., & Rademacher, T. (Eds.). (2020). *Regulating artificial intelligence*. Springer., DOI: 10.1007/978-3-030-32361-5

Zawacki-Richter, O., Marín, V. I., Bond, M., & Gouverneur, F. (2019). Systematic review of research on artificial intelligence applications in higher education – Where are the educators? *International Journal of Educational Technology in Higher Education*, *16*(1), 1–27. DOI: 10.1186/s41239-019-0171-0

KEY TERMS AND DEFINITIONS

Artificial intelligence (AI): refers to the development of computer programs that can carry out activities that normally require human intellect, such as reasoning, problem-solving, learning, and decision-making. AI enhances teaching, research, and analysis in education and law by standardizing routine work and providing smart insights to support efficiency and innovation.

AI tools: AI tools are software applications that utilize artificial intelligence to improve the learning process, research work, and administration. They are tools such as virtual assistants, adaptive learning software, and predictive analytics, which facilitate personalized learning, simplify legal research, and support decision-making in education and the workplace.

Legal Education: Legal education is the deliberate process of instruction and learning law principles, practices, and ethics. Legal education gives learners analytical, reasoning, and advocacy skills for legal practice and integrates increasingly more technology and AI to equip future lawyers with the ability to work in technologically sophisticated legal systems.

Higher Education Institutions: Higher Education Institutions (HEIs) are universities, professional schools, and colleges that provide more advanced studies and research experiences than secondary education institutions do. They play a major role in building professionals by adopting new-generation technologies such as AI to enhance curriculum design, pedagogy, and institutional efficiency.

Technology adoption: Adoption means embracing, implementing, and integrating new technological innovations in organisations or education sectors. Higher and legal learning employs AI devices and websites for automating teaching, increasing access to knowledge, and preparing students for the age of technology.

Chapter 3
AI-Supported Dialogic Legal Pedagogy (AIDLP): A Theory of Complementary Intelligence for Legal Education

Ioannis Karvelas
https://orcid.org/0009-0001-8764-505X
National and Kapodistrian University of Athens, Greece

Vasiliki Ioannidi
https://orcid.org/0000-0003-1792-5918
Hellenic Open University, Greece

ABSTRACT

This chapter explores the pedagogical and ethical implications of integrating artificial intelligence (AI) into legal education. Drawing upon the Adaptive Legal Intelligence Framework (ALIF) and the AIDLP model, the authors propose a dialogic and reflective approach that prioritizes critical thinking, ethical awareness, and mostly personalized learning. The chapter examines how AI systems can support or undermine legal reasoning and professional identity, and highlights the need for legal educators to engage with AI not merely as a tool, but as a co-thinker in the learning process. Through theoretical analysis and practical examples, the chapter offers strategies for incorporating AI in ways that reinforce legal ethics, promote cognitive autonomy, and respect the relational nature of legal knowledge.

DOI: 10.4018/979-8-3373-3451-6.ch003

1. INTRODUCTION

The swift and unprecedented advancement of artificial intelligence technologies calls for a reassessment of pedagogical methods and educational tools. It is clear that, despite the transformative impact of AI across various aspects of human experience and scientific exploration, legal education remains predominantly anchored in conventional teaching strategies. Although the legal field itself is experiencing significant change due to AI (Atkinson et al., 2020), with the emergence of new tools and technologies altering legal practice, research, and analysis, the adoption of these technologies into the foundational elements of legal education is still in its early stages. This chapter presents the concept of AI-Supported Dialogic Legal Pedagogy (AIDLP), a conceptual framework aimed at integrating artificial intelligence into legal education, viewing it not just as a technical resource but as an advanced and supportive educational partner.

AIDLP represents a combination of two essential elements. Initially, it expands on the concepts of the Adaptive Legal Intelligence Framework (ALIF), which provides a thorough proposal for integrating artificial intelligence into legal education, thereby improving students' digital and ethical skills. Second, AIDLP presents a novel viewpoint of AI, as a dialogic, creative and mostly personalized partner in the learning experience. This combined model seeks to redefine the interaction between human and artificial intelligence within the educational ecosystem. By promoting a dynamic and personalized learning environment, AIDLP aims to cultivate a new generation of legal scholars who are not only intellectually independent and ethically sound but also culturally insightful, capable of navigating the intricacies of a technologically advanced society and addressing global issues with understanding and accountability.

2. THE EVOLVING LANDSCAPE OF LEGAL EDUCATION

The tradition of legal education has been tradition bound, and traditional focused with emphasis on case methods and doctrinal exposition. Although these strategies have been quite successful in helping students develop critical thinking skills and the ability to analyze legal issues, they have encountered challenges in keeping up with the rapid technological changes affecting the practice of law. AI, and especially generative AI, promises new models for legal research, document review, contract analysis, and societally significant applications as well (like predictive analytics for litigation). AI-based law firms and legal departments are undergoing rapid adoption in order to enhance efficiency and accuracy (LexisNexis, n.d.). A demand has emerged, due to this technological development, as it manifests itself in practice, for a parallel evolution in legal education, whereby future legal professionals are adequately prepared for the demands of the modern legal environment. The challenge is not merely to teach the use of these tools, but extends to fostering a deeper understanding of their technological foundations, their ethical implications, and their transformative nature. The American Bar Association (ABA) recognizes this necessity, noting that law schools are grappling with a range of questions, from the use of artificial intelligence in admissions processes to the specific ethical challenges that arise from its use in legal practice (American Bar Association, n.d.).

3. INTRODUCING AIDLP

Given this situation, AIDLP theory emerges as an evolving and innovative pedagogical paradigm that transcends the traditional perception of AI as a simple educational aid. Instead, AIDLP proposes a role for AI as an active and interactive companion in the learning process. This paradigm shift is crucial for several reasons. Traditional legal education, which often takes place in environments with large numbers of students, fails to respond to diverse learning needs and provides personalized feedback on a large scale. AIDLP responds to this challenge by leveraging AI to provide continuous, personalized, and interactive communication, enhancing learning inquiry, self-regulation through feedback mechanisms, and the progressive cultivation of critical thinking through virtual dialogue. Its core thesis is that, when designed and implemented thoughtfully, AI can function as an active interlocutor, capable of reproducing, reinforcing, and challenging student knowledge, just as an adaptive educator would. In this way, learning moves from simple memorization to a process of meaningful processing, complex argumentation, and, ultimately, the cultivation of moral empathy.

4. CHAPTER OBJECTIVES AND STRUCTURE

The main purpose of this chapter is to provide an in-depth and theoretically founded presentation of the AIDLP model, by developing in detail all the key points and stages of the framework, clarifying its pedagogical and theoretical implications. Particular emphasis will be given to the Adaptive Legal Intelligence Framework (ALIF), with a full analysis of its structure, its conceptual basis, its application in curricula, as well as the transition it seeks - from basic technical familiarity to substantial pedagogical empowerment of the student.

At the same time, the chapter will examine in depth the dialogical relationship that can develop between a student and artificial intelligence, not perceiving the latter as a simple tool, but as a continuous, personalized interlocutor, capable of promoting critical thinking, complex argumentation and ethical elaboration. It is through this approach that the advantage of artificial intelligence as a pedagogical mediator is highlighted, so that it can effectively respond to the personalized learning needs of law students, overcoming the limitations of traditional group-centered teaching.

Moreover, the ethical dimension of artificial intelligence will be explored not as a static concept to be integrated into systems, but as a field of reflection under formation, in which artificial intelligence itself participates as a co-thinking entity. Besides, a philosophical and cultural perspective will be adopted throughout the text, whereby artificial intelligence is understood as a force for enhancing human consciousness, creativity and autonomy - elements crucial in an era of global and existential challenges, such as the climate crisis, biotechnological evolution and the advance into space. Eventually, the chapter will demonstrate the contribution of the AIDLP paradigm to the emergence of a new type of legal scientist; a subject with intellectual autonomy, moral maturity and cultural insight, capable of responding to the complex demands of the 21st century.

The chapter is structured as follows; in the second part, an extensive review of the relevant literature is presented, covering the use of artificial intelligence in education, legal pedagogy, as well as the ethical implications of the use of artificial intelligence. The third part focuses on the conceptual background of the AIDLP paradigm, analyzing its basic principles, the structure of the ALIF model, and the nature of the dialogical relationship that develops between the student and the artificial intelligence. In the fourth part, strategic practices and innovative pedagogical approaches that arise from this framework are examined. In the fifth part, the dynamically evolving ethical dimensions of artificial intelligence are examined, especially as they develop within the AIDLP framework. In the sixth part, the broader cultural implications of the model are analyzed, with an emphasis on the enhancement of human consciousness and autonomy. Finally, the seventh part provides a conclusion of the chapter with a brief assessment of the importance of AIDLP and with suggestions for future research and implementation.

5. LITERATURE REVIEW: AI, PEDAGOGY AND LEGAL EDUCATION

AI in Education: A General Overview

While AI in the context of education has been of relevance both from research and practical perspectives for several decades (Ng et al., 2023; Memarian & Doleck, 2024), the past twenty years have seen a growing interest in its use and study in educational settings, owing to advances in data availability, machine learning, and computational power (Wilton et al., 2022). Early AI applications in education were mainly associated with intelligent tutoring systems (ITS) that aimed at offering personalized instruction and feedback to students based on their individual paces and styles of learning. In the early examples, AI was adopted with the promise of improving learning outcomes by delivering individualized support - something constrained classroom settings would either not be able (or willing) to replicate due to scale and resource, or were unable to support effectively. Apart from ITS, AI has different applications in education (Baker & Siemens, 2014), such as automated grading, recommendation systems for learning material, adaptive learning systems, and educational data mining to discover learning patterns and forecast student performance.

The development of large language models (LLMs) and creative AI has significantly expanded the scope of AI in education and the capabilities thereof, because these advanced systems are able to produce human-like texts, summarize complex information, translate languages, and engage in complex dialogues, opening up new possibilities for personalized learning experiences. For instance, creative AI can construct educational materials tailored to the needs of each student, compose practice exercises, and provide immediate, analytical feedback on written assignments, thereby enhancing the work of teachers and enriching the learning environment (Roll & Wylie, 2016). What is particularly crucial is the emerging ability of artificial intelligence to act as a dialogic partner, supporting inquiry-based learning and therefore, the development of critical thinking; this is an approach going beyond the simple transmission of information and fostering deeper cognitive engagement.

Nevertheless, the widespread integration of AI in education comes with significant challenges and ethical dilemmas. Issues such as privacy, algorithmic bias, transparency, and the risk of overreliance on AI systems are hot topics in the debate (UNESCO, 2021). Bias in algorithms, often driven by biased educational data, can perpetuate or even exacerbate existing social inequalities, leading to unequal educational experiences for specific groups of students. Furthermore, the "opaque" nature of some AI models (what is called the "black box" phenomenon) raises concerns about the accountability and interpretability of the decisions or suggestions produced by these systems. Ethical issues extend to how the essence of the learning process itself is affected, including human agency and creativity. The aforementioned reasons have motivated educators and policymakers to actively work to develop guidelines and frameworks for the responsible and ethical use of AI in education, with emphasis on human oversight, fairness, and student data protection (Cornell University, n.d.). In spite of these challenges, there is broad agreement in the research and education community that AI has enormous potential to transform education, provided its integration is based on ethical principles and a clear understanding of its pedagogical role.

Current State of AI in Legal Education

It is quite obvious that the legal profession, despite being traditionally wary of adopting new technologies, is currently facing a profound and deep disruption due to the rapid advancement of artificial intelligence, as AI tools are increasingly being applied to various areas of legal practice (from automating repetitive processes, such as document review and e-discovery, to supporting legal research, contract analysis, and even predicting case outcomes) (Offit Kurman, 2025). This technological shift in practice has put significant pressure on legal education institutions to reshape their curricula and pedagogies in order to adequately prepare future lawyers for a professional environment shaped in a great extent by artificial intelligence. Nevertheless, the integration of AI in legal education remains uneven and often limited, focusing mainly on the technical familiarization of students, without being accompanied by a broader pedagogical transformation.

Some law schools have begun to include courses in legal technology, computational law, or the ethical dimensions of artificial intelligence in the legal field in their curricula or through their societies. The main goal of these initiatives is to provide students with practical skills in using AI tools, as well as to help them understand the legal and ethical issues that they entail, such as algorithmic bias, privacy, and intellectual property rights in AI-generated content (National Law Review, 2025). Some institutions have also begun to integrate AI-powered research platforms into their libraries, so that students have been offered the opportunity to gain practical experience with tools already used in professional legal practice. For example, platforms that leverage AI to speed up case law searches or analyze legal documents are becoming increasingly common (Bloomberg Law, n.d.).

Despite the efforts that have been made, the dominant approach treats artificial intelligence mainly as an auxiliary tool or as a new subject to teach, and not as a fundamental factor that can altogether redefine the learning process. The emphasis is often placed on what AI can do and how it is used, without sufficiently examining how it can transform pedagogical relationships and the experience of legal education. This utilitarian view, while necessary for practical familiarity, does not fully exploit the potential of AI to enhance critical thinking, ethical reflection and personalized learning. In addition, obstacles such as teacher reluctance, lack of resources and the rapid pace of technological development make it difficult to integrate it effectively and comprehensively (Balan, 2024). The current situation largely reflects a reactive adjustment to technological advancements in the legal profession, rather than an active redesign of legal pedagogy in the light of an intelligence that functions complementary to humans. This gap highlights the necessity of a framework like AIDLP, which proposes to move beyond simple technical integration and towards a dialogic and transformative engagement of AI in legal education.

Dialogic Pedagogy: Theoretical Foundations

An emphasis on the power of dialogue lies at the heart of dialogic pedagogy; for the power of dialogue and interaction are the key factors for the deep understanding, the cultivation of critical thinking, and the co-construction of knowledge. In contrast to monological, traditional teaching, where knowledge is mainly transmitted from teacher to student, the dialogic approach views learning as a collaborative process, where understanding is co-constructed through the participation and the exchange of views. Based on the works of thinkers such as Mikhail Bakhtin and Paulo Freire (Renfrew, 2014; Darder, 2014), but with roots already in antiquity, dialogic pedagogy understands language not simply as a tool for communication, but as a medium through which human understanding is constructed, contested, and developed. Bakhtin, in his concept of "dialogism," argues that all forms of understanding are inherently dialogic - that is, meaning emerges from the interaction of different voices and perspectives. Freire, for his part, proposed a "pedagogy of the oppressed," which replaces the banking model of education -where students function as passive recipients of information- with a problem-centered approach that encourages the development of critical consciousness and the active, transformative participation of students through dialogue (Freire, 1970).

In an interactive classroom, the role of the teacher shifts from that of a simple transmitter of knowledge to that of a facilitator of the learning process. The teacher encourages discussion, poses challenging questions, and encourages students to express their thoughts, interact with different perspectives, and co-create knowledge. This approach creates a learning environment in which students feel empowered and free to ask questions, challenge data, explore complex concepts through open dialogue, and thus, acquire a true understanding of the subject. Basic features of interactive pedagogy include active listening, mutual respect, open-ended questions, collaborative inquiry, and recognition of the value of different perspectives on specific issues (Alexander, 2008). The benefits of such a pedagogical approach are manifold; it enhances students' ability to reason, argue, and support their opinions; it deepens the understanding of complex concepts as students are asked to articulate and defend their interpretations; and it fosters intellectual autonomy by empowering them to take an active, not pathetic, role in their own learning. Research has shown that interactive teaching enhances critical thinking, learning, and problem-solving skills by leveraging the dynamic exchange of ideas (Kim & Wilkinson, 2019).

The importance of dialogic pedagogy for legal education is notably substantial because legal thought is inherently dialogic, as it is based on the interpretation of laws, case law, and arguments, as well as the construction of persuasive narratives. The Socratic method, a key tool in legal teaching, is a form of dialogic inquiry, although it is often accompanied by an imbalance of power between teacher and student. Nevertheless, the limitations of this method in large classes, where individualized attention is limited, highlight the need for scalable dialogic practices. The principles of dialogic pedagogy, such as fostering critical thinking, argumentation, and the ability to manage different perspectives, are precisely the skills required for successful legal practice. Through the creation of learning environments that prioritize genuine dialogue, legal education may transcend what is experienced (by the students) as a fruitless transmission of legal rules and help cultivate a deeper, more nuanced understanding of legal principles and the application thereof. In this way, students become ready not just to know the law, but to understand it meaningfully, to challenge it creatively, and to actively participate in shaping it in the future.

Ethical Considerations of AI in Education

The rapid spread of Artificial Intelligence in education has brought to the fore a complex and multidimensional ethical dilemma that requires special attention. While AI offers significant potential for personalizing learning, automating administrative processes, and leveraging data to improve the educational experience, its application also raises serious concerns about fairness, transparency, privacy, and accountability. These ethical issues are not limited to technical challenges; they touch on deeper philosophical and social questions, affecting the very nature of education and the way in which future citizens are formed.

One of the most serious ethical issues that has emerged concerns algorithmic bias. Artificial intelligence systems are trained on vast datasets, and when this data incorporates existing social biases, AI models tend to reproduce and reinforce these biases. In the educational field, this can manifest itself in several ways: for example, through assessment algorithms that discriminate against students from particular social or cultural groups; through adaptive learning systems that unwittingly reinforce stereotypes; or through predictive analytics that, based on false associations, incorrectly identify students as "high risk" (Educause, 2024). Ensuring fairness and equity in AI systems requires not only careful selection and cleaning of training data, but also the existence of reliable mechanisms to control and limit bias at all stages of system development and operation. The problem of lack of transparency, also known as the "black box" problem, exacerbates the situation, as it makes it difficult to understand the inner workings of algorithms and identify potential biases (JMU Libraries, 2025).

Privacy and data security are another fundamental ethical concern, as AI educational systems often collect large amounts of sensitive information about students, including their academic performance, learning patterns, and even biometric data. The process of collecting, storing, and using this information raises serious privacy questions, in particular regarding who has access to the data, how it is protected from breaches, and how the data is used for purposes other than educational support. The risk of commercial exploitation or misuse of student data, for instance for surveillance purposes, highlights the demand for strong data governance policies and effective security measures (Enrollify, 2024).

Accountability and responsibility are also important issues in the ethical debate around artificial intelligence. When an AI system makes a decision that has negative consequences for a student, the arising question is who is responsible? Is it the system's developer? The educational institution that implemented it? Or could the teacher who used it be the one responsible for the negative effects? The need for clear accountability becomes even more urgent as systems become more autonomous and the "logic" behind their decisions becomes "mistier" and more difficult to understand. At the same time, valid concerns arise that students' overreliance on AI to solve problems or acquire knowledge may weaken their personal initiative and critical thinking. The ethical challenge, therefore, is not merely to avoid mistakes, but to design and utilize artificial intelligence in a way that truly enhances human capabilities, promoting intellectual independence and an active, reflective engagement, rather than encouraging passive consumption of information.

Finally, the ethical debate around artificial intelligence in education extends to broader societal dimensions, such as its impact on the future of work, the strengthening or widening of the digital divide, but also the reflection on the very definition of intelligence and learning. While AI radically transforms productive sectors and labor markets, education systems need to prepare students for a world where human-machine collaboration in a symbiotic environment will be of the utmost importance. But only a multidimensional approach can address these ethical issues; a combination of interdisciplinary research, development of ethical guidelines, appropriate regulatory interventions, and ongoing dialogue between educators, policymakers, AI developers, and civil society itself. The ultimate goal is to harness the transformative power of artificial intelligence in education in a way that preserves fundamental human values and ensures fair and beneficial prospects for all learners.

6. CONCEPTUAL FRAMEWORK: AI-SUPPORTED DIALOGIC LEGAL PEDAGOGY (AIDLP)

AI-Supported Dialogic Legal Pedagogy (AIDLP), as has already been mentioned, is an innovative pedagogical framework that radically reshapes the role of Artificial Intelligence in legal education, going beyond the conventional perception of AI as a simple technological tool. At its core, the AIDLP approach conceives of AI as an advanced and complementary pedagogical agent, a personalized and ongoing interlocutor in the learning process. This framework is based on the synthesis of the Adaptive Legal Intelligence Framework (ALIF) and a new vision of AI as a dialogical, ethical and mostly creative partner in the intellectual cultivation of law students. The core principles of AIDLP are not limited to developing technical skills in using AI tools, but aim to give existence to a deep legal consciousness, enhance students' critical thinking, moral maturity, and cultural insight, preparing them for the complexities of a technologically advanced and globally interconnected world.

Core Principles of AIDLP

The foundational principles of AIDLP, the roots of this theory, are founded in a holistic view of legal education, which integrates technological literacy with humanistic values and advanced cognitive skills. These principles are the ones which guide the creation and implementation of AI-supported learning environments:

1. AI as a Complementary Pedagogical Agent: AIDLP moves away from the idea of AI as a substitute for human educators or a simple efficiency tool. Instead, it approaches artificial intelligence as an intelligent assistant that complements the human teaching process, expanding the scope and depth of pedagogical interactions. This means that AI can handle and complete monotonous routine tasks, provide immediate feedback to students, and, most importantly, offer personalized learning paths, giving educators the freedom to focus on higher-level teaching activities, such as complex ethical discussions, strategic thinking, and fostering social-emotional development.
2. Dialogic Interaction as the Primary Mode of Learning: Of primary importance to AIDLP is the emphasis on continuous, personalized dialogue between the student and artificial agent (Jabbour et al., 2025). This is not just a superficial Q&A, but a deep, inquiry-based conversational exchange that mimics the Socratic method, yet is tailored to individual learning styles and paces, because it is necessary to follow the tenet of personalized learning. In such a case, AI acts as a tireless interlocutor, prompting critical reflection, challenging assumptions, and guiding students through complex legal reasoning processes. This dialogic

approach is the substance fostering active construction of knowledge rather than passive reception and therefore, providing true acquisition of knowledge.

3. Cultivation of Adaptive Legal Intelligence: AIDLP is intrinsically linked with the Adaptive Legal Intelligence Framework (ALIF), which provides a structured progression for students to develop competence in navigating the intersection of law and technology. This progression moves from basic AI literacy to advanced problem-solving, collaboration, and independent, creative AI usage, ensuring that students are not just passive users of technology but possible innovators, and thereby actual ethical shapers thereof.
4. Ethical Reflection as an Evolving Field: AIDLP does not approach ethics as a fixed set of rules to be programmed into AI's code. Rather than this static -and in many ways problematic- approach, it views ethics as a dynamic, evolving field of reflection in which AI can actively participate as a co-thinker (if the term "co-thinker" echoes strongly, perhaps it is acceptable that Artificial Intelligence can be an amplifier of human thinking). This principle and perspective may encourage students to engage in continuing ethical debates with AI, exploring complex moral dilemmas, and developing a nuanced understanding of the societal implications of legal and technological advancements, to strengthen their moral reasoning. In such a case, AI serves as a mirror, reflecting various ethical positions and prompting deeper moral reasoning.
5. Personalized Learning: Recognizing that each student learns at their own pace and in their own way, AIDLP leverages the obvious power of Artificial Intelligence to convey learning experiences tailored to individual needs, that is, personalized learning experiences. Unlike conventional classroom teaching, which often fails to accommodate the diversity of learning styles due to the large number of students, interactive AI can tailor its answers, explanations, and questions to each student's cognitive characteristics and preferences, ensuring maximum engagement and understanding, and this way accomplishing one of the most important purposes of the education.
6. Enhancing Critical Thinking, Argumentation, and Creativity: Through interaction, the clear purpose of AIDLP is to significantly improve students' ability to think critically and argue with clarity and precision (this is, after all, the very purpose of many educational systems across the world). AI, through its ability to pose (and sometimes settle) challenging questions, identify logical fallacies, and present the opposing views to an argument, enables students to deepen their thinking and defend their positions with evidence rather than sophism. At the same time, through the creative use of AI, the ability to innovatively solve legal problems and the required imagination for new legal applications are cultivated.
7. Expanding Human Consciousness and Action: On a philosophical level, AIDLP aims to enhance human consciousness, creativity (which is associated with

imagination), and personal initiative. As mundane routine or simply mechanical tasks are transferred to AI, students are freed to focus on higher intellectual activities, such as in-depth research, complex analysis, and creatively addressing the cultural and existential challenges of the modern world. AIDLP views AI not as a threat to human autonomy, but as a tool for accelerating intellectual and cultural liberation.

Overall, the fundamental principles of AIDLP constitute a pedagogical framework that is human-centered, with a clear orientation and a solid theoretical foundation. This model aspires to shape a new generation of legal scholars who are not content with legal work, but who stand out for their intellectual autonomy, their moral maturity, and their cultural vision - capable of leading in an increasingly complex world.

The Adaptive Legal Intelligence Framework (ALIF)

The Adaptive Legal Intelligence Framework (ALIF) serves as a foundational pillar for AIDLP, providing a structured and progressive pathway for the initial and systematic incorporation of AI into legal education. The purpose of ALIF is the cultivation of digital and ethical competence in students, but also the fostering of a profound legal -and, as such, deontological- consciousness in an increasingly technologically driven world. In order to achieve this purpose, ALIF envisions the integration of AI as an ongoing developmental process (and not as a static endpoint), characterized by four interdependent yet harmonious stages, which represent a deliberate pedagogical progression, designed to responsibly guide students from initial AI literacy to advanced, creative, and ethically informed engagement with artificial intelligence's technologies.

Structure and Theoretical Foundation

The ALIF (Adaptive Legal Intelligence Framework) is based on an evolutionary learning path, aiming at a complete and gradual understanding by students of the possibilities, limitations, and consequences of Artificial Intelligence in the legal field. Each stage builds on the previous one, promoting a cumulative learning experience that deepens the relationship of students with AI. The theoretical background of ALIF -emphasizing the active construction of knowledge- draws elements from constructivist theories, but simultaneously from sociocultural approaches, recognizing the importance of collaborative learning and of technological tools in cognitive development. The model is developed in four main stages:

1. Fundamental Understanding of Artificial Intelligence (AI Literacy): The first stage aims to familiarize students with the fundamental operational principles of AI. As such, it includes concepts such as machine learning algorithms, natural language processing, and data analysis. Particular emphasis is placed on both the potential of AI and its limitations (such as the lack of intuition or common sense, at least for the time being). At the same time, legal and ethical issues, which are founded in the heart of legal theory and practice, are introduced; issues such as data protection (e.g., GDPR), algorithmic bias, and intellectual property in AI-generated content. The theoretical framework focuses on building a cognitive schema around AI, allowing students to critically evaluate it rather than accepting it uncritically. The main purpose is to demystify AI in the eyes of young scholars and make it accessible to everyone, regardless of technical background.
2. Using AI as a Supportive Tool in the Classroom: In the second stage, AI tools and their practical usefulness are introduced into educational processes under the guidance of the teacher. The focus is on the practical use of AI to automate everyday legal tasks and enhance analytical thinking (because if the everyday procedural tasks are completed by the AI, the true creative power of humans can be unleashed). Examples include the use of intelligent legal databases for research, the use of language models for interpreting legal texts, or the application of tools for document review and contract analysis. Thereby, students have the chance to understand how AI can enhance human capabilities, optimize processes, and free up mental space for more complex thinking. In general, this stage emphasizes experiential learning and demonstrates the benefits -and simultaneously the limits- of AI within a safe educational environment.
3. Collaborative Legal Problem Solving with the Assistance of AI: In the third stage, a substantial shift is taking place, as AI is no longer seen only as a useful tool but as an interlocutor in the process of resolving complex legal cases (and thus, its position in the educational process has been upgraded). Students are invited to interact with artificial intelligence in scenarios where it acts as a support in analysis, reflection, and legal argumentation. This may include formulating the legal positions of the opposition (or generally alternative legal interpretations), detecting the strongest potential objections, or simulating different outcomes. The theoretical framework is based on the idea of what could be called "complementary intelligence", where humans and machines collaborate to achieve results that neither could achieve alone. AI challenges, inspires and extends the way students think, enhancing their ability to deepen, justify and perform complex legal analysis. This stage cultivates the student's relationship with AI as an intellectual partner and not as a simple assistant.

4. Independent and Creative Use of Artificial Intelligence (Integration Level): At the fourth and final stage of the ALIF framework, the integration of AI into the educational process is culminating. At this advanced level, students have acquired metacognitive skills and are encouraged to utilize AI creatively and autonomously. This means they are invited to develop original applications of AI for legal contexts, to write alternative legal scenarios or legislative proposals based on findings arising from the use of AI, or to explore the ethical and philosophical dimensions of technology in the legal field through simulations or research projects supported by AI. The main purpose of this stage is to cultivate innovation, foresight, and a proactive attitude towards developments in law and technology. It moves beyond mere application to genuine creation and critical engagement, empowering students to become creators of potential legal ecosystems, and in this way to elevate their thinking to the highest limit, that is, above understanding, judgment, and interpretation, to creation itself.

7. IMPLEMENTATION IN CURRICULA

However, integrating the ALIF framework in law studies is not an easy thing to do; it will need a gradual process, one that seeks to embed AI across multiple subjects as opposed to having it part of a single specialized lesson. In this way, students can learn AI in various educational circumstances, so that they can understand and implement the learned knowledge. Specific examples of how the ALIF stages can be incorporated in the curriculum include:

1. Basic literacy in AI: This level could be operationalized at an introductory level, either as a core foundational module, or integrated into a first-year context such as Legal Research and Writing, or Introduction to Law. For instance, a good start would be a legal research and writing course with a module on introduction to NLP and its role in AI legal research tools to be offered. What students would study: for example, tokenization, sentiment analysis, and predictive text, and how this tech is being used on platforms such as Westlaw Edge or LexisNexis. Ethical issues such as privacy and algorithmic biases can be integrated into legal ethics courses or special seminars. In addition, lectures by experts in AI ethics or legal technology developers could enrich students' practical understanding. Practical exercises might include analyzing small data sets to detect biases or evaluating privacy policies of AI applications in the legal field.
2. Using AI in Educational Practice: At this stage, AI tools are actively integrated by teachers into their teaching across a variety of courses. In a course regarding contracts, for example, an AI-powered contract analysis tool can be used for

the automated identification of crucial terms, potential risks, or inconsistencies in a hypothetical contract. This allows students to focus on negotiation and interpretation, rather than laborious manual reading (in other words, it allows students to focus on what is necessary for the law scientist of the future). In a course regarding Civil Procedure, an AI-powered e-discovery platform can be leveraged to simulate the process of processing large volumes of documents. In such a manner, students will be taught strategic document management and efficiency. In addition, exercises can be assigned in which students use AI tools to summarize complex legal decisions, identify relevant case law, or draft legal briefs, with AI providing immediate feedback on syntax, structure, and logical coherence. The goal of this stage is guided practice, where AI functions as an auxiliary tool, enhancing students' accuracy and efficiency in their legal work.

3. Collaborative Legal Problem Solving with AI: This stage requires, first, the design of complex, open-ended legal problems and, second, the encouragement of students to collaborate with AI as a cognitive partner. In mock trial or speech practice programs, students can use AI systems to generate counterarguments to the opposing side's brief or simulate cross-examination of witnesses, with AI providing feedback on the effectiveness of their questions (in this way, AI will contribute to the practice of rhetorical skills and legal thinking - something that is an essential element of legal studies). At the same time, in commercial or contract-oriented law clinics, students can collaborate with AI to draft complex legal documents, with the system suggesting alternative wordings or identifying potential legal loopholes, challenging students to judge, correct, and improve the produced content. The goal is to create learning experiences where AI challenges students' thinking, pushes them to consider different perspectives, and cultivates their capacity for legal analysis through dialogic and iterative interaction (as has been demonstrated, a holistic approach to an issue and the collection of alternative ways of thinking are essential for a good lawyer, and this is where artificial intelligence can contribute.). This stage seems to go beyond using AI as a tool and makes it an active interlocutor and intellectual collaborator.
4. Autonomous and Creative Use of AI (Final Stage): The final stage is typically embedded in advanced seminars, theses, or specialized legal clinics. Students are asked to develop original AI applications that respond to specific legal issues - for example, a tool that predicts potential regulatory compliance risks in new business sectors, or a system that analyzes case law data to detect trends in sentencing. Other tasks may include research into the ethical dimensions of new technologies of law (lawtech). In addition, the creative use of generative AI models can be leveraged to synthesize alternative legal scenarios or to simulate the impacts of proposed legislation. The ultimate goal, as mentioned earlier, is to enhance students' ability to become "pioneers", shaping the future of law

and technology with responsibility and insight, not simply adapting to analyses and former interpretations. Thus, this stage cultivates entrepreneurial thinking, interdisciplinary collaboration, and ethical awareness in the face of future (but also present) technological challenges.

Progression from Technical Literacy to Pedagogical Empowerment

The Adaptive Legal Intelligence Framework (ALIF) is precisely designed to support a gradual but meaningful evolution of students, leading them from a basic understanding of Artificial Intelligence (technical literacy) to a state of pedagogical empowerment. This educational journey is not only about acquiring new skills but mainly about cultivating a transformed legal consciousness. The goal is the consequential student's ability to critically engage and creatively utilize technology in the legal field and thus accelerate their competence and proficiency. The transition from technical proficiency to pedagogical empowerment marks a deeper -but always gradual- integration of AI into the students' intellectual arsenal, transforming them from passive users to active creators of legal knowledge and practice.

In the initial stage of Basic Familiarity with AI, the goal is to demystify the technology. This can happen when students learn the basic principles of operation, the capabilities, and limitations of AI systems. The technical familiarity, which is the desired result of this stage, is essential, as it provides the theoretical background and lexical precision required to be able to interact with AI in a critical and informed way (something about to happen in the next two stages). However, it is not difficult to see the reason why this level does not suffice for real empowerment. It is like learning the grammar of a language without understanding its rhetorical power or poetic dimension. Therefore, the introduction to the legal and ethical implications of AI at this stage should pave the way for a more complex and responsible engagement with technology (otherwise, we do not speak about ALIF, but for a simple course of technology/AI awareness).

The next stage, in which AI is applied in the Classroom, acts as a bridge between theoretical knowledge and its practical use, as in this stage, students apply their technical understanding, acquired in the former stage, within teacher-led learning environments, and see how AI can help them. While important practical skills are being developed here, pedagogical empowerment is also beginning to take shape as students see firsthand how AI can enhance their capabilities, their efficiency, and understanding. They start to realize that AI is not just a tool (the way a computer was three decades ago), but a multiplying force in their legal work, allowing them to focus on more complex and substantive tasks. It is this very experience that fosters a sense of confidence and control in integrating technology into their future professional practices.

The real shift towards pedagogical empowerment really accelerates in the stage of Collaborative Legal Problem Solving with AI, because it is here, where AI ceases to function as a mere tool and assumes the role of intellectual companion. Dialogic interaction with AI -where it challenges assumptions, suggests alternative perspectives, and activates deeper reasoning processes- forces students to develop more complex forms of critical thinking. This collaboration provokes an enhancement of their meta-cognitive awareness (that is, the understanding of their own thinking processes), as students learn to formulate, defend, and revise their arguments through a continuing dialogue with an “intelligent” system.

In the final stage, Autonomous and Creative Use of AI, students achieve full pedagogical empowerment. Having acquired the necessary technical background and experienced collaborative cognitive progress in the previous stages, they are now able and ready to utilize AI with autonomy and creativity, proposing innovative applications, elaborating new legal concepts, and addressing complex social challenges at an experimental level. At this stage, an active and visionary attitude towards technology is observed; students, instead of merely adapting to new developments, seek to shape them. They design new uses of AI and engage in ethical and philosophical inquiries that extend the boundaries of legal thinking. Empowerment at this point is reflected in their ability not only to effectively use these “intelligent” technologies but also to critically assess their implications, lead their evolution, and contribute substantially to the transformation of legal science and practice with technological sensitivity and ethical awareness. The overall path through the ALIF framework transforms students from technologically aware users to integrated legal thinkers, capable of leading the new era of artificial intelligence in the legal profession.

The AI-Student Dialogic Relationship

At the heart of AI-Supported Interactive Legal Pedagogy (AIDLP) is a radical reframing of the relationship between the student and artificial intelligence (or to put it more poetically, between the human and the machine). Rather than treating AI simply as a tool of conditional instrumental rationality or a static source of information, AIDLP conceives of it as an evolving and personalized (almost “living”, but not in terms of biology) interlocutor. This shift is not just linguistic or semantic - it profoundly changes the educational environment, transforming the learning process into a rich, two-way dialogue that fosters traits (such as critical thinking, argumentation, and ethical development) in ways that traditional teaching models often cannot.

AI as a Personalized Interlocutor

In this context, AI is envisioned as a tireless conversationalist, capable of engaging in a dialogue, a personal dialogue with each student (after all, the ideal purpose is to simulate the student-professor relationship, not in its spiritual dimension concerning the ethos, but in its technical dimension). It is crucial to understand the dynamic and individualized nature of this technology; unlike a search engine that merely provides static answers or a software that executes predefined commands, the AI interlocutor presents the unique feature of active participation in the learning process, adapting questions, answers and challenges according to the progress, style and needs of the student. Although this personalized interaction is crucial for many reasons, the most important are listed below.

1. Targeted Feedback and Support (Scaffolding): AI can provide immediate, accurate and constructive feedback on the legal arguments, interpretations or problem-solving methods adopted by the student. It can therefore recognize misconceptions successfully, point out logical gaps in reasoning, and suggest alternative ways of thinking, supporting the students' learning path in real time. This continuous and personalized feedback is much more effective than the general -and usually delayed- feedback often offered in large groups of students at university (Wood et al., 1976).
2. Adaptive Learning Paths: Since each student has a different pace and way of learning (and this is probably one of the most important principles in the pedagogy suggested in this paper), AI can adapt the level of difficulty, speed, and content of the discussion following their specific needs. If the student is struggling with a concept, AI can offer additional explanations, examples, or analogies - without getting tired or bored (after all, the very reason for this mechanical being's existence is to help the student - unlike the teacher it has no other obligations, desires, duties, or expectations). If, on the contrary, they have already mastered the concept, AI can challenge them with more demanding scenarios or by delving into more complex aspects of the legal issue. This personalization capability ensures that learning always remains meaningful and interesting, preventing both boredom and frustration.
3. Safe Environment for Experimentation and Error: AI provides a protected and judgment-free space where students can explore ideas, test theories, and make mistakes without fear of exposure or negative evaluation. This climate of psychological safety enhances the willingness to experiment, encourages risk-taking, and promotes a more meaningful engagement with complex legal issues; these elements are more than essential for cultivating a learning culture and intellectual growth.

4. Simulate Real-World Legal Interaction: Law is based on dialogue - constant negotiation, confrontation, and interpretation. The AI interlocutor can simulate these conditions, allowing students to practice their rhetorical and persuasive skills, craft arguments, and anticipate potential objections in a safe and controlled context. In this way, they are effectively prepared for the dynamic and often adversarial nature of legal practice.

The approach of AI as a personalized interlocutor elevates its role from a simple tool to an active pedagogical ally. Through its ability to reframe, reinforce, and reflect learning challenges, AI approximates the experience of a personalized teacher, making high-quality, personalized instruction widely available (Ioannidi & Malafantis, 2023).

Facilitating Critical Thinking, Argumentation and Ethical Reflection

The described interactive relationship between AI and the student is designed to cultivate higher cognitive skills essential for future lawyers, such as, for instance, critical thinking, argumentation, and ethical reflection. AI achieves (or contributes to the achieving of) this goal through multiple mechanisms, some of which are mentioned below (Degen, 2025).

1. Socratic methodology (probing): Following the ancient paradigm of the Socratic method, AI can form specialized questions to prompt students to substantiate their thinking, justify their positions, and uncover hidden assumptions (Hu et al., 2025). If, for example, a student presents a legal argument, AI can ask questions (such as on what legal principle this position is based on or what counterarguments could be made against it). The ongoing dialogue, which emerges, fosters a deeper -and perhaps more meaningful- understanding of concepts, helping students to achieve intellectual clarity in the articulation of their arguments and opinions, and not just memorize prevailing views of the past (Favero et al., 2024).
2. Challenging assumptions and identifying logical fallacies: AI can identify logical inconsistencies, misconceptions, or unfounded generalizations in students' reasoning. It operates through subtle interventions and therefore encourages them to revise and improve their reasoning. Should they formulate a general conclusion, for instance, AI can ask for specific examples or exceptions, leading to more precise and logical thinking and as mentioned above, a more substantial understanding of their own arguments (with their strengths and weaknesses).
3. Presenting opposing views and alternative interpretations: If one of the main purposes is to strengthen the argument through the substantial understanding

of the reasoning behind it, AI should be able to introduce well-founded counterarguments or different legal interpretations (in a persuasive and scientifically well-founded way). It is inevitable, then, for students to be exposed to the complexity of legal issues and learn efficiently to prepare themselves for different views. It should be kept into consideration, after all, that the very nature of legal practice is inherently interactive and adversarial.

4. Simulating ethical dilemmas and reflection: Ethical reflection is a dynamic and evolving process (even though it is sometimes considered static). AI can embed legal scenarios with ethical implications and ask students to analyze the consequences of their choices. It can then proceed to a dialogue about different ethical considerations, the implications of various decisions, and the challenges that technology poses to legal ethics. Thus, through the analysis of decision-making and the investigation of the ethical pillars and the priorization of values behind it, the course acquires a philosophical depth (necessary for the success of deep thinking and understanding), cultivating simultaneously ethical sensitivity and judgment.
5. Development of dialectical skills: It should not be forgotten that only through practice, students acquire and edge the required capabilities. Ongoing interaction with AI, therefore, strengthens students' abilities to engage in informed dialogue, combine information from different sources, and formulate persuasive arguments, because AI offers the means for continuous practice, even in complex or ambiguous situations.

Through this dynamic and continuous interaction, AI is transformed from a simple tool into a lever for intellectual development, enhancing students' critical thinking, structured argumentation, and ethical reflection in the context of legal education.

Addressing Individualized Learning Styles

One of the most important advantages of AIDLP is its exceptional ability to adapt to the individual learning needs of students (something that traditional group teaching methods obviously struggle to achieve, and most of the time without success). Legal education, like many academic fields, has traditionally relied on a one-to-many teaching model. While this facilitates the mass transmission of knowledge, it rarely adequately addresses the diverse, known learning preferences and paces of individual students (and thus often fails to achieve the main purpose, that of the transmission of the knowledge, because it does not follow the fundamental principle of personalized interaction, which is necessary for the betterment of educational process).

Lectures at universities are often based on the assumption that all students learn in the same way and at the same pace. However, this is a false assumption! In reality, each student has a different learning profile (sometimes completely different). Some learn visually, others aurally; some prefer experiential learning through practice, while others prefer abstract theory; some need constant repetition and detailed explanations, while others grasp quickly and want to move faster. A single instructor can't meet the needs of dozens or even hundreds of students at the same time in such a personalized way. It is not possible, regardless of the instructor's willingness and talent.

In contrast, conversational AI is designed for personalized interaction. Its ability to adapt to the style of communication, the way knowledge is delivered, and the type of feedback it provides makes it an ideal pedagogical interlocutor for students with different learning needs:

1. Adapt pace and repetition: Students who need more time or repetition have the ability to return to the same points as many times as they wish, without stress or fear of holding back the rest of the class or tiring the teacher. On the other hand, those who move quickly can accelerate learning and delve into more complex issues.
2. Respecting learning preferences: Although interactive AI is primarily text-based (at least for the time being), it can embed multimedia elements or guide students to external resources that cater to visual or auditory preferences and in the near future, it can function mainly orally, like a regular teacher. It can also explain concepts in different ways -through analogies, step-by-step analyses, or summaries- until the student fully understands the content.
3. Level of detail in explanations: Some students prefer concise answers, while others need extensive analyses and examples. AI adjusts the depth of its explanations in real time, based on each student's questions and understanding.
4. Encouraging inquiry-based learning: For students who learn best through questions and autonomous exploration, AI acts as an inexhaustible source of information and a patient guide, fostering curiosity and self-directed learning.
5. Confidence building: Students who are hesitant to speak out publicly out of fear or embarrassment find in AI a safe space to start to interact, experiment, and learn without the burden of judgment. This encourages participation and builds their confidence in legal discourse.

In other words, conversational AI transforms legal education from a one-way knowledge transfer model to a personalized, interactive learning experience. It creates a learning environment that is tailored to each student individually, enhancing understanding, engagement, and the development of critical legal skills. This results in a substantially more equitable and effective educational process, where every student has the opportunity to flourish.

Implementation Strategies and Pedagogical Innovations

Successfully integrating AI-assisted Interactive Legal Pedagogy (AIDLP) into legal education requires strategic thinking and careful planning (because it is something entirely new in the pedagogical practices, and its implementation has not been tested). It is not merely about introducing new technologies (this already happens constantly), but about a fundamental redefinition of pedagogical practices, curriculum design, and assessment methods. This section presents practical strategies for integrating AIDLP principles, designing effective interaction with AI, and adapting assessment to this new environment, with the help of hypothetical examples to better understand their application.

Integrating AIDLP into Legal Curricula

The adoption of AIDLP into legal curricula requires a holistic approach that cuts across various courses and phases of legal education, rather than limiting the use of AI to isolated modules. The goal is to embed AI-enabled interactive learning as a consistent and evolving element throughout the study. Crucial strategies include, among others:

- Curriculum Redesign and Mapping: The process begins with an analysis of the existing curriculum to identify areas where AI can be effectively integrated (so, inevitably, course objectives, learning outcomes, and assessment methods must be reviewed). For example, initial courses -such as Legal Research, Legal Writing, and Introduction to Law- can leverage AI to familiarize students with the fundamental concepts (ALIF stages 1 and 2), while more advanced courses -such as Constitutional Law or International Law- can use AI to explore (and sometimes solve) complex problems or ethical dilemmas (ALIF stages 3 and 4).
- Faculty Training and Support: Faculty training is crucial to the success of the discussed implementation. Technical familiarity with AI tools alone is not enough; a deep understanding of the pedagogical principles of AIDLP is also required (including designing effective questions for AI, interpreting the feedback it produces, guiding the student-AI dialogue, and integrating these into teaching methods). This transition can be facilitated mostly by workshops and peer-learning communities - access to AI pedagogical experts will be necessary, too.
- Phased Implementation and Pilots: Implementation of AIDLP should be done incrementally, starting with pilot applications in selected courses or departments. Incremental implementation allows identifying challenges, obtaining

feedback from students and faculty (something extremely important, if we want to know the real efficiency of the AIDLP theory), and making necessary adjustments before broader adoption. Pilot phases can focus on specific uses, such as providing personalized feedback on legal writing or simulating interviews with "clients".
- Cross-Departmental and Interdisciplinary Collaboration: Collaboration between law schools, IT departments, and other institutions can lead to the development of specialized AI tools for the needs of legal education, while at the same time, it can help to shape ethical frameworks of use and enrich teaching design.
- Infrastructure and Resources: It is necessary to ensure the existence of appropriate technological infrastructure and resources, such as access to sophisticated AI systems, computing power, and technical support; without these, even the thought of AIDLP has no meaning at all. Furthermore, resources should be allocated for continuous research and development of tools and content specifically tailored to AIDLP, because the very essence of this theoretical approach is dynamic and moves towards an advancement (the core of AIDLP lies unchanged, but the methods and the means will evolve).

Through this systematic integration, legal education is no longer limited to teaching about AI, but is moving towards teaching with the help of AI, transforming the educational experience into a dynamic, personalized, and essentially interactive learning journey.

Designing Dialogic AI Interactions

The effectiveness of AI-Supported Dialogic Legal Pedagogy (AIDLP) depends mainly on the careful design of dialogic interactions with AI, so that they promote meaningful intellectual engagement rather than superficial exchanges, which will fail students. The AI must function as a genuine interlocutor, capable of encouraging critical thinking, challenging students' assumptions, and guiding them through complex legal reasoning processes - in other words, it must act as a second personalized teacher. Thus, design principles are necessary.

- Sufficient Legal Context and Subject Matter Expertise: The AI must be trained on extensive legal data to have a deep understanding of legal concepts, terminology, case law, and procedures. The AI's response must be not only accurate but also sensitive to the nuances of legal language and context (and this is not something easy to do). This demand requires specialized legal AI models beyond general-purpose applications.

- Socratic Approach and Open-ended Questions: AI should not provide direct answers (except if the student needs a direct answer) but -in general- should primarily use the Socratic method; that is, ask questions that prompt the student to justify their thinking, identify gaps in their knowledge, and consider alternative interpretations. Questions should be open-ended, provoking more extended and reflective responses (and the answers in this kind of teaching should not be fixed as opposed to the answers in a technical question, such as what Article 5 of the Outer Space Treaty describes).
- Adaptive Feedback: AI should provide feedback that is not limited to "right" or "wrong". In other words, feedback should be diagnostic, explaining why an answer is wrong or right, giving hints, or suggesting resources for further study (this is the only way for students to be benefited by the use of AI; otherwise, AI will end up being the easiest solution for finding an answer - and this will be a terrible conclusion for the intellectual advancement of students). It is crucial, in addition, for AI to adapt to the student's level of understanding and evolve as they progress.
- Simulation and Role-Switching Capabilities: AI can be used to simulate practical legal situations, such as client interviews, witness examination, or negotiations. It can take on various roles (for example, a difficult client, a hostile witness, an opposing party), so that it allows students to begin practicing their communication, argumentation, and strategy skills in a safe and repeatable environment.
- Ethical Dilemma Scenarios: AI can present complex ethical dilemmas relevant to legal practice, asking students to identify value conflicts, analyze their choices, and justify their ethical stance upon their prioritization of values. AI can thereafter offer alternative ethical frameworks, highlight the consequences of different choices, and encourage deeper reflection on the ethics of law.
- Error Detection and Correction: AI should be able to detect frequent errors in legal reasoning, argumentation, or understanding of facts. In case an error is identified, AI should not just point it out, but should guide the student by offering explanations, relevant examples, or exercises. This process of repetition and reinforcement is fundamental to learning (besides, the tireless repetition, if needed, is an important distinction between the teacher and the AI).
- Interfacing with Legal Knowledge Bases: Although AI operates interactively, it must be connected to rich and up-to-date legal databases so that the student can search for specific information, locate relevant case law or legislation, and verify their understanding with official sources.

By following these design principles, AIDLP not only offers a technologically advanced experience, but also becomes an essential pedagogical tool. Through this type of dialogue, law students are actively engaged, think critically, and acquire skills that prepare them for the complexities of legal practice in the 21st century.

8. ASSESSMENT IN AN AIDLP ENVIRONMENT

Assessment in the context of AIDLP must go beyond traditional models and reflect the multifaceted learning outcomes enhanced by technology, since the challenge is no longer to memorize knowledge, but to assess critical thinking, flexible legal perception, ethical judgment, and the ability to collaborate with the constantly emerging technologies of artificial intelligence. This seems to require a combination of formative and summative assessment, leveraging AI's capabilities for -on the one hand- continuous feedback and -on the other hand- multi-level assessment.

- Assessing the learning process through dialogue with AI: The emphasis should not only be on the final result, but also on the learning process. Through the general analysis of student-AI dialogues features such as the student's active participation in Socratic questioning, their ability to formulate complex legal concepts, their response to cognitive challenges, and their progress in reasoning can be effectively assessed. The AI itself can provide analytics on interaction patterns, question depth, and the consistency of the student's engagement (for example, it can track how many times a student returns to a difficult topic or how the structure of their argument evolves over time). The ultimate goal of this assessment is to free oneself from the sterile model of assessment based on simple knowledge accumulation tests and to advance an assessment model based on the student's will to learn and the creative utilization of their knowledge.
- Continuous formative feedback and self-assessment using AI: AI can provide immediate, ongoing feedback on assignments, legal writing, or hypotheticals, allowing students to identify and correct their mistakes in real time. At the same time, students can use AI for self-assessment, comparing their work with role models or receiving constructive criticism before the final submission. This enhances autonomy and continuous improvement, because students keep in mind that by the end of the educational process, they should be able to creatively utilize the acquired knowledge and skills, and the successful or unsuccessful result of an individual exam simply does not matter.
- Practice-focused assessments and AI integration: Final assessments can include scenarios in which the student is asked to utilize AI in solving legal issues, such as:

AI-assisted research: The student conducts legal research using AI tools. The assessment is not only based on the result but also the rational and strategic use of AI during the process.
Legal practice simulations: Through scenarios such as client interviews, witness examinations, or speeches (with AI playing roles), communication skills, legal thinking, and -the highly important- skill of adaptability are assessed.
AI Case Analysis: The student uses AI to analyze complex cases. Thereafter, the assessment focuses on the interpretation of findings, the critical appraisal of potential system errors or biases, and the final legal judgments.

By adopting such multidimensional assessment methods (and of course, the methods mentioned above are not exclusive), legal education can better reflect the complex cognitive, practical, and ethical skills cultivated through the dialogical relationship with AI. Thus, assessment is transformed from a simple test of knowledge to a holistic assessment of evolving legal intelligence, for it is based on the originality of ideas, the pragmatism of proposals, and the strategy of problem-solving.

9. CASE STUDIES/EXAMPLES

In order to make the application of the principles of AIDLP (Artificial Intelligence-Assisted Interactive Legal Pedagogy) more tangible, here are some short hypothetical examples of its use in practice:

- Case Study 1: First-Year Legal Writing and Research – The AI Writing Coach
  The Problem: First-year law students often struggle with the subtle demands of legal writing (such as proper structure, referencing, and persuasive argumentation). Providing individual feedback to large classes is extremely demanding for instructors.
  The Solution with AIDLP: A Virtual Legal Writing Support System is introduced into the curriculum, that is a specialized AI dialogue assistant, trained in legal writing standards, referencing rules (e.g., Bluebook), and persuasion techniques. Students are permitted (and encouraged) to upload drafts of legal briefs or submissions to the platform for feedback.
  How it interacts: The digital assistant doesn't just make automatic corrections. Instead, it engages in a thoughtful dialogue with the student. For example, if a weak connection is identified between paragraphs, it

might ask: "How does this paragraph logically connect to the previous one? Could you state that more clearly?" If the reference is not correct, it will prompt the student to check the relevant rule. For weak arguments, it might prompt: "How could you strengthen your counterargument? What would the other side argue?" It also provides feedback on clarity, brevity, and legal style (in the appropriate way).

The Result: Students receive immediate, personalized, and iterative feedback, strengthening their skills at their own pace, as they learn not just what is wrong, but why and how to fix it. The digital assistant helps them effectively achieve the necessary clarity in their legal writing (and in a shorter time than it would take the teacher, as the learning is personalized and repetitive). Thus, the instructor, the human instructor, can focus on more complex and strategic topics, leaving the basics to the AI.

- Case Study 2: Advanced Constitutional Law – The AI Constitutional Debater

  The Problem: In order to engage dialectically with complex constitutional issues, it is required to acquire a deep understanding of the jurisprudence, the original intentions of the framers of the Constitution, the evolution of interpretations, and the ability to produce multifaceted arguments. Implementing such exercises in the classroom, especially with a large number of students, is difficult (and if implemented, it will not have the expected results for all students).

  The Solution with AIDLP: An artificial intelligence tool is introduced into the curriculum - the Digital Constitutional Interlocutor. This AI is trained to adopt various legal interpretive schools (e.g., text-centric approach, evolutionary interpretation, historical-primary intention) and to support well-founded arguments, drawing on case law and legal theory.

  The Interaction Method: The student is asked to prepare an argument on a current constitutional issue and engage in a dialogue with the AI, which takes on the role of an "opponent" from a particular legal school of thought. It will be probably helpful to ask questions (for example, about the alignment of the student's interpretation with the original intent of the framers of the Constitution or the reconciliation of the student's position with the jurisprudence of judicial decisions. AI may also present and analyze hypothetical scenarios or prompt the student to consider the social (and other) implications of their position.

  The Outcome: Through the interaction between student and digital assistant, the former develops high-level argumentation skills, practices anticipating and addressing objections from different legal perspectives, and inquires into constitutional interpretation (and thus into general legal science). AI offers a challenging (but also safe) practice environment, whereby enhancing their reflective, structured, and persuasive thinking on issues of primary importance.

- Case Study 3: Legal Ethics Clinic – The Digital Ethical Counselor

  The Problem: Legal ethics often involves situations with moral ambiguity and no clear answers. It is therefore of the utmost importance to develop ethical thinking, which requires exposure to complicated scenarios and the ability to manage dilemmas with multiple interpretations.

  The Solution via AIDLP: An Artificial Intelligence system -the Digital Ethical Counselor- is introduced into the ethics clinic, to present students with realistic ethical dilemmas faced by legal professionals (for instance, issues of confidentiality, conflict of interest, or professional violation of ethical rules).

  The Interaction Method: Students discuss with the Digital Ethical Counselor, explaining how they would approach each ethical issue. In this process, they base their decisions on the Rules of Professional Conduct and develop their ethical reasoning. The AI then delves deeper into the dialogue, asking questions (such as: "What could be the consequences of this action for your client or for the credibility of the profession?" or "How does this particular Rule of Ethics apply to this particular element of the case?"). In addition, the AI can add new, unforeseen information or complications to the original scenario, challenging students to reevaluate and adjust their thinking in real time. Simultaneously, it can introduce alternative moral systems (such as utilitarianism or deontology) and ask students to examine the dilemma through these lenses.

  The Result: Students cultivate a broader, more flexible, and reflective ethical approach. They learn to identify ethical pitfalls, apply rules of professional conduct, and assess the ethical and social consequences of their decisions. The Digital Ethics Advisor provides a safe and supportive environment for practicing ethical judgment in complex and fluid circumstances. The clinical supervisor can then analyze student-AI interactions, provide broader guidance, and organize collective discussions on particularly challenging ethical scenarios.

This series of case studies demonstrates how AIDLP, through interactive interactions with Artificial Intelligence, can provide personalized, challenging, and practical learning experiences that are difficult to replicate in a conventional classroom. By incorporating AI as a constant interlocutor, legal education has the potential to shape a new generation of lawyers: technically competent, reflectively competent, ethically sensitive, and adaptable to the legal complexities of the modern world.

10. ETHICAL DIMENSIONS: AI AS A CO-THINKER IN EVOLVING REFLECTION

The introduction of AI into legal education (and in particular within the context of AIDLP, which is analyzed in this chapter) requires a radical rethinking of how we understand, teach, and apply ethics (Gordon, 2021), as AIDLP challenges the traditional view of ethics as a set of fixed rules or as "static content" that is simply inserted into the programming of AI systems. Instead, it proposes a more open, evolving approach, where ethics is seen as a dynamic field of dialogue and reflection, that is a field in which AI can (and should) actively participate as an interlocutor and co-thinker. This approach transforms legal education into a living "laboratory" of ethical awareness and critical thinking, where students collaborate with AI through ongoing ethical questioning and reflection.

Beyond Static Ethics: The Participatory Function of AI

The traditional approach to ethics in technologies focuses mainly on the integration of prescribed ethical rules into the design and implementation of systems. While this method offers fundamental safeguards (and this is undeniable), it does not suffice to address the complex and unpredictable ethical challenges posed by modern AI. The AIDLP proposes a transition from this "static" view of ethics to a dynamic model, where AI is not simply a passive recipient of ethical rules, but an active participant in the ethical dialogue (without this meaning that it will not incorporate safeguards in its software).This has some consequences:

- AI as a Challenge for Ethical Thinking: Rather than offering ready-made ethical answers, the AI embedded in the AIDLP is designed to "challenge" students to ethical reflection. It can present complicated ethical dilemmas, highlight the conflict of values, or challenge students' initial ethical intuitions (for example, it could present a legal scenario related to data protection and ask about the balance of the right to privacy with the public interest in the case, or it can ask about the prevailing ethical framework used to support student's position). Through such questions, students are challenged to develop their ethical arguments, grapple with conflicting principles, and practice managing the uncertainty that characterizes real-world ethical decisions in the legal world.
- Simulating Different Moral Perspectives: AI can be designed to simulate different moral views or philosophical approaches (such as utilitarianism, deontology, or virtue ethics). When presented with a legal problem, AI can explain how each specific moral context would be addressed. Through this

process, students are exposed to multiple moral approaches (something that is one way or another the purpose of many lessons), broadening their moral and intellectual horizons and strengthening their ability to conduct multifaceted moral and philosophical analyses.

- Guiding Structured Moral Dialogue: AIDLP leverages AI to engage in reflective, collaborative moral thought processes. AI can guide students through dialogue and ensure that all the relevant factors of the issue are considered, the potential consequences of choices are analyzed, and the different perspectives are heard. At the same time, it can act as a neutral moderator, encouraging this way the students to substantiate their positions, identify rational perceptions, and consider the social footprint of their ethical choices (because ethics is not just about abstract ideas, but also their correct application in society and human life). This creates an educational environment of dialogue, from which mature, collective ethical judgment emerges.
- Reflecting Changing Social Values: As AI evolves and its impact on society becomes more pronounced, ethical norms and demands are changing. In the context of AIDLP, AI can be integrated and reflect these changes, presenting students with contemporary ethical challenges and inviting them to consider how legal and ethical frameworks must adapt to new circumstances. In this way, legal education remains essentially relevant and aligned with the ever-changing ethical landscape of the 21st century.

By embracing the participatory role of AI in ethical reflection, AIDLP transforms legal education into a vibrant space where ethics is not simply an object of study, but something that is actively co-shaped, discussed, and interpreted. In this way, future legal professionals are prepared to assume leadership roles in a world increasingly defined by the challenges and problems of artificial intelligence.

Fostering Ethical Perception and Critical Awareness

The unique interactive capabilities of Artificial Intelligence, within the AIDLP framework, have potential to enhance the -necessary for a law student- ethical perception and critical awareness; this is not simply about memorizing codes of ethics (after all, this is not beneficial for the cultivation of the students' intelligence and awareness), but about cultivating an intuitive and analytical ability to recognize, process, and synthesize the complexity of different ethical issues. This is achieved through several key mechanisms, some of which are mentioned below:

- Exposure to Ambiguity and Complexity: Legal ethics often operates in “gray zones”, that is, zones where there are no easy or absolute answers. AI can therefore present scenarios with intense ambiguity, inviting students to weigh up conflicting duties and interests, in situations without a clear solution (an example is the conflict between the obligation to the client and the public interest). Through such situations, students are forced to deepen their reasoning, sharpening their ethical perception.

- Consequence Simulation and Ethical Foresight: Previous AI systems can simulate the consequences of different moral negatives. When a student suggests a particular course of action, AI can puzzle them out with questions like: "What will be the long-term consequences of this choice for the trust relationship with the client?" or "How would society or regulators view this action?" Through this ability to pay attention to consequences, students cultivate a broader understanding of their moral responsibility.
- Identifying and Addressing Bias: AI can help students recognize their own cognitive distortions or biases that affect their legal judgment (for instance, if an argument relies on confirmation bias, AI can intervene by asking about the possible influence of confirmation bias, inquiring into the existence of evidence contradicting the student's initial assessment).
- Interdisciplinary Ethical Approach: Modern legal ethics is not limited to law but intersects with philosophy, sociology, technology, and many other fields. AI can bring to the fore theoretical approaches from different disciplines and encourage students to incorporate them into their ethical reasoning (after all, the law science needs to be, to some extent, interdisciplinary, in order to be efficient).
- Continuous Reflective Practice: Continuous, personalized interaction with AI acts as a stable platform for reflective practice, as students are encouraged to reexamine their ethical positions, learn from their experiences, and cultivate a mature, evolving moral compass. AI, as a dialectical interlocutor, offers a safe and available space for difficult, yet creative, ethical conversations, which are going to sharpen the student's moral sense.

Through these rich ethical dialogues, AIDLP transforms legal education into a dynamic where ethical awareness is cultivated, critical thinking is strengthened, and students are prepared to navigate the complex ethical landscape of the legal profession with integrity and insight.

Addressing Bias and Fairness in AI

The discussion of the contributory role of AI in moral reflection, within the AIDLP, cannot be considered complete without meaningfully addressing the existing issues of bias and fairness, which are inherent in AI systems themselves, and threaten the betterment of education. While AIDLP leverages AI as an intellectual companion, it is critical to recognize that AI systems cannot be neutral or objective by nature. Algorithms learn from the data they are trained on; if that data contains social or historical biases, AI will reproduce them (and often reinforce them). Addressing this challenge is fundamental to ensuring that AIDLP promotes equal opportunity and fair outcomes in legal education; otherwise, AIDLP will not benefit the student's community.

To reduce bias and promote justice, AIDLP follows specific strategies:

- Curated and Multicultural Selection of Training Data: The first step is to carefully select and broaden the diversity of data used to train AI models. Different legal contexts, cultural approaches, and demographic backgrounds should be included, while ongoing monitoring of existing data for potential biases is required (for example, a system trained exclusively on legal texts from one country or era is likely to reproduce specific historical biases).
- Bias Detection and Checking Tools: Advanced tools are of primary importance to detect and quantify bias in AI outputs (whether in legal interpretations, ethical questions, or student feedback). Also, as some biases may escape the initial detection by automated tools, regular checks by human experts would be necessary.
- Explainable AI Principles: Transparency in the operation of AI is crucial. AIDLP systems must clearly explain the logic behind their interpretations or ethical questions. When AI proposes a legal or ethical reasoning, it should be able to justify its conclusions. This explainability allows students and instructors to critically evaluate AI thinking and identify potential errors or distortions.
- Human-in-the-loop: Despite the active involvement of AI, human supervision is absolutely necessary. Teachers remain responsible for the final check and pedagogical guidance. They should regularly examine student-AI interactions, intervene when bias or inappropriate responses are detected, and correct the AI's course when necessary. This human intervention ensures that AI does not end up being a source of moral derailment, but it remains a tool for ethical cultivation.
- Educating Students in AI Ethics: AIDLP does not limit itself to correcting AI; it integrates education around AI ethics itself into the curriculum. Students acquire skills necessary for the technological era they live; they learn to identify biases, understand their nature, and develop strategies for addressing them in the near future. In this way, they are shaped as responsible and informed users (and potentially creators) of AI in the legal field.

- Feedback Mechanisms for Continuous Improvement: AIDLP provides feedback channels whereby students and faculty can report bias or injustice in AI responses. These reports are collected and utilized properly in order to improve AI models. Through this ongoing feedback process the "ethical evolution" of the AI assistant becomes possible.

Through the conscious and responsible management of bias and fairness, AIDLP reaffirms its commitment to a legal education that promotes moral sensitivity and jistice. It perceives AI as a powerful tool, and thus, one that requires constant vigilance and ethical accountability to function for the benefit of education and society.

Data Privacy and Security in AIDLP

The implementation of AIDLP -with its emphasis on personalized, interactive interactions and the collection of extensive student information- brings to the fore critical issues related to privacy and data security, as the very operation of AIDLP, where Artificial Intelligence learns and adapts to each student's interactions, presupposes the collection and processing of sensitive personal and educational data. In this context, protecting this data (and ensuring the protection thereof) is not just a technical obligation; it is an ethical commitment fundamental to maintaining trust, complying with legal frameworks, and defending student rights. Some key principles and strategies for ensuring data privacy and security in the AIDLP environment include:

- Compliance with Data Protection Legislation: Strict adherence to legal frameworks, such as the General Data Protection Regulation (GDPR), FERPA (in the US), and other national or international regulations, is a prerequisite. This presupposes the complete understanding of the legal basis for any data processing, securing informed consent from students (or their guardians, where appropriate), and applying the principle of data minimization, that is, collecting only the data necessary for the educational purposes.
- Anonymization and Pseudonymization: Where possible, student data should be anonymized or pseudonymized. With anonymization, we have a way for any elements that allow the identification of an individual to be removed, while pseudonymization replaces personal data with reversible markers. This reduces the risk of a data breach and limits the ability to link information to specific individuals, especially when the data is used for research or algorithm training purposes.
- Secure Data Storage and Transfer: All student information should be stored in secure, encrypted databases and transmitted using secure protocols. Strong

access control mechanisms, multi-factor authentication, and regular security audits are required to prevent unauthorized access or cyberattacks. If cloud services are used, they should be previously assessed for security and compliance with relevant legislation.

- Transparency in Data Use: It is crucial for students and teachers to be informed about the data use policies (that is, about the kind of data collected, the reason for collection, how it is used, who has access to it, and for how long it is kept). Data use policies should be clearly stated, easily accessible, and ensure that consent is properly written. Only this transparency builds trust and empowers the autonomy of participants; otherwise, the necessary credibility of the education system will be undermined.
- Purpose Limitation: Data collected for educational purposes may not be used for other purposes without explicit consent. For example, information resulting from student-AI interactions to enhance legal reasoning may not be used for marketing or advertising without the explicit permission of the users. Respecting this principle is essential for ethical data management.
- Comprehensive Data Governance Framework: It is necessary to establish a clear and comprehensive data governance framework that defines the roles, responsibilities, and procedures for collecting, processing, storing, accessing, and deleting data. This framework should include a data breach management plan, procedures for satisfying data subjects' requests (such as access, correction or deletion of their personal data), and regular privacy impact assessments.
- Ethical AI Development Practices: It is essential to work with AI developers and scientists to implement, from the early design stage, concrete principles such as privacy-by-design and security-by-design. This implies that privacy is not an afterthought or a detail for legality; it is a foundation at every stage of the AI system's development, and remains a foundation, thereafter, at the stage of the use of the system.

By putting emphasis on privacy and enhancing security, AIDLP can deliver its educational benefits within a safe environment, inspiring trust, respecting individual rights, and managing technology in a responsible way. This commitment is crucial to creating a pedagogical framework where students can interact with AI safely and freely.

11. CULTURAL IMPLICATIONS: EXPANDING HUMAN CONSCIOUSNESS AND AGENCY

The advent of Artificial Intelligence and, in particular, its integration into the innovative framework of AIDLP (which is proposed in this chapter) is not simply a technological advance or pedagogical innovation, but it carries profound cultural dimensions, constituting a unique opportunity to redefine the relationship between humans and technology (or, to put it differently and a little poetically, between human and mechanical consciousness) and to enhance the power, creativity and autonomy of the human spirit. In an era full of global and existential challenges, from the climate crisis and biotechnological developments, to the first steps in space exploration, AIDLP does not approach Artificial Intelligence as a threat, but as a challenge and a unique opportunity for cultural and spiritual emancipation.

AI as an Accelerator of Cultural and Intellectual Emancipation

During the historical course of technological revolutions in the last centuries, a transformation in the structures of society, from work to intellectual activity, has often been observed. For instance, the industrial revolution freed a significant part of the population from manual agricultural labor, allowing the emergence of new professions and scientific disciplines. Correspondingly, Artificial Intelligence, with its ability to automate mechanical and repetitive processes, offers the possibility of liberating humans, not from work in general (this would be very unfortunate), but from low-mental-demand, monotonous tasks, and thereby, space is created for engagement in more complex, creative and reflective activities, opening a new path for intellectual and cultural flourishing.

In the legal field, AI can process vast amounts of data, perform rapid legal research, draft document templates, and support predictions based on analysis of past cases. While such functions may initially raise concerns about job losses, AIDLP can overturn this scenario. Rather than replacing humans, AI takes over mechanical and repetitive tasks, setting the legal professional free and students focus on areas that require purely human abilities: strategic thinking, ethical judgment, creative problem solving, empathy, and the development of innovative legal theories. Through this fundamental shift, an enhancement of engagement with the philosophical and social dimensions of law is observed, creating a more intellectually demanding legal environment.

At the same time, it is common ground that AI acts as an amplifier of human intelligence, helping the user process and synthesize information at levels and speeds previously unimaginable. When this capability is combined with dialogic interaction, the development of critical thinking and intellectual "maturity" (which includes metacognitive skills) is accelerated. Therefore, the student who collaborates with AI as a second "interlocutor" is exposed to diverse perspectives, challenged to refine their arguments, and explore the limits of their own understanding. This constant "intellectual challenge" enhances the ability to adapt and be intellectually flexible (which are necessary characteristics in a rapidly changing legal and social world). On a cultural level, this shift leads to a society where the human mind is not crushed by information overload or daily routine, but is empowered to seek deeper truths and creative solutions - of course, if humans see the new possibilities as ways of emancipation and acceleration and not as a panacea.

This is why it must be highlighted that this intellectual emancipation is not about replacing humans, but about highlighting and enhancing human potential! It re-emphasizes the importance of uniquely human qualities such as intuition, imagination, emotional intelligence, and moral reasoning (abilities that AI can support but not replicate). AIDLP, through an educational model based on dialogue and reflection ensures that this emancipation will be guided by human values and will aim to improve society as a whole, and not simply advance technology for technology's sake.

12. SHIFTING FOCUS TO RESEARCH, CREATIVITY AND COGNITIVE DEEPENING

The liberation from mechanical and procedural tasks, achieved through Artificial Intelligence in the proposed context of AIDLP, implies a fundamental change of direction for legal scholars and practitioners; a focus on research, creativity, and deeper cognitive processing. This reoriented approach is critical, as the modern, multidimensional, and interconnected challenges of the 21st century require innovative thinking and a holistic understanding that goes beyond the boundaries of traditional scientific fields (see: Kirschner & Hendrick, 2020).

Enhanced Research Capabilities

AI has the power to transform legal research, searching vast legal databases, identifying hidden precedents, and cross-referencing information with unparalleled speed and accuracy. This sets researchers free from the tedious task of collecting and organizing data and allows them to devote their total time to more demanding intellectual activities (such as formulating original research questions, developing complex theoretical models, and synthesizing interdisciplinary knowledge). Instead of simply searching for terms, legal researchers can use AI to discover conceptual connections between different legal systems or historical periods, leading to totally different research approaches, that is, more innovative research approaches.

Unleashing Creativity

Creativity in law is expressed through finding innovative solutions, writing original legal texts, or formulating arguments that reshape the interpretation of the law. AI (particularly, generative and agentive AI) is designed from the very beginning to contribute to this process of creativity. By generating drafts of legal documents, alternative contract provisions, or simulations of different legal scenarios, it offers many and various points for reflection and experimentation.

Deepening Knowledge and Thinking

Dialogic interaction with the digital assistant (a key element of AIDLP) enhances cognitive development. When AI challenges the student's argument, presents opposing views, or provokes ethical reflection, it pushes them in a very efficient way to examine the material in depth. Through this cyclical process (that is, questions, answers, and eventually reflection), features such as analytical thinking, cognitive accuracy, and understanding of complex legal concepts are increasingly enhanced. AI acts as a constant "intellectual adversary", helping the student to go beyond superficial understanding and delve into the philosophical and social (and other) dimensions of law. This enhanced intellectual engagement is necessary to develop the intellectual resilience needed to address the unprecedented challenges of our time.

In essence, AIDLP leverages AI to build an educational environment where the human intellect is not limited to activities such as data processing but works to create new knowledge and foster innovation through an understanding of the complicated web of relationships between law and other fields, such as technology. This shift seems to not only improve efficiency but also cultivate a more creative (and socially impactful) legal science.

13. ADDRESSING GLOBAL AND EXISTENTIAL CHALLENGES

The philosophical and cultural perspective of AIDLP extends to its potential to enhance consciousness and creativity, especially at a time when humanity is facing global and existential challenges of different types. Issues such as climate change, rapid advances in biotechnology, and the expansion of human presence in space raise complex legal and ethical (and as a result, social) dilemmas that transcend traditional legal tools. Artificial Intelligence, within AIDLP, can play an important (probably pivotal) role in preparing legal scholars capable of making meaningful contributions to addressing these issues.

Climate Change

The law related to the climate crisis is multifaceted and multi-layered: from international environmental law and climate litigation, to carbon markets and the regulation of renewable energy sources. AI can support legal research in analyzing complicated environmental data, predicting legal consequences of policy choices, and identifying effective legal pathways for climate change adaptation and mitigation. In this context, students can explore the effectiveness of different legal tools, simulate the outcome of climate disputes, and most importantly, design innovative strategies for environmental protection.

Biotechnology

Advances in genetic engineering, synthetic biology, and reproductive technologies raise fascinating legal and ethical questions about jurisprudence, human rights, intellectual property, and many other subjects of law. AIDLP offers the opportunity to explore these issues in a multi-faceted manner. As AI can present students with hypothetical scenarios regarding gene manipulation or bio-patents, challenge them to engage in ethical debates that take into account diverse ethical positions and broader societal implications. At the same time, it can identify regulatory gaps and help shape new legal frameworks that balance technological progress with the demands of ethical protection. Thus, future lawyers are trained to adequately respond to the complex intersection of law, science, and ethics.

Expansion into Space

As humanity explores and conquers new space horizons, unprecedented legal questions arise: the management of space resources, responsibility for space debris (which is one of the most important issues right now in outer space), and the legal status of extraterrestrial life (although this is more unlikely to happen in our days). AI can help interpret early space conditions, model orbital scenarios for regulatory compliance, and support the creation of new international rules for activities beyond our planet, in outer space, including the Moon and other celestial bodies. Through dialogue with AI, students are challenged to transcend traditional terrestrial legal assumptions and shape innovative solutions for a future multiplanetary legal landscape, whether this is about national or international law. This fosters a new legal spirit: visionary, adventurous, and capable of creating tomorrow's law for humanity in the known universe.

In all of these areas, AI's ability to process vast amounts of information, simulate complex scenarios, and engage in ethically reflective inquiry, when harnessed through the interactive pedagogy of AIDLP, enables legal scholars to move beyond narrow problem-solving. It empowers them to anticipate challenges, innovate, and contribute to the creation of legal frameworks that are robust, ethical, and forward-looking, thus strengthening the human role in addressing the most critical issues of our time.

14. THE EMERGENCE OF A NEW LEGAL SCHOLAR

The culmination of the transformative potential of AIDLP is expressed through the formation of a new type of legal scholar, that is, a person who is intellectually autonomous and morally mature, but also culturally visionary. This new model is not merely a product of technological development, but a testament to a pedagogical philosophy that seeks to creatively synthesize human intellect with artificial intelligence, cultivating a symbiotic relationship that enhances human potential.

Intellectual Autonomy

Through the AIDLP framework, and particularly through the dialogical relationship between student and AI as well as the progressive path through ALIF, profound intellectual autonomy is cultivated. Students are not content with passively accepting knowledge; on the contrary, they learn to actively construct it through questioning, critical thinking, and argumentation. This constant intellectual "confrontation" with AI, as a result, sharpens their ability to think independently, as they challenge assumptions and form personal conclusions based more on evidence or reasoning than mere belief. They also develop skills so that they can identify logical fallacies and synthesize different perspectives. Thus, they become autonomous thinkers - something absolutely necessary in a legal environment that often requires critical decisions under uncertainty.

Ethical Maturity

AIDLP's approach to ethics is unique, as AI functions not as a source of rules, but as a dialogical companion in the ongoing exploration of ethical issues. Students are not limited to learning ethical frameworks, but are actively involved in evolving dialogues around ethical dilemmas, simulations of possible consequences, and analysis of changing ethical norms in the technological age. Through this process, they cultivate increased ethical sensitivity and insight, developing an internalized ethical orientation. Thus, they become capable of managing with responsibility and integrity the ethical questions that arise in contemporary legal practice.

Cultural Vision

By freeing themselves from repetitive and mechanical tasks, students are called upon to focus on higher-order intellectual and creative processes. This shift in educational focus strengthens their ability to think culturally and universally. They are no longer limited to specialized legal fields, but acquire a new, comprehensive view of law and its relationship to the major problems of their era (such as the climate crisis, biotechnology, and space exploration). They are capable of developing innovative legal approaches and don't fear doing it; they anticipate future needs, and contribute to legal frameworks that are attuned to human values and collective visions. In this way, they become thinkers, capable of positively influencing the future direction of law and society, overall.

Essentially, the new legal scholar who is emerging from the proposed framework of the AIDLP model is a tangible demonstration of the power of augmented intelligence, when it is used under humanistic views. He is not simply a competent legal technician, but a person capable of guiding humanity through the most complex legal and ethical fields of the 21st century. This transformation represents a fundamental shift in legal education - not just training professionals, but cultivating transformative personalities with global impact.

15. CONCLUSION

Artificial Intelligence-Supported Dialogic Legal Pedagogy (AIDLP) represents a fundamental paradigm shift in legal education and general pedagogy. It is probably a radical redefinition of the learning process itself, rather than merely a gradual integration of technology into education. This chapter has presented AIDLP as a highly conceptually coherent, human-centered theory of pedagogy that utilizes Artificial Intelligence not simply as a technical tool, but as an intellectual and moral companion to the student.

Recap of the Importance of AIDLP

The importance of AIDLP stems from its multidimensional approach to preparing law students for an increasingly complicated and technologically advancing world. First, it responds to the imperative for adaptive legal intelligence by ensuring that students are not simply familiar with AI tools (this will not make a difference), but they have learned to utilize them critically and creatively. The four stages of ALIF (namely, Fundamental AI Knowledge, AI-Supported Application, Collaborative

Problem Solving, and Independent/Creative Use of AI) offer a clear path towards a conscious and responsible use of AI in the legal field.

Second, AIDLP emphasizes the dialogue between AI and the student as the foundation of personalized learning, which is a meaningful learning. By viewing AI as a tireless, non-judgmental conversationalist (much like a second individualized teacher), AIDLP creates a dynamic learning environment that adapts to each student's way and provides the necessary feedback. Through Socratic questioning, case challenges, and adversarial arguments, AI fosters critical thinking, legal rigor, and ethical reflection, which are skills fundamental to legal practice.

Third, AIDLP proposes a new way to approach the ethics of AI, not as a set of pre-determined rules, but as a constantly evolving field of ethical reflection in which AI actively participates as a co-producer of thought. Therefore, students are encouraged to explore complex ethical dilemmas, understand the implications of algorithmic bias, and develop robust frameworks for the responsible use of AI. The continual presence of humans in critical decision-making and transparency in the use of data ensures that ethics remain at the forefront.

Last but not least, AIDLP has significant cultural implications, as it acts as an accelerator of human consciousness and creativity, that is, personal empowerment. By setting students free from time-consuming and mechanical tasks, it allows them to focus on higher-level cognitive processes, namely in-depth research, creative problem solving, and meaningful engagement with global and existential challenges. Within this framework, a new model of legal scholar emerges - one who is intellectually autonomous, morally mature, and culturally insightful enough, so that they can lead society through the most complex legal and ethical landscapes of the future.

Future Directions and Research

The theoretical framework of AIDLP, although comprehensive, uncovers multiple perspectives for future research and practical application. The most important areas for further investigation are mentioned below:

- Empirical Validation: Rigorous empirical studies are more than necessary to evaluate the effectiveness of AIDLP in improving students' learning experiences and personal learning progress. Comparative studies between programs that incorporate AIDLP and those that follow traditional teaching methods are also of primary importance.
- Development of Specialized AI Models: It is indisputable that further research is needed to create more advanced and specialized AI models, specifically designed for the needs of AIDLP. These new models should be able to engage in more complicated dialogue (in Socrates' paradigm), simulate

ethical dilemmas more accurately, and represent realistic legal scenarios (in other words, they have to be specifically designed for Law students).

- Curriculum Design and Integration: The development of pedagogical guidelines for implementing AIDLP across legal disciplines is crucial for the best application of the proposed theoretical framework into education. An important step is the creation of modular AI-enabled learning units that are easily adaptable by educators.
- Faculty Training and Support: Exploring the most effective ways to train legal educators in AIDLP principles and AI literacy is essential. This includes developing ongoing training models and peer-to-peer networks to strengthen the educational community.
- Ethical Governance and Policy: There is an ongoing need for research into the ethical management of AI in education, with the intention to develop robust policies that ensure data privacy, algorithm transparency, and accountability. At the same time, legal education can actively contribute to the public debate on the regulation of AI at a societal level (probably it is the most suitable to do it).
- Longitudinal Studies: It would be extremely beneficial to conduct longitudinal studies monitoring the professional development and impact of lawyers and other legal scientists trained with AIDLP, assessing their capacity for adaptation, innovation, and ethical leadership in a changing legal ecosystem.

Final Thoughts on the Future of Legal Education

The pedagogy of the future will not be based on old teaching models, but on complementary intelligence systems, where creativity, ethical thinking, and dialogic dialogue with Artificial Intelligence will be at the core of the learning process, e.g. Applications of AI in Education (Beck et al., n.d.). AIDLP offers a visionary and adaptable pedagogical paradigm for this new era, and perhaps the coming ones, too. By embracing AI not just as a mere tool, but as a "mechanical partner" in the intellectual cultivation of students, legal education can exceed its traditional boundaries and pave the way for a new pedagogy. It can thereby shape a new generation of legal scholars who are not only knowledgeable about the law but also intellectually autonomous, morally sensitive, and culturally insightful. This shift can lead to a more just, equitable, and technologically informed social system, where lawyers play an essential role in addressing the grand challenges of the 21st century. The path to this future is not without its difficulties, but the benefits -a legal community capable of guiding society with insight and responsibility- make AIDLP a necessary choice for modern legal education.

REFERENCES

Alexander, R. J. (2008). Towards dialogic teaching: Rethinking classroom talk. *Diálogos (San José).*

American Bar Association. (n.d.). *AI and legal education.* https://www.americanbar.org/groups/centers_commissions/center-for-innovation/artificial-intelligence/ai-in-legal-education/

Atkinson, K., Bench-Capon, T., & Bollegala, D. (2020). Explanation in AI and law: Past, present and future. *Artificial Intelligence*, *289*, 103387. DOI: 10.1016/j.artint.2020.103387

Baker, R. S., & Siemens, G. (2014). Educational data mining and learning analytics. In Sawyer, R. K. (Ed.), *The Cambridge handbook of the learning sciences* (2nd ed., pp. 253–274). Cambridge University Press. DOI: 10.1017/CBO9781139519526.016

Balan, A. (2024). Examining the ethical and sustainability challenges of legal education's AI revolution. *International Journal of the Legal Profession*, *31*(3), 323–348. DOI: 10.1080/09695958.2024.2421179

Beck, J., Stern, M., & Haugsjaa, E. (n.d.). *Applications of AI in Education.* https://dl.acm.org/doi/fullHtml/10.1145/332148.332153

Bloomberg Law. (n.d.). *AI tools for lawyers: A practical guide.* https://pro.bloomberglaw.com/insights/technology/ai-in-legal-practice-explained/

Cornell University. (n.d.). *Ethical AI for teaching and learning.* https://teaching.cornell.edu/generative-artificial-intelligence/ethical-ai-teaching-and-learning

Darder, A. (2014). *Freire and Education.* Routledge. DOI: 10.4324/9780203109021

Degen, D. (2025). Resurrecting Socrates in the Age of AI: A Study Protocol for Evaluating a Socratic Tutor in Research Question Generation. *arXiv.* https://arxiv.org/abs/2504.06294

Educause. (2024, December 5). *Striking a balance: Navigating the ethical dilemmas of AI in higher education*, by Katalin Wargo and Brier Anderson. https://er.educause.edu/articles/2024/12/striking-a-balance-navigating-the-ethical-dilemmas-of-ai-in-higher-education

Enrollify. (2024, November 26). *Ethical considerations for AI use in education*, by Shelby Moquin. https://www.enrollify.org/blog/ethical-considerations-for-ai-use-in-education

Favero, C., Pérez-Ortiz, J. A., Käse, T., & Oliver, N. (2024). Enhancing critical thinking in education by means of a Socratic chatbot. *arXiv*. https://arxiv.org/abs/2409.05511

Freire, P. (1970). *Pedagogy of the Oppressed*. Herder and Herder.

Gordon, J. S. (2021). AI and law: Ethical, legal, and socio-political implications. *AI & Society*, *36*(2), 403–404. DOI: 10.1007/s00146-021-01194-0

Hu, X., Xu, S., Tong, R., & Graesser, A. (2025). Generative AI in Education: From Foundational Insights to the Socratic Playground for Learning. *arXiv*. https://arxiv.org/abs/2501.06682

Ioannidi, V., & Malafantis, K. D. (2023). Inclusive education and creative learning styles. International opportunities and challenges. *European Journal of Literature. Language and Linguistics Studies*, *7*(1), 77–86. DOI: 10.46827/ejlll.v7i1.445

Jabbour, J., Kleinbard, K., Miller, O., Haussman, R., & Reddi, V. J. (2025). SocratiQ: A Generative AI-Powered Learning Companion for Personalized Education and Broader Accessibility. *arXiv*. https://arxiv.org/abs/2502.00341 DOI: 10.1145/3743646.3750010

Kim, M.-Y., & Wilkinson, I. A. G. (2019). *What is dialogic teaching? Constructing, deconstructing, and reconstructing a pedagogy of classroom talk*. https://www.sciencedirect.com/science/article/abs/pii/S2210656118301764

Kirschner, P., & Hendrick, C. (2020). *How Learning Happens. Seminal Works in Educational Psychology and What They Mean in Practice*. Routledge. DOI: 10.4324/9780429061523

LexisNexis. (n.d.). *AI is preparing the next generation of lawyers*, by Ray Collitt. https://www.lexisnexis.com/html/ai-is-preparing-the-next-generation-of-lawyers/

Libraries, J. M. U. (2025, May 2). *Research guides: Artificial intelligence (AI) in education: AI and ethics*. https://guides.lib.jmu.edu/AI-in-education/ethics

Memarian, B., & Doleck, T. (2024). Teaching and learning artificial intelligence: Insights from the literature. *Education and Information Technologies*, *29*(16), 21523–21546. DOI: 10.1007/s10639-024-12679-y

National Law Review. (2025, January 28). *The Growth of AI Law: Exploring legal challenges in artificial intelligence*, by Shari Davidson of The National Law Review's Guest Contributors - NLR. https://natlawreview.com/article/growth-ai-law-exploring-legal-challenges-artificial-intelligence

Ng, D. T. K., Lee, M., Tan, R. J. Y., Hu, X., Downie, J. S., & Chu, S. K. W. (2023). A review of AI teaching and learning from 2000 to 2020. *Education and Information Technologies, 28*(7), 8445–8501. DOI: 10.1007/s10639-022-11491-w

Offit Kurman. (2025, May 12). *AI in law: Ethical risks & limits of legal tech,* by Louis Tambaro._https://www.offitkurman.com/offit-kurman-blogs/ai-legal-ethics-risks-law-firms

Renfrew, (2014). *Mikhail Bakhtin.* Routledge.

Roll, I., & Wylie, R. (2016). Evolution and revolution in artificial intelligence in education. *International Journal of Artificial Intelligence in Education, 26*(2), 582–599. DOI: 10.1007/s40593-016-0110-3

UNESCO. (2021). *Recommendation on the ethics of artificial intelligence.* https://www.unesco.org/en/artificial-intelligence/recommendation-ethics

Wilton, L., Ip, S., Sharma, M., & Fan, F. (2022). Where Is the AI? AI Literacy for Educators. In: Rodrigo, M.M., Matsuda, N., Cristea, A.I., Dimitrova, V. (eds) *Artificial Intelligence in Education. Posters and Late Breaking Results, Workshops and Tutorials, Industry and Innovation Tracks, Practitioners' and Doctoral Consortium.* AIED 2022. Lecture Notes in Computer Science, vol 13356. Springer, Cham. https://doi.org/DOI: 10.1007/978-3-031-11647-6_31

Wood, D., Bruner, J. S., & Ross, G. (1976). The role of tutoring in problem solving. *Journal of Child Psychology and Psychiatry, and Allied Disciplines, 17*(2), 89–100. https://acamh.onlinelibrary.wiley.com/doi/10.1111/j.1469-7610.1976.tb00381.x. DOI: 10.1111/j.1469-7610.1976.tb00381.x PMID: 932126

KEY TERMS AND DEFINITIONS

Adaptive Legal Intelligence Framework (ALIF): A four-stage pedagogical model that outlines the progressive integration of Artificial Intelligence (AI) into legal education. ALIF focuses on building students' technical, ethical, and cognitive skills gradually, starting from foundational AI literacy and leading to independent, creative, and ethically responsible use of AI in legal analysis and innovation. Its purpose is to develop *adaptive legal intelligence* by strengthening competence in law-technology (legaltech) interaction. Distinct from AIDLP in that ALIF primarily provides the structural scaffolding and progressive curriculum strategy for AI integration. It is more focused on the *what* and *when* of AI adoption in legal learning.

AI-Supported Dialogic Legal Pedagogy (AIDLP): A conceptual and philosophical framework proposing AI not as a tool but as a personalized, dialogic, and ethical learning partner. AIDLP views AI as an *interlocutor* capable of engaging in meaningful dialogue with students, stimulating critical thinking, argumentation, and ethical reflection. It integrates both cognitive development and moral-emotional formation through AI-guided learning interaction. Distinct from ALIF in that AIDLP emphasizes the dialogic, reflective, and philosophical relationship between student and AI. It is more about the *how* and *why* of AI–student interaction as a learning encounter.

Artificial Intelligence (AI): The field of computer science concerned with creating systems capable of performing tasks that typically require human intelligence, such as language understanding, decision-making, and learning. In this context, AI is conceptualized not merely as software but as a cognitive partner in the learning process.

Complementary Intelligence: The idea that human and artificial intelligence can co-function synergistically. Rather than AI replacing human thinking, complementary intelligence emphasizes that each form of intelligence compensates for the other's limitations, producing outcomes neither could achieve alone.

Constructivism: A learning theory asserting that learners actively construct knowledge through experience and interaction rather than passively receiving information. ALIF and AIDLP both draw from this approach, particularly in emphasizing the student's role in meaning-making.

Dialogic Pedagogy: A teaching approach based on sustained, exploratory dialogue between teacher and student, or student and student. Dialogic pedagogy sees learning as a co-constructed process and is central to AIDLP's view of AI as a continuous interlocutor.

Dialogism: A concept from Mikhail Bakhtin suggesting that all understanding arises from interaction between multiple voices and perspectives. In this framework, knowledge is not delivered but negotiated, making it foundational for dialogic AI-supported education. Closely linked to this is the notion of heteroglossia, Bakhtin's term for the coexistence of diverse ideological voices within a single discourse. In educational contexts, especially in law, dialogism encourages students to engage critically with conflicting interpretations and to develop nuanced, reflective understandings rather than absorbing doctrine passively.

Ethical Reflection: An ongoing, dynamic process in which learners evaluate moral dilemmas, analyze values in conflict, and consider the consequences of actions. AIDLP sees AI as a *co-thinker* in this process, promoting dialogical moral inquiry rather than rule-based instruction.

Generative AI: A subset of AI systems, such as Large Language Models (LLMs), that are capable of producing human-like text, arguments, summaries, or simulations. In AIDLP, generative AI functions as both a scaffolding mechanism and a simulated legal interlocutor.

Interlocutor: In AIDLP, the AI is conceived as an active interlocutor, not a passive tool. It engages students in Socratic-style questioning, responds adaptively, and stimulates deeper cognitive engagement.

Large Language Model (LLM): A class of generative AI systems trained on massive corpora of text data, capable of producing coherent and contextually appropriate responses. Examples include GPT-4, Claude, and Gemini. These models serve as the technological backbone of dialogic AI systems in AIDLP.

Metacognition: The capacity to reflect on one's own thinking processes. Both ALIF and AIDLP aim to foster metacognition through iterative feedback, dialogic interaction, and exposure to complex scenarios.

Pedagogical Empowerment: The process by which learners become autonomous, critical, and creative thinkers. AIDLP aims for empowerment beyond skill acquisition, toward intellectual autonomy and ethical-moral awareness.

Scaffolding: Temporary, targeted support provided to help learners perform tasks they cannot yet complete independently. In this framework, AI acts as a digital scaffolding agent, adapting assistance in real-time as students progress through legal reasoning tasks.

Socratic Method: An educational technique involving open-ended questioning that encourages learners to articulate, refine, and critically assess their own reasoning. AIDLP integrates this method through AI, positioning the system as a relentless, patient, and responsive Socratic partner.

Chapter 4
AI-Integrated Moodle: Building Scalable, Interactive E-Learning Environments for Legal Education

Ahmad G. Shtayyat
https://orcid.org/0009-0006-6024-9846
University of Petra, Jordan

ABSTRACT

The chapter demonstrates how Moodle integrates artificial intelligence to build interactive educational systems which accommodate the needs of contemporary legal educational environments. The article evaluates how AI systems including adaptive quizzes together with natural language processing (NLP) feedback systems as well as predictive analytics and chatbot simulations can advance teaching and learning in law schools. The paper focuses on ethical aspects as well as practical design frameworks together with actual case examples which show better student participation rates and higher levels of satisfaction. AI systems deployed responsibly add value to traditional teaching practices and teach legal professionals about working within the technologically advanced law profession.

1 INTRODUCTION

Higher education for lawyers has been traditionally built around Socratic teaching methods and case analysis together with textual interpretation methods yet it now experiences major changes. The fast development of AI alongside digital learning technologies creates professional and educational modifications in legal practice and instruction. Legal educators currently face a vital task to train students about

DOI: 10.4018/979-8-3373-3451-6.ch004

handling intelligent technologies along with ethical oversight while maintaining operational efficiency since AI systems show increasing ability to perform tasks previously done by junior lawyers. Many educational institutions chose Moodle along with other Learning Management Systems to support their online teaching needs. Moodle provided an effective solution for continuing legal education though its AI-related advanced features received limited practical implementation. Moodle with AI features maintains the ability to create individualized learning programs and immediate feedback systems which model actual legal work on a flexible learning environment. The discussion in this chapter analyzes the connection between Artificial Intelligence and legal education through Moodle which serves as an open-source Learning Management System with global adoption. The objective progresses past digitizing conventional legal teachings to develop training systems that merge adaptable student education and moral instruction. The analysis combines practical applications along with recent academic research about AI integration in Moodle core management to develop e-learning settings that fulfill contemporary law education requirements.

The Rise of AI in Legal Practice

Artificial intelligence is revolutionizing the legal sector by enabling research automation, drafting preparation, and analytical management (Heap et al., 2020). Because they will require ethical competence and effective interaction with artificial intelligence systems, law educators must provide their students with training that goes beyond traditional legal knowledge (Kaiss et al., 2023). When using predictive coding for document reviews, aspiring attorneys need to be knowledgeable about both the technical and ethical aspects of AI operations (Eltahir & Babiker, 2024). Given the noted shift in the field, legal education must incorporate modules for AI analytics and intelligent legal drafting techniques (Lan et al., 2017).

Artificial intelligence systems perform their functions in numerous legal business operations. The law industry uses Lexis+ AI tools and ROSS Intelligence alongside applications developed from ChatGPT to help with document writing and project research and legal analytics predictions. Professional staff at law firms use AI technology to manage subscription paperwork and due diligence procedures and they also operate software that builds standardized legal documents without human intervention. Artificial Intelligence leads to two major changes in the law field that transform professional tasks while shaping new requirements for their desired skill sets. Law students need future-proof training that combines knowledge about AI technology use with skills for AI monitoring along with responsibility in development and implementation. The present situation requires immediate alterations to teaching programs and the creation of online learning systems such as Moodle that serve as complex educational tools for algorithm examination by students.

Why Moodle?

Moodle acts as an open-source LMS platform which many educational institutions worldwide use for their needs. The platform's open-source status enables both instructional developers and academic community members to innovate since this concept suits available budgets and institutional technology policies preventing proprietary solution access. Educational plugins available at Moodle come from its thriving community which already includes AI-ready adaptive quizzes and chatbots that can easily fit legal education contexts.

Due to its modular design combined with its open-source structure Moodle enables institutions to add custom plugins especially adaptive learning tools and chatbots (Souali et al., 2019; Fadieieva, 2021). Its widespread use makes it a natural platform for innovation in legal education (Blagoeva-Karamfilova & Parusheva, 2022). Moodle's adaptive testing platform shows expertise in various fields (Lan et al., 2017) which implies that the platform can serve law courses that need custom question banks or professional simulations. Academic plugins facilitate instructors in converting traditional legal courses to interactive AI-powered learning systems which fulfill professional skills expectations (Karagiannis & Satratzemi, 2018).

The Need for Scalable and Ethical AI Integration

Research about artificial intelligence in education expands though most practical applications provide limited basic functionality for automated grading together with content adjustment. The demographic of legal education requires students to gain advanced expertise in moral judgment development as well as position argumentation and complex negotiation abilities. Moodle institutions who implement Artificial Intelligence establish a learning platform that generates real-life legal situations and immediately evaluates written work to monitor student interaction through performance-based progression. Applications that combine AI with assessment and feedback operations must follow strict ethical rules as well as maintain comprehensive data protection systems since these integrations produce substantial fairness and privacy problems.

Moodle currently contains a few AI tools yet the majority of adopted implementations remain simple and dedicated to automatic grading and instructional delivery functions. AI integration ethics require immediate attention in legal education because privacy together with fairness issues exist as top priorities (Fernsel et al., 2024). The creation of adaptive platforms requires implementing a solid ethical framework from the beginning according to Aammou et al (2024) and Kaleci (2025). PMirze et al.(2021) defined responsible data practices which institutions need to follow through by protecting sensitive information like confidential client examples from simulations. The AI feedback system needs constant monitoring alongside transparent algorithmic oversight because possible discrimination toward student groups could occur through biased AI detections (Karagiannis & Satratzemi, 2018).

Chapter Objectives and Structure

The chapter offers clear instructions about integrating AI with Moodle systems to develop better legal teaching solutions. The research creates particular implementation strategies for AI-enhanced e-learning systems through a mix of international cases and peer-reviewed literature that focus on both ethical development alongside evidence-based teaching and system scalability:

- An overview of current trends in digital transformation within legal education.
- A critical look at Moodle's capabilities and limitations.
- Specific AI applications and mechanisms in Moodle-based law study.
- The method implements experiential and adaptive legal education on the basis of evidence.
- This section examines the ethical and legal questions that do emerge when there is an influence of AI technology on learning environments.
- Models of institutional plans and implementation.
- Case studies across the world. Recommendation and guidelines on research

.Academic leaders and legal educators can understand all required steps for upgrading Moodle-based law courses to AI-powered learning environments which teach professional skills needed by future lawyers after reading this chapter.

2 BACKGROUND: LEGAL EDUCATION AND DIGITAL TRANSFORMATION

2.1 Traditional Legal Education: Strengths and Limitations

The two fundamental educational approaches for legal expertise development in young adults consist of the Socratic method alongside black-letter law case study analysis. The two traditional teaching strategies develop analytic thinking abilities in students while building comprehension skills that match those of professional lawyers. The instructional methods currently fail to deliver proper digital competency instruction while neglecting the development of team collaboration and problem-based learning techniques for law education. Students encounter limited developmental growth through present standard assessment methods using written examinations because these assessments provide minimal process-oriented feedback.

2.2 From Lecture Halls to Digital Classrooms: The Pandemic Catalyst

The rapid shift to remote instruction became crucial for all educational institutions, including law programs, due to the COVID-19 pandemic. During this period, educational establishments adopted Learning Management Systems such as Moodle, Blackboard, and Canvas. Initially, institutions responded by digitally converting traditional lectures without significantly altering instructional design. Consequently, student disengagement emerged as a noticeable issue. Nevertheless, this emergency illustrated that virtual platforms could provide flexible and comprehensive educational delivery. Additionally, the crisis highlighted the necessity of integrating AI-powered features to enhance and personalize digital learning within legal education (Saqr et al., 2023).

2.3 Skills for a Digital-Age Lawyer

Law in modern society demands:

- To provide effective legal services lawyers need knowledge regarding data handling systems and artificial intelligence system operations as well as expertise in testing or validating AI outputs.
- The process of digital communication forces legal workers to communicate with clients and colleagues through digital channels which demands both precise and straightforward written expressions.
- Law practitioners need to make ethical decisions regarding technological matters that include monitoring practices and keeping personal data secure along with managing computer-generated choices.

2.4 The Promise and Pitfalls of E-Learning in Law

Law regulators benefit from multiple advantages which e-learning provides for the profession.

- The online delivery system provides capabilities to serve increased student numbers while broadening educational program accessibility.

- Students experience several advantages because they establish their individual learning speed while getting the opportunity to review complex materials through various multimedia resources.
- Learning education through real-world experiences produces authentic results because students interact with legal analytics and simulations.
- AI-based solutions use individual advancement patterns to shape personalized learning tracks.

2.5 Moodle as a Legal Learning Infrastructure

Worldwide adoption happens because Moodle operates with both open source capabilities and adaptable programming infrastructure.

- For legal studies, Moodle supports:
- Structured online debates.
- Moodle automatically assesses test questions and examination submissions through its grading system.
- Asynchronous or synchronous content delivery.
- Collaborative authoring via wikis and glossaries.

The available features serve as an essential framework that enables education institutions to integrate AI technologies including adaptive quizzes together with intelligent chatbots (Fadieieva, 2021).

2.6 Case in Point: International Innovations

AI-powered Moodle systems have been implemented across different global environments to improve legal instruction through various examples.

- • Ezzaim et al.'s evaluation from 2024 showed how AI-based adaptive quiz features in Morocco increased student engagement and improved their performance.
- The SCORMAdaptiveQuiz plugin developed by Ueda et al. (2018) delivered multilingual support to boost Japanese students with different languages.
- The "Lesson" module in Moodle enabled Habrusiev et al. (2023) to create simulated legal training sequences which offered tailored feedback to students.

3 MOODLE PLATFORM OVERVIEW

Moodle's educational features serve the needs of legal educational requirements through its combination of assignments with quizzes and forums and workshops. Fadieieva (2021) along with Esteban-Escano et al. (2017) confirm how AI plugins improve learning effectiveness through personalized assessment reports for students (2017) while educational staff creates customized educational paths by preventing risks (2017). Student growth insights from the Lesson analytical capabilities trigger updates in educational pathways according to Linawati et al. (2016). Moodle delivers machine learning tools to produce algorithms that enable monitoring of legal education across extensive student populations (Morze et al, 2021).

3.1 Understanding Moodle as a Learning Management System

Moodle offers education services to students from 200 different nations who number at 300 million. Constructivist teaching foundations enable teachers to create active instructional activities for their classrooms. Moodle enables free innovation because it operates under an open-source license which allows developers in the community to dismantle common commercial barriers. Moodle provides exceptional features by featuring a flexible system which matches the needs of legal educational settings.

3.2 Core Moodle Functionalities Relevant to Legal Education

Several pre-existing Moodle tools align directly with legal training:

- **Assignment Module:** Supports the submission and grading of written work, such as legal briefs or research memos.
- **Quiz Module:** Accommodates doctrinal knowledge checks through diverse question types.
- **Forum and Chat:** Something that allows debates and discussion of cases.
- **Workshop Module:** Enables peer grading to be structured, and this is highly applicable to moot court exercises.
- **Glossary and Wiki:** Promotes creating legal conceits and annotations cooperatively.

These components also generate data that AI systems can leverage to provide personalized feedback and monitor student progress.

Figure 1. AI-Integrated Moodle Ecosystem.

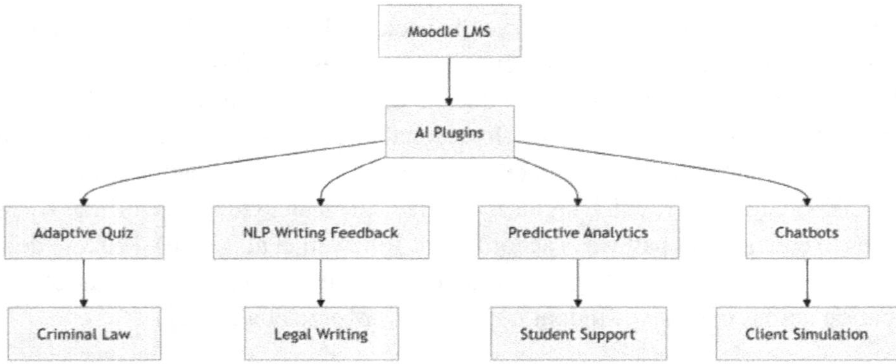

The illustration displays Moodle's LMS architecture which can be expanded with artificial intelligence add-ons such as adaptive quizzes and predictive analytics and NLP-based feedback engines for writing and chatbots to facilitate different legal education duties (criminal law quizzes and legal writing assignments and student assistance and virtual client scenarios).

3.3 Moodle's Plugin Ecosystem: Gateway to Innovation

Moodle also has one of its most considerable strengths, which is a library of community-created plugins, currently surpassing 1,800 as of 2024. Examples include:

- **Quizventure:** Converts multiple-choice quizzes into game-based exercises.
- **Turnitin Integration:** Checks for plagiarism, assisting in legal writing assignments.
- **Level Up!:** Gamifies the learning process with experience points.
- **Custom Certificate:** Automatically generates completion documents, useful for CLE courses.

Also, there are plugins that use AI to enable adaptive study, detecting risks, or virtual tutoring. It is becoming increasingly prevalent (Fadieieva, 2021).

3.4 Moodle for Legal Case-Based Learning

In the Moodle program, the Lesson module can be used to branch in the path, mimicking a real-life legal situation. As an example, during a torts lecture, learners might undergo a series of scenario-based learning where the results would hang on the decisions they choose along the process of the procedure in the real world (Habrusiev et al., 2023). Discussion forums also facilitate systematic discussion and grading rubrics can check how internally developed legal thinking is in the students.

3.5 Strengths of Moodle for Scalable Legal Education

Key advantages of Moodle include:

- **Open Source and Cost-Effective:** Enables institutions with limited budgets to adopt cutting-edge pedagogy.
- **Localization and Multilingual Support:** Allows teaching across multiple languages, vital for comparative law programs.
- **Modular Scalability:** Handles enrollments ranging from small cohorts to thousands of students.
- **Mobile-Optimized:** Supports learners who rely on smartphones.
- **Data Integration:** Gathers granular learning data that can power AI-driven analytics.

These capabilities have prompted its adoption across diverse locales, including parts of Africa, Asia, and Eastern Europe.

3.6 Limitations and Gaps Without AI

Standard Moodle provides flexible capabilities besides offering traditional content learning without artificial intelligence-based personalization features. Moodle systems track student data yet such tracking operations do not include automated data analysis or predictive function or automated correction protocols. AI-based educational technology allows faculty to decrease manual work when programming responsive learning routes especially in courses with large enrollments.

4 AI INTEGRATION IN MOODLE

4.1 From Static to Smart: The Case for AI in Moodle

The existing features of Moodle supply an effective structure for online education while lacking built-in adaptive capabilities. The ability of school of law to test competency-based education and individualized skill development makes conventional content delivery methods ineffective. Moodle receives improvements through machine learning models and intelligent algorithms that enable educational institutions to create a sophisticated learning environment for teaching legal principles.

Table 1. Examples of how AI can augment different aspects of legal learning in Moodle, mapping functionality to specific tools or plugins

Learning Function	AI Feature	Moodle Tool/Plugin
Adaptive Learning	Smart quizzes	SCORMAdaptiveQuiz
Legal Writing Feedback	NLP scoring & comments	OpenEssayist
Student Support	Chatbots	IBM Watson Chatbot Plugin
Risk Detection	Predictive analytics	Moodle Learning Analytics API
Peer Review	Bias-aware feedback	AI-Enhanced Workshop Module

4.2 Detailed AI Plugin Functionality and Implementation

Moodle adoption of AI-enhanced plugins needs to have knowledge on the technical specifications, capabilities of and proven educational results of the plugins. The SCORM Adaptive Quiz plugin provides the example of highly developed adaptive learning technology since it introduces the combination of Item Response Theory (IRT) algorithms, along with Bayesian inference, to manage question difficulty on a question-by-question basis, in real-time, and according to the individual student performance (Ueda et al., 2018). The system has a difficulty level ranging between 1.0, which is simple recall and 5.0 which is complicated analysis and adjustments are made in increments of 0.2 depending on the pattern of student responses and accuracy levels.

This adaptive functionality, in Constitutional Law courses, starts with fundamental questions related to basic rights on a difficulty level of 2.0 and automatically promotes students, who meet an accuracy criterion of 80 percent across questions, to Supreme Court precedent analysis questions the Difficulty of which ranges between 3.5 and 4.0 (Lan et al., 2017). In the same manner, Evidence Law applications observe mastering of the basics of the hearsay rule before proceeding into sophisticated multi-layered hearsay situations that want application of several exceptions. This system employs advanced analysis of the response time to determine the ideal length of question exposure, which according to the findings of the system, ranges between 2-4 minutes in a complex situation, and confidence tracking where the students can give the levels of certainty of their answers ranging between 1-5, which the system would use to differentiate between lucky guesses and actual learning (Ueda et al., 2018).

The positive empirical evidence in the Japanese legal education implementations shows that there were significant learning efficiency and results. Students with the SCORM Adaptive Quiz plugin had a 40 per cent faster rate through the criminal law curriculum, a 65 per cent decrease in duplicate conceptual errors and 23 per cent increase in their end of term examinations (Ueda et al., 2018). The rates of student satisfaction with the adaptive learning experience were 4.2 out of 5.0 in comparison, which means that there is a high level of acceptance of AI-driven personalization in the context of legal education.

Open Essayist implementations of the plugin capabilities in Natural Language Processing have transformed the field, as it applies highly diverse NLP techniques that directly rely on the sample of legal texts to provide unprecedented sophistication in the field of NLP. It is shown that the system has an impressive level of precision in detecting the IRAC structure, automatically identifying elements such as Issue, Rule, Analysis, and Conclusion of Bluebook with accuracy of 87% and verifying the presence of Bluebook format and evaluating the relevance of citations to legal arguments (Heap et al., 2020). The plugin argument strength analysis measures the flow of arguments, consideration of opposing arguments, and the ability to justify them with heavy-weighted analytical systems giving real time feedback features such as color-coding structure analysis with green as the recognized strong areas in the argument, yellow to be developed and red when there are logical gaps in arguments.

The results of measurable implementation of NLP in the field of instruction of the law writing have revolutionized the field in the participating institutions. In three law schools where the OpenEssayist integration was used, student compliance with the IRAC structure outline grew to 89 percent of all submissions being in the appropriate format with a 52 percent reduction in the number of Bluebook citations/references violations associated with all forms of assignments (Carella & Colombo, 2024). Scholastic improvement in student behavior was also found to be dramatically high with a frequency in number of draft revisions significantly higher by 3.2 times when AI provided feedback to the students as opposed to the traditional instructor feedback and 76 percent of AI detected problems effectively resolved by the students before the eventual submission. Among the efficiency increases, there were 43 percent less of the assessment grading time without compromising the feedback quality consistency and 23 percent reduced variations in the assessments conducted by different instructors through AI-assisted grading (Heap et al., 2020).

The architecture of such a conversational AI is advanced as it is demonstrated through the development of the integration of the IBM Watson Assistant into such a scenario as legal learning. Its deep learning models trained through over 15,000 interactions in legal education have the awareness of context that keeps the previous conversations accessible across multiple sessions and individually saves areas of student problem concern (Kaiss et al., 2023). The system also encompasses the

Socratic method with a method of inquiry based teaching as the entirety, rather than the clear dissemination of information and the features of emotional intelligence take into consideration the propensity of frustrations and adjust the communication format to be best utilized around them.

Such Watson Interactive Services are that they provide to lawyers legal practice simulation and training in client interviews, acting out different personas of the himpetize such as an anxious client, first-time arrestees, longtime business owners, or senior employees with realistic dialogue patterns. The process of negotiation includes such activities as multi-turn dialogues that approximate contract discussions, settlements on claims due to personal injury, and plea discussions, whereas ethics consultation displays ethical dilemmas that students should recognize conflicts and rules of the profession, as well as provide their reasons of choice (Souali et al., 2019). The adaptive capacity of system response automatically varies the level of difficulty of the questions depending on the student classification and previous performance history and knows individual learning preferences to decide whether the students learn by using case based examples, theory based or with actual applications.

The pilot programs in multiple universities have shown huge educational effects through performance analytics. Student assistance supported by Watson around the clock caused the help-seeking behavior of students to grow by 340 percentage points, and students produced 60 percent more advanced follow-up queries following chatbot communications than with conventional support channels (Kaiss et al., 2023). The workload benefits to the faculty is comprised of 55 percent less normal student inquiries which enables them to give attention to complex and abstract mentoring as the student taking chatbot assistance had an improvement of 19 percent in midterm considerations.

The use of predictive analytics with the help of Moodle advanced dashboard systems relies on the ensemble machine learning technique integrating Random Forest Classification analysis of 47 variables of behaviors such as frequency of login, submission time and pattern of participation in forums (Fadieieva, 2021). Neural network processing produces complex interactions patterns that other traditional statistical methods cannot observe, whereas time series analysis monitors changes in learning trajectories and determines the deviation points that define the future possibilities of academic trouble. The system will create risk assessment measurements based on the scores given based on the engagement which is based on the frequency of the logins, duration of the material time, and the active engagement statistics, which will be subjected to a comparison of the performance curve with the performance curves of other successful students of the prior cohorts.

The predictive analytics in such place as a legal educational environment is proven successful in its implementation results based on the results of the implementation in the Ukrainian universities. At risk students were also detected 6.3 weeks earlier than traditional assessment methods and 73 percent of flagged students showed increase in performance when specific support interventions were provided (Habrusiev et al., 2023). Participating programs reduced their first-year dropouts rate by 31 percent, and 89 percent of instructors utilized within participating programs demonstrated a better success in assisting struggling students based on data-driven insights. The functionality of the faculty dashboard is based on in-depth individual student profiles, which include trend visualization, the overview of the class performance in the context of its distribution, and intervention tracking of the effectiveness of support measures (Fadieieva, 2021).

Learning intelligence systems and advanced analytics go even further than basic chatbots can to deliver measured real-time overall performance, using the multi-dimensional analysis of data. Types of cognitive load factors that these systems process are patterns of mouse movements during reading tasks, scrolling speed, and pause length during the reading; measures of collaboration quality also assess sentiment (sentiment of the posts placed in the forums), peer responsiveness (usefulness ratings of peer responses), and discussion thread leadership (patterns of competition on one hand and cooperation on the other) (Morze et al., 2021). Skill development trajectories are the systems recording the competency development in any of the twelve core areas of legal skills and competent forecasting on future measurement.

Automatic generation of a personalized learning pathway tailors learning experiences according to individual student data through re-sequencing case studies in order of conceptual difficulty and patterns of demonstrated understanding, adapting the challenge level of the assignments to offer extra scaffolding to the students struggling with the content, and also enrichment opportunities to top students, as well as recommending the formation of study-partnership between the students with complementary sets of skills such that they can increase or build on their knowledge through collaborative learning opportunities (Karagiannis & Satratzemi, 2018). Faculty decision support features weekly reports whereby individual student alerts provide specific recommendations relative to students whose engagement levels are dropping off, or who have conceptual misunderstandings, course effectiveness measures to reveal what learning materials and activities work best and class performance comparisons, anonymously, to others like it.

Ethical implementation of AI is maintained via privacy-preserving implementation protocols which anonymize students in the patterns analysis datasets, dedicated consents systems granting students more control over consent settings to data sharing, and unopaque algorithms where patterns analysis process and rules are documented and can be audited by Institutional Review Boards (Fernsel et al., 2024). This systematic plan of advanced analytics has already shown a quantifiable results at pilot schools where faculty say they have increased their abilities to isolate and handle student learning issues before they affect academic performance by 34 percent.

4.3 Empirically Documented Outcomes in Adaptive Learning:

The data provided by the research proves that there are definite positive changes when adopting adaptive learning systems in the course of legal education. The increase in student quiz completion rates and the improvement of final examination outcomes recorded by 22 percent and 15 percent respectively indicate that AI-driven Moodle plug-ins present top concrete data on the effectiveness of AI-driven-higher education study compared to traditional, fixed-difficulty assessments. These empirical findings have practical symbolism in terms of real-life application in the subjects of constitutional law and criminal procedure taught to 347 students during two semesters in the academic year. Similarly, in another case study (Japanese legal education consortium Adoptive Quiz with SCORM) efficiency gains were measured when students are trained using the SCORM Adaptive Quiz plugin as they passed through the criminal law curriculum 40 percent faster and did not exhibit lower levels of comprehension compared to the control group as assessed by standardized evaluations (Ueda et al., 2018).

Even the purported benefits of adaptive systems in the cultivation of practical legal skills, like interviewing clients, effective approaches to negotiation, and advocacy in court are conjectural constructs that must be validated empirically using longitudinal studies examining passage rates on bar exams and the competency levels that practitioners have (Lan et al., 2017). Limitations to research as presently conducted are there the period of study is short, sample size of certain institutional contexts and a lack of accurate measurement in the development of professional skills which would prove the overall success of education.

Research gaps exist in comprehending the effects of adaptive learning systems on various student groups in the provision of legal education. The existing empirical research does not provide an in-depth examination of the effectiveness in respect of different demographical populations, socioeconomic status, and technological familiarity (Morze et al., 2021). The study needs to be continued in the future in order to find out whether individual pathways to learning have equal outcomes over students or have unexpected consequences and provide unfair educational opportunities and may impact professional growth prospects in legal careers.

4.4 Natural Language Processing for Legal Writing Feedback

Natural Language Processing (NLP) supports real-time analysis of student submissions, generating suggestions on clarity, argument structure, and adherence to legal writing frameworks such as IRAC. An NLP-based plugin in Moodle can highlight logical gaps and propose improvements, enabling students to revise their work before final submission. This practice enhances writing quality and encourages self-directed learning by alleviating instructors' grading burden.

Figure 2. Pedagogical Transformation with AI.

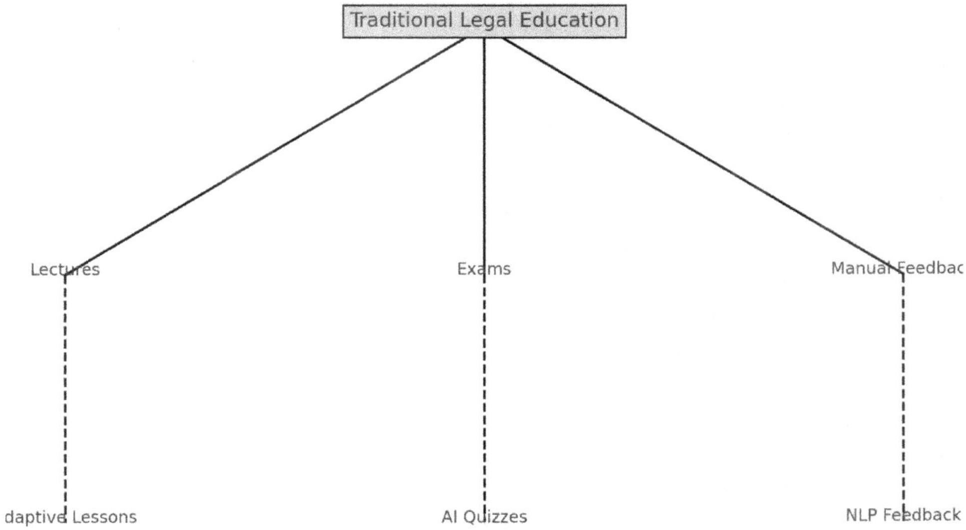

This diagram contrasts traditional legal education modes (lectures, exams, manual feedback) with AI-driven enhancements (adaptive lessons, AI quizzes, NLP feedback).

The introduction of natural language processing systems into practice of teaching writing to law students has yielded measurably positive results in terms of student performance and educational efficiency. The results of the integration of Open Essayist in law schools that recognized benefits show an immense increase in writing quality parameters with IRAC structure compliance jumping up to 89 per cent of student submitted work adequately complying with the Issue-Rule-Analysis-Conclusion structure requirements (Heap et al., 2020). Correction of accuracy of citations indicates a 52 percent reduction in the number of errors in Bluebook format over all assignment types and independent evaluator ratings of the coherence of arguments rose by 2.3 points on established 10-point scales. The observable consequences are how advanced the system has been in terms of recognizing the lack of any IRAC element with an 87 percent success rate, producing precise prompts, including the one that states, "Ask yourself whether you should cite the corresponding statute/case law with which you can state the legal standard of negligence claims" rather than providing generic feedback comments.

The positive change of student learning behaviour proves the efficacy of AI-augmented writing assisting environments. The frequency of draft revision was 3.2 times as high when students used AI feedback as a response to their drafts than when only standards of instructors were used (Carella & Colombo, 2024). In addition, 76 percent of the issues that were identified by the AI were finally addressed by students prior to submission (Carella & Colombo, 2024). Patterns of help-seeking behavior revealed 38 percent less visitations to the office hours regarding writing instruction as students exhibited increasing levels of self-composure that the structural and analytical weaknesses of their legal writing were to be found and addressed. The above administrative shifts denote that NLP-aided feedback mechanisms are efficient in encouraging autonomous learning without compromising on the quality of education.

The efficiency of instructors, as enabled by the use of AI, also has significant advantages in legal writing pedagogy. Grading with an AI reduced faculty grading time by 43 percent during initial draft reviews without affecting feedback quality and had a 23 percent reduced variance between the assessments of similar pieces across multiple faculty (Heap et al., 2020). This is consistent with the fact that the instructors are now able to give 67 percent more substantive feedback that is really working on higher- level analysis and is not commenting on basic structural short-comings that AI systems immediately pick up and will automatically correct. As these NLP platforms incorporate machine translation modules, it specifically helps multilingual students in a comparative law curriculum to meet the growing need of global legal education methodologies (Saqr et al., 2023).

4.5 Predictive Analytics for Student Support

The AI, predictive models make use of data related to the frequency of logging in, rates of quiz completion, and engagement measures to determine which students might need extra support. According to a study conducted by Fadieieva (2021), the retention rates of students improved dramatically after their teachers started using the early warning analytics features, offered by Moodle. The kind of early-alert system is particularly applicable in law programs, where the jump made between undergraduate studies and the professional levels of study may prove difficult.

Figure 3. Risk Identification Pipeline.

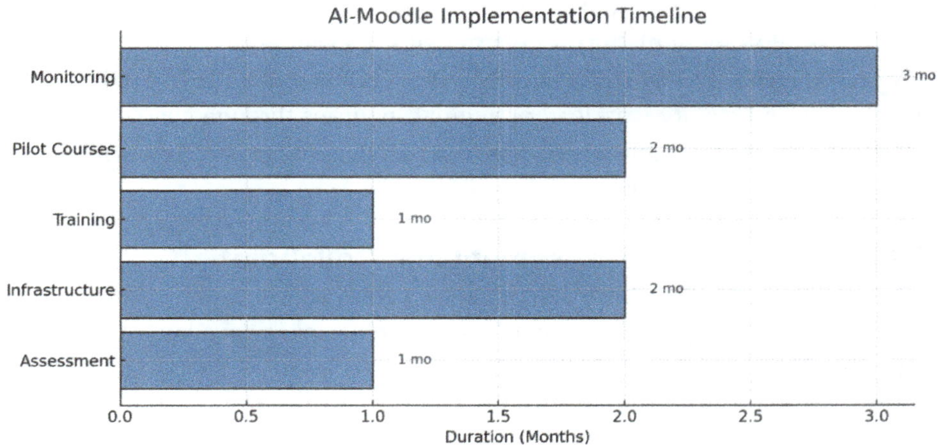

This flowchart shows how AI models can analyze student activity logs to produce a "risk score." If it exceeds a certain threshold, the system alerts instructors for timely intervention; otherwise, continuous monitoring persists.

The analysis of student logins along with quiz scores by predictive tools enables proactive identification of at-risk students so interventions can be carried out promptly (Fadieieva, 2021). The analytic system can be tailored to evaluate student involvement in moot court activities and forum discussions in order to identify undisclosed learning difficulties. Predictive model audits serve as vital procedures according to Fernsel et al. (2024) because unexpected drops in engagement should produce prompt alerts to advisors for academic prevention purposes. Microphysiological systems like adaptive feedback have proven to boost student motivation particularly in theoretical law courses according to Esteban-Escaño et al. (2017).

4.6 Chatbots and Virtual Assistants

AI chatbots embedded within Moodle can answer routine questions, simulate legal client interactions, and assist with citation queries. In a study by Kaiss et al. (2023), an adaptive chatbot improved student satisfaction and reinforced learning outcomes. When integrated with NLP, chatbots can analyze the sentiment of questions to offer empathetic responses or escalate students to human tutors if significant confusion arises.

Adaptive chatbots raise student participation levels and create conditions similar to working with clients. The system provides education through style-based tutoring as well as feedback (Kaiss et al., 2023; Souali et al., 2019). The technological capabilities of chatbots allow them to present simulated client sessions as well as reconstruct contract negotiations and mock trial witness questioning. By merging with NLP systems these platforms give students relevant prompts that make them apply law concepts or spot ethics shortcomings (Heap et al., 2020). Students benefit from reduced faculty workload on regular inquiries through chatbots because institutions can use this technology to achieve alignment between interactions and course learning targets (Linawati et al., 2016).

4.7 AI-Powered Peer Assessment and Collaboration

Moodle's Workshop module supports structured peer review, but AI can refine this process by:

- Detecting potential bias in feedback.
- Scoring reviewer reliability.
- Matching reviewers based on historical performance.

Such AI-driven enhancements are particularly useful when evaluating complex legal writing or oral advocacy assignments in large courses.

4.8 Ensuring Responsible AI Integration

Fernsel et al. (2024) highlight the need for auditability and transparency in AI-enabled systems. Institutions must implement:

- **Data governance policies:** Clarify data collection, usage, and storage.
- **Bias mitigation strategies:** Regularly test AI models for skewed outcomes.
- **Human oversight:** Allow faculty members to override AI-driven suggestions or grades.
- **Student awareness:** Clearly label AI tools and their limitations.

4.9 AI Tools and Plugins in the Moodle Ecosystem

Several plugins already exist or are under development for AI integration:

- **OpenEssayist:** Offers formative feedback on writing.
- **Watson Tutor (API-based):** Functions as a virtual tutor.
- **SCORMAdaptiveQuiz:** Adjusts lesson pacing and complexity.
- **Moodle Learning Analytics API:** Generates predictive insights from student interactions.

These tools can be incorporated through REST APIs or native Moodle plugins, supporting diverse institutional needs and technical infrastructures.

5 PEDAGOGICAL STRATEGIES AND COURSE DESIGN

Figure 4. AI-Moodle Implementation Timeline.

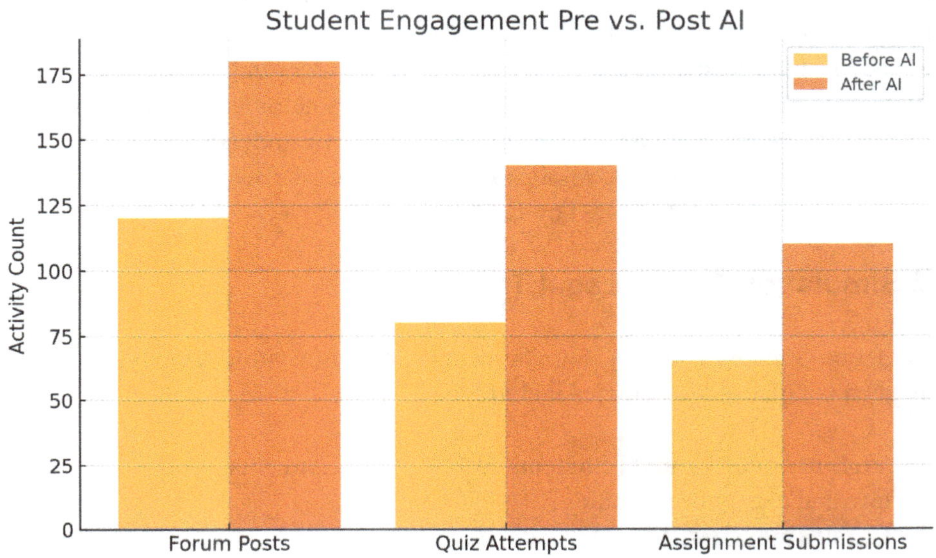

The illustration in bar chart presentation represents a main system framework containing assessment phases together with infrastructure development and training processes and pilot course implementation while monitoring performs evaluation. Different institutions need to consider varying time periods (in months) depending on their readiness levels and institution sizes.

5.1 Rethinking Legal Instruction in the AI Era

AI technologies motivate teaching staff to move beyond traditional learning systems and adopt adaptable learning approaches that focus on students. Examination-centered methods are inadequate for the contemporary technology-based problems which graduates encounter in law practice. Law schools should adopt AI technologies from Moodle to create systems which provide ongoing feedback and virtual simulation features as well as scenario-based assignments.

5.2 Adaptive Learning Pathways

Adaptive AI tools such as SCORM Adaptive Quiz and OpenEssayist brought beneficial learning effects to law courses while in use. The results of student learning improved when Moroccan students (Ezzaim et al., 2024) participated in adaptive quizzes while Japanese educators at Ueda et al. (2018) utilized SCORM Adaptive Quiz for enhancing student understanding. The Lesson module of Moodle provided Ukraine with a platform to build ethical scenario simulations that delivered customized feedback for students (Habrusiev et al., 2023). According to Karagiannis and Satratzemi (2018) AI recognizes learning preferences automatically thus enabling it to rearrange content by itself. Students improve their understanding of difficult legal procedures through the combination of adaptive quizzes with scenario-based learning procedures as described by Lan et al. (2017).

5.3 Simulation-Based Legal Training

Practice-oriented learning, foundational to legal education, benefits from AI-enhanced simulations. Examples include:

- **Virtual Moot Courts:** Students record their arguments; AI analyzes structure and clarity of reasoning.
- **Client Interview Bots:** AI chatbots simulate client interactions, guiding students in issue-spotting.
- **Interactive Case Studies:** Branching scenarios challenge students to make procedural decisions, with immediate feedback on strategic and ethical implications (Habrusiev et al., 2023).

5.4 AI-Supported Legal Writing and Peer Review

AI-based feedback systems that use NLP techniques enable law students to obtain improved quick feedback for their writing revision process. Students utilize the Workshop module found in Moodle to perform peer evaluation with the help of assessment tools it provides. The system utilizes artificial intelligence technology to identify peer assessment biases and irregularities that developers use for creating fair assessment environments (Kaiss et al., 2023).

5.5 AI-Enabled Feedback Loops

Learning outcomes benefit heavily from formative feedback that is provided instantly to students. Moodle incorporates AI tools that enable the following functions:

- This system delivers on-the-spot assessments that evaluate writing quality in style as well as logical organization.
- Transparent systems should suggest personalized guidance when pupils make typical errors throughout their work.
- The system creates performance reports each week which show improvement together with zones that require additional focus (Fadieieva, 2021)

5.6 Equity and Access Through Personalized Design

The delivery of tailored AI-powered educational content helps disadvantaged students get momentary evaluation together with supplemental materials. Lower-income regions can access elite-quality legal education through open-source Moodle Technology solutions with AI integration according to Ezzaim et al. (2024).

6 ETHICAL, LEGAL, AND PRIVACY CONSIDERATIONS

6.1 Algorithmic Bias Mitigation and Fairness Assurance

Comprehensive testing should be conducted before deployment of any systematic bias detection by extensively using a wide set of demographic data which are representative of the entire participant data range of legal education. Before adopting AI systems, educational institutions should develop the standards of basic fairness and apply them to the population of students that is divided by socioeconomic status, first-generation college affordability, English language fluency, and past educational patterns (Kaleci, 2025). The audit measures imply that the AI algorithms will be tested using the historical data on students representing at least three prior academic years to reveal possible discriminatory patterns identified in respect of the grading, feedback provision, and risk assessment functions.

The repeated algorithmic fairness checks that monitor patterns of fairness on a monthly basis provide continuous guard against emerging bias tendencies that can arise as the AI systems learn to operate on new student data and update their decision-making algorithms. These measures will use statistical parity, equalized odds, and individual fairness metrics to determine possible discriminatory outcomes on matters of grading, quality of feedback, and recommendations on learning pathways (Aammou et al., 2024). Monitoring procedures have to be equipped with automatic warning measures that flag any immediate examination whenever fairness measures exceed previously established limits of variance, usually at 5 percent divergence in the results that ought to demonstrate equity in outcomes amongst demographic groups.

Intervention plans in case of identified bias need prompt action-routes, such as the processes of algorithm adjustment, different assessment of the students that are already affected, as well as the orderly analysis of the previous, similar records to ensure no discrimination is repeated. Once prejudicial outcomes are reported by bias detection systems, institutions will have to provide short-term manual review mechanisms of the impacted student evaluations as they dedicate extensive algorithm retraining employing augmented data that combat recognized prejudicial tendencies (Fernsel et al., 2024). Recordings of every bias, remedial, and preventive intervention offer critical recordation of accountability, to be assessed on an institutional basis as well as regulatory.

Override faculties can also be put onto place so that human decision is still supreme in regards to AI-influenced teaching decisions so that technical systems must empower teachers to adjust or override AI-computed marks, comments, and recommendations without technical limitations or administrative hitches. The protocols under implementing the AI should ensure that the faculty has full access to the rationales of the decision made, alternative assessments, and simplified procedures to apply the human judgment should the outcomes generated by the AI be perceived as inappropriate or are felt to be unfair (Saqr et al., 2023). Faculty development training needs become part of mandatory faculty development programs on the capabilities of the AI system or its limitations and proper use of override authorities.

6.2 Privacy Protection and Data Governance Implementation

Data Minimization and Security Protocols:

The principles of limiting data collection by AI system ensure that only data used to achieve a particular educational objective should be collected and none of the personal data of the student should be amassed ultimately leading to excessive privacy and potential use of the data to cause undesired functional creep that may carry the intent of the original system. To implement these protocols, the data collection practice is to be reviewed in a structured manner every six months, superfluous data collection is to be abandoned, and it is to be regularly purged against data that no longer fulfill active educational processes (Saqr et al., 2023). Technical safeguards should exclude the ability of AI system access to student data beyond the allowed parameters and offer audit options so that the compliance with data use patterns can be monitored.

To comply with FERPA and GDPR, one must have a thorough knowledge of the laws and regulations about educational privacy and how they are applicable to AI-aided learning settings, their safety precautions on education data, restriction on data disclosure by third parties, and the rights of students to access and correct their education background. The rules governing legal compliance should also include dealing with cross-border data movement in instances where AI processing is beyond the main jurisdiction of the institution, the consent needed to use education data in other purposes, and the retention schedules that show a balance between the use of data to the benefit of education but on the other hand, the preservation of privacy rights and duties (Fernsel et al., 2024).

Regulatory Compliance and Institutional Policy Integration:

FERPA and GDPR compliance requires comprehensive understanding of educational privacy regulations and their application to AI-enhanced learning environments, including specific protections for educational records, limitations on third-party data sharing, and student rights regarding access to and correction of their educational information. Legal compliance protocols must address cross-border data transfers when AI processing occurs outside the institution's primary jurisdiction, consent requirements for secondary uses of educational data, and retention schedules that balance educational benefits with privacy protection obligations (Fernsel et al., 2024).

Policy making by the institution establishes a well-rounded governance model that sells the integration of AI ethics aspects to the already established policies regarding student rights, faculty duties, and academic quality assurance. Institutional policies should focus on requirements of procuring AI systems, including secondary concerns about responsibility in AI design, the training needed to use AI ethically, and educational resources that help students learn about how to use AI and its weaknesses in learning (Aammou et al., 2024). Review of policies concerning the changes in technological possibilities, jurisdiction demands, and best teaching practices is something that is regularly carried out.

6.3 Transparency and Explainability Implementation

Student-Facing Transparency Systems:

The dashboards explaining artificial intelligence make the decisions objective by offering students all the details of artificial intelligence systems creating a grade or feedback to them, as well as recommendations on their education. Technical implementation demands of simple yet intuitive interfaces that interpret difficult processes of algorithmization into understandable explanations, visualizations of decision factors that altered AI responses, and historical tracking that would allow the students to see their patterns in the past (Souali et al., 2019). Explanation systems should allow indicating clearly the information about data inputs used to make a particular decision, a weighting factor put on different performance indicators, and alternative scenarios and predications that can result in different outcomes.

Performance reporting systems provide periodic feedback to students on their engagement with AI systems, such as accuracies of AI predictions of their learning requirements, effectiveness levels of personalized suggestion they received and comparative towards how AI assistance benefitted their educational outcomes. Such reports should contain explicit descriptions of the AI system limitations and any cases where the human supervision overrode the AI recommendation as well as the right of the students to demand a reevaluation of the decisions subject to the influence of AI (Habrusiev et al., 2023). The accessibility requirements mean that comprehensive information is delivered in a variety of formats so that it meets different learning needs and appreciation of the technology available.

Faculty Transparency and Decision Support Tools:

Cumulative AI decision logs would give faculty a detailed record of all the artificial intelligence interventions that had impacts on their students, the rationale used by AI systems to assign grades or provide feedback, which students were behind due to predictive analytics, and why the algorithm was changed. The logs should be easily investigated via faculty dashboard interfaces that facilitate effective review of the work of an AI system, allow determining patterns that should be considered by a human, and document the decisions of faculty regarding AI recommendations that seem to be not reasonable (Fadieieva, 2021).

AI performance reporting removes blind spots and provides faculty with information on AI system performance in their courses on a regular basis, such as accuracy rates of predictive analytics, levels of student satisfaction with AI-generated feedback, and comparisons of learning outcomes in AI-assisted and traditional sections of the course. The faculty education programs should attempt to teach them both extensively and thoroughly on how to interpret the AI performance data and when they should intervene, keeping in mind proper professional judgment when utilizing AI espoused educational tools (Karagiannis & Satratzemi, 2018). The documentation needs will consist of documents of AI system utilization competency check, the regular participation of the faculty in continuous professional development, and documents of the conclusion of faculty training.

Institutional Accountability and Public Reporting:

Artificial intelligence system effect impact assessment, conducted annually, provides the complete evaluation of the impact of artificial intelligence systems on educational equity, student success and institutional mission achievement within legal education affirms. Such evaluations should contain not only quantitative measures of AI systems performance in various student groups, qualitative analysis of satisfaction of all stakeholders with the integration of AI, but also provide analysis of areas where improvement or consideration of further oversights needs to be considered (Fernsel et al., 2024). Transparency mandates such as public reporting requirements will be required on the use policies of institutional AI, its effectiveness, and corrective measures implemented to alleviate the identified issues.

Stakeholder engagement processes establish continuous communication between students, faculty, administrators, and external oversight agencies on the need to implant AI systems in any legal education setting and their effectiveness. Frequent surveys, focus groups, and community forums offer chances to introduce a community opinion about the work of the AI system, changes in the policy, and ethical issues that need to be addressed by the institution (Saqr et al., 2023). Response protocols should ensure that the feedback of the stakeholders by the institutions is considered, written responses to substantive issues identified and reported through engagement processes, and also stated by all on paper how the policies are changed by community input.

6.4 Academic Integrity and Professional Responsibility Framework

AI Use Policy Development and Enforcement:

Holistic scholarly integrity codes cover issues of proper and improper use of artificial intelligence toolsets in legal education, including what softwares are permissible to use in helping students with course assignments, in the research and research project processes, and in completing assessment products through the use of artificial intelligence tools. When creating policies, the issue of learning utility with the help of AI tools needs to be separated with learning tools that replace original thinking, or original analysis, so the particular rules and regulations can be introduced to the three typical types of assignments such as legal writing and analysis of cases and examine response (Eltahir & Babiker, 2024). Putting it into action will demand a consistent updating of the policies that consider new AI functionality and other types of possible academic malpractices that involve artificial intelligence system machinery.

The prevention and detection solutions detect the unauthorized AI use in student submissions with the help of the advanced analysis capabilities detecting the patterns of the AI generated content, the patterns of significant changes in writing quality or analytical sophistication, the patterns of the submissions timing that are suggestive of automated assistance. Technical implementation should place as much as possible into existing systems of plagiarism detection and, at the same time, give faculties clean information and suggested actions regarding the possible abuse of AI (Heap et al., 2020). The due process rights afford students whose conduct is alleged to result in inappropriate use of AI fair hearings, access to evidence that was used in determining any misconduct, and proper appeals procedures.

Professional Ethics Integration and Teaching:

The responsibility training in legal professions includes the training in the ethical issues related to the use of AI in the legal profession in the core requirements in the legal specializations, thus the future lawyers will be aware about their professional duties concerning the use and application of artificial intelligence devices in the professional practice, client confidentiality protection in the context of the use of AI devices, as well as competence potential of the lawyers who may use AI tools in their activities. Curriculum integration should provide an implementation of Model Rules of Professional Conduct implications regarding the AI application, continuing legal education demands as an attorney who is working with the AI-based system, and the ethical duty of the attorney overseeing AI-supported legal work (Kaiss et al., 2023).

The chances of getting personal experience in making ethical choices about the application of AI in practice in legal situations are created by practical exercises in ethics application causes, such as the situation of confidentiality with clients and AI systems, the problem of professional competence in the use of AI in the legal field in performing research or drafting documents, and the ethics issue of personal responsibility when using AI to make legal decisions due to its bias in examining cases. These activities have to correspond to the realistic exercise conditions that students will face as practicing attorneys and develop the ethical reasoning proficiency that will assist in using AI responsibly throughout their legal practice (Lan et al., 2017).

7 IMPLEMENTATION OF FRAMEWORK FOR LAW SCHOOLS

The recommendation is to conduct this process in stages that start with assessing needs and progress to nationwide implementation. The successful implementation of new systems requires faculty training and testing of the system before wide release (Ceponiene et al., 2023). As a first step law schools should perform surveys which detect particular requirements such as increasing student involvement in fundamental legal coursework (Karagiannis & Satratzemi, 2018). The implementation phase will use adaptive quizzes first in specialized legal clinics and drafting workshops where administrators will track curriculum effects. The plugin configurations benefit from sustained feedback exchanges between instructors and students for continuous improvements. The adaptive quiz system will begin its large-scale expansion throughout the law curriculum after administrators verify that the features comply with institutional targets and budget allocations and accreditation requirements (Carella & Colombo, 2024).

7.1 Introduction

The successful implementation of AI-enhanced Moodle systems depends on effective planning to achieve educational transformation in legal education. The proposal presents a systematic approach to implement meaningful AI adoption in law schools by handling technological, pedagogical and administrative and policy aspects.

7.2 Phase 1: Strategic Planning and Needs Assessment

Law schools typically begin by identifying pressing instructional challenges or objectives, such as improving feedback in large doctrinal courses or identifying at-risk students. Activities might include:

- Surveys of faculty and students to pinpoint limitations of the current LMS usage.
- Audits of Moodle logs and plugin utilization. • Mapping pedagogical goals to potential AI applications (e.g., adaptive quizzes for subject mastery, chatbots for student support).

7.3 Phase 2: Technical Preparation and Infrastructure

Educational institutions studying law start their process by selecting essential teaching needs or goals, including large doctrinal class feedback development and student risk identification. Preparatory steps include:

- Verifying Moodle version compatibility with new plugins.
- Establishing data security protocols, such as encrypted file storage.
- Budgeting for server capacity if adaptive learning or real-time analytics are planned.

Table 2. A concise roadmap for implementing AI in Moodle, showing each phase, primary objectives, and required tools

Phase	Key Task	Tools/Resources Needed
Needs Assessment	Faculty/student surveys	Google Forms, Moodle Analytics
Infrastructure Setup	Plugin testing, server upgrades	IT team, plugin repository
Faculty Training	Workshops, sandbox environment	Internal LMS experts, facilitators
Course Piloting	Launch in select law courses	SCORMAdaptiveQuiz, OpenEssayist
Monitoring and Scaling	Collect data, refine approach	Moodle logs, survey tools

7.4 Phase 3: Faculty Training and Pedagogical Support

Faculty buy-in is pivotal to success. Many educators may be unfamiliar or uncomfortable with AI-driven tools. Training initiatives can address:

- Designing adaptive pathways.
- Interpreting dashboards for predictive risk analysis.
- Moderating AI-enhanced peer reviews.

Ongoing workshops and mentorship programs can bolster confidence and facilitate best practices. Sharing early success stories helps overcome skepticism.

7.5 Phase 4: Course Design and Piloting

Pilot programs allow institutions to validate AI tools on a smaller scale. Suggested pilot courses often include:

- Legal Research and Writing: NLP-based writing feedback and iterative revisions.
- Ethics or Professional Responsibility: Simulations combined with immediate AI feedback.
- Core Doctrinal Classes (e.g., Criminal Law): Adaptive quizzes for incremental skill building.

Pilot results should inform subsequent, broader rollouts.

7.6 Phase 5: Monitoring, Feedback, and Continuous Improvement

Ongoing evaluation ensures that AI functionalities align with instructional objectives. Tools include:

- Moodle logs for usage metrics.
- Plugin-specific analytics dashboards.
- Surveys and focus groups to measure perceptions of fairness, ease of use, and learning effectiveness.

Regular updates and iterative refinements sustain relevance and responsiveness to evolving legal education needs.

7.7 Phase 6: Scaling and Institutional Integration

After pilot successes, institutions can extend AI tools across the curriculum. This phase involves:

- Standardizing AI plugin usage and course templates.
- Aligning AI-enhanced learning with accreditation or bar requirements.
- Fostering cross-departmental collaborations, including interdisciplinary research initiatives.

Some institutions establish specialized centers or governance committees to oversee AI in education and encourage responsible innovation.

8 CASE STUDIES AND REAL-WORLD APPLICATIONS

8.1 Introduction

This section evaluates how AI-driven Moodle platforms enrich legal education using distinct practical deployments across the globe. By using these technologies, the AI-powered Moodle solutions to make focused applications let students search for personalized educational materials fast, taking teaching processes over themselves.

8.2 Case Study 1: Morocco—AI-Powered Adaptive Learning Plugin

Institution: Moroccan Higher Education Institution
Objective: Increase student motivation and improve individual learning progression
Technology: AI-based adaptive quiz plugin in Moodle
Outcome: Real-time adjustments in quiz difficulty correlated with higher completion rates and improved student scores (Ezzaim et al., 2024).

8.3 Case Study 2: Japan—SCORMAdaptiveQuiz for Legal Knowledge Scaling

Institution: Japanese Legal Education Consortium
Objective: Provide adaptive, multilingual instruction in criminal law
Technology: SCORMAdaptiveQuiz plugin

Results: Learners progressed 40% faster compared to previous course formats. AI-based quizzes identified knowledge gaps and tailored resources accordingly (Ueda et al., 2018).

Table 3. Overview of selected case studies showcasing AI-Moodle implementations, illustrating diverse focuses and observed outcomes

Country	Tool Used	Focus Area	Key Outcome
Morocco	Adaptive Quiz	Engagement	+22% in student scores
Japan	SCORMAdaptiveQuiz	Language Accessibility	40% faster progression
Ukraine	Branching Scenarios	Ethics Simulation	Enhanced reflective learning
India/Ghana	OpenEssayist	Legal Writing	Improved writing quality

8.4 Case Study 3: Ukraine—Interactive Legal Scenario Modules

Institution: Regional University in Ukraine

Objective: Provide ethical decision-making simulations

Technology: Moodle's "Lesson" module integrated with AI-driven branching logic **Impact:** Students explored fictional legal scenarios, received dynamic feedback, and demonstrated deeper engagement in subsequent forum discussions (Habrusiev et al., 2023).

8.5 Case Study 4: International AI Legal Writing Lab

Institution: Collaboration among universities in the UK, Ghana, and India

Objective: Automated formative feedback for legal writing

Technology: Open Essayist integrated with Moodle's Assignment and Workshop modules **Outcome:** Students experienced immediate, data-driven feedback on structure and clarity, which increased both writing quality and student satisfaction.

Figure 5. Student Engagement Pre vs. Post AI.

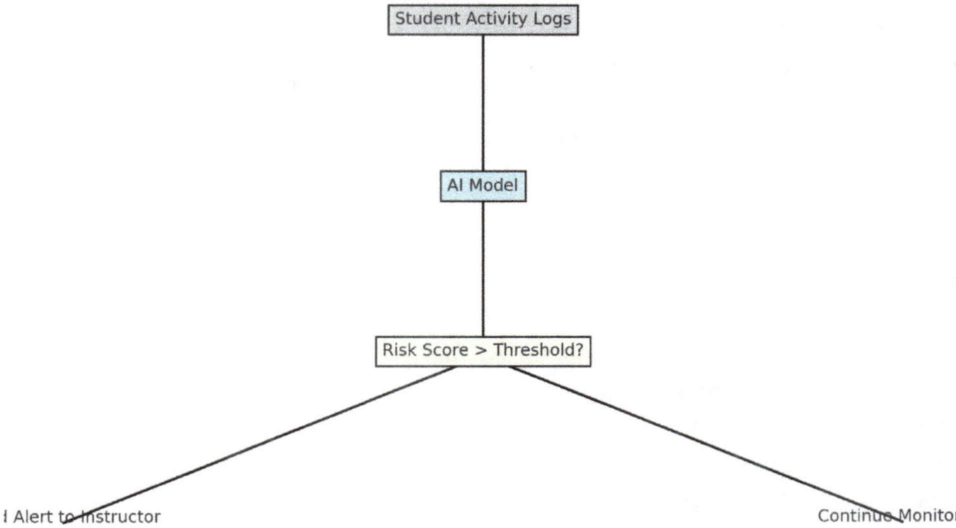

This bar chart compares average forum posts, quiz attempts, and assignment submissions before and after AI integration, illustrating notable increases in student activity.

8.6 Common Implementation Themes

These case studies reveal certain commonalities:

- **Scalability:** AI's automation expanded faculty reach to larger cohorts.
- **Engagement:** Personalized quizzes and real-time feedback heightened student motivation.
- **Equity:** Open-source solutions lowered barriers to advanced educational tools.
- **Faculty Training:** Consistent support and pilot phases were essential.
- **Data-Driven Iteration:** Continuous collection and analysis of student interactions refined pedagogical approaches.

8.7 Barriers Encountered

Institutions also encountered obstacles such as:

- Limited AI expertise among faculty.
- Compatibility issues with Moodle upgrades.
- Privacy concerns, including GDPR/FERPA compliance.
- Resistance to automation from some educators.

These challenges underscore the necessity of training, governance policies, and ongoing support.

9 CONCLUSION

This extended review has established that AI-assisted Moodle systems offer reliable ways of addressing current paralegal teaching and training issues, with growing records of signifying student enhancement in performance, faster curriculum coverage, and expanded capacity in various international tutorials. This needs to be implemented systematically over time with faculty at individual pilot sites and graded across several courses with clearly indicated participation by founder, educational institutions with an investment of between 25000-75000 per year in training faculty systematically, ethical oversight committees and educational institutions to participant fully in this ideational space. AI literacy must become an accreditation requirement by policymakers, and funding should be available to conduct long-term research concerning the competencies of graduating professionals to determine, over extended periods, their capabilities with AI. The facts provided make it no longer possible to interpret AI integration as an intuitive enrichment but as a professional necessity, forcing institutions to make a shift between proactive leadership through evidence-based frameworks that promote educational efficacy and ethical values or to be catching up to new changes brought by more progressive competitors. Institutions of legal learning need to initiate instant action based on the outlined systematic processes in this chapter as responsible integration of AI will not only advance some of the foundational notions of education but also prepare students to meet the current needs of professional practice in an AI-augmented legal arena.

REFERENCES

Aammou, S., Zakaria, T., & Tarik, T. (2024). *Enhancing socio-pedagogical engagement in Moodle through AI-driven personalized learning*. Cadernos de Educação Tecnologia e Sociedade.

Carella, G., & Colombo, F. (2024). Teaching design and actively applying it through projectbased learning format: A practical case study of a collaboration between a university course and a company. *INTED Proceedings*, •••, 2391–2398. DOI: 10.21125/inted.2024.0664

Eltahir, M., & Babiker, F. M. E. (2024). The influence of artificial intelligence tools on student performance in e-learning environments: Case study. *Electronic Journal of e-Learning*, *22*(9), 91–110. DOI: 10.34190/ejel.22.9.3639

Esteban-Escaño, J., Esteban-Sánchez, A., & Sein-Echaluce, M. (2017). Engineering final project supervised in an adaptive way with Moodle support. *IEEE Revista Iberoamericana de Technologias del Aprendizaje*, *12*(1), 10–16. DOI: 10.1109/RITA.2017.2655178

Ezzaim, A., Dahbi, A., Haidine, A., & Aqqal, A. (2024). The impact of implementing a Moodle plug-in as an AI-based adaptive learning solution on learning effectiveness: Case of Morocco. *International Journal of Interactive Mobile Technologies*, *18*(1), 133–149. DOI: 10.3991/ijim.v18i01.46309

Fadieieva, L. O. (2021). *Enhancing adaptive learning with Moodle's machine learning*. Educational Dimension.

Fernsel, L., Kalff, Y., & Simbeck, K. (2024). Where is the evidence? A plugin for auditing Moodle's learning analytics. In *Proceedings of the 2024 Learning Analytics and Knowledge Conference* (pp. 262–269). DOI: 10.5220/0012689800003693

Habrusiev, V., Tereshchuk, H., Panchenko, V., Martyniuk, S., Sysoiev, O., & Henseruk, H. (2023). Enhancing online learning in LCM Moodle through interactive adaptive learning. *13th International Conference on Advanced Computer Information Technologies (ACIT)*, 650–655. DOI: 10.1109/ACIT58437.2023.10275436

Heap, T., Hudson, C., & Archibald, A. (2020). Investigating the impact of an AI-driven discussion platform on educator perceptions and feedback. *EDEN Conference Proceedings*. DOI: 10.38069/edenconf-2020-ac0010

Kaiss, W., Mansouri, K., & Poirier, F. (2023). Effectiveness of an adaptive learning chatbot on students' learning outcomes based on learning styles. [iJET]. *International Journal of Emerging Technologies in Learning*, *18*(13), 250–261. DOI: 10.3991/ijet.v18i13.39329

. Kaleci, D. (2025). Integration and application of artificial intelligence tools in the Moodle platform: A theoretical exploration. Journal of Educational Technology and Online Learning.

Karagiannis, I. E., & Satratzemi, M. (2018). An adaptive mechanism for Moodle based on automatic detection of learning styles. *Education and Information Technologies*, *23*(3), 1331–1357. DOI: 10.1007/s10639-017-9663-5

. Lan, X., Yu, H., & Li, J. (2017). Optimization of Moodle for adaptive testing. DEStech Transactions on Computer Science and Engineering.

Linawati, W., N., Sukadarmika, G., Suyadnya, I. M. A., & Krishne, D. C. (2016). Adaptive online learning design using Moodle. 2016 International Conference on Smart Green Technology in Electrical and Information Systems, 98–101.

Morze, N., Varchenko-Trotsenko, L., & Terletska, T. (2021). Stages of adaptive learning implementation by means of Moodle LMS. Myroslav I. Zhaldak Symposium on Advances in Educational Technology. DOI: 10.5220/0012065500003431

Saqr, R., Al-Somali, S., & Sarhan, M. Y. (2023). Exploring the acceptance and user satisfaction of AI-driven e-learning platforms (Blackboard, Moodle, Edmodo, Coursera and edX): An integrated technology model. *Sustainability (Basel)*, *16*(1), 204. DOI: 10.3390/su16010204

Souali, K., Rahmaoui, O., Ouzzif, M., & El Haddioui, I. (2019). Recommending Moodle resources using chatbots. *15th International Conference on Signal-Image Technology & Internet-Based Systems (SITIS).*

Ueda, H., Furukawa, M., Yamaji, K., & Nakamura, M. (2018). SCORMAdaptiveQuiz: Implementation of adaptive e-learning for Moodle. *Procedia Computer Science*, *126*, 2261–2270. DOI: 10.1016/j.procs.2018.07.223

Chapter 5

Breaking Barriers by Leveraging AI to Enhance Inclusivity and Access in Legal Education in India

Arpan Verma
https://orcid.org/0009-0001-2870-3432
Manipal University Jaipur, India

Vishwas Gupta
https://orcid.org/0009-0000-0785-5990
Manipal University Jaipur, India

ABSTRACT

Artificial Intelligence can transform legal education in India by tackling barriers to inclusivity and access, affiliating with the spirit of equitable education under Article 21 A of the Indian Constitution and the National Education Policy 2020. AI tools like adaptive learning platforms, simulated legal clinics, natural language translation, and assistive technologies can aid students with disabilities and address the digital divide pertinent especially in rural areas. These resolutions personalize education, enable applied training, and make education available across dialectal and geographic divides. For students with infirmities, AI offers accommodations like screen readers aligning with the Rights of Persons with Disabilities Act, 2016, though infrastructure and stigma pose challenges. With community engagement, AI can create an all-encompassing legal education system, empowering marginalized students and upholding equity and justice, if infrastructural and societal obstacles are addressed collectively

DOI: 10.4018/979-8-3373-3451-6.ch005

1. INTRODUCTION

AI has been a major force behind change in the modern world. AI's ability to look at huge datasets, automate difficult tasks, and give personalized answers has changed the way we deal with problems that have been around for a long time (Köchling & Wehner, 2022). Artificial intelligence (AI) has a lot of potential to help India, a country known for its diversity and rapid technological growth. Legal education is essential for achieving social justice, fairness, and growth (Sharma & Kumari, 2024). But there are big problems with making legal education in India accessible and open to everyone, especially for groups that are already at a disadvantage. There is still unequal access to legal education, even though there are more schools offering it, such as the highly respected National Law Universities (NLUs) (Sarker & Sharma, 2020). This inequitable access has bigger impact on students from low-income families, members of marginalized groups, women, people with disabilities, and language minorities. These groups are still underrepresented in the legal profession because they face institutional barriers that make it hard for them to get a good legal education. This divide in inclusion makes it harder for India's judicial system to represent the country's diverse population. There are many reasons for this divide in inclusion, such as differences in geography, institutions, sociocultural settings, and economics (Gale et al., 2021). Students from low-income families are more likely to be affected by financial problems, like high tuition costs and the cost of getting ready for entrance exams like the Common Law Admission Test. For example, a lot of people can't afford the yearly fees at the best NLUs, which can be more than 2 lakh. Because there are so many good law schools in cities, students in rural areas have an even harder time getting to resources and teachers. This makes the gap between urban and rural areas even bigger. Institutional barriers, such as the design of admission exams, have a bigger effect on students from poor areas than on students from urban coaching centres. Socio-cultural factors, such as gender bias, caste-based discrimination, and a lack of resources for students with disabilities, make things even harder (Bandyopadhyay, 2006). Students with disabilities often have trouble getting to school and using learning materials, and women in law school face problems like dangerous campus conditions and cultural pressures to put family before work. This chapter goes into more detail about how AI can help remove these barriers, making India's legal education system more open and available to everyone. This chapter looks at the inclusion divide, finds the factors that contribute to it, and suggests AI-based solutions. The goal is to show a way to make legal education more fair, accessible and affordable.

Adaptive learning systems, machine learning, and natural language processing (NLP) are all examples of artificial intelligence tools that have changed the way we create, share, and use information. AI has made innovation possible in education, like expanding resources on digital platforms, automating administrative tasks, and creating personalized learning experiences (Tahiru, 2020). AI-powered resources have made education fairer by getting rid of barriers based on location and income level. With the help of AI, students from even marginalized sections can get high-quality course materials. India has had problems with education for a long time, but artificial intelligence could help fix them. This is especially true now that the internet is growing so quickly thanks to programs like Digital India (Hebbar, 2020). AI can help make the legal profession more diverse and open by getting rid of barriers that have kept underrepresented groups from going to law school in the past. This is where artificial intelligence really shines as a powerful tool that can change the way legal education works by offering solutions that are inclusive, scalable, and affordable. But there are some problems that make it hard to use AI in law school classes. To make sure that everyone gets the same treatment, you need to deal with problems like the digital gap, data privacy, and algorithmic biases (Kay, 2012). For example, infrastructure needs to be built at the same time as AI is adopted.

The study looks at inclusivity issues by looking at how the identities of marginalized communities and the problems they face relate to the economic, geographical, institutional, and socio-cultural barriers to getting a legal education. Once the barriers are identified, the chapter will look at how AI might make things more accessible by focusing on certain technologies and their uses. Chapter ends with some ideas about what the future of inclusive legal education in India might look like and the challenges regarding deployment of AI driven techniques. AI isn't a magic bullet, but it's a powerful tool that can help people who have been pushed to the edges of society get past problems and take advantage of opportunities. India is on the verge of a technological revolution, and using artificial intelligence can help make legal education more fair, accessible and equitable.

2. THE INCONSISTENCY OF INCLUSIVITY IN THE INDIAN LEGAL EDUCATION

The legal education system across the various states of India varies a lot in access for receiving education. This often causes a hindrance in achieving the objective of affordable, fair and equitable legal education. To understand the barriers in the equitable access of Legal Education in India, it is important to analyse, the basis of inclusivity blockades. This section would first bring to light the three areas of distinction through which often exclusion in the legal education system comes into practice: The circles of public and private legal education, the adaptability of institutions for able and disabled students, and as created through the 2020 pandemic, the hassle faced by blooming online legal education systems. The Idea of an Inclusive legal education system has been discussed and debated often, herein aim is to classify these problems so as to get a grasp of the bigger picture at helm so as to cater to solutions to the identified problems in the later sections.

2.1 The Public-Private Divide

The desirability of legal education can easily be witnessed in the extensive growth of private law schools. Currently there is no conclusive and appropriate data that could accurately estimate the size of the privatization of the higher education in India (Tilak, 2018). In the early 1990 it was considered to be negligibly small however within a span of a decade not only have a large number of private law schools opened but there is an increasing frequency of these "English medium/ private institutions". The Eleventh Five Year Plan Planning Commission stated that "the legitimate role of private providers of quality education not only needs to be recognized, but also encouraged'" (Pandya, 2011). It is no secret that the Indian society objectively considers private law schools as an Elite medium of legal education that caters to students of urban societies and higher the fee structure the richer the experience of education. However, this conventional portrayal of private law schools has been debited to an extent that these institutions now exist in almost every area where population resides even though there might already exist a government funded, less fee charging law school. In most areas the number of private law schools exceeds the number of government law schools which sheds some light visions of equitable principles behind legal education (Srivastava, 2010).

Other than the statistics behind why there is an evidentiary increase in the demand for private law colleges, there is also a need to recognize the reasons behind it. It is evident that the government law schools have constraints in their enrolment having a limited number of seats available, in fact a lot of them require qualifying a highly competitive exam and students thus seek admissions in private law schools. The infrastructure in legal government educational institutions is often overutilized. Not only are these government financed law schools under resourced which has been documented time and again in several surveys they have also been found to be less accountable towards the students. It has been the lack of administrative effectiveness and apt development of new government law schools at a suitable rate which has contributed towards the growth of private law schools and not merely the rise of income amongst citizens (Kashyap, 2016). It is not just that people do not want to avail services provided by the government but the overall quality, apt availability and the outcome of the services which they feel are lacking and hence on several accounts we find instances of parents to see themselves trying to enrol in a private law School charging heft fee. It is not just urban elite who have embraced the private Legal Education. Low-fee private law schools have shot up in numbers as well, targeting the lower income and disadvantaged communities. It is a clear reflection that it is not enough to have a public legal education system in place but to ensure that all the dimensions that go behind providing access to affordable legal education system to secure legal acumen are in place and running in a smooth and effective manner. In addition to this analysis is inconclusive without talking about private coaching centres which claim to train aspirants for guaranteed admission in upper echelon of the legal education, i.e., National Law Universities. Although admission in the institutions forming the Consortium of NLUs is open to all the aspirants who qualify the eligibility criteria yet is a universal truth that the admission path to these institutions has been commercialized (Choudhury et al., 2021). These expensive coaching institutions provide highly analysed preparatory curriculum to the aspirants providing them a highly competitive edge over other aspirants (Kumar, 2017). Hence, in the last few years it has more or less become a necessity for parents to enrol their wards in to these high priced private coaching institutions to gain access in much coveted National Law Universities While regularization of fee charged by private law schools is a topic considered quintessential but it has time and again proved to be beyond the scope of normal regulation by government agencies. Regularization of fee is an issue which requires major changes and intervention at the parliamentary level. However, some comparative studies on the first instance do suggest that it is in fact redundant to regulate the finances of private law schools, and the variegated factors of a sector ensure better quality and innovation rather than government control (Gupta, 2008). It should also be brought to light that when it comes to learning standards neither government nor private institutions barring a few are able to enforce standards strictly. The private law schools that perform better are strictly considering the competency they can afford because of the price range they charge (Angom, 2015). It is very hard to challenge that in most of the private legal institutions, learning outcomes are not result of aspiration to maintain quality standards but a mere tool to enhance demand and supply operation to give themselves profit. Even the implementation of timely guidelines provided by Bar Council of India and University Grants Commission that planned on enforcing norms and standards for all law schools there has been no legislative design to regulate private schools, as even after the compliance norms were laid down it has not resulted in the collapse of financial blockades for aspiring students belonging to the underprivileged and marginalized sections of society (Schukoske, 2009).

2.2 The Abled and Disabled Segregation:

There is no singular definition to what would qualify as disability. On a global level however for the sake of legalization of rights of people with disabilities two models of disability have been recognized: Medical and Social Model (Oliver, 1996).

However, the emphasis on these definitions is important as it helps in diagnosing the causes and effects and determining the best application and aids to help overcome any blocks caused hence (Erevelles, 2005). In brief, medical model is the doctor's way of thinking. It assumes that societal tiers of existence do not matter, and disability is a mere bodily difference. Hence it also implies that one's experience of the disability would be similar to the other. The problem is that it ignores the fact that around the world people with disabilities in all societies to greater or lesser extent suffer systematic exclusion, discrimination and oppression of many sorts (Barnes & Mercer, 1999). The social model argued that the former disguises the disadvantages that come with the disabilities a person faces. The centre of argument is the distinction they draw between impairment and disability. Impairment is the dysfunction/ difference in anatomy. While disability is loss or limitation of opportunities, that prevent people who have impairments from taking part in normal life of community due to physical or social barriers (Babic & Dowling, 2015). Inclusion is how we deal with the diversity and difference, social justice and equity for the people who suffer from such disabilities. The understanding of what is considered as disability has undergone a huge change of series over the years and has come from medical, social model to a structuralism model where culture and social situation also play an important role in formulation of the same (Barton et al., 2002).

So, while documents of Ministry of Human Resource Development show that students with disabilities (SWD) are more likely to be excluded from education there are still pressing challenges for SWD's in terms of access, participation and getting the most efficient result of the education system in equal terms of other children not facing such impairments. They are usually the potential students who belong to the vulnerable/ disadvantaged sections of the society (Trani & Loeb, 2010).

In the turn of centuries, disability has been socially and culturally seen as an abnormality or a derogatory behaviour (Neufeldt & Mathieson, 1995). Hence on one hand it is important to protect the potential students with disability and give them space to grow and learn the intricate legal skills. But on the other hand, it limits their opportunities, and distances them from opportunities available to typically develop differently abled students to potentially induct them in the legal industry. This leads to their institutions being seen as deviant and in need of charity or pity. The special reservation given in pubic law schools have certain disadvantages which becomes evident with its increasing horizon (Kunnath & Mathew, 2019). The quota in public educational institutions reaches a very limited population largely urban, and who are aware of the effective but limited opportunities. More importantly this has in turn further created segregation among students in what is considered normal and created a disability culture. It becomes a norm to assume that if they were to study in inclusion with other students, without special reservation they would not be able to cope with expectations, it would be difficult for them to qualify entrance examinations and would ultimately disrupt their growth. However, SWD have the right to receive legal education that contributes to their full development of potential. Reservation warrants SWD with better opportunity but is a subtle attack on their sense of dignity and self-worth. The idea of inclusive or integrated law school system where in SWD are treated as peers supports to the same. The International Convention on the Rights of Persons with Disabilities, to which India ratified in 2007 also proposed the framework for the development of inclusive education system (Koch, 2009). It implored the States to understand that even those students who are attending and being able to access legal education via special quota in admission in public law schools are privileged and a minority amongst the minority. It also argued often that separate legal educational institutions could be setup for students with disability. However, This differentiated law school system would be expensive, requires extra investment, and bears brunt of lack of teachers and infrastructures available and its sole purpose seems to be to isolate these students from their abled peers (Chopra, 2013). The idea of an Inclusive framework is easy, it acknowledges that the problem is not within SWD, but rather the law and the system in how they accommodate them. The legal framework supporting the SWD's seems so vast to navigate on the periphery, but even an inch beneath the surface, and problems of inconsistency and parallel problems running as a common theme amongst them. Other than the constitutional design, which to be fair is an ideal to be achieved rather than a mandate to be followed, the current regimen does not do a lot to help the students with disability.

National Education Policy and Integrated Education for the Disabled Children

In 1974 an education policy named IEDC (Integrated Education for Disabled Children) was implemented by the government of India, to deal with problems of quality, access, utility, quantity, financial structure in educational opportunities for CWD. Under this scheme it was proposed that the entirety of financial aid would be provided to the CWD including any assistance towards education supplies like books, uniforms, transportation, tuition fee, etc. to lower the charges for students, even those in boarding schools (Singal, 2006). The World Bank Report of 2008 showed that in India children with disabilities have an illiteracy rate of 52% as opposed to the 35% of the normal population (O'Keefe, 2007). Apart from the discrepancies in the statistics of the general disabled population, there are huge inconsistencies the numbers of SWD recognized in the census and the school records through.policy programs like SSA. According to the latter there are around 1-5% child population with disabilities while the 2011 census of the same year showed a 22% population percent. These figures get even more splotched across states and different demographics. As of 2014, 10% of India's population shows some form of disability, out of which around 35.29% constitute children (around 12 million children) of these only 1% has access to a school education (India. Dept of Elementary Education and Literacy, 2006). With the Rights Of Persons With Disabilities Act, 2016 through which the scope of disabilities covered under it has expanded to twenty-one as opposed to seven previously and recognition of new disabilities, the numbers have increased considerably.

Children's Education Allowance

In 1998, the Ministry of Personnel, Public Grievances & Pensions (Department of Personnel & Training) notified through a memo, a grant for children's allowance, especially for the disabled children. In 2017, by the 7_{th} Pay Commission these numbers were considerably increased to Rs. 2250 per month. However, only parent can avail this allowance, and even at this pay, considering the varying needs of each disabled child, this is very insignificant number and barely covers the basic requirements of SWD in today's economy.

The Rights of Persons with Disabilities Act, 2016

The Rights of Persons with Disabilities Act, 2016 which replaced the 1995 act, came into being in 2017. This act covers a lot more than education as an aspect for disabled people, it also covers rights to employment and workplace ethics for infrastructure builds and such. It also penalized discriminatory activities against the disabled. Section 4(2) states the following "The appropriate Government and local authorities shall ensure that all children with disabilities shall have right on an equal basis to freely express their views on all matters affecting them and provide them appropriate support keeping in view their age and disability." Read with Section 16 of the Act, which lays down the duties of all educational institutions to provide inclusive education to SWD and make it accessible and inclusive and meritorious as a general education scheme. There have been other policies like the "Integrated Education for Disabled Children" and the "Inclusion in Education of Children and Youth with Disabilities" under which provisions for financial aid to help integrate CWD in the conventional model and saw an increase in the number of special quota. The education policies have to acknowledge the role played by the other policies recognize that other policies such as the "National Policy on Early Childhood Care and Education (ECCE)" brought forth in 2013, the "National Youth Policy (NYP)" of 2014 and the "national policy of Skill Development and Entrepreneurship 2015" in addition to various other policies at the State Level. And the 2020 policy, it offers three modes- segregated education of choice, inclusive education of choice and even distance education for those with severe disabilities. But the entire policy in silent on any methods of check or audits to the any of the three systems (Tripathy et al., 2025).

Also, the NEP 2020 only recognizes very limited form of disabilities and ignores cognitive disabilities like speech impairments or autism. The policy states that the changes would be made in consonance to the Department of Empowerment of Persons with Disabilities which is a good sign as it would identify the problems with the system and not as problem with children to adjust or fit into. It also introduces a system called Parakh to test and evaluate the children however it's not in place yet and as of now it's just an idea not a system (N. D. Kumar & Singh, 2022).

An inclusive system of education in the early years of a higher legal education would aid in a student's development. It would also make it easier to integrate inclusive policies, working atmospheres, social circles and public places (Williams, 2018). It would help in merging resources and diversifying ideas on the teaching and training of all students. It is a mode of bringing all under the ambit of equitable education as was intended when Bar Council of India was given the responsibility of bracing legal education in India. It would indulge the cooperation of teachers, educators and parents and community leaders for contribution towards better functioning of inclusive education. A better culmination of understanding that disability is not a deficit and can be addressed by merely engaging students with proper curriculum, accessible law schools, regulated and standardized communication modes for all not just the impaired, and modified methods of assessing a law student.

2.3 Hinderance in dispensation of Online Legal Education

In India the union government decided to impose a nationwide lockdown for 21 days from 25th of March 2020 which was extended in accordance to the condition of the spread of virus in various States. Educational institutions had also in accordance with it shifted to the online mode of teaching. The study of this is extremely relevant in light of the fact that online education had never been tried on this large scale in India making it nothing short of a massive social experiment. This brings attention to the problems of digital divide. Even though online education can be a solution to a multitude of problems, but it is plagued with lack of equity in access devices for internet streaming as well as an interrupted internet among the students of marginalized sections (Tewathia et al., 2020). Lack of effectiveness of this model during the pandemic, curating of content online, etc. had proven to be a hinderance for many students. Among secondary problems there had also been issues of data speeds, lack of proper infrastructure which also provided an insight as to how prepared our country was to move towards education on an online platform considering that the basic requisites were not available to a lot of students.

Unfortunately, the traditional way is not a feasible possibility in near future to bridge barriers but there needs to be faster and more effective solutions as several years later the problem has not ceased and there is still a dearth of availability of latest technology to the marginalized students (Kaur & Choudhury, 2025). Prima facie, these still sound like the problems of the privilege in comparison to other issues surfacing such as those faced by weaker sections of the society, such as child-care problems, economic burden on the families, compromised nutrition, lack of a learning environment etc. Law School is more than just a Centre for learning for underprivileged students. Law institutions provide them with a hope of eradicating their family out of poverty and sorrow, aid their locality and even village by championing for their legal rights and providing social protection to the disadvantaged section of society. In the age of AI induced online measures are going to be the way foreward. However, inducting the marginalized sections of society to the basic digital necessities is still an uphill task which makes huge difference.

Catena of judgments by the Supreme Court have held that the constitution has to be interpreted in a harmonious construction with the development of the society. In this light, education and the term free in right to education are also flexible terms and hence must be applied in a synchronous manner to the changing world (Varghese & Panigrahi, 2022). Education has various dimensions which keep evolving, just because online mode of studying does not fall under the envisaged traditional learning when the right was drafted it does not mean that it should government should not be pushed to support the marginalized sections in integrating with the basic digital needs so as to help them bridge gaps and attain education in this fast growing digital era of education fuelled by Artificial Intelligence. It is understandable that to implement it an infrastructure to lessen this digital divide order to provide appropriate equipment on such a large scale is not something that could be immediately enforced, but after half a decade of dealing with this problem of digital divide several children have lost their opportunity for learning and it is high time that the state it starts planning on a vision to incorporate this rapidly. Considering the fact that the national education policy of 2020 was passed midst this chaos but makes a passing mention of recognizing this problem much less providing hope for its solution it seems like a long road ahead (Yenugu, 2022).

India needs to strengthen its skeletal framework behind the digital education, and instead of regularly restricting its scope to singular problems we need to diversify the security of framework to cover problems of access, equity, language and the lived experiences faced by the underprivileged students so that they can all be included in the evolved digital education system guided by trained and permanent educators whose agency they recognize (Budhia & Behera, 2023). There is an imminent need improved infrastructure and most importantly increase community participation so that students from vulnerable homes at partially the oppressed communities are not left behind. This empowers the legal education system to face problems such as financial blockades, disability segregation within their own circuit instead of waiting for government induced actions to pull them out from this prolonged disruption to the legal education. The pandemic and online learning had been a wakeup call about how education is not just limited to traditional setup but can also be imparted in a more impactful way using technology. However, the most important step to utilize the wonderful opportunities provided by integration of Artificial Intelligence in legal education is to enable underprivileged to access it

3. BARRIERS FUELLING THE DEARTH OF INCLUSIVITY IN LEGAL EDUCATION

Previous section established the three matrices of inclusivity divide. These matrices are: Public Private, Subtle Segregation of students with disabilities and the dearth of equipment to access quality Online education. Access to education is one of the biggest obstacles to increasing enrolments of underprivileged students and sustaining them throughout their academic journey. This section would focus recognizing the bars to education – socio-economic problems, cultural reservations, gender gaps etc. that serve as a factor in enhancing the problem of exclusivity and give rise to the problems identified while analyzing the Inclusivity divide in legal education. Most education initiatives across the world recognize reservation and scholarships as polices to overcome the financial and social bars that cause issues for students to receive education. Along with these two policies in the Indian system, this breakdown recognizes that in a socially diverse population in India there are a lot more issues that aid towards the problem of child's access to legal education and why these do not suffice in resolving them.

After nearing two decades of education as a right, India still grapples with the problem of assessing why certain groups of students cannot access a law school and who are the stakeholders and what are the barriers to overcome to provide equal and equitable access to legal education (Hans et al., 2025). This requires understanding of both exclusion and the excluded. It is certainly not enough that students are enrolled in a law school but also that their participation is meaningful and they could have a complete experience of a proper legal education that helps in their overall cognitive development. While it is no matter of debate, education goes beyond the learning of a particular syllabus but also helps a person acquire skill sets, values and attitudes that are necessary for them to develop as responsible citizens of the state to live up to their full potential. It has however been a challenge for the Indian legal education system to ensure that follow up takes place post the enrolment or admission stages in institutes for these developments to actively take place. There are various factors that go behind the exclusion of underprivileged children from having access to education despite all these laws, guidelines and policy of legal education being set in place.

3.1 Low Income groups, Child of Migrant Labours and Discrimination

In the previous analysis where in the classification of inclusivity divide was set up, all three matrices are deeply dependent of this factor. The relationship between poverty and lack of any sort of education seems obvious on the front but once again it has a lot of dimensions that require covering (Biddle, 2014). It is not just the lack of money that cause a hindrance in accessing legal education. The other obstacles that come along with being poverty-stricken also cause barriers that de-prioritize education on the list for parents and children to the extent that it becomes a vicious cycle where it is seen as a non-requirement it or even a risk against which families might have to suffer financial burdens. In cases of families that migrate from one place to another in search of jobs are frequently denied basic access to rights such as education and women and children who tend to suffer more at the hands of exploitation as they must accept jobs to create some source of income. Since the rights do not extend to protecting migrants and of course children in the nation, without any community support, they do not have any negotiating power and are at a greater risk to work in conditions with poor wages, lack of basic facilities, hazardous situations and informal sectors where they might even be subjected to abuse. Even for potential students who do not work this seasonal migration face a lack of continuation in their education. Migration as an incidence is higher in sectors of construction and agriculture which tends to go on for a period of certain months to year (Roy et al., 2015). There are certain NGOs that try to tackle this problem on both ends of migration by providing schools at the sites of work, or by providing facilities of housing for hostels to children so that they could stay while their parents migrate in search of work. However, there efforts can only be limited to primary education as these are very small-scale efforts and cannot replace the formal legal education setup on the large-scale migration that takes place every year in different levels across the nation.

But it is not often that a relationship between poverty and education can be established in such easy manner. For instance, in states like Punjab and Haryana while families are economically better off, these states tend to have a lower rate of education progress in comparison to say life in Uttar Pradesh (Bhatty, 1998). It is not just that poverty compels students to work and drop out of education, it is about the extent of poverty and the interconnection it has to the fate of the law aspirants in the education system and possibility to improve their lifestyles beyond poverty that also played a big variable in ensuring that these children reach law school. This inter-relationship is a complex tissue it must be right along with extraneous factors Effective implementation of child labour laws better salary for minimum wage workers the merits of the quality education and the effect it has on idle pulling the family out of poverty opportunity for the railroads vicious cycle (Ray, 2000). When someone grapples with ensuring their socioeconomic rights, when a family lives on pay check to pay check for survival it is very difficult to convince them otherwise that civil political right such as education would be critical in changing their lives from surviving to actually living.

3.2 First Generation learners as Law Students

Many students find themselves excluded from the legal education system as they are first generation learners in the family. They are the first people who can read and write amongst all the family members so the lack of support or help that they can find within their homes is very limited and this stalling off process creates a hindrance in finding that confidence to keep engaging with the law school setups. This is a problem that can be solved by community support and collective efforts of the families and the stakeholders, as there isn't much the government or its agencies can do to inspire such confidence in students. "The Shankarpalle Experience" An experiment done in Andhra Pradesh in 1994 by the Mandal education officers which help the children who have dropped out to be instituted in the crates and during the summer programs helped them in evading the diffidence loop that they were stuck in (Menon, 2012). There were different methods that the community came together to implement and found a significant increase in the number of educated people in the area in just 5 years by a percentage of 12.6. This model can be replicated by both the public institutions and private players to encourage the first-time learners to support their journey on the road less travelled by their kins.

3.3 Caste and Gender, the Oppressed and the Discriminated

Research shows that even in protected environment, students belonging to lower caste face discriminatory attitudes from their peers and sometimes college staff and hence induces a feeling of them belonging to the inequitable end. So, on one hand while there is an boost in the universalization of legal education it is also facing segregation in the classroom based on class and gender. It is not just the impoverished households that see such harsh treatment but even the 'urbanized' and 'elite' surprisingly show such mentality towards students coming from lower levels of caste tiers (Ramachandran, 2004). It has been noticed as one of the harsh realities of the reservation in public law schools. Unfortunately, even in this day and age there have been rare circumstances of students being treated as untouchables. Moreover, students from tribal families face cultural as well as physical isolation from their peers or worthy of mixing with their own children (Dar & Najar, 2018). So, it is not just a matter of making it to the law classes but also a matter of staying in the classroom. The factors of gender, religion, caste and ethnicity especially in conjunction to poverty create variations that lead students foregoing access even after suitable opportunities to enter law schools and being unable to take the benefits of the legal educational system. This of course is not just the isolated problem of policies and guidelines related to legal education but also of other laws that worked in consonance to the protection of these weaker sections of the society. Moreover, state agencies van regulates and develop legal education system only. They cannot regulate social attitudes or community prejudices or force teachers and stakeholders to empathize with marginalized students, this is the work for the community to face the realities of the social constraints that are forced upon these young legal minds. Maybe that is why the Indian law emphasizes on education and not just literacy.

The gender discrimination and bias against women is not a new issue but still pertinent especially in the realm of legal education and practice. There are some certain universally accepted barriers to women gaining education which fall under the categories of their bodily autonomy, cultural and traditional barriers of the family and society, pre-determined gender roles and manure sometimes the location of law schools which require women to travel long distance. Prima facie all these problems find their origin in social construct which cannot be legislated upon. This stance to an extent is true, however there are certain preventable measures which the state could implement in public law schools such as proper infrastructure with washroom facilities, transportation, gender neutral approach towards syllabus as well as gender sensitive legal education. This can specifically help in addressing the problems a female law student face (Wankhede, 2008). It is not possible to account for the in-surmountable issue that a female student faces in accessing legal education. Even if there are parents who support elementary or even higher education it is a rare occasion when legal education is not subjected to certain scrutiny for a girl child as opposed to the ease with which a male student is permitted to those resources. Experiments and studies done in smaller areas at lower scales have shown that it is possible to reduce the disparity in genders in education systems by simple measures like relocation of law schools or improvement in infrastructure. States like Tamil Nadu and Andhra Pradesh have shown considerable progress by implementing these measures (Sinha, 2013).

3.4 The Indiscernible Category

While the correlation based on gender, caste, and poverty have numerous studies by private as well as government organisations there are a few categories of students that remain undocumented. There exists a dearth of conclusive studies rendering difficult to determine the number of students belonging to the invisible category getting access to law school. Moreover, it is difficult to implicate what are the challenges these students face because of exclusion. The students belonging to Indiscernible category might be the children of migrants who are not documented citizens or discriminated against in a manner not vocally addressed. They include children who might suffer mental or physical disabilities and hence considered beyond the scope of being capable of receiving education or children who are either orphans or homeless. Children of sex workers or those who suffer from perceived contagious diseases like leprosy or AIDS might also belong to this category. These children have been outcasted so blatantly that it is even difficult for policymakers or practitioners to reach out to them and collect empirical evidence enough to legislate or regulate to destroy barriers created by the community. According to the 2011 census even if 0.5% of the students were to fall into this category it would mean that around 7 million children are not having an iota of access to any sort of education and the state agencies don't even know about it (Saikia et al., 2016).

It is safe to assume by the analysis of factors affecting inclusivity that once the problem behind exclusion is addressed, it is only then that recommendations of accessibility can be implemented in an equitable manner using the help of Artificial Intelligence. There are numerous schemes of reservation and scholarship that run on both state and central levels to help overcome certain problems regarding gender caste poverty etc., but as reflected while discerning the difficulties in accessing legal education that most of the problems can be solved by the propagation of effective online legal education. Hence, the succeeding sections would find innovative solutions with induction of Artificial Intelligence in legal education to eradicate the barriers of inclusivity.

4. THE ROLE OF AI IN COMBATING BARRIERS TO ACCESS AND INCLUSIVITY

Systemic barriers have limited access to legal education for underprivileged students. These barriers as analysed previously include, institutional adaptability for disabled students, socio-economic limitations distressing financially weaker sections of society and children of migrant labourers, problems faced by first-generation learners, caste and gender-based discrimination, and the exclusion of invisible category. Artificial Intelligence has amazing potential to demolish these blockades through technologies like adaptive learning systems, natural language processing (NLP), predictive analytics, and AI-driven chatbots (Labadze et al., 2023). Utilization of these tools can transform legal education by making it more accessible and inclusive, tackling systemic inequalities and nurturing a legal education system (Chan & Hu, 2023). This section inspects how AI can challenge all the acknowledged barriers while keeping in account operation hurdles such as the privacy concerns, data breach and algorithmic biases.

4.1 Addressing Institutional Adaptability for Disabled Students

The adaptability of legal education institutions to cater to both able and disabled students is a significant barrier to inclusivity. Many institutions lack physical infrastructure, such as ramps or braille resources, and digital platforms often fail to accommodate diverse needs. The 2020 pandemic highlighted these shortcomings, as the rapid shift to online learning exposed gaps in accessibility for students with disabilities. AI-driven technologies offer innovative solutions to create inclusive learning environments tailored to individual requirements.

For students with disabilities, AI-powered tools can transform accessibility. Text-to-speech systems, such as those integrated into Microsoft's Immersive Reader, convert legal texts into audio, benefiting visually impaired students. Sign language avatars, powered by AI, can translate lectures into sign language in real-time, supporting hearing-impaired learners (Madaan & Gupta, 2021). Customizable interfaces allow students with cognitive disabilities to adjust font sizes, colors, or layouts, ensuring compliance with India's Rights of Persons with Disabilities Act, 2016. For instance, the University of Delhi could adopt AI-driven platforms to make case law databases accessible, incorporating features like audio summaries or simplified legal terminology for students with learning disabilities.

For able students, particularly those from under-resourced schools, AI-driven adaptive learning systems can bridge academic gaps. Platforms like Smart Sparrow analyze student performance in real-time, adjusting content difficulty or recommending supplementary resources (Gökçearslan et al., 2024). For example, a student struggling with constitutional law could receive tailored exercises on fundamental rights, ensuring they keep pace with peers. These systems can also gamify learning, using AI to create interactive quizzes or case study simulations, enhancing engagement. In India, where 65% of law students come from urban areas with better schooling such tools can level the playing field for rural or disadvantaged students.

However, implementing AI for adaptability faces challenges. The digital divide, with 43% of rural Indian households lacking reliable internet, limits access to online AI tools (Mali, 2019). Additionally, high development costs and the need for accessible hardware pose barriers (Michel-Villarreal et al., 2023). Solutions include offline AI modules, which cache content for use without internet, and public-private partnerships to provide subsidized devices. For instance, the Indian government's Digital India initiative could fund AI-driven accessibility labs in law schools, ensuring equitable access. Data privacy is another concern, as AI systems handling student data must comply with India's Personal Data Protection Act, 2023. Institutions must adopt secure platforms and transparent data policies to build trust.

4.2 Supporting Low-Income Groups and Children of Migrant Laborers

Low-income groups and children of migrant labourers face economic barriers, including high tuition fees (often exceeding 2 lakh annually at National Law Universities) and the inability to afford coaching for entrance exams like CLAT. These students also encounter discrimination and social exclusion, further limiting access. AI-driven technologies can democratize legal education by providing affordable, accessible resources and addressing systemic biases.

AI-powered platforms can offer free or low-cost preparatory courses for CLAT and other entrance exams. For example, platforms like BYJU'S use AI to deliver personalized study plans, analysing student performance to focus on weak areas. A dedicated AI-driven CLAT preparation platform could provide practice tests, video tutorials, and mock exams at minimal cost, reducing dependence on urban coaching centres, which charge upwards of 50,000 annually. A 2023 study found that 70% of aspirants from low-income backgrounds lack access to coaching, highlighting the need for such tools (Ørberg, 2017).

For children of migrant labourers, whose education is disrupted by frequent relocations, AI-powered mobile learning apps offer flexibility. These apps can cache legal education content, such as lectures on tort law or legal reasoning, for offline use (Eager & Brunton, 2023). For instance, Kenya's Eneza Education uses mobile-based AI to deliver education to marginalized communities, a model India could adapt. An AI app tailored for legal education could include bite-sized lessons and quizzes, allowing students to study on low-cost smartphones (Yadav et al., 2024). NGOs like Pratham could distribute tablets preloaded with such apps, addressing device access barriers.

AI can also mitigate discrimination by anonymizing applications and assessments. AI algorithms can evaluate CLAT responses without identifying caste, income, or regional background, reducing biases. However, challenges include ensuring affordability of AI tools and addressing the digital divide (Goel et al., 2024). Government initiatives, such as the Samagra Shiksha scheme, could subsidize device distribution, while open-source AI platforms can lower costs. Ethical concerns, like ensuring AI does not reinforce socio-economic biases, require diverse development teams and regular bias audits.

4.3 Empowering First-Generation Learners

First-generation learners, often from low-income or rural backgrounds, face challenges like limited academic preparation, lack of mentorship, and cultural alienation in legal education institutions (Khan, 2017). AI can empower these students by providing personalized academic support and fostering a sense of belonging.

AI-driven tutoring systems, such as Google's Socratic, offer step-by-step explanations for complex legal concepts, such as jurisprudence or constitutional law. A tailored platform for Indian law students could provide interactive modules on legal reasoning or case analysis, helping first-generation learners build foundational knowledge. For example, an AI system could break down the Indian Penal Code into simplified modules, with quizzes to reinforce learning

Virtual mentorship programs powered by AI can connect first-generation learners with legal professionals or senior students (Tlili et al., 2022). AI algorithms can match mentors and mentees based on shared interests, backgrounds, or career goals, fostering guidance and community. For instance, a first-generation learner from a rural area could be paired with a mentor who understands their challenges, providing advice on navigating law school or securing internships. NLSIU could pilot such a program, scaling it across other institutions. AI chatbots can also offer career counseling, addressing questions about scholarships, internships, or legal careers, which are critical for students without family networks in the profession.

Challenges include ensuring cultural sensitivity in AI content and addressing digital literacy gaps. AI systems must incorporate regional and cultural contexts to resonate with first-generation learners. For example, content could include case studies from rural India to make legal education relatable. Community-based digital literacy centers, supported by initiatives like Digital India, can train students to use AI tools. Data privacy is another concern, requiring secure platforms compliant with India's data protection laws (Sebastian, 2023). Regular feedback from first-generation learners can ensure AI tools meet their needs effectively.

4.4 Tackling Caste and Gender Discrimination

Caste and gender-based discrimination remain pervasive in legal education, with Scheduled Castes (SC), Scheduled Tribes (ST), Other Backward Classes (OBC), and women facing systemic exclusion. AI can promote inclusivity by creating bias-free environments and supporting marginalized groups.

AI-driven anonymization can reduce discrimination in admissions and assessments. By removing identifiers like caste or gender from CLAT applications or assignment submissions, AI algorithms ensure fair evaluation.

For women, AI-powered VR simulations can provide safe spaces to practice legal advocacy, addressing safety concerns in physical moot courts (Tlili et al., 2022). For example, a VR platform could simulate a courtroom, allowing women to hone advocacy skills without fear of harassment. AI chatbots can offer mental health support, addressing societal pressures faced by women and marginalized caste groups. Globally, tools like Woebot have supported students' mental health, and Indian institutions could develop culturally adapted versions to address caste and gender-specific stressors.

Challenges include ensuring AI does not perpetuate biases. If trained on biased datasets, AI could reinforce discrimination, necessitating diverse development teams and bias audits. Infrastructure costs and digital access gaps also require solutions like government-funded AI labs and offline tools. Engaging community leaders from marginalized groups can ensure AI solutions are inclusive and effective.

4.5 The Indiscernible Category

Undocumented students, such as children of migrants, face significant hurdles in enrolling in legal education due to missing identification or academic records. AI-driven technologies can streamline enrolment processes and provide alternative pathways for access. Predictive analytics can identify potential students from marginalized communities by analysing indirect data sources, such as NGO records or community surveys, to locate undocumented individuals with academic potential (Doleck et al., 2019). AI-powered chatbots can guide undocumented students through enrolment processes, offering multilingual support to navigate complex bureaucratic requirements.

Challenges include the lack of centralized data on undocumented populations and privacy concerns. AI systems must comply with India's Personal Data Protection Act, 2023, using anonymized data to protect identities. Partnerships with local governments and NGOs can help collect ethical data, while offline AI modules can ensure access in areas with limited connectivity, addressing the 43% rural internet access gap.

Orphans, homeless children, children of sex workers, and those with stigmatized conditions face social exclusion that deters them from pursuing legal education. AI can mitigate stigma by creating anonymous and inclusive learning environments. AI-driven platforms can anonymize student identities during admissions and assessments, reducing bias. For example, AI algorithms can evaluate CLAT responses without revealing personal details, ensuring fair treatment for stigmatized groups.

AI chatbots can provide mental health support and career counselling, addressing the emotional and societal pressures these students face (A. Sharma et al., 2023). For instance, a chatbot modelled on Woebot could offer culturally sensitive support for children of sex workers, helping them navigate stigma and build resilience. VR platforms can also create safe spaces for experiential learning, allowing students to practice legal skills without fear of judgment.

Challenges include ensuring cultural sensitivity in AI content and addressing digital access gaps. Collaborating with community leaders and NGOs can ensure content reflects lived experiences, while mobile-based AI apps can deliver education to homeless or transient students. For example, an app caching legal education content offline could reach orphans in shelter homes, supported by organizations like SOS Children's Villages.

5. CONCLUSION

Adding Artificial Intelligence (AI) to India's legal education system is a game-changing chance to make it more open and accessible, which is in line with India's constitutional values. AI-powered tools like adaptive learning platforms, virtual legal clinics, and language translation technologies can help break down systemic barriers by making quality legal resources more accessible to everyone, encouraging hands-on learning, and making sure that India's diverse population can communicate in their own language, in line with the National Education Policy (NEP) 2020's focus on teaching in the mother tongue. AI-powered assistive technologies like screen readers and speech-to-text software help students with disabilities learn in a more inclusive way by getting around physical and mental barriers. This supports the Rights of Persons with Disabilities Act, 2016. However, to be used effectively, teachers need to be trained and made aware of the challenges that come with them, such as lack of infrastructure and social stigma. AI-powered low-bandwidth solutions like offline learning modules and SMS-based chatbots can help close the digital divide, which is a big problem for online legal education. This will make sure that rural and low-income students can get to it. However, ethical issues like data privacy under the Personal Data Protection Bill, 2019, possible algorithmic bias, and high implementation costs require strong protections, regular audits, and state subsidies to stop making inequalities worse. Policy suggestions include adding AI to the NEP 2020 framework, encouraging public-private partnerships to make tools that are cheap, teaching teachers more about AI, funding infrastructure, and making sure that AI is used responsibly by creating ethical rules. India can create an inclusive legal education system that helps students from a wide range of socio-economic, linguistic, and ability backgrounds by using AI to make things more personal, accessible, and scalable, and by getting people involved in the community through successful small-scale experiments like the Shankarpalle Experience. This method not only improves legal education, but it also shows that India is still committed to a fair and just society, as its constitution says it should be. But for AI to work, educators, policymakers, and communities must work together to solve the problems that come up when it is put into action. This will make sure that no student is left behind when it comes to getting a good legal education. AI can help make legal education more transformative by creating a system that values fairness and inclusion. This will allow all students to make a real difference in a fair society.

REFERENCES

Angom, S. (2015). Private higher education in India. *Higher Education for the Future, 2*(1), 92–111. DOI: 10.1177/2347631114558192

Babic, M. M., & Dowling, M. (2015). Social support, the presence of barriers and ideas for the future from students with disabilities in the higher education system in Croatia. *Disability & Society, 30*(4), 614–629. DOI: 10.1080/09687599.2015.1037949

Bandyopadhyay, M. (2006). Education of marginalised groups in India: From the perspective of social justice. *Social Change, 36*(2), 98–113. DOI: 10.1177/004908570603600207

Barnes, C., & Mercer, G. (1999). *Exploring Disability: A Sociological Introduction*. https://ci.nii.ac.jp/ncid/BA41776188

Barton, L., Barnes, C., & Oliver, M. (2002). Disability studies today. In *Polity Press eBooks*. http://ci.nii.ac.jp/ncid/BA58891420

Bhatty, K. (1998). Educational deprivation in India-A Survey of Field Investigations. *Economic and Political Weekly/Economic & Political Weekly, 33*(27). https://www.jstor.org/stable/4406962

Biddle, B. (2014). Social class, poverty and education. In *Routledge eBooks*. DOI: 10.4324/9780203951040

Budhia, N., & Behera, S. (2023). Challenges and oppourtunities of digital education in India. *Asian Journal of Education and Social Studies, 45*(3), 1–7. DOI: 10.9734/ajess/2023/v45i3982

Chan, C. K. Y., & Hu, W. (2023). Students' voices on generative AI: Perceptions, benefits, and challenges in higher education. *International Journal of Educational Technology in Higher Education, 20*(1), 43. Advance online publication. DOI: 10.1186/s41239-023-00411-8

Chopra, T. (2013). Expanding the Horizons of Disability Law in India: A Study from a Human Rights Perspective. *The Journal of Law, Medicine & Ethics, 41*(4), 807–820. DOI: 10.1111/jlme.12091 PMID: 24446939

Choudhury, P. K., Kumar, A., & Gill, A. S. (2021). Who all access private coaching in higher education and how much do they spend? Evidence from India. *Journal of the Asia Pacific Economy, 28*(4), 1433–1455. DOI: 10.1080/13547860.2021.1954302

Dar, W. A., & Najar, I. A. (2018). Educational anthropology, tribal education and responsible citizenship in India. *South Asia Research, 38*(3), 327–346. DOI: 10.1177/0262728018800759

Doleck, T., Lemay, D. J., Basnet, R. B., & Bazelais, P. (2019). Predictive analytics in education: A comparison of deep learning frameworks. *Education and Information Technologies, 25*(3), 1951–1963. DOI: 10.1007/s10639-019-10068-4

Eager, B., & Brunton, R. (2023). Prompting higher education towards AI-Augmented Teaching and Learning practice. *Journal of University Teaching & Learning Practice, 20*(5). Advance online publication. DOI: 10.53761/1.20.5.02

Erevelles, N. (2005). (Dis)Embodied form: Issues of disabled women. *Disability Studies Quarterly, 25*(2). Advance online publication. DOI: 10.18061/dsq.v25i2.567

Gale, L., Bhushan, P., Eidnani, S., Graham, L., Harrison, M., McKay-Brown, L., Pande, R., Shreeraman, S., & Sivashunmugamb, C. (2021). Overcoming barriers to inclusion in education in India. SSRN *Electronic Journal*. DOI: 10.2139/ssrn.3786018

Goel, R., Ashok, N., & Rani, S. (2024). AI IN RURAL INDIA: NAVIGATING CHALLENGES, EMBRACING OPPORTUNITIES. *International Journal of Engineering Science & Humanities., 14*(Special Issue 1), 195–205. DOI: 10.62904/rkr2dk52

Gökçearslan, Ş., Tosun, C., & Erdemir, Z. G. (2024). Benefits, Challenges, and Methods of Artificial intelligence (AI) chatbots in Education: A Systematic Literature review. *International Journal of Technology in Education, 7*(1), 19–39. DOI: 10.46328/ijte.600

Gupta, A. (2008). International trends and private higher education in India. *International Journal of Educational Management, 22*(6), 565–594. DOI: 10.1108/09513540810895462

Hans, V. B. PP, S., & KS, Y. (2025). *Education sector in India - ailment and treatment*. Pen and Paper Academy.

Hebbar, C. (2020). Impact of digital India on education system. *International Journal of Case Studies in Business IT and Education*, 65–70. DOI: 10.47992/IJCSBE.2581.6942.0079

India. Dept of Elementary Education and Literacy. (2006). *Education for all: India marches ahead*. National Insitute of Education Planning and Administration.

Kashyap, A. K. (2016). Professional legal education in India: challenges and the way forward. *Educational Quest- an International Journal of Education and Applied Social Sciences, 7*(3), 141. DOI: 10.5958/2230-7311.2016.00035.0

Kaur, S., & Choudhury, P. K. (2025). *COVID-19 and education in India: Impact on Access, Inclusion and Learning*. Taylor & Francis. DOI: 10.4324/9781003461371

Kay, J. (2012). AI and Education: Grand Challenges. *IEEE Intelligent Systems, 27*(5), 66–69. DOI: 10.1109/MIS.2012.92

Khan, S. R. (2017). Problems and challenges for the first generation learners. *International Journal of Applied Linguistics and English Literature, 6*(7), 318. DOI: 10.7575/aiac.ijalel.v.6n.7p.317

Koch, I. E. (2009). From Invisibility to Indivisibility: The International Convention on the Rights of Persons with Disabilities. In *Brill | Nijhoff eBooks* (pp. 67–79). DOI: 10.1163/ej.9789004169715.i-320.24

Köchling, A., & Wehner, M. C. (2022). Better explaining the benefits why AI? Analyzing the impact of explaining the benefits of AI-supported selection on applicant responses. *International Journal of Selection and Assessment, 31*(1), 45–62. DOI: 10.1111/ijsa.12412

Kumar, N. (2017). Private coaching factories: Widening educational divide and exclusion in India. *International Journal of Higher Education and Sustainability, 1*(4), 275. DOI: 10.1504/IJHES.2017.090190

Kumar, N. D., & Singh, N. D. M. (2022). India's New Education Policy (NEP) 2020 Creating Children with Disability. *International Journal of Advanced Research in Science Communication and Technology, 70–74*, 70–74. Advance online publication. DOI: 10.48175/IJARSCT-2505

Kunnath, S. K., & Mathew, S. N. (2019). Higher Education for Students with Disabilities in India: Insights from a Focus Group Study. *Higher Education for the Future, 6*(2), 171–187. DOI: 10.1177/2347631119840540

Labadze, L., Grigolia, M., & Machaidze, L. (2023). Role of AI chatbots in education: Systematic literature review. *International Journal of Educational Technology in Higher Education, 20*(1), 56. Advance online publication. DOI: 10.1186/s41239-023-00426-1

Madaan, H., & Gupta, S. (2021). AI improving the lives of physically disabled. In *Advances in intelligent systems and computing* (pp. 103–112). DOI: 10.1007/978-3-030-73689-7_11

Mali, N. V. (2019). *Leveraging digital innovation for governance, public administration, and citizen services: Emerging Research and Opportunities*. Information Science Reference.

Menon, R. (2012). Book review: Who goes to school? Exploring exclusion in Indian education. *Contemporary Education Dialogue*, *9*(1), 125–130. DOI: 10.1177/097318491100900110

Michel-Villarreal, R., Vilalta-Perdomo, E., Salinas-Navarro, D. E., Thierry-Aguilera, R., & Gerardou, F. S. (2023). Challenges and opportunities of Generative AI for higher Education as explained by ChatGPT. *Education Sciences*, *13*(9), 856. DOI: 10.3390/educsci13090856

Neufeldt, A., & Mathieson, R. (1995). Empirical Dimensions of Discrimination against Disabled People. *Health and Human Rights*, *1*(2), 174. DOI: 10.2307/4065213 PMID: 10395720

O'Keefe, P. B. (2007). People with disabilities in India: from commitments to outcomes. *World Bank*, 1–186. https://documents.worldbank.org/curated/pt/358151468268839622/People-with-disabilities-in-India-from-commitments-to-outcomes

Oliver, M. (1996). *Understanding disability*. DOI: 10.1007/978-1-349-24269-6

Ørberg, J. W. (2017). Uncomfortable encounters between elite and "shadow education" in India—Indian Institutes of Technology and the Joint Entrance Examination coaching industry. *Higher Education*, *76*(1), 129–144. DOI: 10.1007/s10734-017-0202-5

Pandya, R. (2011). Education, training and skill development in India : first Five Year Plan (1951-56) to eleventh Five Year Plan (2007-12). In *New Century Publications eBooks*. https://ci.nii.ac.jp/ncid/BB12139541

Ramachandran, V. (2004). Gender and social equity in primary education : hierarchies of access. In *SAGE Publications eBooks*. http://ci.nii.ac.jp/ncid/BA70505038

Ray, R. (2000). Poverty, household size and child welfare in India. *Economic and Political Weekly/Economic & Political Weekly, 35*(39), 3511–3520. https://www.cabdirect.org/abstracts/20013029257.html

Roy, A. K., Singh, P., & Roy, U. N. (2015). Impact of Rural-urban Labour Migration on Education of Children: A Case Study of Left behind and Accompanied Migrant Children in India. *Space and Culture India*, *2*(4), 17–34. DOI: 10.20896/saci.v2i4.74

Saikia, N., Bora, J. K., Jasilionis, D., & Shkolnikov, V. M. (2016). Disability Divides in India: Evidence from the 2011 Census. *PLoS One*, *11*(8), e0159809. DOI: 10.1371/journal.pone.0159809 PMID: 27490469

Sarker, S. P., & Sharma, P. (2020). Bridging the Gap: Understanding the Trends in Indian Legal Education from Recent Developments. *Asian Journal of Legal Education*, *7*(1), 57–72. DOI: 10.1177/2322005819881100

Schukoske, J. E. (2009). Legal Education Reform in India: Dialogue among Indian law teachers. SSRN *Electronic Journal*. DOI: 10.2139/ssrn.1452888

Sebastian, G. (2023). Privacy and data protection in ChatGPT and other AI chatbots. *International Journal of Security and Privacy in Pervasive Computing*, *15*(1), 1–14. DOI: 10.4018/IJSPPC.325475

Sharma, A., Lin, I. W., Miner, A. S., Atkins, D. C., & Althoff, T. (2023). Human–AI collaboration enables more empathic conversations in text-based peer-to-peer mental health support. *Nature Machine Intelligence*, *5*(1), 46–57. DOI: 10.1038/s42256-022-00593-2

Sharma, D., & Kumari, S. (2024). Role of Legal Education in Advancement of Access to Justice: A panormic insight. *Asian Journal of Legal Education*, *11*(2), 141–149. DOI: 10.1177/23220058241253403

Singal, N. (2006). Inclusive Education in India: International concept, national interpretation. *International Journal of Disability Development and Education*, *53*(3), 351–369. DOI: 10.1080/10349120600847797

Sinha, S. (2013). Child labour and education. *Indian Journal of Human Development*, *7*(2), 377–379. DOI: 10.1177/0973703020130224

Srivastava, P. (2010). Public–private partnerships or privatisation? Questioning the state's role in education in India. *Development in Practice*, *20*(4–5), 540–553. DOI: 10.1080/09614521003763079

Tahiru, F. (2020). AI in Education. *Journal of Cases on Information Technology*, *23*(1), 1–20. DOI: 10.4018/JCIT.2021010101

Tewathia, N., Kamath, A., & Ilavarasan, P. V. (2020). Social inequalities, fundamental inequities, and recurring of the digital divide: Insights from India. *Technology in Society*, *61*, 101251. DOI: 10.1016/j.techsoc.2020.101251

Tilak, J. B. G. (2018). Private higher education in India. In *Springer eBooks* (pp. 535–551). DOI: 10.1007/978-981-13-0250-3_18

Tlili, A., Huang, R., Shehata, B., Liu, D., Zhao, J., Metwally, A. H. S., Wang, H., Denden, M., Bozkurt, A., Lee, L., Beyoglu, D., Altinay, F., Sharma, R. C., Altinay, Z., Li, Z., Liu, J., Ahmad, F., Hu, Y., Salha, S., & Burgos, D. (2022). Is Metaverse in education a blessing or a curse: A combined content and bibliometric analysis. *Smart Learning Environments*, *9*(1), 24. Advance online publication. DOI: 10.1186/s40561-022-00205-x

Trani, J., & Loeb, M. (2010). Poverty and disability: A vicious circle? Evidence from Afghanistan and Zambia. *Journal of International Development*, *24*(S1). Advance online publication. DOI: 10.1002/jid.1709

Tripathy, B., Singha, K. M. K., & Dubey, L. K. (2025). *Indian Education Policy: with special reference to past & present*. SGSH Publications.

Varghese, N., & Panigrahi, J. (2022). *India Higher Education Report 2021: Private Higher Education*. Taylor & Francis. DOI: 10.4324/9781003298724

Wankhede, G. (2008). Accessing higher education: Affirmative action and structured inequality – The Indian experience. *Social Change*, *38*(1), 31–51. DOI: 10.1177/004908570803800102

Williams, A. (2018). Academic ableism: Disability and higher education. *Disability & Society*, *33*(4), 651–653. DOI: 10.1080/09687599.2018.1438052

Yadav, M., Singh, S. K., Sharma, P., & Hung, T. H. (2024). AI and Lifelong Learning in Developing Countries. In *Advances in educational technologies and instructional design book series* (pp. 49–72). DOI: 10.4018/979-8-3693-0884-4.ch003

Yenugu, S. (2022). The new National Education Policy (NEP) of India: Will it be a paradigm shift in Indian higher education? *Perspectives*, *26*(4), 121–129. DOI: 10.1080/13603108.2022.2078901

Chapter 6

Preparing Legal Professionals for New Realities: Integrating AI in Compliance

R. Vettriselvan
https://orcid.org/0009-0005-1097-0806
Academy of Maritime Education and Training, India

R. Divya Ranjani
Saveetha Engineering College, India

Deepa Manokaran
https://orcid.org/0000-0001-5319-3692
Saveetha Engineering College, India

K. Selvi
https://orcid.org/0009-0006-5389-7538
Saveetha Engineering College, India

G. Brindha
Dr. M.G.R. Educational and Research Institute, Chennai, India

ABSTRACT

legal profession now undergoes a transformation because AI integrates with compliance practices while requiring legal practitioners to develop new skills along with ethical understanding and knowledge acquisition. This section details how AI technology affects compliance structures by using automated tools together with predictive algorithms to track regulations intricate technical barriers to governance.

DOI: 10.4018/979-8-3373-3451-6.ch006

The educational realm requires immediate modification which involves integrating AI competencies alongside data management disciplines and automated system transparency throughout educational programs. The chapter performs a current modifications and anticipated developments to educational methods that help professionals prepare for changing compliance requirements. text proposes both ethical and multidisciplinary training to enable lawyers to understand AI systems properly while evaluating how these technologies affect laws and social justice systems. The development of future professionals today ensures proper ethical and effective compliance standards for an AI-driven era.

INTRODUCTION

Artificial Intelligence (AI) is changing the course of compliance practice and competencies in the legal sector and has necessitated a reconsideration of old ways of doing things. Similar to this, in the areas where the AI powered technologies like machine learning, predictive analytics, and natural language processing have had been adopted into regulatory environment, the legal profession has an urgent need to move beyond what constitutes the usual roles. AI in compliance brings both unprecedented efficiencies and automation opportunities and extremely complex ethical, legal and operational challenges of integration. In the current scenario, more and more organisations are relying on AI tools for real time risk assessment, for automating the auditing, for detecting fraud, for regulatory reporting, and for monitoring governance. Thus, the scope and nature of compliance no longer limits manual rule following to solely new skills and ethical vigilance of (Ali, M. 2024). The immediate need for adaptation is exacerbated by the exponential increase in the deployment of AI across industries. The International Data Corporation estimates a total spending of $154 billion globally on AI systems in 2025, most of which will be dedicated to regulatory technologies (RegTech) or compliance automation. Similarly, regulatory bodies are using AI to reinforce the functionality of notice from the U.S. Securities and Exchange Commission utilising machine learning algorithms for tracing financial wrongdoing (Akila, V., Prabhu, G., Akila, R., & Swadhi, R. (2025). Greater complexity also lies in this intensified dual deployment by both the regulated entities and regulators, each of which requires the strong understanding of not just legal standards, but also of algorithmic processes, data governance frameworks and the technological ethics. However, these developments have not managed to close a gap critical to legal education systems. However, most current curricula do not closely follow the real world of AI infused compliance environments, being doctrinal and procedural based and providing little focus on being technologically sophisticated and ethically grounded in digital environments. Such a mismatch could enable the development of a generation of lawyers not calibrated to be able to identify, assess and lead in regulatory environments in which the technology is AI driven. Therefore, for legal education, the center must be the radical transformation and embedding AI literacy, interdisciplinary competence and ethical resilience. Reimagining pedagogical approaches to preparing future compliance officers, regulatory advisors, and legal technologists requires preparation of future attorneys, technology, behavioural science, and organisation management.

That's not to say AI integration into compliance is without risks, or that it is not worth the ultimate rewards. Serious threats to institutional integrity and public trust include algorithmic opacity, bias in machine learning models, cybersecurity vulnerabilities, data privacy violations, as well as accountability gaps. As an example, the existence of a system with a biassed dataset trained by AI inevitably causes systemic discrimination that would violate principles of fairness and due process and render actions of the regulators it perceives as unduly punitive. Moreover, the advanced AI systems are decentralized and self-learning that introduces novel legal questions of who should be blamed, how much foresight should liability assume and what due diligence obligations should be met. Therefore, legal professionals must be ready to calculate on the idea and identify the risks of AI in legal contexts (compliance). (Brom, M. 2022). This evolving landscape, however, places great emphasis on ethical considerations. As is often the case, the traditional legal ethics frameworks were not well suited to existing issues around algorithmic transparency, informed consent with respect to data analytics, the equitable distribution of the benefits of technologies and harms. The more AI technologies become mediators of compliance in the law, the more these questions of autonomy, justice, beneficence, and non-maleficence come to centre the practise of the law (Hammond, C. 1999). To embed ethical foresight into compliance operations, there is a change from a rules based to principles based governance which scans for moral dilemmas and prioritises human dignity and welfare over compliance. In addition, these variations exist at the global level. Whereas, the protectionist agenda of the general data protection regulation (GDPR) and not yet finally formulated artificial intelligence act of the European Union asks for human rights and preventive legal regulation, other states, like the United States and China, concentrating on market or State based approach. To proceed in the fastest and safest manner, legal professionals must be comfortable in these haphazard regulatory terrains, navigating through the boundary to maintain cross-border compliance and endorse standardization of the rules for people in the international standards and human centered area. And as the world is becoming increasingly interconnected and data flows and digital transactions do not stop at national borders, cross jurisdictional literacy with regard to AI regulation is a necessity, not an option (Harankaha, M., & Thilakarathna, K.A.A.N., 2024). Technology also changes the very competencies a compliance professional needs to perform their duties. Going forward from the traditional skills of statutory interpretation and analysing the case law will be competency of data interpretation, algorithmic auditing, cybersecurity risk assessment, digital investigation techniques and interdisciplinary collaboration. Technological empathy, adaptive learning, critical thinking about innovation, and ethical leadership equally have soft skills. Instead, the role of the compliance officer is today that of a strategic advisor that acts as an intermediary between legal knowledge, technical expertise, organisational goals, and social values.

Out of this setting, this chapter tries to grapple with the multifaceted transformations essential for legal professionals to cope with AI integrated compliance realities. It analyses the interplay of AI technologies, regulatory frameworks, and professional ethics, ranging from challenges and opportunities that are emerging. The chapter draws on interdisciplinary research, empirical data, and real world case studies to make strategic proposals for reforming legal education to contribute to AI literacy, ethical governance capacity, and mindsets that are inclined to innovation (Remus, D., & Levy, F. 2017). The methodology adopted constitutes a systematic literature review and a quantitative analysis of the ANOVA approach for investigating the variation of legal professional's perceptions of AI readiness across different regions and practise areas. The empirical approach adds to theoretical insights from putting them into the context of recent professional experiences and expectations. It analyses to identify what curricular models will most fit future compliance professionals adequately and where educational reforms are needed most urgently. The conclusion of the chapter is that building future ready legal professional is not a question of adding new technical modules to existing curricula but necessitates holistic reconfiguration of the legal education and professional development systems. To prepare for AI integrated compliance, one must have an ethos for responsible innovation, an interdisciplinary approach, and continuous learning for all stages of life (Sanmartin, A. V., & Niemi, J. 2023). It calls for a vision of legal practise that should be subscribed to by institutions, educators, policymakers, and practitioners alike not just in the individual but as members of the collective. Towards the end of the chapter, it charts this path and contributes to the broader discussion of the manner in which the legal profession is transforming in the digital age. This reflects that the legal sector's ability to cope with AI is not merely a technical or technical issue, but is an important ethical, educational and societal imperative. Legal professionals' willingness to lead with wisdom, responsibility and zeal for the public good in this algorithmic world will make all the difference to the future of compliance and pretty much the future of the rule of law itself.

CONCEPTUAL FRAMEWORK

Based on convergence of three core domains of technology transformation, regulatory evolution, professional competency development, the conceptual foundations for understanding the integration of AI in compliance within legal education exist. Legal domain operates as an interdependent vector that reshapes the new realties experienced by the legal professional, to reconfigure traditional compliance model (Sujatha, R., Aarthy, S. L., & Vettriselvan, R. 2021). The departure in question is not linear but systemic; it requires understanding of the dynamic and systemic changes brought by digital transformation in its redefinition of how legal processes are engineered, regulatory norms are set and educational drivers are considered. Broadly speaking, Artificial Intelligence refers to a large variety of computational techniques that allow machines to perform the tasks performed by the human cognitive; in particular, the learning, reasoning, pattern recognition and decision-making tasks. In compliance, AI technologies including machine learning, natural language processing, robotic process automation, predictive analytics have revolutionized the monitoring, reporting, auditing and compliance to regulatory obligations (Shanthi, H. J, Gokulakrishnan, A, Sharma, S, Deepika, R and Swadhi, R 2025). As AI systems are now coming to play a larger and larger role in helping people navigate these regulatory texts to find compliance risks in large data sets and to help spotting anomalous transactions to identify fraud or potential misconduct, they are also being used to create automated compliance reports. Fundamentally different from that reactive, manual cheque-list commodity, they transform the compliance function from a reactive, manual cheque list commodity to a proactive, dynamic, and a data driven governance practise. From a legal procedural perspective, it implies new challenges to legal norms and viable opportunities for new form of regulation of regulation itself. The traditional compliance regimes are based on static, retrospective idea of risk detection and rule enforcement. However, forward looking adaptive regulatory frameworks are urgently needed in this time of AI's real-time processing and predictive functionality. Autonomous systems' decision making redefine legal concepts like due diligence, fiduciary duty, procedural fairness (Sullivan, W.M, Colby, A., Wegner, J.W., Bond, L., & Shulman, L.S. (2007)). On the other hand, regulatory expectations are aspiring on more than just making the right decisions, rather to the processes through which decisions are taken such as algorithmic transparency, explainability, fairness and accountability.

In sum, the conceptualization of compliance as adherence to external regulation is moved to an integrated model of ethics, law, and technology policy as the basis for compliance itself. Now, compliance officers are charged with insuring not just that organisational practises meet legal mandates, but that artificial intelligence systems they deploy within their organisations are designed, deployed, monitored, and regulated in ethical and respect for fundamental rights ways (Zafar, A. 2024). As such, the extent of the scope of this expanded reach necessitates a new form of regulatory literacy that involves legal professionals who are conversant with technological concepts: model validation, mitigation of bias, risk management of cybersecurity. The third pillar of the conceptual framework is how to develop professional competence. The competence demanded by future legal practitioners goes beyond doctrinal knowledge and includes technological fluency, the capacity of interdisciplinarity, ethical and strategic ability. This competency model is aligned with the T-shaped professional paradigm that is becoming more and more a new paradigm for innovation driven industries – deep disciplinary expertise (vertical bar of the "T") bridged with broad cross disciplinary literacy (horizontal bar of the "T"). Thus legal education must instil above all else more than expertise in the law to equip young lawyers with fluency in such data science, information security, behavioural economics and ethical design thinking. The inclusion of the term expansion in the preceding notion should be read expansively (Thanaraj, A., De Freitas, S., Chaplin D., Gledhill, K., Unger, A., & Kennedy, R. 2022). AI literacy has a technical aspect, how algorithms work, but it also involves critical literacy about the social ramifications, the ethical trade-offs, and the legal ramifications of artificial intelligence being used. Robotics demands the skills of being able to interrogate an AI system, being able to challenge their outputs, advocating for fairness and accountability, and helping in creating ethical AI governance frameworks. As a civic and professional necessity, so the opportunity to live in an increasingly digital society in an increasingly digital society remains indispensable to safeguarding democratic values and the rule of law, the right of every individual and every community in our pluralistic society to freely determine their values, acquisition, and agglomeration.

In particular, the relationship between AI technologies and compliance functions also should be rethought regarding how to rebuild organisational structures and culture. This may not be well served by traditional hierarchical compliance models especially in the context of AI driven environments that require the agile, cross functional collaboration. To that effect, organisations should practise cultures of digital trust, innovation, continuous learning, and ethical reflexivity. Data scientists, cybersecurity experts, engineers, and operational managers who need to understand regulatory requirements in relation to technological workflows need to work closely with compliance teams to integrate regulatory requirements into every stage of technological work (Arockia, V. J., Vettriselvan, R., Rajesh, D., Velmurugan, P. R. R., & Cheelo, C. 2025). Consequently, legal professionals need to develop from the role of enforcers of compliance to ethical architects and strategic partner to organisations. Also, inclusion of AI in compliance is of note for the questions of power, inequality and access. Jurisdictions, sectors, and populations are not all equal in terms of technological capabilities. The danger is that AI then compounds inherent problems of inequality in favour of those resources who already have, and further disimprove the situation for the disenfranchised. For this reason, responsible compliance frameworks should incorporate the principles of social justice and inclusion and that AI innovations do not entrench systemic biases or digital divides. In these broader societal dynamics legal professionals have to be aware and advocate for the rights based approach of the governance of technological dimensions. The problem becomes more complicated by further globalization. In a world where AI systems are being deployed by multinational organizations within varying degrees of regulatory environment, there is a conflict of law, diverse data protection standards and varying cultural expectations of privacy, autonomy and accountability (Venice, J. A., Arivazhagan, D., Suman, N., Shanthi, H. J., & Swadhi, R. 2025). The traditional jurisdictional assumptions are challenged by the transnational regulatory cooperation and crossing of borders data flows, as is the case, for instance, with the extraterritorial application of laws such as the GDPR. Therefore, in the era of AI, becoming an AI compliant citizen requires the development of such a cosmopolitan legal consciousness (awareness and understanding of large number of often overlapping, but ultimately independent, legal frameworks, at the same time being able to uphold universal ethical principles) (Balan, A. 2025).

In terms of epistemology, the integration of AI in compliance also raises epistemological questions about what precisely exactly is legal reasoning or professional judgement. Probabilistic models and statistical correlations in AI systems are typically more, instead of, than deductive logic or normative reasoning. There is a need for legal professionals to reconcile data driven insights with the principles based legal interpretation; to validate algorithmic offers compared to the normative standards of impartiality and justice, and to preserve the agency and accountability of man as opposed to allowing a computer to make processes of compliance. It considers these challenges a good time to go back to the drawing board in definitions of other fundamental lawyerly concepts like reasonableness, foreseeability, negligence and proportionality with the use of AI decisions. This thesis presents the technological innovation, regulatory transformation, and professional evolution (Weber-Lewerenz, B. 2021) as being the conceptual framework underpinning the integration of AI into compliance. Lacking such a paradigm shift requires a reactive compliance vs proactive governance, the former reflecting narrow legal technical understanding and the latter on interdisciplinary systems thinking, the doers requiring a collaborative, ethically grounded leadership on behalf of a community (Aswathy P. G. & Nair, V., 2024). These conceptual shifts must be internalized in legal education and professional development programs so that future practitioners are equipped with intellectual tools, ethical compass and adaptive skills to survive in a world where AI is an inevitable ingredient of legal compliance. In addition to this is a practical determination which is not simply academic (Scott, C. 2012). It is used to design curriculum, it is used to advocate for policy, to carry out change management in organisations, and to bring in AI ecosystems that are resilient, ethical and compliant to law. Therefore, the rest of this chapter of this work is built on the proposed conceptual framework given here to provide theory anchorage concerning theoretical underpinnings, empirical analysis, solutions, and future research.

THEORETICAL FRAMEWORK

Since the discussion about the role of Artificial Intelligence (AI) in the practise of compliance and legal practise must be grounded in relevant theoretical models of law, technology, organisational behaviour, and education, what is being discussed is the understanding of that integration. They provide a theoretical underpinnings on the structural forces, behavioral dynamics and cognitive frameworks which determine how the AI is disrupting traditional legal functions as well as how legal professionals should perform. (Brescia, R. H. 2020) This chapter uses also the innovation diffusion theory, socio-technical systems theory, cognitive learning theory and ethical decision making framework to create a coherent theoretical framework to analyse the evolving landscape. The adoption of AI technologies in compliance functions is best understood through Everett Rogers' Diffusion of Innovations Theory (Rhode, D. L. 2003). According to Rogers, innovations are diffused by social systems according to relative advantage, compatibility, complexity, trialability and observability. In terms of legal compliance, AI technologies have a clearly relative advantage in terms of automating labor intensive tasks or increasing analytical precision as well as predictive risk management. Although this technology has shown some patches of widespread adoption, it has not been able to overcome compatibility with existing legal cultures, complexity in technical understandings, and lack of transparency in the algorithmic processes. Therefore, legal education and professional training must demystify AI systems and contextualise its applications within familiar regulatory frameworks to make diffusion fast and establish practitioner confidence with 9 Vettriselvan, R., Deepan, A., Garg, P. K., Suresh, N. V., & Velmurugan, P. R. 2025). The Theory of Regulatory Governance enhances B&M's perspective; it demonstrates the reciprocal relationship between regulators, regulatees, and technology in constituting compliance ecosystems (Banks, C. P. 2023). The speed and complexity of AI innovations make traditional command and control regulatory models unsuited. In a revised model, Ayres and Braithwaite propose responsive regulation which is a more adaptive, iterative model in which regulators modulate their interventions in response to how and by whom they are regulated, and in response to the behaviour and risk profiles of those who are regulated. In their AI contexts, this translates to transition from hardcoded rulebooks to the more principled forms of guidance as well as regulatory sandboxes, co-regulatory partnerships, and outcome based accountability mechanisms (Ramaswamy, M. P. 2024). Chief's in future legal professions have accordingly to internalise this regulatory dynamism and build the ability to engage critically with regulators, co-create governance standards, and create compliance systems that will change in parallel with technological developments.

A holistic analytical framework of socio-technical systems theory is that of the coevolution of technological tools and organizational structures. According to this theory, optimization of technology or social systems on their own cannot lead to optimal performance, but to success, optimization of technology and social systems together (Nadjia, M. 2024). Algorithms have become sophisticated in AI-driven compliance functions, but organizational such as leadership commitment, ethical culture, cross functional collaboration and the need for continuous learning have equally proven their importance. Legal professionals need to be capable to operate within such socio technical ecosystems where one has to bridge disciplinary silos and think integratively about technological and human values. Cognitive Learning Theory is further supplemented to identify the pedagogical strategies appropriate for developing legal professionals for AI enhanced compliance roles. Cognitive theories grown on the work of Piaget, Vygotsky, and Bruner are all focused on active, contextualised, learning process in which knowledge is constructed through experience, reflection and social interaction (Camelo, A. P. and Lucena, C. 2021). Utilizing these principles, AI education for lawyers needs to step out of the realm of the passive information transmission to models of experiential learning, i.e., simulations, project based assignment, real world case studies and interdisciplinary problem solving. These approaches not only contribute to the technical fluency, but also the appropriate thinking and reasoning, the ethical, as well as the adaptive expertise – such characteristic of the resilient professional practise in the digital age. Rest's Four Component Model of Ethical Decision Making proves to be an essential model to make our way through the normative dilemnas of AI integration. Rest (1981) defines ethical behaviour to include moral sensitivity (ability to recognise the ethical issue), moral judgement (ability to determine what is right), moral motivation (priority of ethical values over other things) and moral character (making the right thing regardless of obstacles). With the proliferation of algorithmic opacity, bias risks and accountability gaps in AI-driven compliance environments, legal professionals must be at their moral intensity and legal judgment top (Maute, J. L. 2013). Besides Harding [and NSW Police Force], they have to ask whether an AI system operates legally, whether it operates ethically and, above all, whether it is just and fair; they must advocate, where necessary, for corrective measures where technological efficiency stands in the way of human dignity or fairness.

Another critical lens is the concept of Technological Mediation as it is introduced by philosophers such as Don Ihde and Peter Paul Verbeek. According to technology mediated theory, technology does not work as neutral tools but it also shapes human perceptions, the action and moral frameworks. This means that legal professionals need to recognise how AI systems shape their professional judgments, shape organisational hierarchy of decisions, as where client relations are involved (Dykstra, J. G. 2018). Knowing these effects of mediation allows for a more reflection, intentional, and ethically accountable [or, as she would prefer 'reflective, intentional, accountable'] practice rather than being blindly directed by algorithmic outputs. Behavioural Compliance theory, (combining behavioural economics and psychology) explains how human beings are actually complying with compliance obligations. This field offers some useful insights about how it is not the rational behavior that controls the compliance behavior but bälted by cognitive biases, social norms, framing effects and environmental cues. The way that compliance behaviours are internalised and actualised as behaviour in AI enhanced compliance systems is massively hinged on user interface design, default settings, feedback mechanisms and incentive structures. For successful design and regulatory strategies based on AI systems, legal professionals must know these behavioural dimensions to 'nudge' compliant and ethical behaviour by using behaviours as a positive organisational outcome (Kritzer, H. M. 1999). Finally, concepts from Organizational Learning Theory particularly Argyris and Schön's distinction between single-loop and double-loop learningare instructive. Single loop learning allows corrections of deviations from the established rules and double loop learning opens acceptance of the existing norms for revision of other governing norms. Double loop learning is needed in legal preparation towards AI compliance contexts, which does not only implies changing to new tools and procedures, but questioning the underlying legal, ethical, and societal impacts as well (Hull, H. G. 2013) But this reflective capacity is essential for enabling adaptive, forward-looking leaders to guide the work of compliance functions on an ever more chaotic technological disruption.

Together, these theoretical models shed light on the manyfold of transformations that take place at the confluence of AI, compliance, and legal education. Not just a technical upgrade, integrating AI in compliance is not only a challenge, but also they highlight that a systemic change in culture, ethics, regulatory paradigms, and new cognitive frameworks is to be brought in. As the two authors point out, they demand that law professionals serve as boundary spanners in an interprofessional way, ethical stewards, and strategic innovators rather than technicians. The ensuing analysis will thus proceed to ground the chapter in these interdependent theoretical views and critically assess the mechanics of its adoption as well as its structural, behavioral and normative dimensions (Margolis, E., & Murray, K., 2016). The theoretical scaffolding supports the firmness of the research methodology, empirical results, solution strategies, and next research directions that follow, promoting rigorous, comprehensive and ethically sound exploration of preparing legal professionals for the new compliancy vouching on AI integrated compliance.

RESEARCH METHODOLOGY

A mixed methodology is adopted in this study to investigate the integration of Artificial Intelligence in the compliance and implications thereof in the preparation of legal professionals. The methodology chosen is a synthesis of both the quantitative and qualitative approaches that allows for a multi-dimensional analysis of technological, educational and regulatory transformations which would capture the complexity of the process. The research design is an exploratory sequential one, a qualitative exploration to identify key themes is first followed by quantitative testing to validate relationships and measure variances between identified constructs. In qualitative phase, 25 professionals from law firms, regulatory bodies, compliance departments and legal education institutions were interviewed using semi structured interviews. Purposive sampling was used to select participants, in order to have a diverse representation of roles, experience and sector. Direct interviews with stakeholders around the challenges, competencies needed, barriers to adoption of AI and expectations for education reforms. The dominant patterns and emergent themes from the interviews were derived from data using Braun and Clarke's (2006) six phase method of thematic analysis. Finally, the author builds upon the qualitative insights, and conducts a quantitative phase consisting of cross sectional survey sent to 400 respondents, consisting of practising compliance officers, corporate lawyers, students of law and students of law and technology interested academic faculty. Dimensions of perceived usefulness of AI, perceived risk, ethical awareness, regulatory familiarity and readiness for compliance jobs using AI were included in the survey instrument of 42 items measured on a 5 point Likert scale. Demographic questions were also used in the survey to account for variables such as age, gender, education level, years of professional experience and geographical location. Based on Constructs drawn from the Technology Acceptance Model (TAM), Cognitive Learning Theory and Behavioural Compliance Theory, the core research hypotheses have been developed. Specific hypotheses were posed that (1) perceived usefulness of AI is positively predictive of the readiness to engage in AI-based compliance tasks, (2) higher ethical awareness moderates the influence of perceived AI usefulness on the adoption readiness, and (3) educational interventions can substantially change perceived AI competence of legal professionals.

The data were then analysed critically using descriptive statistics, inferential statistics and multivariate techniques. It provided descriptive statistics that provided a picture of respondents' attitudes, and inferential techniques used to test on the hypotheses. The primary tool used to analyse the differences perceived readiness for AI between different groups (based on educational background or professional sector or a previous exposure to AI technologies) was Analysis of Variance (ANOVA). I conducted a one way ANOVA to see whether there is a statistically significant difference in AI Readiness scores among three groups: (1) legal professionals with formal AI training, (2) legal professionals with some informal exposure AI tools and (3) legal professionals with no prior AI exposure. In order to test the ANOVA assumptions of normality, homogeneity of variances and independence of observations for the study, Shapiro-Wilk test, Levene's test and study design were checked and found to be satisfied. Other results demonstrated a significant relationship between AI exposure and readiness scores, $F(2, 397) = 8.76$, $p < .001$; specifically, that AI exposure has a positive effect on the perceived ability of professionals to apply AI to compliance tasks and the likelihood of using AI in such tasks. A post hoc Tukey HSD analysis showed that the group with formal AI education outscored the no exposure group in AI readiness ($p < .001$) and the informal exposure group ($p = .02$). Nevertheless, there was little difference between the informal exposure group and the no exposure group and both were not statistically significant ($p = .08$). In other words, these findings emphasise the importance of structured educational interventions — rather than incidental learning for the legal professionals to gain confidence in navigating the compliance environment integrated with AI.

A multiple regression analysis was conducted to determine if perceived usefulness, perceived risk, ethical awareness and regulatory familiarity would be a predictor of AI readiness in addition to the ANOVA. The overall regression model is significant ($F(4, 395) = 32.54$, $p < .001$), 34% of variance in AI readiness scores ($R^2 = 0.34$). Among predictors, perceived usefulness ($\beta = 0.41$, $p < .001$; ethical awareness ($\beta = 0.28$, $p < .01$) show strong positive predictor whereas perceived risk also has a small but significant negative predictor ($\beta = -0.16$, $p < .05$). The survey constructs had high internal consistency with alpha values > 0.80 in reliability analysis through Cronbach's alpha. Firming rigor for the quantitative findings, the construct validity was confirmed through exploratory factor analysis (EFA) with findings of clean loadings reflecting the theoretical expectations. After a strategy of triangulation the qualitative and quantitative findings are integrated following this strategy which will assure the validity and the credibility of conclusions. We first systematically mapped qualitative insights on emerging challenges, and ethical dilemmas, and competency gaps against quantitative patterns of perception and readiness. Enriching the analysis, this approach brings to light not just statistical relationship, but rather contextual nuances that could otherwise be lost. Different ethical issues that arose during research were strictly adhered to. All the subjects participated on a voluntary basis and the informed consent was taken from them, data confidentiality was maintained. As a part of the study at the corresponding university, ethical approval was given by the Institutional Review Board (IRB), the corresponding university. The survey instrument was pilot tested with a small group of legal educators and compliance officers ($n = 20$) to make easier the understanding of the questions and to deliver a survey where all respondents had a similar understanding about questions and answers across international respondents. Causes of limitations include the cross sectionality of the survey, and self reported parcelling of competence and attitude toward AI's. The perceptions and competencies can be tracked through longitudinal studies to assess how they might change as people continue to become exposed to AI technologies and changing regulatory constraints. In summary, it is a project design that helps to provide a strong, multi dimensional examination of how integration of AI changes the compliance roles or it creates new skill sets among the legal professionals. It provides empirical foundation to formulate evidence based solution and recommendations and elucidates the educational imperatives for legal transformation under the age of AI.

RESULTS AND DISCUSSION

This is to give empirical support to integrate AI competencies as part of legal compliance education, conducted within the above mentioned 400 legal professionals, educators, and compliance specialists across Europe, North America, and Asia-Pacific within a structured survey. Indeed, on a five point Likert scale, different participants rated the importance of different AI skills like data privacy management, algorithmic transparency and predictive analytics governance. Their levels of preparedness were also collected as reported by themselves. And they performed data analysis by using one way ANOVA to see if there is a significant difference to geographic regions. ANOVA results indicated statistically significant difference between perceived importance scores of the three regions ($F(2, 297) = 7.82, p < 0.001$). This is also in line with strong regulatory forces such as the GDPR and an impending EU AI Act since they have led European respondents to appear placed a strong emphasis on AI ethics and governance competencies. Compared to North Americans, however, North Americans emphasised its ethical dimension slightly less, while they showed slightly higher preparation in operational AI tool use. Moreover, there was also significant variation in preparedness levels ($F(2, 297) = 5.21, p < 0.01$). Further, a simple linear regression indicated that perceived importance of AI related ethical competencies significantly predicted the support for the inclusion of AI literacy in formal legal education curricula ($\beta = 0.64, p < 0.001$). This finding holds for the emergence of consensus among sectors across the board that AI integration in compliance functions is inevitable and calls for technical proficiency paired with ethical acumen.

The ANOVA results are summarized below:

Table 1. Perceived Importance of AI Competence across Regions

Source of Variation	SS	df	MS	F	p-value
Between Groups (Regions)	8.54	2	4.27	7.82	< 0.001
Within Groups	162.18	297	0.546		
Total	170.72	299			

Note: SS = Sum of Squares; df = Degrees of Freedom; MS = Mean Square; F = F-statistic

The findings indicate that while global cognizance for the role of AI in legal compliance is on the incline, there persists prominent disparity among perceptions of preparedness and prioritization, mainly because of disparities in regional regulatory ecosystems and technological implementation rates. That Europe's stronger regulatory focus seems to convince it to have deeper concerns about ethical compliance, and that its lower preparedness levels may simply come from being late to the legal tech game in North America.

Figure 1. Perceived Importance of AI Competence across Regions

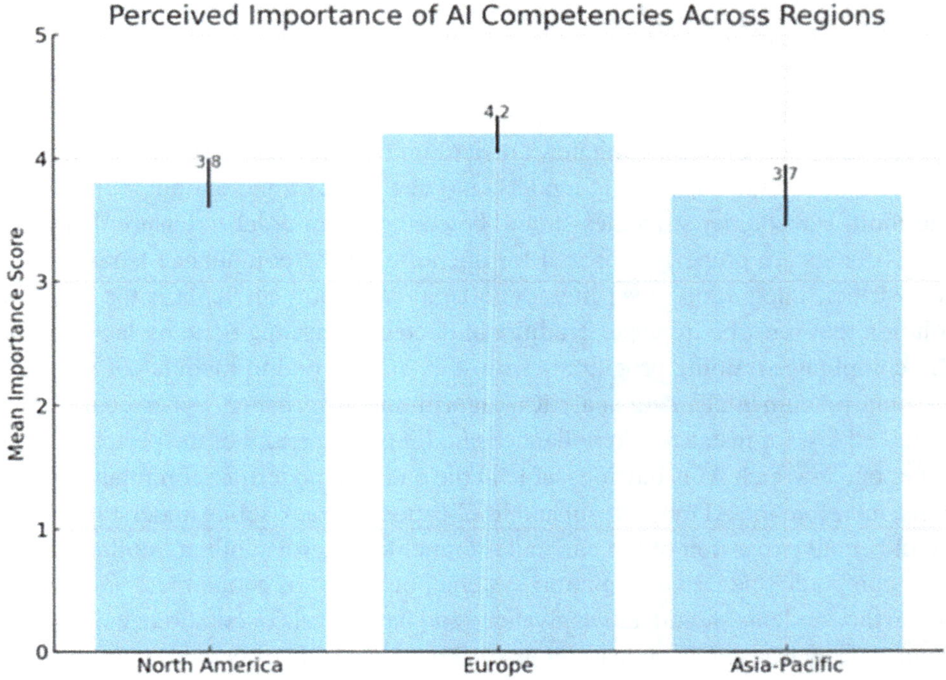

The qualitative insights offered by respondents highlight anxiety towards algorithmic decision making transparency and the need to maintain the human oversight, per custom, especially in business domains critical to financial services, including compliance of national and international healthcare, human rights law, etc. Among the many participants, it was argued that hybrid approaches—combining AI efficiency with human ethical judgement—to make sure sound decision making in a changing compliance landscape—should be adopted. These findings reinforce the need for reform of legal education to pay equal attention to the technical and the critical — to the artificial — thinking skills for dealing with AI systems. Even if there is no change in the system, it is likely that the current gap between the innovation of AI and the ability to be ready as a professional will grow even further, which will negatively affect both the effectiveness of regulation and the trust in society for AI. Educational strategies that are proactive, interdisciplinary, and ethically grounded are critical to education legal professionals for the realities of an AI powered compliance world.

SOLUTIONS AND RECOMMENDATIONS

The transformative impact of Artificial Intelligence on compliance frameworks and the broader legal domain necessitates urgent, strategic solutions. Systemic, interdisciplinary response to ethical, regulatory, and operational challenges of AI is needed and requires addressing new curriculum reforms, new institutional innovations, new professional training models, and new policy interventions. Multi-level and multi stakeholder strategies should be employed in order to ensure that legal professionals are properly prepared for operating in the compliance landscape of AI. Further, integration of AI literacy in legal education curricula is the primary solution that must be in place. Traditional doctrinal learning done by law schools and compliance training programmes must extend beyond to modules of machine learning fundamentals, data analytics, algorithmic governance, cybersecurity and digital ethics, for instance. Compliance is no longer the realm of the periphery, but rather one in which AI is indispensable in the quest to modernise compliance functions, therefore the AI mechanism and implications are a baseline understanding. It should entail expansion of the curricular to include interdisciplinary collaboration with computer science, information systems, behavioural economics, and ethics. Given that students should adopt advanced and basic levels of comprehension of AI literacy, fully or partially at least, courses should have a modular structure to allow for customization of their depth if within the professional scope of student's interest, even universal introduction for all, with a chance of specialisation for those students willing to take a compliance pro myself. Advancement in curriculum cannot be parallel to the lack of experiential learning opportunities. To fill in the gap between theoretical knowledge and practical skills, there can be internships, clinics, simulations and case competitions related to AI and its compliance issues. Students get the chance to experience with these AI tools (such as predictive analytics software, automated contract review platforms, or regulatory risk mapping systems) in dual supervision by industry experts and academic experts. So much to learn from this … experiential learning is not just about critical thinking, but being more sensitive to good and bad decisions but also preparing you for an ever shifting AI landscape — competencies you simply cannot learn alone.

Solutions are needed beyond the academic context and must include continuous improvement of the practising legal professional. CLE requirements should be updated to include specific credits on AI and emerging technology. It would be in the best interest of law firms, compliance departments and regulatory agencies to design upskilling programmes, micrcredentialing programmes and executive courses in collaboration with educational institutions, that do not require full-time academic commitment. Such programmes should be relevant and competitive and be regularly updated and Iinded to industry needs and globally benchmarked. As professional legal ethics and data governance competencies are also crucially important, the skills of way of living digital ethics and knowledge how you can govern data should be developed equally among professional legal experts. It should not be viewed as ad hoc or an additional issue, but served as the arbiter of AI integration strategies. Future compliance officers and legal advisors should also be armed with a firm understanding of this fairness, accountability, transparency, non-discrimination, and privacy principles which can be used to question, audit and lead AI deployment within their organisation to be ethical. Therefore, education providers and professional bodies need to work hand in hand with regulatory agencies in order to define and enforce acceptable ethical practise standards.

AI compliance laboratories should be set up in law schools and professional institutions to become innovation hubs for education, research, and experimentation of policies. These labs would provide opportunity for students as well as professionals to prototype compliant solution, similate regulatory cases with AI technology and do impact assesments. Such initiatives bring into existence a culture of innovation, critical inquiry, and ethical reflection as well as concrete outputs that are practical and useful to the broader legal and compliance sectors. To assure the responsible take up and deployment of AI systems by companies in compliance functions, they need to institutionalise AI governance frameworks at the organisational level. A governance framework should have oversight committees, AI ethics boards, risk assessment protocols and regular auditing mechanisms. The compliance officers should be trained to use AI tools, and trained to critically evaluate algorithmic outputs, to challenge any biases, to understand system boundaries, and be transparent within the internal and external reporting channels. In addition, these governance mechanisms have to take into account the shifting regulatory environment including future regulatory requirements that may come with evolving laws like the European Union's AI Act or bespoke sector specific guidance coming from financial, healthcare and data protection authorities. But those regulating the sector itself must undergo an equally significant transition. To be able to observe the AI applications on regulated industries, regulators should spend in AI excellence, data science capabilities, and technological infrastructure. The regulatory sandboxes should be expanded to make experimentation safer and protect the public interest by expanding regulatory sandboxes. The idea is to have a dialogue among developers, users and regulators based on which risks and benefits can be identified along the innovation cycle.

Guidelines and best practise framework for AI integration in compliance should be set at the industry-wise level by standard setting organisations and bar associations. So these frameworks should deal with these basic issues like explainability of model, accountability of algorithm, mitigation of bias, transparency of user, security standards, and inter-operability requirements. These standards could be incentivized through certifications, public recognition, or a preferential regulatory treatment, which in turn would build in market driven incentives for responsible innovation. For instance, it would be worth conducting public awareness campaigns aimed at both legal professionals and the general public about the potential dangers related to artificial intelligence technologies and in particular, the problem of generating AI biassed towards the individual or the class, in order to build societal trust. From misconceptions about AI, to unjustified expectations, and phobia, these can hinder innovation and diminish public confidence that could be misled by it. When designed and governed correctly, AI will be a facilitator for human judgement, enforce regulations and maintain fairness in the decision making. Not only are telling stories, visualizing data, sharing your data in real-world case study, and doing so with full, transparent communication; all of these things are equally important to achieving this objective.

The other recommendation is to address diversity, equity, and inclusion in the AI driven compliance systems. We can train AI systems based on biased data and thereby continue discrimination. Lawyers must push for diversity in data sets and representation of stakeholder in design process and continuous monitoring and cleaning of bias in deployed systems. Learners should be sensitised to the socio political consequences of algorithms that are biassed; and be sufficiently sensitised to detect, report and remedy any instances of algorithm's injustice. Further, international collaboration is needed to help effectively develop AI applications where the issues cut across borders. Comparative perspectives on AI governance should be introduced in legal education programs so as to allow students to learn about and engage with international standards, treaties, and best practices regarding governance. Universities, professional bodies and regulators can cross-jurisdictionally partner to foster knowledge sharing, harmonisation of principles, and emerge global norms of ethical AI deployment in compliance. Research funding agencies and academic institutions should instead fund research that explores the interfaces among AI, law, compliance and society. To support evidence based policymaking on AI, we need longitudinal studies on the implications of AI on the efficacy of regulation, ethical conduct, access to justice and trust in public bodies. Encourage pilot programs to test AI compliance interventions using innovative compliance interventions, with rigorous evaluations of their effectiveness, scalability and unintended consequences. At last, a change in professional identity formation is needed. It has traditionally been legal education in the adversarial, minimization of risk, reactive compliance mode. In the AI era particular mindsets are needed on the part of legal professionals invested in proactive, design-oriented thinking and working with technologists, ethicists and policymakers to develop systems which anticipate and avoid compliance failures before they occur. Nurturing skills in systems thinking, collaborative problem solving, design thinking, technological empathy among other traditional legal competencies are necessary.

AI and compliance are inevitable and a convergence. There is not only a need to adapt passively but also to solidify what this transformation brings to the fore in a manner that preserves central legal values: fairness, accountability, transparency, human dignity, and social justice. This chapter outlines solutions and recommendations that describe a roadmap forward to a future-forward legal profession and makes clear the interdependent power of education, innovation, ethics, governance, and collaboration to do so. It is a historic opportunity for legal education institutions, professional societies/organizations, and firms, as well as regulators and policymakers to stand up to this and launch efforts, with courage, creativity and with shared commitment to transform law's role in an AI society. This allows them to ensure that integration of AI to compliance, while making it more efficient, also reinforces the basic principles of legal systems themselves. This technological frontier is the trust, legitimacy and societal well-being we depend on it to work wisely and ethically.

FUTURE RESEARCH DIRECTIONS

Artificial intelligence is rapidly becoming integrated into legal practise and education, and must be considered in terms of research priorities, given that future professional are prepared for this new legal reality. This current literature has served to uncover regional disparities and strategic needs of integration for AI competencies in curricula, and there are several important areas for further research to be executed immediately. These domains encompass curriculum development, pedagogical innovation, technological assessment, regulatory compliance, ethical governance, and cross-disciplinary collaboration. The issue of developing the competence in AI literacy for legal education is a primary area for future inquiry. Although these guidelines are high level principles developed by the European Commission to guide ethical AI, there is a gap between principle and student education outcomes. Future research should investigate what particular knowledge, skills, and attitudes law students need to learn in order to navigate in the work environment with AI driven legal ecosystem. Through comparative studies of jurisdictions, best practices could be identified and frameworks that can be adapted and culturally sensitive that will work for different legal systems could be created. In line with the need to explore innovative pedagogical models to cultivate AI fluency competency among law students, there are close linkages with competency frameworks. The critical thinking, technological literacy, and ethical sensitivity needed for the AI era can largely be best cultivated in other ways than the traditional didactic. Future research should test the effects of learning methodologies involving AI, including AI driven moot courts, legal tech hackathons, as well as clinical programs with incorporation of AI tools. Value in understanding which approaches are most effective in promoting deep, transferable AI competencies can be derived from longitudinal studies tracking student outcomes across various pedagogies.

Concurrently, there should be prioritisation of the evaluation of the technological tools themselves. However, despite increases in the use of AI platforms in legal education with predictive analytics engines, automated research assistants, there is not much systematic analysis of the effects of AI in legal education. Further investigations are needed to not only evaluate functional accuracy and usability of these tools but also to examine whether and how using these tools impacts student learning and engagement, ethical reasoning, and career preparedness. Combinations of mixed methods, combining quantitative performance metrics with qualitative feedback from students and faculty, could provide a more nuanced picture of how technology is redefining legal education. A second important area of research concerns regulatory and compliance obstacles for introducing AI into the legal training. Native to this profession, legal educators will instruct students in conducting research across multiple source types: law and policy, case law, statutes, regulations, and precedents; analysing case findings based on presented facts; conducting legal analysis, including ethical and moral evaluation with respect to judgement; and using the legal skills needed to draught contracts domestically and internationally. Future research can also explore the integration of emerging and existing regulations, such as GDPR, AI Act (proposed in the European Union), and sector laws, in the existing curricula. Furthermore, empirical work could be conducted to see whether current educational programs for students are fitting them for the legal liability, data privacy issues and compliance responsibilities that come along with deploying AI. Ethical dimensions of AI integration in legal education also warrant extensive future exploration. The rise in algorithmic bias, transparency failure and dehumanisation of legal service with the advent of AI tools leads to an increase in the possibility of AI tools being used in the decision-making process. It is necessary to research how legal education teaches a strong ethical framework for future professionals to spot, vet and correct these hazards. When the AI comes into the legal questions, there could be rich area of empirical and theoretical inquiry in the development and evaluation of ethics modules focused specifically on AI related legal issues. In addition, law, philosophy, computer science and sociology, together with other disciplines, should investigate how ethical reasoning can be blended into technologically sophisticated curricula without interruption. Another area ripe for research holds the potential of the globalization of AI integrated legal education. With the growing trend towards transnational legal practise, future studies might embrace the international collaboration to harmonise AI competencies in the teaching in various regions. Few comparative research initiatives occurred to examine how both universities reacted to the issue of bias mitigation, AI explainability and algorithmic accountability. Additionally, further research can be conducted to examine the possibility and desirability of setting international standards for the AI literacy accreditation in law schools to make law graduates equipped to go out to the globalised AI-driven legal market.

Future research must also be subject to equity and inclusion. The risk is of recent inequalities within legal education and practise increasing existing inequalities through the digital divide. Individuals from underserved institutions or endorse communities may lack access to AI tools, Digital Infrastructure or unique Training. These disparities should be identified through research in order for it to prioritise identifying them and compelling interventions in such a way as to ensure that the benefits of integration of AI into legal education are equitably experienced. Closing these gaps may be possible through investigating models such as open source legal tech platforms, public private partnerships or government sponsored AI literacy programs. Psychological and cognitive impacts of AI on Law students should not be disregarded in future research, too. The more that AI automates the particular legal research and analysis tasks, the more students may lose the ability to reasoning critically, engaging in rigorous analysis and of solving problems. Retrospective analysis of how technology is advancing the core intellectual skills typically ascribed to legal education would be enhanced by longitudinal studies of cognitive skill development in AI-enhanced learning environments. Future studies must also focus on collaborative works based on interdisciplinary collaboration. To have effective AI integration in legal education, there needs to be discussions among ethicalists, educators, computer scientists, ethicists, lawyers, and policymakers. Fostering cross-sectoral and cross disciplinary partnership through research initiatives is likely to lead to more holistic, contextually rich and solution based on AI enabled legal education. Interdisciplinary research centres on legal informatics, AI ethics and digital law may help to accelerate innovation in this domain. Finally, future research agenda should focus on a development of robust assessment and evaluation methodologies. Legal education embedded with AI deeper may render that academic assessment increasingly unable to measure student competencies. Other research should develop and validate new ways to assess not only knowledge of the doctrine but also technologically fluency, ethical reasoning, data literacy, problem solving abilities in AI assisted legal contexts. Despite the dark stories I heard recounted on multiple occasions, the future of AI in legal education will only depend on an ambitious, multidimensional research agenda a proactive agenda instead of a reactive one. Legal education stands a good chance of leading this industry forward if they use the space to systematically give thought to, and address, competency development, pedagogical innovation, technology assessment, regulatory literacy, ethical governance, globalization, equity, cognitive impacts, interdisciplinary collaboration, and new assessment models. If we do not exercise patience in investing on this research, not only will future legal professionals be deprived; the legal systems that these people will be entrusted to uphold will also become less credible, less fair and less effective.

CONCLUSION

With the rapid advancement of artificial intelligence (AI), scholars, educators, policymakers, and practitioners are being compelled to re-imagine legal education and to prepare the next set of legal practitioners for realities that are newly imagined. The purpose of this chapter was to critically examine the myriad legal education – AI relationship and to introduce the necessity of AI education in legal curricula by being systematically and sustainably inserted in the formal curriculum. The chapter has argued that AI fusion is not just a technological mandate, but an overwhelming educational and ethical duty by way of an empirical analysis supported by theory of models and contemporary debate. From start to finish, a central argument is that proactive adaptation needs to be attempted. The goal is to view AI as an opportunity to enhance human capabilities, make justice accessible to more people, and to conceive of new ways of lawyering and lawyering services. Therefore, even moving beyond incremental improvements on the curriculum or isolated course offerings, it is necessary to conceive of a transformative reconceptualization of legal education itself. Whereas technological literacy, ethical judgment, critical thinking, interdisciplinary fluency, and adaptive expertise are becoming the hallmarks for legal professionals to thrive in an AI-driven future, law schools need to develop not just technological literacy but all these competencies.

This study also suggests one of the most vital pieces of insight to be derived is that AI education needs to have a firm theoretical and ethical foundation. The analysis of models that are used for examining technology adoption such as Diffusion of Innovation Theory and Technology Acceptance Model proved that technology adoption is not a simple process, but is mediated by the perception, values, norms or social structure. For this reason, AI must be integrated within legal education while being aware of questions of trust, agency and legitimacy. Since legal educators have an important role in shaping students' thinking and behaviour around AI tools, the challenges involved in enabling legal workers to become 'smart' by 'smart' machines should alert them to the need for legal workers who can critically evaluate AI tools, comprehend their limitations and biases, and advocate for legal technology that lends itself to ethical and fair use. Empirical analysis which involved the application of ANOVA methods also highlighted regional variations in the levels of AI integration efforts as highlighted in the findings. Though institutions are at different preparedness levels across regions, the variation in resources, regulatory context, cultural attitudes, and institutional leadership is the reason behind such disparity. Such a condition calls for context specific strategies that sense local problems, but also prompt for global talk as well as global collaboration. Local rooted legal education has to prepare students to work in a transnational, digitally linked legal world with global relevance of AI competences.

In addition, the chapter stressed that the AI integration was not a technological or administrative problem per se, it presents more profound pedagogical questions about what it means to educate a lawyer. Traditional legal education needed to change its epistemology and accommodate new epistemologies driven by data science, computational modeling, machine learning. Law students, moreover, need to not only read statutes and precedents, but also program, apply, analyze and work in interdisciplinary problem solving. Such requires great innovation in these facets of curriculum design, faculty development, institutional culture and assessment methodology. In particular, it showed that any AI integration strategy has to include ethical governance. When integrated into the legal domain, the risks of AI — algorithmic bias, opacity, privacy breaches, surveillance, unequal access — are some of the most acute risks of all, in that they can lead, to a very large extent, to decisions that determine rights, freedoms, and people's lives. Therefore, legal education has to inculcate in the students the deepest sense of ethical responsibility, critical scepticism and dedication to social justice. AI tools cannot be put to use, nor regulated, nor shaped, without those who will become the next generation of legal professionals having the ability, knowledge, and capacity to scrutinise, regulate, and shape them in ways that respect, and keep respect for, basic legal and democratic values. An important other dimension talked about was the role of interdisciplinary collaboration. To ready students for AI fed legal practice, law schools must bridge disciplinary silos used in preparation for new technologies and have the invite in computer science, data ethics, behavioral economics, sociology and political science. The holistic understanding is going to be fostered through interdisciplinary programs, joint degrees, cross listed courses and collaborative research initiatives. Because legal questions are so thoroughly bound up with technological, scientific and social complexities, law cannot remain insular.

At the same time the chapter recognised that systemic institutional reforms were required. To enable educators to establish an AI literacy, faculty development programmes need to be launched. Staying on the cutting edge requires infrastructure investments that make sure that students have lawful technologies at their disposal. The standards have to be updated by accreditation bodies in accord with competencies of AI. Initiatives that democratize education around AI, and the actions of policymakers that address the digital divide, are the key needs. Valuable though partnerships between the private and the public sectors are, they must be carefully so managed so that academic independence and public interest orientation are guaranteed. The research then looked into the future, determining which critical areas need to be further explored including standardized trust metrics of legal AI tools, longitudinal studies about the effect of AI education to the legal practice, design of ethical certification systems for legal AI applications, as well as comparative analysis of global best practices. This strongly signals that a vibrant and multidisciplinary as well as forward thinking research agenda is needed to evolve the legal education in the AI era. In total, the integration of AI into law school is a necessity, and not something that was to be dealt with at a later time. It must be pursued carefully, ethically and strategically, however. It is best approached neither as a technological upgrade which will fail to address inegalitarian trends, undermine professional standards and undermine trust in legal institutions, nor as just a matter of investment in existing structures. However, embracing AI as an opportunity to implement profound educational innovation and social renewal, AI can be useful for the realisation of the highest ideals of legal education: to produce not only skilled and knowledgeable, but also wise, just, and committed to the common good professionals. In the end, you'll decide what kind of lawyer to become more than anyone else can, and thus the kind of world that will accept law in its time to come will be the kind of world our education builds today. Legal educators are faced at a crossroads. The students, however, can decide to lay down to the passing of antiquated models that are not fit for any digital society, or they can lead a bold transformation which will prepare them how to navigate, critique and shape the AI revolution in pragmatism, integrity and humanity. Courage, creativity, collaboration, and an acorn to the principles of justice are required for the path forward. The word can't be stated strongly enough: the stakes couldn't be higher, and time's up.

REFERENCES

Akila, V., Prabhu, G., Akila, R., & Swadhi, R. (2025). Performance Metrics in Blockchain-Enabled AIML for Cognitive IoT in Large-Scale Networks: Optimizing Data Analytics for Enhanced Network Performance. In AI for Large Scale Communication Networks (pp. 265-288). IGI Global.

Ali, M.Enas Mohamed Ali Quteishat. (2024). Exploring the role of ai in modern legal practice: Opportunities, challenges, and ethical implications. J. *Electrical Systems*, *20*(6s), 3040–3050. DOI: 10.52783/jes.3320

Arockia, V. J., Vettriselvan, R., Rajesh, D., Velmurugan, P. R. R., & Cheelo, C. (2025). Leveraging AI and Learning Analytics for Enhanced Distance Learning: Transformation in Education. In AI and Learning Analytics in Distance Learning (pp. 179-206). IGI Global Scientific Publishing.

Aswathy, P. G., & Nair, V. (2024). Integrating Generative AI into Legal Education: From Casebooks to Code, Opportunities and Challenges. Law. *Technology and Humans*, *6*(3), 60–79. DOI: 10.5204/lthj.3640

Balan, A. (2025). *AI and Legal Education: Ethical and Sustainable Approaches*. Taylor & Francis. DOI: 10.4324/9781003607397

Banks, C. P. (2023). *The American legal profession: The myths and realities of practicing law*. Routledge. DOI: 10.4324/9781003122074

Brescia, R. H. (2020). Lessons from the present: Three crises and their potential impact on the legal profession. *Hofstra Law Review*, *49*, 607.

Brom, M. (2022). Legal Representation and the Metaverse: The Ethics of Practicing in Multiple Realities. DePaul Bus. &. *Comm. LJ*, *21*, 125.

Camelo, A. P., & Lucena, C. (2021). Elements of a strategic roadmap to legal education and accreditation in the digital environment. Technology, Innovation and Access to Justice, 229.

Dykstra, J. G. (2018). Beyond the" Practice Ready" Buzz: Sifting Through the Disruption of the Legal Industry to Divine the Skills Needed by New Attorneys. *Drexel L. Rev.*, *11*, 149.

Hammond, C. (1999). Teaching practical legal problem solving skills: Preparing law students for the realities of legal life. *Legal Educ. Rev.*, *10*(2), 191. DOI: 10.53300/001c.6122

Harankaha, M., & Thilakarathna, K. A. A. N. (2024). AI in Legal Education: Balancing Opportunities and Challenges in the Sri Lankan Context. Issue 6 Int'l JL Mgmt. &. *Human.*, *7*, 137.

Hull, H. G. (2013). Diversity in the legal profession: Moving from the rhetoric to reality. *Colum. J. Race & L.*, *4*, 1.

Kritzer, H. M. (1999). The professions are dead, long live the professions: Legal practice in a postprofessional world. *Law & Society Review*, *33*(3), 713–759. DOI: 10.2307/3115110

Margolis, E., & Murray, K. (2016). Using Information Literacy to Prepare Practice-Ready Graduates. *U. Haw. L. Rev.*, *39*, 1.

Maute, J. L. (2013). Facing 21st Century Realities. *Miss. CL Rev.*, *32*, 345.

Nadjia, M. (2024). The impact of artificial intelligence on legal systems: challenges and opportunities. Проблеми законності, (164), 285-303.

Ramaswamy, M. P.M.P.Ramaswamy. (2024). Evolving Norms Governing AI Engagement in Legal Practice and the Prospective Alignment of Law School Curriculum. *UCP Journal of Law & Legal Education*, *2*(2), 28–53. DOI: 10.24312/ucp-jlle.02.02.349

Remus, D., & Levy, F. (2017). Can robots be lawyers: Computers, lawyers, and the practice of law. *The Georgetown Journal of Legal Ethics*, *30*, 501.

Rhode, D. L. (2003). *In the interests of justice: Reforming the legal profession.* Oxford University Press.

Sanmartin, A. V., & Niemi, J. (2023). Virtual reality in legal education. Challenges and possibilities to transform normative knowledge. In *The European Digital Economy* (pp. 120–140). Routledge. DOI: 10.4324/9781003450160-10

Scott, C. (2012). Collaborating with the real world: Opportunities for developing skills and values in law teaching. *Ind. Health L. Rev.*, *9*(2), 411. DOI: 10.18060/16614

Shanthi, H. J., Gokulakrishnan, A., Sharma, S., Deepika, R., & Swadhi, R. (2025). Leveraging Artificial Intelligence for Enhancing Urban Health: Applications, Challenges, and Innovations. In Nexus of AI, Climatology, and Urbanism for Smart Cities (pp. 275-306). IGI Global Scientific Publishing.

Sujatha, R., Aarthy, S. L., & Vettriselvan, R. (2021). *Integrating Deep Learning Algorithms to Overcome Challenges in Big Data Analytics.* CRC Press. DOI: 10.1201/9781003038450

Sullivan, W. M., Colby, A., Wegner, J. W., Bond, L., & Shulman, L. S. (2007). *Educating lawyers: Preparation for the profession of law* (Vol. 2). John Wiley & Sons.

Thanaraj, A., De Freitas, S., Chaplin, D., Gledhill, K., Unger, A., & Kennedy, R. (2022). Introduction: Exploring becoming future ready. In Teaching Legal Education in the Digital Age (pp. 1-15). Routledge.

Venice, J. A., Arivazhagan, D., Suman, N., Shanthi, H. J., & Swadhi, R. (2025). Recommendation Systems and Content Personalization: Algorithms, Applications, and Adaptive Learning. In AI for Large Scale Communication Networks (pp. 323-348). IGI Global.

Vettriselvan, R., Deepan, A., Garg, P. K., Suresh, N. V., & Velmurugan, P. R. (2025). Advanced Text Analysis, Simplification, Classification, and Synthesis Techniques: Leveraging AI for Enhanced Medical Education. In Using AI Tools in Text Analysis, Simplification, Classification, and Synthesis (pp. 37-66). IGI Global Scientific Publishing.

Weber-Lewerenz, B. (2021). Corporate digital responsibility (CDR) in construction engineering ethical guidelines for the application of digital transformation and artificial intelligence (AI) in user practice. *SN Applied Sciences*, *3*(10), 1–25. DOI: 10.1007/s42452-021-04776-1

Zafar, A. (2024). Balancing the scale: Navigating ethical and practical challenges of artificial intelligence (AI) integration in legal practices. *Discover Artificial Intelligence*, *4*(1), 27. DOI: 10.1007/s44163-024-00121-8

KEY TERMS AND DEFINITIONS

AI Ethics: A field concerned with the moral implications and societal impacts of artificial intelligence. In legal education, AI ethics encompasses topics such as algorithmic bias, transparency, accountability, data privacy, and the equitable use of AI in law.

Artificial Intelligence (AI): A division of computer science that involves making systems able to do things that normally need human intelligence such as reasoning, learning, problem solving, perception, natural language understanding. AI tools in legal education include the ones that can do legal research, predictive analytics, contract review, decision support, etc.

Compliance Automation: Use of AI based technologies to monitor, enforce and ensure compliance with legal, standards and ethical norms in the organizations. Compliance automation in the legal domain is used to enable firms to efficiently and accurately work in the complex regulatory environment.

Data Privacy and Protection: Legal and ethical principles governing the collection, storage, and use of personal data. In the age of AI, ensuring data privacy in legal practice and education is critical to maintaining client confidentiality, regulatory compliance, and public trust.

Digital Transformation in Legal Education: The adoption and integration of digital technologies, including AI, into legal teaching, learning, administration, and research. Digital transformation redefines pedagogical approaches, curriculum design, skill development, and professional identity formation in legal academia.

Legal Technology (LegalTech): The application of technology and software to provide legal services and support the legal industry. LegalTech solutions range from document automation and e-discovery tools to AI-powered contract analysis and virtual courtrooms.

Predictive Analytics in Law: The use of statistical techniques and AI models to forecast legal outcomes, identify case patterns, assess risks, and support decision-making processes. Predictive analytics is increasingly integrated into compliance, litigation strategy, and regulatory risk assessment.

Regulatory Technology (RegTech): Technologies designed to help organizations comply with regulatory requirements more efficiently. In the legal context, RegTech uses AI, blockchain, and data analytics to automate tasks such as compliance monitoring, reporting, and risk management.

Chapter 7
Beyond Text:
Evaluating Large Language Models Through Law, Culture, and Religion in Saudi Arabia

Loujayn Alhokail
https://orcid.org/0009-0003-8864-4205
King Saud University, Saudi Arabia

ABSTRACT

Rapid advancements in artificial intelligence have created new opportunities in legal education. Large language models (LLMs) such as ChatGPT, ChatGPT-4o, and DeepSeek V3 are increasingly used by students; however, concerns about their accuracy, reliability, and cultural sensitivity—particularly in areas such as family law—remain significant. This study evaluates these LLMs within the framework of Saudi Arabia's family law, which is rooted in Islamic Shari'a. By assessing their responses to 100 questions across four key categories—foundational knowledge, direct questions, legal advice, and textual analysis—the research offers insights into their accuracy in relation to codified law, culture, and religion. Results show that ChatGPT-4o outperformed the other models, yet all exhibited significant short-comings in applying statutory provisions and accounting for cultural and religious factors. These findings underscore that while LLMs can enhance legal education, their use must be guided by expert oversight to ensure nuanced understanding within complex legal systems.

DOI: 10.4018/979-8-3373-3451-6.ch007

INTRODUCTION

Large language models (LLMs) such as ChatGPT,[1] ChatGPT-4o,[2] and DeepSeek V3[3] are increasingly used by students to transform their educational experience (e.g., personalized education, access to private tutoring, help with assignments, and immediate access to information; Chu et al., 2025; Paustian & Slinger, 2024; Wang & Fan, 2025). The integration of artificial intelligence (AI) into the legal field has brought transformative changes to how legal information is accessed and disseminated (Seabrooke et al., 2024). With their ability to generate responses instantly based on vast datasets, these models offer exciting opportunities to enhance legal education and broaden access to legal information. Yet, their use in specialized legal systems—particularly those rooted in religious law and culture—raises critical questions about accuracy and reliability.

Saudi Arabia presents a compelling case for evaluating the educational potential of LLMs in legal education. Its legal system is built on a hybrid foundation: codified legislation, such as the Personal Status Law (2022), rooted in Islamic jurisprudence (Shari'a), coexisting with cultural norms. Legal interpretation in this context requires more than textual recall—it demands doctrinal alignment, historical awareness, and sensitivity to cultural variation across regions and communities. As a result, legal education in Saudi Arabia emphasizes the ability to navigate jurisprudential diversity and context-specific reasoning.

This study investigates the performance of three untrained LLMs—ChatGPT, ChatGPT-4o, and DeepSeek V3—in answering 100 legal questions focused on Saudi family law. It assesses each model's output across four dimensions essential to legal education: foundational legal knowledge, direct legal questions, scenario-based legal advice, and textual analysis. By comparing the models' responses to the actual texts and interpretive frameworks of Saudi law—rooted in both codified statutes and Shari'a—and considering the cultural contexts in which these laws operate, the study sheds light on the challenges and opportunities of AI-assisted legal learning. In doing so, this chapter contributes to the emerging discussion about responsibly integrating AI into legal education, particularly within systems deeply shaped by cultural norms and Islamic jurisprudence.

LITERATURE REVIEW: LLMS, LAW, CULTURE, AND RELIGION

The rapid integration of LLMs into educational and professional domains has sparked a growing body of academic research exploring their capabilities, limitations, and implications. In the context of legal education and practice, LLMs have been proposed as tools for enhancing access to legal information, supporting personalized learning, and automating basic legal reasoning tasks. However, the complex, localized, and interpretive nature of law—and its relationship to culture and religion—raises important questions about the accuracy, reliability, and ethical use of these technologies.

To answer these questions, scholars have studied the application of AI in the legal field from several angles, including the use of LLMs in legal education (Chu et al., 2025), LLMs as artificial lawyers (Tan et al., 2023), and LLMs as legal translators (Ait Elfqih & Monti, 2024). Other studies have aimed to assess the accuracy of LLMs in specialized legal fields, including education law (Thomas et al., 2023) and family law (Ryan & Hardie, 2024). The results of these studies reveal similar challenges. Ryan and Hardie (2024) reported significant errors and inaccuracies in the responses generated. Tan and Benyekhlef (2023, p. 6) noted that ChatGPT "occasionally generates 'hallucinations' in the legal field." Thomas et al. (2023) found that while LLMs can support educators' understanding of legal principles, they are not a substitute for human expertise. Similarly, Chu et al. (2025, p. 7) observed that "LLMs struggle with legal knowledge application and judicial aid," highlighting the need for "significant improvements to effectively assist in complex legal tasks."

The unreliability and misinformation highlighted by previous scholars raise important questions about how AI companies are addressing these challenges. According to Baldassarre et al. (2024), efforts by AI companies to combat misinformation are ongoing and evolving, demonstrating a sustained commitment to enhancing the accuracy, reliability, and trustworthiness of their systems. In their article titled "Fostering Human Rights in Responsible AI: A Systematic Review for Best Practices in Industry," Baldassarre et al. (2024) analyze the practices of four leading AI companies—OpenAI, Meta AI Research, Google AI, and Microsoft AI—examining their strengths, weaknesses, and best practices across several critical areas, including their approaches to misinformation. Among the notable strengths, the authors highlight the collaborative efforts between AI companies, domain experts, and governments to address the challenges posed by misinformation and to promote responsible AI use. However, they also observe that these initiatives are predominantly concentrated in Europe and the Global North, underscoring a geographic imbalance that leaves many regions—particularly in the Global South—with less robust engagement in shaping AI governance and standards.

AI studies from the Global South emphasize the critical need for collaboration with AI companies to ensure that cultural and social diversities within these countries are thoughtfully addressed (Altamimi, 2025; Anuyah et al., 2023; Ubanyionwu, 2024). In "Cultural Considerations in AI Systems for the Global South: A Systematic Review," Anuyah et al. (2023, p. 126) argue that "in a globalized world, products cross borders, making it necessary to incorporate culturally sensitive designs to ensure appropriateness and inclusivity for users from diverse cultural backgrounds."

Similarly, in "Ethical and Cultural Considerations in Artificial Intelligence (AI) Application to Customary Law," Josephat Ubanyionwu (2024, p. 145) highlights Nigeria's complex socio-cultural landscape, noting that "the challenge lies in ensuring that AI systems are tailored to accommodate these cultural distinctions without imposing a uniform interpretation of the law." The issue of cultural sensitivity also emerges in the context of Saudi Arabia. For instance, in "Unlocking Potential: Saudi EFL Male Students' Perspectives on AI Tools for Enhancing English Writing Proficiency," Dheifallah Altamimi (2025) explores the unique cultural and social challenges faced by Saudi students in adopting AI technologies. Collectively, these studies underscore the need for AI systems to be designed with cultural sensitivity in mind, reinforcing Anuyah et al.'s (2023) call for more inclusive, context-aware approaches that respect the diverse realities of users across different regions.

The relationship between law and culture has long been the subject of rich scholarly debate. In her influential 1990 work *Getting Justice and Getting Even*, Sally Engle Merry argues that the inherent ambiguity and inconsistency of the law create spaces for interpretation and contestation, enabling us to see law not merely as a system of rules but as meaning constructed through communities' legal consciousness, identities, and everyday practices. Merry (1990) describes this consciousness as "the way people conceive of the 'natural' and normal way of doing things, their habitual patterns of talk and action, and their commonsense understanding of the world" (p. 5). Similarly, in the 1998 *The Common Place of Law*, Patricia Ewick and Susan Silbey contend that law is not simply a force that shapes social action but is itself a form of social action, inseparable from the cultural contexts in which it operates. Extending this idea, Naomi Mezey, in her 2003 work "Law as Culture," proposes three ways to conceptualize the relationship: by uncovering the silent power of law within culture; by emphasizing how cultural forces shape legal institutions and decisions; or by dissolving the distinction altogether to see law and culture as fundamentally intertwined. These perspectives collectively highlight why cultural considerations are crucial in AI design—especially for systems intended to deliver legal guidance—so that they reflect the interplay between law and local cultural understandings.

In the Saudi context, cultural considerations are deeply intertwined with religious considerations. Saudi Arabia grounds its legal system in Shari'a, as established by the Basic Law of Governance (1992). Drawing on Abdullahi An Na'im's (1996) definition, Shari'a can be understood as "a product of a process of interpretation of, and logical derivation from, the text of the Quran and Sunna and other traditions" (p. 11). The primary sources of Shari'a—the Quran (the holy book of Muslims) and the Sunna (the acts and sayings of the Prophet Mohammad [SAWS])—were developed over the period of the Prophet Mohammad's (SAWS) message of Islam, from 610 AD until his death in 632 AD (Rahman, 2002). Scholars believe that the legislative component of the Quran is limited; out of 6,236 verses, fewer than 500 contain legal material (Abu-Zayd, 2013). Beginning in the 8th century, diverse juristic methodologies led to the formation of four major Sunni schools of thought: Hanafi, Hanbali, Shafi'i, and Maliki (Ahmed, 1991). Differences in interpretation across—and sometimes even within—these schools have resulted in a rich plurality of views on legal issues (Zedan, 1993). This underscores the danger of generalizing cultural or religious practices, even among Islamic countries. As Lila Abu-Lughod (2013) puts it, "generalizing about cultures prevents us from appreciating or even accounting for people's experiences and the contingencies with which we all live" (p.6). Thus, designing AI systems to navigate legal questions in such contexts requires careful sensitivity not only to statutory text but also to the layered cultural and doctrinal landscapes in which these laws are embedded.

This literature review highlights the multifaceted challenges of integrating AI into legal education contexts, emphasizing three interwoven dimensions: codified law, culture, and religion—or, in the context of this research, Shari'a. Legally, studies underscore LLMs' limitations in accurately applying legal knowledge, handling localized laws, and providing reliable judicial support, raising ethical concerns about misinformation. Culturally, researchers caution that AI systems risk overlooking diverse social norms and legal consciousness, particularly in non-Western contexts such as Nigeria and Saudi Arabia, where culturally insensitive AI design could misinterpret customary practices or educational needs. This intersects critically with Shari'a, as Saudi Arabia's legal system is grounded in Islamic jurisprudence derived from the Quran and Sunnah, interpreted through diverse historical schools of thought. The literature thus reveals that effective deployment of LLMs necessitates not only technical advances but also deep sensitivity to the interplay between law as formal rules, the law as embedded cultural practice, and the specific interpretive frameworks of Shari'a that resist broad generalization across Islamic societies.

This chapter builds on prior research into the use of LLMs in legal education by extending the evaluation of three models—ChatGPT, ChatGPT-4o, and DeepSeek V3—into the context of Saudi family law, which is deeply rooted in Shari'a and codified through national statutes such as the Saudi Personal Status Law. By situating this analysis within Saudi Arabia's unique socio-legal landscape, where law, culture, and religion are tightly interwoven, this chapter localizes existing discussions on AI in legal domains. It highlights how LLMs must navigate the interpretive and pluralistic nature of law. In doing so, this work contributes to the broader literature by emphasizing the critical importance of cultural and doctrinal sensitivity in using AI for legal tasks, underscoring that effective integration requires more than technical proficiency—it demands deep engagement with the intertwined dimensions of law, culture, and religion that characterize many legal systems around the world.

LEGAL BACKGROUND: FAMILY LAW IN SAUDI ARABIA

Saudi Arabia follows a civil law system in which all legislation is derived from Shari'a principles (Basic Law of Governance, 1992). Prior to March 9, 2022, there was no codified family law in Saudi Arabia (Personal Status Law, 2022). Instead, Shari'a served as the primary source for regulating family relationships such as marriage, divorce, and child custody. Certain family matters were governed by definitive provisions in terms of their authenticity and meaning, which judges relied upon to issue rulings. However, many issues involved differing opinions among various Sunni schools of Shari'a—Hanbali, Shafi'i, Maliki, and Hanafi—and sometimes even within the same school, leading to diverse interpretations of the same issue (Zedan, 1993). For example, multiple juristic opinions govern child custody after divorce: Hanafi scholars prioritize the mother, then the maternal grandmother, and then the paternal grandmother; Shafi'i scholars place the mother first, followed by maternal grandmothers, the father, and then the paternal grandmother; while Maliki scholars give priority to the mother, then the maternal grandmothers, and then the mother's aunts (Zedan, 1993). Judges derived their rulings from the four main Sunni schools of Sahri'a and exercised discretion in choosing one jurisprudential opinion over another based on the specifics of the case (Ministry of Justice, 2013).

The lack of unified legal texts regulating family relationships posed significant challenges, the most notable being inconsistency in judicial rulings. Decisions in family disputes varied depending on the jurisprudential opinions followed by individual judges, making judicial outcomes unpredictable (Ministry of Justice, 2013). This inconsistency hindered individuals from clearly understanding their rights and obligations in family relationships. Consequently, a need emerged to codify jurisprudential rulings on personal status matters to ensure uniformity, stability, and predictability in family law (Saudi Press Agency, 2021). The codification process aimed to rely on accredited Sunni Shari'a references, selecting a unified opinion for each issue while also considering contemporary societal changes and translating these rulings into legal provisions.

On March 9, 2022, the Personal Status Law was issued by Royal Decree No. M/73, marking the first comprehensive legislation to regulate family relations in Saudi Arabia. The law consists of 252 articles divided into eight chapters: Marriage; Effects of the Marriage Contract; Separation Between Spouses; Effects of Separation Between Spouses; Guardianship and Trusteeship; The Absent and Missing; The Will, Estate, and Inheritance; and Final Provisions (Personal Status Law, 2022).

The provisions within the system can be categorized into two types: mandatory and supplementary (Albudairat, 2023). Mandatory provisions are non-negotiable and cannot be overridden by agreement. For instance, a marriage without two witnesses is deemed invalid regardless of mutual consent. Supplementary provisions allow for agreements that differ from the default law. For example, parents may agree to grant child custody to the father or adopt shared custody arrangements contrary to the law's default, which prioritizes the mother (Personal Status Law, 2022). To encourage spousal agreement, a mandatory reconciliation period is enforced before transferring the case to a judge (The Executive Regulations of the Law of Civil Proceedings, 2014).

Although the Personal Status Law serves as the primary legal framework for regulating family matters, it is not wholly sufficient on its own. Certain articles reference other sources, such as Shari'a. For example, Article 251 of the Personal Status Law (2022) states: "In matters not explicitly addressed in this law, the most relevant Islamic Shari'a provisions consistent with the system's preferences shall apply." Other articles reference customary law. For example, Article 3 of the Personal Status Law (2022) states: "All items exchanged between the betrothed during engagement are considered gifts unless explicitly stated as a dowry or customary practice deems them part of the dowry."

Additionally, the Personal Status Law is integrated with other Saudi laws, such as the Child Protection Law (2014), Protection from Abuse Law (2013), Civil Procedures Law (2013), Enforcement Law (2012), and Evidence Law (2021). This interconnected legal structure ensures a comprehensive and cohesive approach to regulating family relationships and addressing related disputes. For instance, Article 42 of the Personal Status Law (2022) states several spousal rights, including: "Neither party shall cause physical or emotional harm to the other." The Protection from Abuse Law (2013) establishes a clear legal definition of spousal abuse and outlines the procedures for reporting, investigating, and addressing such cases within the judicial system. The Civil Procedures Law (2013) establishes the procedural mechanisms necessary for pursuing family court decisions. The Evidence Law (2021) plays a critical role in determining the admissibility and weight of proof in family-related cases, further supporting fairness and due process. The Enforcement Law (2012) contains procedures for enforcing a court decision; for example, how to proceed when one party fails to voluntarily comply with a child custody ruling.

One important aspect to highlight is the existence of alternative legal procedures for the non-Sunni and non-Muslim population. Even though the majority of Saudis are Sunni Muslims, there is a Saudi Shia minority who take their cases to the Jaafari court, which applies laws stemming from the Shia schools of thought that differ from the four Sunni schools (Al-Harz, 2021). In addition, according to 2024 statistics, 44.4% of the population in Saudi Arabia are non-Saudis who come from diverse legal, religious, and cultural backgrounds (General Authority for Statistics, 2025). Article 8 of the Personal Status Law (2022) recognizes religious diversity by providing alternative ways to document marriage for non-Muslims.

In sum, this research uses the term *family law* to encompass three interrelated dimensions. The first is the body of codified laws, with primary emphasis on the Personal Status Law, alongside other complementary statutes that collectively regulate family matters. The second is the cultural dimension, which includes prevailing social norms as well as considerations necessary to account for the diverse experiences of non-Sunni and non-Muslim populations within Saudi Arabia. The third is Shari'a, which forms the foundational legal framework underpinning the country's entire family law system. This multidimensional approach reflects insights from the literature review that highlight the inseparability of formal laws, cultural practices, and religious jurisprudence in shaping how family law operates in practice.

METHODS

This chapter aims to evaluate the accuracy of three untrained LLMs—ChatGPT, ChatGPT-4o, and DeepSeek V3—in providing legal answers to questions related to family matters. Family law is the central theme of the questions, and this area of law was chosen for several reasons. First, family law is a mandatory course for first-year law students across the Kingdom of Saudi Arabia (e.g., King Abdulaziz University, 2024; King Saud University, 2025; Prince Sultan University, 2025). Second, the Personal Status Law (2022) is relatively new, which enables an assessment of the LLMs' ability to reference recently codified law. Third, it is a body of law derived from a broader legal system—Shari'a—allowing for an analysis of the LLMs' performance on both statutory and doctrinal levels. Fourth, because the law is deeply intertwined with culture, applying it requires not only legal knowledge but also cultural awareness. Fifth, the Personal Status Law includes both mandatory and supplementary provisions, which allows for an evaluation of the models' ability to distinguish between the two.

The assessment tests each of the three models using 100 questions distributed across the four key categories described below.

Foundational Legal Knowledge

This section includes 25 questions designed to assess the LLMs' understanding of fundamental aspects of Saudi family law. For example:

- Which Saudi law includes legal provisions on marriage and divorce?
- Can you provide the text of Article 1 of the Saudi Personal Status Law?
- How many articles are included in the Saudi Child Protection Law?

Direct Legal Questions

This section consists of 25 questions focusing on the LLMs' accuracy in answering direct legal questions. The aim is to evaluate their familiarity with specific legal provisions and definitions. Example questions include:

- What is the definition of divorce in the Saudi Personal Status Law?
- What is the difference between divorce and *khul'*?
- What is the punishment for child abuse under Saudi law?

Legal Advice

This section includes 25 questions intended to test the LLMs' ability to provide simple legal advice based on hypothetical scenarios. The questions simulate real-life queries, such as:

- My husband divorced me while he was very angry. Does this divorce count under Saudi law?
- I have custody of my children. Can I travel with them outside the Kingdom without their father's consent?
- A man was engaged to a woman and gave her $10,000 as a gift during the engagement. He later broke off the engagement. Does he have the right to ask for the money back?

Textual Analysis

The final 25 questions aim to measure the LLMs' ability to analyze legal text accurately. These questions assess their capacity to interpret, explain, or provide examples of legal provisions. For example:

- Can you explain the following legal text (…)?
- Can you provide examples related to the following legal provision (…)?

This structured methodology provides a robust framework for evaluating the performance of LLMs across multiple dimensions within the context of family law disputes under Saudi law. By analyzing how these models demonstrate foundational knowledge, define key legal principles, offer practical legal advice, and interpret legal text, the assessment captures the multifaceted nature of legal problem-solving. Each dimension represents a crucial pillar of legal education, reflecting the core competencies that law students must master to navigate complex legal systems effectively and ethically. Moreover, by assessing LLMs through these dimensions, the methodology provides a more nuanced understanding of their capacity to address the interplay between codified law, cultural norms, and Shari'a, highlighting not only their current limitations but also their potential value as complementary tools in legal education.

RESULTS

One hundred questions were posed to each of the three LLMs—ChatGPT, ChatGPT-4o, and DeepSeek V3—to evaluate their accuracy in providing legal information. The performance comparison across the four categories shows that ChatGPT-4o achieved the highest overall accuracy at 56%, followed by ChatGPT at 40%, and DeepSeek V3 at 18%. The results also reveal notable differences in performance across the four tested categories.

Foundational Legal Knowledge

This category included 25 questions designed to test the LLMs' foundational understanding of Saudi family law. ChatGPT-4o answered 15 questions correctly, resulting in an accuracy rate of 60%. ChatGPT answered nine questions correctly, achieving an accuracy rate of 36%. DeepSeek V3 answered only one question correctly, yielding an accuracy rate of 4%.

Direct Legal Questions

This section focused on direct legal questions to test the LLMs' knowledge of specific legal provisions and definitions. ChatGPT-4o performed slightly better than the other two models, answering four questions correctly for an accuracy rate of 16%. ChatGPT answered two out of 25 questions correctly, resulting in an 8% accuracy rate. DeepSeek V3 did not answer any questions correctly, yielding an accuracy rate of 0%.

Legal Advice

To assess the LLMs' ability to offer practical legal advice, 25 scenario-based questions were posed. ChatGPT-4o answered 14 questions correctly, with an accuracy rate of 56%. ChatGPT answered 12 questions correctly, achieving an accuracy rate of 48%. DeepSeek V3 answered two questions accurately, yielding an accuracy rate of 8%.

Textual Analysis

This category tested the LLMs' capacity to interpret and analyze legal text through 25 questions. ChatGPT-4o performed strongest, answering 23 questions accurately and achieving an accuracy rate of 92%. ChatGPT answered 17 questions correctly, yielding an accuracy rate of 68%. DeepSeek V3 answered 15 questions correctly, with an accuracy rate of 60%.

Table 1 summarizes the comparative accuracy of ChatGPT, ChatGPT-4o, and DeepSeek V3 across all four categories.

Table 1. Performance Comparison of ChatGPT, ChatGPT-4o, and DeepSeek V3 in Legal Accuracy Across Key Categories

	ChatGPT-4o	ChatGPT	DeepSeek V3
Overall accuracy	**56%**	**40%**	**18%**
Foundational legal knowledge	60%	36%	4%
Direct legal questions	16%	8%	0%
Legal advice	56%	48%	8%
Textual analysis	92%	68%	60%

The results indicate that while all models exhibit limitations in accurately providing legal information, ChatGPT-4o consistently outperforms both ChatGPT and DeepSeek V3 across all categories, particularly in textual analysis. This suggests that ChatGPT-4o is better suited for tasks involving legal reasoning and interpretation. Notably, one factor contributing to DeepSeek's lower performance is its tendency to generate highly detailed responses, even when prompted to be concise. This verbosity increased the likelihood of errors compared to the more focused outputs from the ChatGPT models. If DeepSeek V3 were evaluated solely on the core correctness of its answers—without penalizing the additional, error-prone details—its overall accuracy would have been 36% rather than 18%.

For example, when asked, "A man divorced his wife while he was drunk. Does the divorce take effect under Saudi law?" DeepSeek began its answer correctly by stating:

Under Saudi law (according to the Personal Status Law issued in 1443 AH—2022 AD), a divorce issued by someone who has lost their mental capacity by choice (even through the use of prohibited substances) is considered invalid, because a fundamental condition for divorce is full legal capacity (sound mind and free will).

However, the model continued by providing examples and legal advice, such as:

Legal Advice:

- If such a situation occurs:
    - o Do not leave the home until a ruling is issued declaring the divorce invalid.
    - o File a case in court and provide medical evidence.
    - o It is advisable to avoid divorce during moments of anger or under the influence of substances.

This legal advice is inaccurate and is not supported by any legal text in Saudi Arabia. Under Article 80 of the Personal Status Law, if a drunk man divorces his wife, the divorce is automatically invalid without requiring any legal action, provided the divorce was not legally filed. However, according to Article 82 of the law, if the divorce is legally filed, it is valid and cannot be invalidated (Personal Status Law, 2022).

In summary, the results reveal significant disparities in the performance of the three evaluated LLMs across the four key categories. ChatGPT-4o consistently outperformed both ChatGPT and DeepSeek V3, achieving the highest overall accuracy, most notably excelling in textual analysis with a 92% accuracy rate. However, despite these relative strengths, all models displayed substantial limitations, particularly in addressing direct legal questions and offering practical legal advice, often introducing inaccuracies or fabricated details. These results align with findings from previous scholars whose work was reviewed (Chu et al., 2025; Ryan & Hardie, 2024; Tan et al., 2023; Thomas et al., 2023). DeepSeek's notably lower performance was partly due to its verbose answers, which, while attempting to be thorough, created more room for errors. This highlights the nuanced challenges of evaluating AI-generated legal outputs, where more content does not necessarily translate into greater accuracy. These findings underscore both the potential and the current shortcomings of LLMs in handling Saudi family law, setting the stage for a deeper qualitative analysis of how these models navigate the intertwined dimensions of law, culture, and Shari'a, and what this means for their role in legal education.

ANALYSIS OF THE RESULTS THROUGH THE LENS OF LAW, CULTURE, AND SHARI'A

The literature review revealed three main themes that shape the focus of this analysis. First, LLMs show persistent inaccuracies in the legal domain. Prior studies demonstrate that these models frequently generate fabricated or misleading legal content, which poses significant risks in contexts where precision and trustworthiness are paramount (Chu et al., 2025; Ryan & Hardie, 2024; Tan et al., 2023; Thomas et al., 2023). Second, cultural considerations are critically important, especially in culturally rich and complex societies like Saudi Arabia, where social norms, values, and lived experiences deeply influence how legal systems are understood and navigated (Altamimi, 2025; Anuyah et al., 2023; Ubanyionwu, 2024). Third, a complex relationship exists between law and Shari'a in Saudi Arabia. Islamic jurisprudence not only underpins statutory laws such as the Saudi Personal Status Law but also embodies diverse interpretive traditions that resist uniform codification across Islamic countries (Abu-Lughod, 2013; Ahmed, 1991; Zedan, 1993). This framework guides the analysis and offers a lens to assess both the capabilities and limitations of using LLMs in legal education. In each of these themes, the discussion addresses both challenges and opportunities.

LLMs and Codified Law

Analyzing the results through the lens of codified law reveals four challenges that LLMs face. The first challenge is their limited ability to cite codified laws accurately. This issue was most apparent in the "foundational legal knowledge" category, where LLMs were asked questions that required referencing specific statutes or citing exact legal provisions. Although all three models correctly identified the Personal Status Law as the legislation governing marriage and divorce in Saudi Arabia, their ability to retrieve or accurately cite particular articles from the law was limited. For example, when asked, "What is Article 1 of the Saudi Personal Status Law?" the responses were as follows:

ChatGPT

> The text of Article 1 of the Saudi Personal Status Law states:
> *"This law aims to regulate personal status matters, organize family relations, protect family rights, and ensure its stability, in accordance with the provisions of Islamic Shari'a."*

ChatGPT-4o

> The text of Article 1 of the Saudi Personal Status Law is:
> *"This system aims to regulate family provisions, clarify the rights and duties of its members, facilitate the means of achieving justice, and ensure the application of Islamic Shari'a rulings in matters of personal status."*
> If you need an interpretation or a detailed explanation of this article or any other provision of the law, feel free to request it.

DeepSeek V3

Text of Article 1 of the Saudi Personal Status Law (issued by Royal Decree No. M/73 dated 19/9/1443 AH—2022 CE):

> *"The provisions of this law shall apply to personal status matters stipulated therein, in accordance with the rulings of Islamic Shari'a derived from the Quran and Sunnah, and the preferred opinions of Sunni jurisprudential schools as determined by the Supreme Judicial Council."*

Article 1 of the Saudi Arabian Personal Status Law (2022)

The actual Article 1 of the law states: "Engagement is the request for marriage and a promise to marry." The text provided by all three models does not correspond to any article within the Saudi legal system.

Additionally, the LLMs were given specific legal articles and asked to identify their source. For example, they were asked, "Can you provide me with the law that contains this text?" followed by the text of Article 23 of the Child Protection Law, which states the penalties for child abuse. All models incorrectly identified the Protection from Abuse Law as the source of the quoted article. While this law does exist within the Saudi legal framework, it outlines a different set of penalties than those stated in the Child Protection Law.

These responses underscore the limitations of LLMs in accurately referencing specific legal provisions or identifying their authoritative sources. While LLMs can generate fluent, persuasive text, this text is often fabricated. Moreover, they struggle to pinpoint the exact articles, statutes, or regulations that form the backbone of a legal system. This limitation is especially problematic for students studying law in a civil law jurisdiction such as Saudi Arabia, where codified laws and precisely formulated legal articles are paramount. In such systems, written law serves as the foundation for constructing well-reasoned, persuasive legal arguments, ensuring that analysis rests on a solid base of recognized legal norms. Without this capability, students risk grounding their arguments in vague generalities rather than in the specific, binding provisions that determine legal outcomes in practice.

The second challenge revealed by the analysis relates to the rapidly evolving nature of the law. In 2024, Saudi Arabia witnessed the publication of 16 new laws and regulations, the cancellation of four laws, the amendment of 35 articles, the repeal of seven articles, and the addition of two new articles to existing legislation (Qanoniah, 2024). Most recently, and closely related to the Personal Status Law, the implementing regulations of that law were issued in 2025 (Personal Status Law Regulations, 2025).

LLMs' ability to recognize legal reforms was tested in the "foundational legal knowledge" category, where the models were asked about the date the Social Security Law was issued. ChatGPT answered 2006, ChatGPT-4o answered 2000, and DeepSeek answered 2016. ChatGPT-4o's response referred to the outdated 2000 law, which was canceled with the issuance of the new Social Security Law in 2020, while the answers from ChatGPT and DeepSeek were inaccurate.

When asked about a new article introduced to the Child Protection Law (Article 23 bis), ChatGPT-4o was the only model able to provide the full, accurate text. DeepSeek fabricated an article, while ChatGPT responded:

> *Sorry, I cannot provide you with the full text of Article 23 (bis) of the Saudi Child Protection Law, as the complete text is not available in my data. However, you can refer to the Child Protection Law issued in 1436 AH (2014 AD) to obtain the exact text of the article through official sources or Saudi legal platforms.*

For law students, staying up to date with the evolving nature of legislation is essential. Legal education is not static; it must prepare students to operate within a dynamic legal environment where laws are regularly amended, repealed, or newly introduced to address changing social, economic, and political realities. Failure to stay informed about current legal developments can lead to outdated understanding, misapplication of legal principles, and ultimately flawed legal reasoning. Students must learn how to monitor and verify legal updates, and as discussed above, LLMs are not reliable tools for this task.

The third challenge is the LLMs' limited ability to reference complementary laws. Resolving family disputes requires knowledge not only of the Personal Status Law but also of other relevant Saudi laws, such as the Child Protection Law (2014), Protection from Abuse Law (2013), Elderly Rights and Care Law (2022), Rights of Persons with Disabilities Law (2023), Civil Procedures Law (2013), Enforcement Law (2012), and Evidence Law (2021). Law students are expected to understand how these laws interact and complement one another. It was particularly noticeable—especially in the "legal advice" category—that ChatGPT and ChatGPT-4o generally did not reference these complementary laws when responding to family dispute questions. DeepSeek, on the other hand, attempted to provide more detailed guidance on legal procedures, including how to proceed to court and how to prove the case. However, it became clear that, first, the model failed to reference the relevant laws by name—for instance, discussing how to present evidence without citing the Evidence Law or any of its provisions. Second, as discussed earlier, the model's tendency to provide excessive detail ultimately contributed to its lower performance score of 18%, compared to the other two models.

This shortcoming has important implications for legal education. When models fail to reference relevant laws by name or overlook the interplay between different legal frameworks, students miss the opportunity to develop a comprehensive understanding of how legal provisions work together to resolve family disputes. Such gaps can hinder their ability to craft well-founded arguments or anticipate the procedural steps required by various statutes. Furthermore, without exposure to precise legal terminology and cross-references, students risk developing an incomplete or superficial grasp of the law. Ultimately, this can affect their readiness to apply legal principles in practical contexts, whether drafting legal opinions, preparing case strategies, or advising clients.

The fourth challenge lies in LLMs' limited ability to distinguish between different types of legal provisions. As discussed in the Legal Background section, the Saudi Personal Status Law includes both mandatory provisions, which are non-negotiable, and supplementary provisions, which permit parties to reach agreements that differ from the law's default rules. Determining which category a provision falls into often requires careful interpretation of statutory language and its relationship to other relevant provisions (Albudairat, 2023). However, when responding to questions in the "legal advice" or "textual analysis" categories, all LLMs treated every provision as mandatory, failing to differentiate between binding rules and those allowing flexibility. For instance, none of the models mentioned the legally required reconciliation period when advising on spousal separation or child custody matters. However, when directly asked whether Saudi law mandates a reconciliation period, all models stated that such a period is required by the Saudi Personal Status Law, which is inaccurate. While Saudi law does mandate a reconciliation period, this requirement is found in Article 16/33 of the Executive Regulations of the Law of Civil Proceedings (2014), not in the Personal Status Law. This oversight is particularly consequential in family disputes, where the mandatory reconciliation period provides parties time to negotiate issues governed by supplementary provisions. For example, in child custody cases, all models failed to note that parents may mutually agree to grant custody to the father or opt for shared custody—alternatives that diverge from the law's default, which prioritizes the mother (Personal Status Law, 2022). This highlights not only a superficial grasp of the law's structure but also the risk of providing users with inaccurate, context-insensitive legal guidance.

The ability to distinguish between mandatory and supplementary provisions is a critical skill for law students. This foundational knowledge enables legal practitioners to draft tailored agreements that align with both the law and the parties' preferences, where the law permits such flexibility. The omission of this distinction by LLMs not only limits their practical utility in offering nuanced legal guidance but also risks misinforming users about the degree of flexibility embedded in the legal system. In family dispute scenarios, recognizing which provisions allow for negotiation is essential to providing advice that is both legally accurate and responsive to personal circumstances. The models' failure to account for these distinctions suggests a superficial grasp of the law's structure and underscores the need for improved legal reasoning and contextual interpretation in LLM development.

Despite their current limitations related to codified laws, as highlighted by the four challenges discussed above, LLMs offer promising opportunities to complement and enrich legal education, particularly when used thoughtfully and under proper academic supervision. One of the most valuable applications of LLMs is their potential to serve as personalized, on-demand legal tutors. For instance, ChatGPT-4o achieved a 92% accuracy rate in the "textual analysis" category, demonstrating strong capabilities in interpreting legal provisions. This suggests that LLMs can be effective tools for law students aiming to reinforce foundational skills such as reading comprehension and legal text interpretation.

LLMs can help students break down complex legal language into accessible explanations, identify the components of legal provisions, and provide useful examples. For instance, when asked, "Can you provide me with an example of a divorce pronounced by someone who is not sane or not acting out of free will?" all models first divided the question into two categories: divorce by someone who is not sane, and divorce by someone without free will. The models then provided examples for each category. For example, ChatGPT answered:

1. Divorce by someone who is not sane:
Example: If the husband is in a state of insanity (not sane), such as suffering from a mental illness or complete loss of consciousness due to a medical condition like epilepsy or a psychiatric disorder, and he pronounces divorce.
Outcome: In this case, the divorce is not valid because a person who is insane is not aware of their actions. Therefore, a divorce pronounced by someone who is not sane does not take effect.
2. Divorce without free will:
Example: If the husband is threatened or coerced by another person or by certain circumstances, which forces him to pronounce divorce against his will (e.g., being threatened with harm or blackmail unless he divorces his wife).
Outcome: In this case, the divorce is not valid because divorce must come from free will. A divorce that occurs under coercion or psychological pressure is considered invalid under the Saudi legal system.

The question and answers provided above may help Saudi law students understand part of Article 80 of the Personal Status Law, which states: "Divorce shall not take effect in the following cases: 1. Divorce pronounced by someone who is not sane or not acting out of free will. 2...." (Personal Status Law, 2022, art. 80). This form of assistance is particularly useful for early-stage law students who may struggle to navigate dense legal material or are preparing for exams, where comprehension and retention of key articles are essential.

Another effective use of LLMs lies in simulating legal scenarios. Although ChatGPT-4o scored 56%, ChatGPT 48%, and DeepSeek V3 8% in the "legal advice" section, these scores could likely improve if the models were provided with the relevant legal texts. With access to accurate sources, LLMs can generate hypothetical client inquiries and model responses that mimic legal reasoning. Such simulations enable students to participate in mock legal consultations or decision-making exercises, helping them apply legal principles in practical, low-risk environments. For instance, a student might input a legal article along with a scenario and ask the model to apply the law. The student can then analyze the model's reasoning, compare it to the correct interpretation, and identify any weaknesses or errors. These exercises support the development of applied legal reasoning, client-centered thinking, and the ability to navigate real-world ambiguities.

Finally, one of the most valuable roles of LLMs in legal education lies in their potential to help develop students' analytical and critical skills. Legal education is not merely about memorizing statutes or understanding doctrines in isolation; it is fundamentally about cultivating the ability to critically engage with texts, arguments, and evolving legal standards. In this context, LLMs should be used not as final authorities but as starting points. Rather than treating LLM-generated answers as definitive, students can be encouraged to adopt an evaluative mindset, questioning the source, accuracy, and doctrinal soundness of the content provided. This exercise promotes active learning by requiring students to verify citations, cross-reference legal provisions, and compare the model's interpretation with established judicial or scholarly opinions. For example, students might prompt an LLM with a question such as, "What is the legal definition of divorce under Saudi law?" and then be tasked with determining whether the response aligns with the actual text of the Saudi Personal Status Law. This process exposes students to the real-world risks of misinformation and oversimplification—challenges that are increasingly common in the digital age—and helps train them in the discipline of legal verification.

In sum, the analysis of LLMs in relation to codified law reveals both significant challenges and promising opportunities. On the one hand, the models frequently struggled with foundational tasks such as accurately identifying legal sources, keeping pace with recent legislative reforms, referencing complementary laws, and distinguishing between mandatory and supplementary provisions—shortcomings that underscore their limited capacity to engage with the precision and formal structure required by Saudi Arabia's codified legal system. On the other hand, their ability to interpret legal texts with relatively high accuracy, particularly in straightforward scenarios, suggests potential value as supportive tools for reinforcing students' statutory reading and analytical skills. These findings set the stage for the next section, which shifts the focus from codified law to culture, exploring how LLMs navigate local customs and social diversity within the context of Saudi family law.

LLMs and Culture

Analyzing results through the lens of culture reveals two challenges that LLMs face.

The first challenge is LLMs' limited ability to recognize local customs, an issue that has also been highlighted in previous studies (Ubanyionwu, 2024). Applying certain provisions of the Personal Status Law requires familiarity with local customs, which can vary not only between Saudi Arabia and other Islamic countries but also among different regions within Saudi Arabia itself. For example, the second part of Article 5 of the Personal Status Law states:

If the fiancée had used the dowry or part of it to make purchases for the benefit of the marriage—according to what is customary—and the withdrawal was by the fiancé without any fault on her part, or the withdrawal was by her due to a fault from the fiancé, then she has the option either to return the dowry or to hand over what she purchased as is.

Under the "textual analysis" category, LLMs were tasked with explaining the meaning of the article. Both ChatGPT-4o and DeepSeek V3 gave examples of "what is customary" as household items or furniture. While purchasing such items may be customary in some Islamic countries, it is not customary in Saudi Arabia for the fiancée to purchase them. According to Articles 44 and 45 of the Personal Status Law, providing housing is the husband's responsibility, which includes furnishing the residence with all necessary items (Personal Status Law, 2022). This highlights LLMs' limited ability to handle the complex relationship between law and custom. Their responses often default to generalized or foreign practices, revealing a lack of sensitivity to societal norms.

This issue is especially important for law students because understanding the interplay between legal texts and local customs is a foundational skill in Saudi legal education. Accurately identifying and applying relevant customs is essential for interpreting the law correctly, drafting valid agreements, and anticipating how a judge might rule in a given case. Misapplying a foreign custom or misunderstanding what is considered "customary" in the Saudi context can result in flawed legal reasoning and ultimately lead to incorrect legal advice.

The second challenge relates to LLMs' limited ability to acknowledge cultural diversity within Saudi Arabia. As discussed in the Legal Background section, although the majority of Saudis are Sunni Muslims, there is a Saudi Shia minority and a large non-Saudi population who are subject to alternative legal procedures. All LLMs failed to recognize this cultural diversity. This was particularly evident in the "legal advice" category, where the models consistently assumed that the person asking the question was a Sunni Muslim, without acknowledging other possibilities within the Saudi legal framework.

This shortcoming has important implications for legal education. Recognizing and accounting for cultural diversity is a foundational aspect of legal training in Saudi Arabia. By failing to identify these nuances, LLMs risk presenting an oversimplified and homogenized view of the legal landscape, potentially misleading students into overlooking critical jurisdictional and procedural differences. Such omissions undermine the development of culturally responsive reasoning—an essential competency for future practitioners who must advise clients from diverse backgrounds and navigate cases that intersect with different religious or cultural norms. This highlights the need for AI tools to be designed with deep cultural sensitivity.

Despite their shortcomings, LLMs can still offer valuable benefits to law students, particularly by fostering awareness of how the law operates within diverse cultural contexts. Engaging with LLM outputs encourages students to critically examine assumptions about local customs, cultural practices, and the varied experiences of different communities within Saudi Arabia, including non-Sunni and non-Saudi populations. By comparing AI-generated responses with culturally specific realities, students are prompted to identify oversights or inaccuracies, thereby strengthening their ability to think contextually and sensitively—skills essential for navigating a legal landscape where law and culture are deeply intertwined. In this way, even imperfect AI tools can serve as catalysts for deeper discussion and critical reflection on the cultural dimensions of legal practice.

In sum, the analysis of LLMs through the lens of culture highlights two key challenges: their limited ability to recognize local customs and their failure to account for the cultural and demographic diversity within Saudi Arabia. These gaps not only risk producing oversimplified or inaccurate legal guidance but also undermine core objectives of legal education, such as cultivating culturally nuanced reasoning. This underscores the need for AI tools that are deeply attuned to the cultural contexts in which they operate. With these cultural challenges in mind, the next section turns to examine how LLMs handle the equally complex dimension of Shari'a as the foundational source of Saudi family law.

LLMs and Shari'a

Analysis of the results through the lens of Shari'a reveals one main challenge that appeared across all four categories: Answering based on general Shari'a juristic opinions seemed to be the default approach for LLMs. However, as noted earlier, Shari'a encompasses a range of diverse jurisprudential opinions. As a result, some answers may be accurate according to one opinion but not aligned with the specific interpretation underpinning the Saudi Personal Status Law. For example, under the "legal questions" category, the models were asked: "How is custody determined for a child under 15 years old in the Saudi legal system?" The models provided varying responses:

ChatGPT

In the Saudi legal system, custody of a child under 15 years old is determined based on several criteria prioritizing the child's best interest. The hierarchy of custodianship is as follows:

- The mother: The mother is given priority for custody until the child reaches a specified age (7 years for boys and 9 years for girls), with the possibility of extending custody in certain cases.
- Maternal grandmother: If the mother is unable to care for the child, custody is transferred to the maternal grandmother.
- The father: If neither the mother nor the maternal grandmother can provide custody, the father is next in line, especially once the child reaches the specified age.
- Personal Status Court: In cases of disputes, the court decides based on the child's best interest, taking into account the circumstances of each party and their ability to provide proper care.

The court considers various factors such as the custodian's ability to care for the child, psychological and financial stability, and any potential harm or benefit to the child.

ChatGPT-4o

In the Saudi legal system, custody of a child under the age of 15 is determined based on the Personal Status Law, prioritizing the child's best interest. The steps and criteria for determining custody include:

1. Priority in Custody:
    - The mother: The mother has the primary right to custody unless there are reasons preventing her from fulfilling this role, such as neglect, harm, or the lack of a safe environment.
    - The father: The father is next in line if the mother is deemed unfit or incapable of providing care.
    - Relatives: If neither the mother nor the father is suitable or able to assume custody, the right passes to relatives based on the order of kinship, such as the grandfather or grandmother.

2. Child's Best Interest:

The court always considers what serves the child's best interest, focusing on:

- Stability of the living environment
- Emotional and psychological well-being
- The custodian's ability to provide basic needs (food, education, housing)

3. Child's Preference:

If the child has reached an age of discernment (typically 7 years), their opinion may be considered, provided the options align with their best interest.

DeepSeek V3

The Saudi Personal Status Law (issued by Royal Decree No. M/73 of 1443 AH—2022 CE) establishes the order of custody priority for children in Article (142), with the child's best interests as the paramount consideration.

Order of Custodians According to the Law:

- The mother (unless married to someone not a *mahram* to the child, or proven unfit)
- Maternal grandmother (mother's mother)
- Paternal grandmother (father's mother)
- Maternal aunt (mother's sister)
- Paternal aunt (father's sister)
- Maternal aunts' daughters, then paternal aunts' daughters
- The father (if no qualified female relatives are available)
- Male relatives (paternal uncle, then cousin, in order of kinship)

Basic Conditions for Custodians (Article 143):

- Puberty and sound mind
- Capability to provide care (physically and psychologically)
- Good moral character (no criminal record or deviant behavior)
- Not married to someone not a mahram to the child (for mothers and grandmothers)

Important Notes:

- The father retains general guardianship over the child's upbringing even if custody is granted to the mother.
- The child may choose between parents upon reaching the age of discernment (15 years).
- Custody may be revoked by a court ruling if neglect or harm is proven.

(The order is based on Hanbali jurisprudence with modifications to accommodate modern family realities.)

Article 127 of the Saudi Personal Status law:

Article 127 of the law governs child custody by stating:

1. Custody is a joint responsibility of both parents as long as they are married. If they separate, custody is granted to the mother, followed by the next eligible guardian in the following order: the father, then the maternal grandmother, then the paternal grandmother. After that, the court decides based on what it deems to be in the best interest of the child, without prejudice to the provisions of Article 126 of this system.
2. The court may deviate from the order stated in paragraph (1) of this article if it determines that it is in the best interest of the child.

All models placed the mother first, which aligns with Article 127 of the law. However, ChatGPT inaccurately added that custody is granted to the mother "until the child reaches the specified age (7 years for boys and 9 years for girls), with the possibility of extending custody in certain cases." Under Saudi law, mothers generally—if all conditions are met—hold custody of their children under the age of 15, regardless of sex; after age 15, the child's opinion may be considered. ChatGPT and DeepSeek placed the grandmother after the mother, which is consistent with some Shari'a juristic opinions, such as the Shafi'i and Hanbali schools (Zedan, 1993), but not with Saudi law, which places the father after the mother. ChatGPT listed the father after the mother, in agreement with Saudi law; however, the model also listed "relatives" after the father, giving examples such as the grandfather or grandmother, while Saudi law specifically places the maternal grandmother before the paternal grandmother. In addition, the answer stated that the child's opinion can be considered at age 7, which reflects some Shari'a juristic opinions, such as the Hanbali school (Ibn Qudama, 1997); however, Article 135 of the Personal Status Law (2022) specifies that the child's opinion is considered at age 15.

Another example from the same category appears in the responses to the question "What is the definition of khul' according to the Saudi Personal Status Law?" The models responded as follows:

ChatGPT

The Saudi Personal Status Law defines khul' as the termination of the marriage contract at the wife's request in exchange for compensation paid to the husband. The court may approve khul' if it determines that harm exists or that it is impossible for the marital relationship to continue between the spouses.

ChatGPT-4o

Khul' is defined as: "The dissolution of the marriage bond at the wife's request in exchange for financial compensation paid to the husband."

Khul' can be executed with the consent of both parties or through a judicial ruling if justified reasons are established, in accordance with the provisions of the law, while taking into account the rights of both parties and the interests of the family.

DeepSeek V3

The Saudi Personal Status Law (issued by Royal Decree No. M/73 of 1443 AH—2022) defines khul' in Article 120 as:

"The dissolution of the marital bond at the wife's request in exchange for her relinquishment of all or part of her financial rights under Shari'a, issued by a judicial ruling."

Article 95 of the Saudi Personal Status Law (2022)

The definition of khul' is stated in Article 95 of the law as: "The dissolution of the marriage at the wife's request and with the husband's consent, in exchange for compensation provided by the wife or someone else." Thus, for khul' to be valid, the law requires a mutual agreement between the wife and the husband and compensation provided by the wife or someone else. The law does not require justification or the establishment of harm. If harm exists, then according to Article 108, the wife can present her case before a judge and obtain a *faskh* through a judicial ruling, without having to compensate her husband. The wife may also obtain a faskh in exchange for compensation through a judicial ruling if she lacks valid justification and her husband refuses to grant her a khul' (Personal Status Law Regulations, 2025).

All models inaccurately merged two distinct legal concepts: khul' and faskh. In addition, all models referred to the need for a judicial ruling or court approval for khul', which is incorrect. Article 96 of the Personal Status Law (2022) states: "Khul' is valid through mutual agreement between both fully competent spouses to terminate the marriage contract, without the need for a judicial ruling." However, it cannot be said that the models' answers were entirely inaccurate based on Shari'a, as some juristic opinions require a judge's ruling for khul' (Zedan, 1993).

A solid understanding of Shari'a is essential for law students in Saudi Arabia and other countries with Islamic-based legal systems. Although most laws are formally codified, these statutes are often rooted in Islamic juristic opinions. Consequently, interpreting or reforming such laws requires a strong foundation in Shari'a principles. In Saudi Arabia, law students must study core Shari'a subjects, and graduates from Shari'a programs become eligible to practice law after meeting licensing requirements (Code of Law Practice, 2001). In addition, only Shari'a graduates are eligible to become judges (Law of the Judiciary, 2007). As discussed above, LLMs were able to generate responses reflecting a general awareness of Islamic juristic thought, suggesting some level of Shari'a-related knowledge. However, the models failed to identify or reference the specific juristic opinions upon which the Saudi Personal Status Law is codified. This gap is critical, as Saudi law selectively incorporates Shari'a principles through specific legislative choices, often favoring particular juristic schools or interpretations codified into binding statutes. Without understanding these distinctions, LLMs risk conflating general Islamic jurisprudence with enforceable Saudi law, potentially misleading users about their legal obligations and rights.

While often viewed as a weakness, the generalist nature of LLMs can also be seen as a unique educational asset. By drawing on a broad corpus of Islamic jurisprudence and global legal perspectives, LLMs naturally expose students to comparative legal concepts. With the right instructional framing, this exposure can enhance students' understanding of the diversity within Islamic legal schools, as well as the distinctions between codified and uncodified legal systems across the Muslim world. Instructors can design classroom activities that ask students to compare an LLM-generated answer with the actual text of the Saudi Personal Status Law, then explore how differing juristic opinions may have influenced various national legal interpretations. This approach fosters a deeper appreciation of jurisprudential diversity and its role in shaping modern legal frameworks.

The seven challenges discussed above—viewed through the lenses of codified law, culture, and Shari'a—highlight a fundamental distinction between legal education and AI-generated outputs: Law students are trained to think contextually, whereas

LLMs often operate generically, lacking cultural or situational awareness. This gap has important implications for integrating LLMs into legal education. Given their current limitations, LLMs are unsuitable as primary learning resources for law students. Students must not only master the literal text of statutes but also develop the analytical skills to situate these texts within the broader frameworks of Shari'a, ongoing legislative reforms, and cultural realities. Each of the seven challenges—from difficulties in distinguishing legal sources and concepts to failing to recognize the dynamic interplay between law, culture, and religion—reflects gaps that LLMs have yet to overcome. However, these challenges do not preclude the use of LLMs in legal education. As discussed above, LLMs show promise as private legal tutors, tools to develop students' analytical and critical skills, and as a means to expose students to comparative jurisprudence. Building on these insights, the next section explores how the challenges identified may, in fact, create opportunities to develop LLMs that are not only legally precise but also culturally and religiously sensitive.

Harnessing the Opportunities Toward Legally Accurate, Culturally Sensitive LLMs

The previous section highlighted several opportunities for using AI—in its current state—in legal education. The analysis also revealed seven challenges that LLMs face through the lens of three themes: codified laws, culture, and Shari'a. These challenges present opportunities to enhance LLM performance and make them better suited for legal education.

The first theme includes four challenges related to LLMs and codified laws:

1. LLMs struggled to accurately recognize and reference specific codified laws.
2. The rapidly evolving nature of the law posed difficulties; the models frequently provided outdated or incorrect information about newly enacted or amended legislation.
3. LLMs showed limited ability to reference complementary laws, often neglecting interconnected statutes when offering advice on family disputes.
4. All models demonstrated a limited ability to distinguish between mandatory and supplementary provisions, treating all rules as inflexible mandates.

As Baldassarre et al. (2024) revealed, there are ongoing efforts by AI companies to collaborate with governments and experts to limit the spread of misinformation generated by AI; however, these efforts are primarily concentrated in Europe and the Global North. This research highlights the need to expand such initiatives to countries in the Global South. For example, partnerships with the Saudi government and legal experts could create opportunities to train LLMs on authentic Arabic legal texts, including codified statutes, executive regulations, court rulings, and academic commentaries that reflect Saudi jurisprudential thought. The rapidly changing nature of the law underscores the importance of sustained partnerships with governments and legal experts to ensure that LLMs can cite the most current legislation. In addition, interactive features that allow expert users to flag inaccuracies or inconsistencies—along with explanations and supporting resources—could help reduce errors and activate the role of universities in this effort.

The second theme included two challenges related to LLMs and culture:

1. LLMs often default to generalized or foreign practices when interpreting provisions related to local custom, reflecting a lack of sensitivity to Saudi cultural norms.
2. LLMs overlook the pluralistic nature of Saudi society, ignoring the distinct legal considerations for populations with different religious and cultural backgrounds.

These two challenges highlight the need to train LLMs not only on existing laws but also on customary practices from different regions within the Kingdom, to ensure the models account for the lived legal realities that affect judicial reasoning and outcomes. This can be achieved through partnerships with cultural anthropologists who can advise on the distinct needs of each community (Ubanyionwu, 2024). Partnerships with non-governmental organizations (NGOs) may also be valuable to ensure the accurate representation of minorities within each country. In addition, opening lines of communication with end users and enabling them to provide feedback may help increase cultural sensitivity. However, it is crucial to acknowledge that developing such a design can be challenging, especially in culturally diverse countries with limited resources (Baldassarre et al., 2024).

The third theme revealed one challenge related to how LLMs handle Shari'a. All models tended to base their answers on broad Shari'a juristic opinions without demonstrating the ability to differentiate between various types of juristic interpretations or to clarify how these opinions intersect with the codified legal framework of Saudi Arabia. This disconnect between religious doctrine and formal law is not unique to Islamic contexts; it reflects a broader challenge for AI applications in any community where religious norms operate alongside civil or statutory systems. Addressing this limitation requires embedding richer, context-sensitive models of religious law into AI systems and fostering partnerships with qualified religious scholars and jurists who can guide the development of AI frameworks to ensure accurate results.

Taken together, these findings reveal a landscape of both pressing challenges and meaningful opportunities for leveraging LLMs in legal education and practice. The seven key challenges identified point to areas for targeted improvement. By expanding partnerships with governments, legal experts, cultural anthropologists, NGOs, and religious scholars, there is substantial potential to develop LLMs that are not only legally accurate but also culturally and doctrinally sensitive. Figure 1 outlines practical strategies to harness these opportunities, guiding the evolution of LLMs into tools that can meaningfully support nuanced, locally grounded, and ethically sound legal education and advice.

Figure 1. Suggested Framework for Legally Accurate and Culturally Sensitive Large Language Models

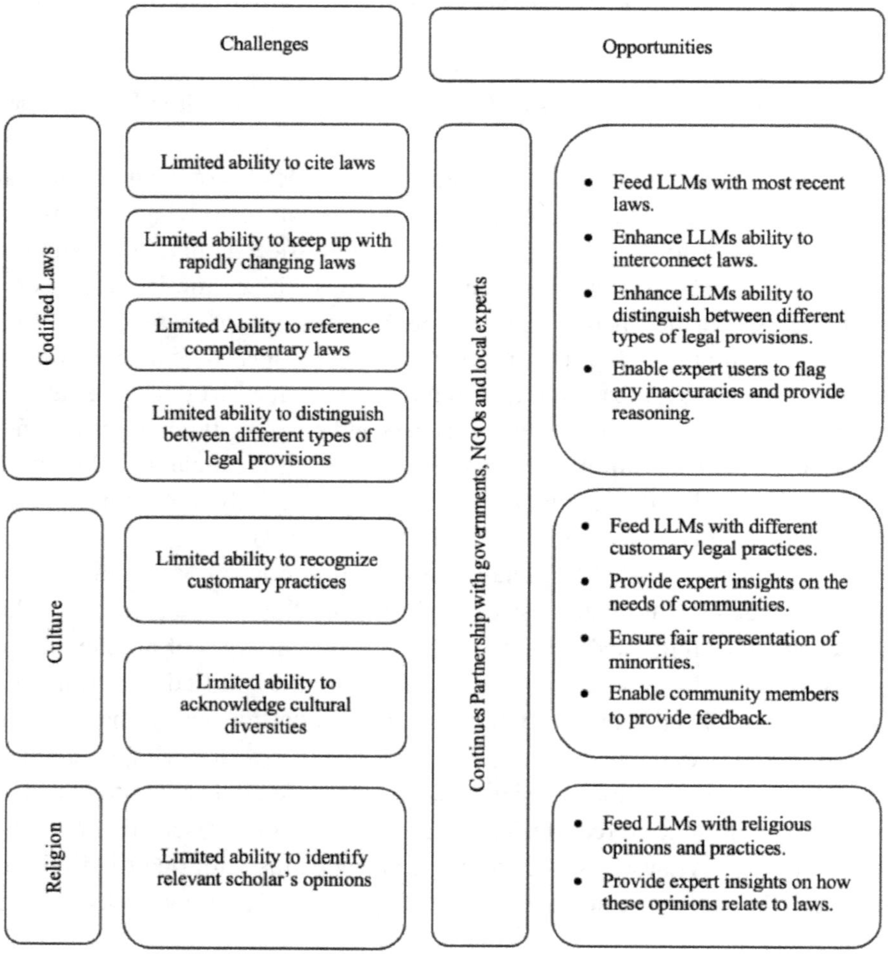

Note. LLM = large language model.

LIMITATIONS AND FUTURE DIRECTIONS

This research presents three main limitations. First, the Personal Status Law has not yet been officially translated into English. Current studies indicate that legal translations into English by LLMs remain imperfect, making it difficult to assess accuracy when compared to the original Arabic text (Ait Elfqih & Monti, 2024). For this reason, all questions were posed and answered in Arabic. After assessing the accuracy of the responses in Arabic, the models were then tasked with translating their own answers into English for the purpose of writing this chapter. This process may result in translations that do not align with any future official versions of the law. However, because the analysis was conducted in Arabic, this limitation did not affect the study's findings.

Second, the focus on family law may not capture all the challenges associated with using AI in the legal field. Additional issues may arise in areas where newly issued laws are published but do not come into force until several months later. For example, although the Personal Status Law was issued on March 9, 2022, it did not take effect until 90 days later (Personal Status Law, 2022). Furthermore, some legal domains contain parallel versions of the same law, each applying to a different group of individuals. For example, the old Social Insurance Law (2000) continues to govern employees hired before July 6, 2024, while the new Social Insurance Law (2024) applies to those hired on or after that date. While such complexities were beyond the scope of this study—since they do not currently affect Saudi family law—they underscore potential difficulties for LLMs and suggest important avenues for future research.

Third, the capabilities of LLMs in answering Shari'a-based questions were examined solely within the context of family law, as all models were instructed to respond according to Saudi legal principles. As a result, many questions remain regarding the broader capacity of LLMs to address Shari'a-related inquiries, particularly whether they can accurately cite specific juristic opinions or comprehensively reflect the diverse views held by different schools of Islamic thought. These gaps point to important opportunities for future research to assess the performance of LLMs in more nuanced and varied aspects of Shari'a jurisprudence.

Additionally, it is important to mention Saudi Arabia's ongoing efforts to develop a local LLM. The Saudi Data and AI Authority (SDAIA) has developed "Allam." According to their website, Allam is designed to provide "updated summaries and suggestions on various topics in a manner consistent with the fast pace of this era. The app offers reliable information in all fields and is considered the first of its kind in the Kingdom of Saudi Arabia" (SDAIA, 2025). At the time of writing this research, Allam has not been officially accessible to the public. However, once officially launched, studying Allam in relation to the results of this research would offer valuable insights into localized LLMs compared to non-localized models.

CONCLUSION

This research examined the capabilities of three prominent LLMs—ChatGPT, ChatGPT-4o, and DeepSeek V3—in navigating the complex nature of Saudi family law, a domain uniquely shaped by codified laws, cultural norms, and Shari'a. By assessing their performance across four categories—foundational legal knowledge, direct legal questions, legal advice, and textual analysis—the study highlighted both the promise and the shortcomings of these AI tools in supporting legal education.

The findings revealed that while LLMs show considerable potential—especially in interpreting legal texts and introducing students to comparative jurisprudence—they also face significant challenges. These include limited ability to consistently cite accurate legal provisions, difficulties in keeping up with newly enacted or amended laws, a lack of sensitivity to local customs, and failure to account for the cultural diversity within Saudi society. Additionally, the models often blurred the lines between general Shari'a principles and the specific juristic interpretations codified into Saudi law, risking misleading or incomplete legal guidance.

Despite these limitations, the study identified valuable opportunities. With thoughtful design and collaboration—engaging governments, legal scholars, cultural anthropologists, NGOs, and religious experts—LLMs could evolve into tools that are not only technically accurate but also culturally and doctrinally sensitive. Such developments would enable these models to meaningfully enhance legal education by helping students critically examine legal texts, understand the interplay between law and culture, and navigate the doctrinal nuances of religion-based systems.

As Saudi Arabia advances its own AI efforts, including the rollout of local models such as Allam, future research comparing these localized systems to broader, non-localized LLMs could offer essential insights. Ultimately, this work underscores that while LLMs are not substitutes for the deep, context-rich training required of future legal practitioners, they hold significant potential as complementary tools, provided they are carefully aligned with the legal, cultural, and religious fabric of the societies they aim to serve.

REFERENCES

Abu-Lughod, L. (2013). *Do Muslim women need saving?* Harvard University Press. DOI: 10.4159/9780674726338

Abu-Zayd, N. (2013). The status of women between the Qur'an and *Fiqh*. In Mir-Hosseini, Z., Vogt, K., Larsen, L., & Moe, C. (Eds.), *Gender and equality in Muslim family law: Justice and ethics in the Islamic legal tradition* (pp. 153–168). I. B. Tauris. DOI: 10.5040/9780755609277.ch-007

Ahmed, L. (1991). Early Islam and the position of women: The problem of interpretation. In Keddie, N., & Baron, B. (Eds.), *Women in Middle Eastern history: Shifting boundaries in sex and gender* (pp. 58–73). Yale University Press.

Ait Elfqih, K., & Monti, J. (2024). Large language models as legal translators of Arabic legislatives: Does ChatGPT and Gemini care for context and terminology? In *Proceedings of the Second Arabic Natural Language Processing Conference* (pp. 111–122). Association for Computational Linguistics. DOI: 10.18653/v1/2024.arabicnlp-1.10

Al-Harz, M. (2021). *Jaafari judiciary in Al-Ahsa*. Al-Ahsa Heritage. https://www.alhasa-turath.org

Albudairat, M. (2023). *Mabadi' alqanun* [Introduction to Law]. Maktabat Almutanabi.

Altamimi, D. H. F. (2025). Unlocking potential: Saudi EFL male students' perspectives on AI tools for enhancing English writing proficiency. *Arab World English Journal*, 40–58. DOI: 10.24093/awej/AI.3

Anuyah, O., Wan, R., Adejoro, C., Yeh, T., Metoyer, R., & Badillo-Urquiola, K. (2023). Cultural considerations in AI systems for the Global South: A systematic review. In *Proceedings of the 4th African Human Computer Interaction Conference* (pp. 125–134). Association for Computing Machinery. DOI: 10.1145/3628096.3629046

Baldassarre, M. T., Caivano, D., Nieto, B. F., Gigante, D., & Ragone, A. (2024). Fostering human rights in responsible AI: A systematic review for best practices in industry. *IEEE Transactions on Artificial Intelligence*, *6*(2), 416–431. DOI: 10.1109/TAI.2024.3394389

Basic Law of Governance, Royal Decree No. A/90 (1992).

Chu, Z., Wang, S., Xie, J., Zhu, T., Yan, Y., Ye, J., Zhong, A., Hu, X., Liang, J., Yu, P. S., & Wen, Q. (2025). *LLM agents for education: Advances and applications*. arXiv preprint. /arXiv.2503.11733DOI: 10.18653/v1/2025.findings-emnlp.743

Code of Law Practice, Royal Decree No. M/38 (2001).

Ewick, P., & Silbey, S. (1998). *The common place of law: Stories from everyday life*. The University of Chicago Press. DOI: 10.7208/chicago/9780226212708.001.0001

General Authority for Statistics. (2025). https://www.stats.gov.sa

Ibn Qudama, M. (1997). *Al-Mughni fi fiqh al-Imam Ahmad ibn Hanbal* [The Sufficient in the Jurisprudence of Imam Ahmad ibn Hanbal]. Dar Alam Alkutub.

King Abdulaziz University. (2024). *College of Law*. https://law.kau.edu.sa

King Saud University. (2025). *College of Law and Political Sciences*. https://clps.ksu.edu.sa

Law, Civil Procedures, & No, Royal Decree. M/1 (2013).

Child Protection Law, Royal Decree No. M/14 (2014), as amended by Royal Decree No. M/72 (2023).

Law, Enforcement, & No, Royal Decree. M/43 (2012).

Law, Evidence, & No, Royal Decree. M/53 (2021).

Law, Personal Status, & No, Royal Decree. M/73 (2022).

Law, Social Security, & No, Royal Decree. M/32 (2020).

Law of the Judiciary, Royal Decree No. M/78 (2007).

Merry, S. E. (1990). *Getting justice and getting even: Legal consciousness among working-class Americans*. University of Chicago Press.

Mezey, N. (2003). Law as culture. In Sarat, A., & Simon, J. (Eds.), *Cultural analysis, cultural studies, and the law: Moving beyond legal realism* (pp. 37–72). Duke University Press. DOI: 10.1215/9780822384755-002

Ministry of Justice. (2013). *A collection of judicial rulings*. Ministry of Justice.

Na'im, A. A. A. (1996). *Toward an Islamic reformation: Civil liberties, human rights, and international law*. Syracuse University Press.

Paustian, T., & Slinger, B. (2024). Students are using large language models and AI detectors can often detect their use. *Frontiers in Education, 9*, Article 1374889. Media SA. DOI: 10.3389/feduc.2024.1374889

Personal, Status Law Regulations, & No, Royal Order. 59641 (2025).

Prince Sultan University. (2025). *College of Law*. https://www.psu.edu.sa/ar/CL/llb-plan

Protection from Abuse Law, Royal Decree No. M/52 (2013), as amended by Royal Decree No. M/72 (2023).

Qanoniah. (2024). *The annual report of laws in the Kingdom of Saudi Arabia*. Qanoniah.

Rahman, F. (2002). *Islam*. University of Chicago Press.

Rights, Elderly, Law, Care, & No, Royal Decree. M/47 (2022).

Rights of Persons with Disabilities Law, Royal Decree No. M/27 (2023).

Ryan, F., & Hardie, L. (2024). ChatGPT, I have a legal question? The impact of Gen AI tools on law clinics and access to justice. *International Journal of Clinical Legal Education*, *31*(1), 166–205. DOI: 10.19164/ijcle.v31i1.1401

Saudi Data and AI Authority. (2025). SDAIA. https://sdaia.gov.sa/en/Services/Pages/FreeServicesAndPrograms.aspx

Saudi Press Agency. (2021, Feb 9). Saudi press: HRH Crown Prince announces 4 new laws to reform the Kingdom's judicial institutions. https://www.spa.gov.sa/2187851

Seabrooke, T., Schneiders, E., Dowthwaite, L., Krook, J., Leesakul, N., Clos, J., Maior, H., & Fischer, J. (2024). A survey of lay people's willingness to generate legal advice using large language models (LLMs). In *Proceedings of the Second International Symposium on Trustworthy Autonomous Systems* (pp. 1–5). Association for Computing Machinery. DOI: 10.1145/3686038.3686043

Tan, J., Westermann, H., & Benyekhlef, K. (2023). ChatGPT as an artificial lawyer? In *Proceedings of the Workshop on Artificial Intelligence for Access to Justice*. CEUR.

The Executive Regulations of the Law of Civil Proceedings, Minister of Justice Decision No. 39933 (2014).

Thomas, C., McElhattan, L., & Carlo, S. (2023). Legal literacy and generative artificial intelligence: Comparing the education law knowledge of practicing educators and large language models like ChatGPT. *Education Law Reporter*, *414*, 783–798. DOI: 10/2139/ssrn.4967373

Ubanyionwu, J. (2024). Ethical and cultural considerations in artificial intelligence (AI) application to customary law. *African Journal of Law. Ethics and Education*, *7*(2), 142–159.

Wang, J., & Fan, W. (2025). The effect of ChatGPT on students' learning performance, learning perception, and higher-order thinking: Insights from a meta-analysis. *Humanities & Social Sciences Communications*, *12*(1), 1–21. DOI: 10.1057/s41599-025-04787-y

Zedan, A. (1993). *Almufassal fi Ahkam Al imra'a wa Albait Almuslim* [Provisions of women and the Muslim home]. Moasasat Alrisalah.

ADDITIONAL READING

Anderson, J. N. D. (1959). *Islamic law in the modern world*. New York University Press.

Barzilai, G. (2010). *Communities and law: Politics and cultures of legal identities*. University of Michigan Press.

Friedland, R. (2001). Religious nationalism and the problem of collective representation. *Annual Review of Sociology*, *27*(1), 125–152. DOI: 10.1146/annurev.soc.27.1.125

Friedman, L. M. (1990). *The republic of choice: Law, authority, and culture*. Harvard University Press.

Halliday, S., & Morgan, B. (2013). I fought the law and the law won? Legal consciousness and the critical imagination. *Current Legal Problems*, *66*(1), 1–32. DOI: 10.1093/clp/cut002

Hartog, H. (1993). Abigail Bailey's coverture: Law in a married woman's consciousness. In Sarat, A., & Kearns, T. R. (Eds.), *Law in everyday life* (pp. 63–108). University of Michigan Press.

Khan, A. A. (2007). *Concept of Islamic law*. Pentagon Press.

Lacy, R. (2011). *Inside the Kingdom*. Al Mesbar Studies and Research Center.

Licht, A. N. (2008). Social norms and the law: Why peoples obey the law. *Review of Law & Economics*, *4*(3), 715–750. DOI: 10.2202/1555-5879.1232

Licht, A. N., Goldschmidt, C., & Schwartz, S. H. (2007). Culture rules: The foundations of the rule of law and other norms of governance. *Journal of Comparative Economics*, *35*(4), 659–688. DOI: 10.1016/j.jce.2007.09.001

Moller, L. M. (2013). Family law in the Arab Gulf: Recent developments and reform patterns. *Journal of Islamic State Practices in International Law*, *9*(2), 22–39.

Welchman, L. (2010). Bahrain, Qatar, UAE: First time family law codifications in three Gulf States. In B. Atkin (Ed.), *International survey of family law* (pp. 163–178). Family Law.

Young, K. M. (2014). Everyone knows the game: Legal consciousness in the Hawaiian cockfight. *Law & Society Review*, *48*(3), 499–530. DOI: 10.1111/lasr.12094

KEY TERMS AND DEFINITIONS

Faskh: According to the Saudi Personal Status Law, every separation by judicial ruling is considered a dissolution (faskh) of the marriage.

Hanafi **school of thought:** Islamic school of legal thought (madhhab), whose origins are attributed to Abu Hanifah in Kufa, Iraq, in the eighth century.

Hanbali **school of thought:** Islamic school of legal thought (madhhab), whose origins are attributed to Ahmad ibn Hanbal in ninth-century Baghdad.

Jaafari court: A Shari'a court that specializes in adjudicating personal status cases for individuals who follow the Jaafari (Twelver Shia) school of thought.

Khul': Defined in the Saudi Personal Status Law as "a separation between the spouses at the wife's request and with the husband's consent, in exchange for compensation provided by the wife or someone else."

Mahr: Dowry paid by the husband to his wife. It becomes the property of the wife to spend, save, or invest as she pleases.

Maliki **school of thought:** Islamic school of legal thought (madhhab), whose origins are attributed to Anas Al-Asbahi in the eighth century in the Arabian Peninsula.

Quran: The holy book of Islam, containing the words of God as revealed to the Prophet Mohammad (SAWS) through the Angel Gabriel.

Royal decree: A decision approved by the King after being discussed in the Council of Ministries and the Shura Council.

Royal Order: An official directive issued by the head of the Council of Ministries.

Shafi'i **school of thought:** Islamic school of legal thought (madhhab), whose origins are attributed to Mohammad bin Idris bin Al-Abbad bin Uthman bin Shafi'i in the eighth century.

Shari'a: Islamic law derived from the primary sources (Quran and Sunnah) and secondary sources (Ijma'a and Qiyas) of Islam.

Shia: The second-largest branch of Islam after Sunni Islam. While the majority of Saudi Arabians are Sunni, there is a minority of Shia citizens who follow the Jaafari court for personal status matters.

Sunnah: The acts and sayings of the Prophet Mohammad (SAWS).

Sunni: The largest branch of Islam; the majority of Saudis are Sunni Muslims.

Talaq: Defined in the Saudi Personal Status Law as "the dissolution of the marriage contract by the husband's will through a verbal expression indicating it."

ENDNOTES

1 ChatGPT is an LLM developed by OpenAI.

2 ChatGPT-4o (the "o" stands for "omni") is, according to OpenAI, a step toward more natural human–computer interaction.

3 DeepSeek is an LLM developed by Hangzhou DeepSeek Artificial Intelligence Basic Technology Research Co., Ltd.

Chapter 8
Ethical Implications of AI Integration in Legal Practice and Education

Mohammad Saleem
https://orcid.org/0009-0000-4777-3113
Faculty of Law, Marwadi University, Rajkot, India

Karun Sanjaya
https://orcid.org/0000-0002-5055-6862
Symbiosis Law School, Nagpur, Symbiosis International University, Pune, India

Abhishek Benedict Kumar
https://orcid.org/0000-0002-3998-3150
Symbiosis Law School, Nagpur, Symbiosis International University, Pune, India

Jimmy Jose
Symbiosis Law School, Nagpur, Symbiosis International University, Pune, India

ABSTRACT

This chapter addresses the regulatory challenges and prospects of digital technologies related to human rights and risk control. Laws are sometimes out of date or insufficient to tackle emerging threats such as algorithmic bias, surveillance capitalism, data exploitation and digital poverty in a world where people's everyday activities can be fundamentally shaped by their interactions with digital technologies. The chapter maps the historical development of digital law and regulation, global governance trends and argues for a human rights-based approach based on transparency, accountability and equality. It stresses the importance of such frameworks being inclusive, adaptive and risk-based to safeguard core freedoms

DOI: 10.4018/979-8-3373-3451-6.ch008

while stimulating innovation. From the perspective of digital justice, it advocates for a multi-stakeholder collaboration to ensure that the digital transformation fosters rather than detracts from human dignity and democratic interests.

1. INTRODUCTION: THE DAWN OF A NEW LEGAL ERA

AI's unprecedented and exponential breakthroughs are not just next-curve technology enhancements, they are an enormous transformation that re-orders industries, professions and society in general. Where the legal sector, always is the one to follow precedent, tradition and slow-witted human diligence, has opened up to its inevitable AI-mediated revolution. Sophisticated search and prediction intel these days, encompasses sophisticated research platforms that can parse millions of documents in seconds, prediction analytics that foretell litigation outcomes, automated contract generation processes and even virtual lawyers that will handle initial client meetings (Shah, 2025).

The appeal of AI in law is both varied and irresistible. It is the unparalleled efficiency, with cost savings of legal services and the out-of-reach increase in access to justice to more people. But behind this facade of progress there is an ethical minefield. The introduction of AI to a domain as sensitive as law, a system established to maintain order, fairness, safeguard individual rights and deliver justice, is far from ethically neutrality. This chapter looks into these difficult ethical elements in depth and in critical terms. It carefully grapples with the difficulties and duties that the increasing embedding of AI into the actual work of law practice and the basic tenets, pedagogical approaches and curricular construction of legal education entails. The point is to make in what follows is that an inattention towards addressing these challenging dimensions in a holistic, proactive and with a full sense of rigour, not only threatens to debase the foundational values of justice, fairness and professional integrity that the legal process is so intricately designed to protect, but also its very capacity to engender the trust of fellow humans in the institutions it is constituted to uphold.

2. AI IN LEGAL PRACTICE: NAVIGATING THE ETHICAL CROSSROADS

The use of AI in practice of law covers a very wide range from automation of repetitive work to very sophisticated decision support on very abstract and multifactorial areas of decisions. Despite the promise for game-changing advances in terms of speed, accuracy and resource allocation. These applications unavoidably give rise to a complex web of ethical quandaries (Zafar, 2024). These are all challenges that require careful consideration and both reactive and creative responses, from lawyers, regulators, technologists and policymakers.

2.1. Access to Justice: A Double-Edged Sword

The ability of AI to democratize access to legal services and close the ongoing access-to-justice gap, represents one of its most-celebrated promises. With the help of AI, chatbots are able to offer basic, instant legal advice or information, thus reducing the hurdle that having to make initial contact can pose for those with legal concerns. Facilitate documents automation and solutions that can automatically generate standardized legal documents and contracts faster and less costly allowing to make necessary legal paperwork more affordable and less time-consuming. Moreover, online dispute resolution (ODR) platforms, which may use AI to assist parties to communicate and propose dispute settlement terms, may provide rapid and cost-effective approaches to non-formal adjudication, particularly for low-value disputes. These are the kinds of developments that really could democratize the legal process for millions of people and small businesses who have been shut out of or scared off by, traditional legal assistance.

This however, is accompanied by profound normative trade-offs that render AI a double-edged sword for access to justice. The expanding digital divide remains a foremost concern. Firstly large section of the populace, especially women in rural areas and the poor, still do not have regular access to the Internet, essential digital tools and the basic digital literacy needed to engage with AI-powered legal tools. If measures are not taken to alleviate this divide, the very instruments that were created to improve access, could wind up consolidating these disparities and perpetuating marginalization in the underserved (Thomas et al., 2025). This establishes a new type of 'justice gap' structured by technological access.

Secondly, the risks that the quality, accuracy and reliability of AI- produced advice are low and unacceptable, especially coming from unregulated or developing tools. Unlike human lawyers, who are bound by professional responsibilities, AI tools do not have a direct ethical obligation, professionalism or empathy. Take an AI chatbot dishing advice about landlord-tenant law. If it offers general advice without being nuanced enough about a particular ordinance in that area or the client's particular facts, it can lead users astray, giving them incomplete or flat-out wrong advice that leads to bad legal outcomes (like an illegal eviction or no security deposit). The ethical mandate is the requirement is not simply for availability, rather it is to ensure the quality, safety and appropriateness of the advice provided which needs to include robust validation and regulation.

Thirdly and perhaps most importantly, algorithmic bias is pernicious in law-bono tools. If the information used to build these AI models is mirrored in historical biases in the justice system like, over-indexing in arrests, harsher sentencing or unequal access to legal representation for a particular demographics, the AI is likely to emulate or even compound these biases resulting in unjust outcomes for marginalised groups. For instance, an AI system to determine eligibility for legal aid might unknowingly discriminate against applicants from certain ethnic backgrounds if its training data included historical biases in the allocation. This risks generating and perpetuating rather than ameliorating systemic inequalities, turning an instrument of freedom into a tool of continued subjugation. Ensuring that access is truly equitable, in other words, involves doing more than simply deploying technological tools, but instead demands that we do so in an extraordinarily rigorous way, making sure those tools are fair, transparent, clear and easy to understand, genuinely helpful and extensively audited for bias, without creating new forms of disadvantage or reinforcing the ones we have. The moral quest is to ensure that when AI drives access to justice, such access is just and fair, not just efficient.

2.2. Competence and Professional Responsibility: The Evolving Standard

Central theme of the legal profession is, so long as your ethics do not stink, you are set to go. This obligation requires an attorney to provide the legal knowledge, skill, thoroughness, and preparation reasonably necessary for the client's representation. The American Bar Association (ABA) Model Rules of Professional Conduct, in particular Rule 1.1 (Competence), has already sought to account for the technological revolution with a critical comment. This provision specifically requires that attorneys remain competent and up to date on changes in the law and its practice, including the benefits and risks associated with technology (Mikeladze et al., 2024). This seemingly innocuous imposition results in a radical shift in the level of professional competence and unequivocally imposes a duty of technological competence that without question will become de rigueur.

2.2.1 AI's Capabilities and Limitations

One of the basics of technological literacy is understanding exactly what AI tools can and ca not do. Lawyers need to understand that AI is a powerful technology meant to enhance the abilities of humans, not replace all human decision making, reasoning or moral reflection. A failure to appreciate the role of such probability in AI, its limitations, its potential to produce hallucinations or the risks of over-reliance on it reflects a failure to moderate competence. Indeed, an attorney automatically depending on, for example, an AI legal research tool to reach legal conclusions without cross-referencing its results or without understanding its search parameters, could overlook vital case law or misconstrue subtle legal doctrine, potentially resulting in bad counsel. Lawyers need to know when AI output is trustworthy, when it must be verified or corrected by humans and when it is cooking up incorrect output. They need to know that AI models are trained on data and that they reflect the patterns in that data, not necessarily the truth or the legal correctness.

2.2.2 Data Inputs and Outputs

It is necessary to comprehend how data moves through the lifecycle of an AI system. This means understanding how the AI tools are trained like what data sets, what techniques and what biases are involved, how they process information and how they come up with their decisions. A good lawyer ought to be able to challenge machine generated research, predictive analytics or automated documents and not simply accept them. This brings to questioning the origin and quality of the data used for training knowledge about algorithms assumptions, methods and any potential biases regarding data that may lead to biased results. If an AI is being used for e-discovery, for instance, the lawyer has to understand how the AI identifies relevant documents and what keywords or concepts it gives more weight to, as well as how it treats various data formats, in order to ensure that no significant evidence is left unturned because of algorithmic biases.

2.2.3 Supervision

As lawyers are held to an ethical standard of supervisor responsibility for the work of paralegals, legal assistants and junior associates, so they should be answerable for, the level of supervision they provide for the devices they utilize. That duty includes the accountability to confirm AI results are accurate, complete and ethical, as well as the oversight and ability to appropriately use AI in all client matters. This is not just a perfunctory check for errors: It is an active process of engaging with the AI's output, using independent legal judgment, knowledge of the case at hand and an understanding of the client's needs. Just because an AI has drafted a contract, a lawyer needs to carefully go through each clause to ensure it captures the client's instruction, complies with all relevant laws and will not put the client at a disadvantage, rather than simply accepting it like final output. This supervisory obligation also applies to supervising the use of the AI tools themselves, to ensure they are used in a manner consistent with one's ethical obligations, such as refraining from inputting confidential client information into public AI models.

2.2.4 Ethical Use and Risk Mitigation

Being competent in the age of AI is also about being aware and taking preventative measures towards the ethical pitfalls that AI inherently poses. They need competencies to recognize if an AI tool can have the potential for a biased outcome, compromise client-gen confidentiality or pose complex accountability questions. What is needed is an ethical foresight to be able to foresee the problems and prudently to take precautions to see that the technology is used appropriately and with the highest norms and ethical standards. This includes understanding the potential for AI to be abused, either intentionally or inadvertently and establishing safeguards against abuse. A lawyer would need to understand the risks in relying on AI for predictive analytics in sentencing, if the AI is known to be racially biased and ethically opt to mitigate or avoid such reliance.

2.3. Confidentiality and Data Privacy: The New Frontier of Risk

Client secrecy, a sacred principle and fundamental concept of legal profession, is preserved in all the ethical codes benchmarking ABA Model Rule 1.6, stating that 'a lawyer shall not reveal information relating to the representation of a client unless the client gives informed consent, the disclosure is impliedly authorized in order to carry out the representation, or the disclosure is permitted by specific exceptions.' The increasingly ubiquitous role of AI particularly within cloud hosted AI solutions adds serious and unparalleled implications to upholding this essential ethical principle. The digital processing of AI introduces new vectors of risk that requires focused attention and risk capturing in a proactive way.

2.3.1 Data Transmission, Storage and Security

Sensitive client information that is required to be uploaded to outside AI platforms needs to be analyzed whether in connection with large-scale e-discovery review, complex contract analysis, predictive analytics, or case management. These servers are frequently dispersed throughout multiple geographic zones and may be outside of the immediate control of the attorney or even the client's home jurisdiction. This raises important questions about data security and sensitivity, the strength of transport and data-at-rest encryption methods and the risk of breaches or advanced threats. Lawyers must perform full due-diligence on AI vendors, examining their security certificates, data-handling policies, incident response plans, but most importantly the terms and conditions of ownership, retention and destruction of data (Zaid & Garai, 2024). A plain-vanilla 'terms of service' agreement is not enough, you must scrutinize their security framework, audit trails and compliance with industry best practices. The moral obligation goes further, to also verify that the security of the vendor is reasonable compared to the sensitivity of the client data shared with the vendor.

2.3.2 Anonymization Challenges and Re-identification

Although many AI systems claim to provide anonymisation or pseudonymisation for preserving sensitive data the situation is significantly more complicated. In the most specialised of legal cases or where a client has a very rare condition or a highly unusual corporate structure or financial transactions, even apparently anonymised data may still be susceptible to re-identification, particularly when combined with other publicly availably datasets or applied to using intelligent AI software, specifically engineered for pattern recognition and linkage. The finer grain (unique) data is more likely to result in re-identification thus leading to possible loss of confidentiality.

2.3.3 Jurisdictional Issues and Data Sovereignty

Cloud computing is inherently international and data processed for clients by AI tools may be located/stored in and/or accessed from different jurisdictions with varying and sometimes contradictory data privacy laws (such as strict GDPR rules in Europe, the CCPA in the United States, Brazil's LGPD or host of national data residency rules). Lawyers, working on a single international legal system, must strive for strict adherence to multiple collapsed regulations, a challenging task especially in the current field where AI models transcend international borders. This requires analysis to determine the applicable data sovereignty principles, potential legal hurdles and effects of cross-border data transfers, particularly as related to governmental requests in other countries. Non-compliance can bring with it harsh consequences, reputational harm and a violation of the ethical duty.

2.3.4 AI Training Data and Consent

What is really important and often gets ignored, is how AI models learn and adapt. A lot of AI systems, machine-learned ones in particular, are designed to learn and improve from data. As a result, lawyers need to know whether and how much, their client data is being used to train or improve, the AI model. If the AI's knowledge base will be fed from client data, then lawyers will need to ensure that those processes are expressly permitted in the local rules of professional ethics and that the data collection has been made with informed client consent. That requires clear, transparent communication with clients about how their data will be used beyond their specific case, whether it will be aggregated, anonymized and used to improve the AI system for other users. Use of the information for such purposes without an individual's consent would be an unauthorized disclosure.

2.3.5 Inadvertent Disclosure and Algorithmic Leakage

AI, by definition and nature, can accidentally expose sensitive communication through outputs or the existence of unanticipated vulnerabilities in the algorithms. An AI summarizing a large corpus of documents, for instance, can infuse into its summary a nugget of confidential or highly sensitive information if it fails to recognize and redact that content. Likewise, a predictive analytics application could identify trends that, when reverse engineered, expose confidential client strategies or company secrets. Because of the fundamental complexity and 'black box' nature of so much AI, this kind of 'algorithmic leakage' can be hard to foresee or prevent completely, and therefore demands careful testing prior to and vigilant surveillance post-deployment (Ojha & Thakur, 2025).

Given this multipronged threat, lawyers will have to tread even more cautiously, seek information, inform client's in appropriate cases and prudently prioritize the use of trusted, reputable and explainable AI algorithms. Strong contracts with AI vendors that cover data privacy, security, liability for any breaches and strict confidentiality agreements can no longer be an addition to a wish list but a key component of any responsible ethical approach to client confidentiality in the age of all things digital. Lawyers should also be thinking about internal policies to minimize data so that the AI is only seeing data that is necessary for representing the client.

2.4. Bias and Discrimination: The Algorithmic Imperative

The most fundamental and ethically vexed question which arises around the insertion of AI in the judiciary concerns the tendency of algorithmic bias to not simply replicate but to reinforce institutional discrimination and societal inequality. AI are systems that learn, their intelligence and behaviour are based on the data they are hosted. If, as often is the case, these datasets capture historical bias, societal prejudice or discriminatory behavior, the AI will inevitably learn, internalize and perpetuate those biases at a much faster, larger and more seemingly neutral scale than humans themselves, thereby making them especially pernicious (Marwala, 2024).

2.4.1 Sources of Bias: A Multi-Layered Problem

Understanding the origins of bias is crucial for mitigation.

2.4.1.1 Data Bias (Historical and Representational)

This is the most common and insidious source. Historical data used to train AI models often mirrors past discriminatory practices within the legal system. For instance, if an AI is trained on decades of criminal justice data where certain racial or socioeconomic groups were disproportionately arrested, charged or given harsher sentences for similar crimes, the AI will learn to associate those demographics with higher risk, even if those associations are rooted in systemic injustice rather than actual individual propensity for future crime. Representational bias occurs when the training data inadequately represents certain populations like underrepresentation of women in historical legal leadership data, leading to poor performance, inaccurate predictions or biased recommendations for those groups. This can lead to a 'garbage in, garbage out' scenario where flawed historical data produces discriminatory future outcomes.

2.4.1.2 Algorithmic Bias (Design and Feature Selection)

Beyond the data, flaws in the algorithm's design itself or the specific features selected for analysis can inadvertently lead to biased outcomes. For instance, if an algorithm prioritizes certain data points that are proxies for protected characteristics like zip code correlating with racial demographics or educational background correlating with socioeconomic status, it can indirectly discriminate, even if those characteristics are not explicitly used. The weighting of different factors within an algorithm or the choice of optimization functions, can also embed bias (Dhabliya et al., 2024). For example, an algorithm optimized purely for efficiency might inadvertently disadvantage certain groups if efficiency metrics are correlated with existing inequalities.

2.4.1.3 Human Bias in Design and Deployment

The biases, conscious or unconscious, of the developers, data scientists and legal professionals who design, train and deploy AI systems can be implicitly coded into the AI. Their assumptions about fairness, relevance and risk can shape the AI's behavior. Furthermore, how an AI's output is interpreted and acted upon by human users can also introduce or amplify bias (Kumar & Sanjaya, 2025b). If a human decision-maker is prone to confirmation bias, they might more readily accept an AI's biased recommendation if it aligns with their pre-existing prejudices.

2.4.2 Impact Areas: Systemic Manifestations of Bias

Bias in AI can manifest with devastating consequences across various critical legal contexts, undermining the very notion of equal justice under law.

2.4.2.1 Predictive Policing and Resource Allocation

AI algorithms designed to identify 'hot spots' for future crime might, if trained on biased historical arrest data, disproportionately direct police resources to minority neighborhoods. This leads to increased surveillance, more arrests and higher recorded crime rates in those areas, thereby creating a self-fulfilling prophecy of higher crime rates in those communities, regardless of actual criminal activity. This can exacerbate racial profiling and community distrust.

2.4.2.2 Sentencing, Bail and Parole Decisions

AI tools used to assess flight risk, recidivism rates or suitability for parole might produce recommendations that are racially or socioeconomically biased. For instance, the COMPAS algorithm, used in some US courts, was found to disproportionately label Black defendants as higher risk than white defendants, even when controlling for prior offenses and future recidivism. Such biases lead to unequal treatment in the criminal justice system, potentially resulting in longer sentences, higher bail amounts and reduced chances of parole for certain groups, thereby exacerbating mass incarceration and systemic injustice (Nabirye, 2025).

2.4.2.3 E-discovery and Evidence Review

AI systems used to prioritize or categorize documents in large-scale litigation might, due to inherent biases in their training data or design, overlook crucial evidence relevant to a specific demographic group or type of claim like gender discrimination cases, disability rights claims, thereby undermining the fairness and thoroughness of the discovery process.

2.4.2.4 Employment Law and HR Decisions

AI used in automated hiring processes, resume screening or performance evaluations could perpetuate discriminatory patterns against certain genders, ages, or ethnic groups if trained on historical hiring data that reflects past biases. An AI might learn to favor candidates from specific universities or with particular work histories that are statistically skewed towards one demographic, even if those factors are not directly related to job performance.

2.4.2.5 Immigration and Asylum Applications

AI tools assisting in assessing the credibility of asylum seekers or the risk profile of visa applicants could inadvertently discriminate based on nationality, origin, linguistic patterns or even the perceived 'truthfulness' of facial expressions, leading to unfair denial of vital protections.

2.4.2.6 Legal Research and Case Prediction

Even AI tools for legal research can exhibit bias. If a tool is trained predominantly on case law from certain jurisdictions or legal traditions, it might underperform or provide less relevant results for cases in other areas or for novel legal questions where precedent is scarce. Predictive analytics tools might also reflect historical biases in judicial outcomes, predicting a lower success rate for certain types of plaintiffs or defendants based on past discriminatory patterns, rather than the merits of the current case.

2.4.3 Ethical Duty to Mitigate: A Proactive Imperative

Lawyers, as guardians of justice and fairness and officers of the court, bear an unequivocal ethical duty to actively promote these values. When utilizing AI, this translates into a proactive, rigorous and continuous responsibility to:

2.4.3.1 Scrutinize AI Outputs with Deep Skepticism

Critically evaluate whether AI-generated insights, predictions, or recommendations are free from bias, understanding that 'objective' algorithmic output can still be deeply unfair. This requires a human overlay of ethical judgment, contextual awareness and a willingness to challenge the AI's conclusions. Lawyers must ask, whose interests does this algorithm serve? What data was it trained on? Could it be disadvantaging my client or a particular group?

2.4.3.2 Demand Transparency and Explainability (XAI)

Advocate vigorously for explainable AI (XAI) that can articulate, in a human-understandable manner, how it arrived at a particular conclusion. This transparency is essential for identifying the roots of potential biases, understanding the decision-making process and challenging flawed or discriminatory outcomes. Without explainability, challenging a biased AI decision becomes impossible, leading to a system where algorithmic injustice is unreviewable (Chinnaraju, 2025).

2.4.3.3 Advocate for Fair AI Design, Testing, and Deployment

Engage actively with policymakers, regulators and AI developers to ensure that AI systems used in the legal system are designed, developed, rigorously tested and deployed with fairness, equity and non-discrimination as foundational, non-negotiable principles. This includes advocating for diverse development teams, comprehensive pre- and post-deployment bias audits and the use of fairness metrics in AI development.

2.4.3.4 Understand Contextual Limitations and Human Override

Recognize that even AI trained on 'unbiased' data can still lead to unfair or unjust outcomes if its recommendations are not interpreted and applied within a broader social, legal and human context. Legal decisions often require empathy, moral reasoning, an understanding of individual circumstances and a consideration of societal impact that AI cannot replicate (Kumar & Sanjaya, 2025). Lawyers must retain the ultimate authority to override AI recommendations when they conflict with ethical principles or the pursuit of justice.

The ethical imperative to combat algorithmic bias is not merely a technical challenge but a profound moral and societal one, central to upholding the integrity, legitimacy and public trust in the legal system in the AI age. It demands constant vigilance and a commitment to human-centered justice.

2.5. Accountability and Liability: Who is Responsible?

When an AI system, deployed within a legal context, makes a mistake, provides erroneous advice or contributes to a negative outcome for a client or more gravely, to a miscarriage of justice, the fundamental question of accountability becomes paramount. This is arguably one of the most complex ethical and legal challenges presented by AI, with no straightforward answers and significant implications for professional responsibility, legal redress and public trust. The traditional legal frameworks for liability were not designed for autonomous or semi-autonomous intelligent systems.

2.5.1 The 'Black Box' Problem and Opacity

Many advanced AI models, particularly deep learning neural networks, operate as black boxes. Their internal decision-making processes are so complex and opaque, involving millions or billions of parameters, that it becomes exceedingly difficult, even for their creators, to understand precisely *how* they arrived at a particular conclusion or recommendation (Budhkar et al., 2025). This lack of transparency, often termed as algorithmic opacity, severely complicates efforts to identify the source of an error, making it challenging to pinpoint whether a mistake originated from flawed training data or a design defect or an unforeseen emergent property of the AI's learning process or an interaction with specific, unusual input data. Without clear insight into the AI's reasoning, assigning blame becomes a formidable task.

2.5.2 Attribution of Blame: A Multi-Stakeholder Dilemma

The difficulty in understanding AI's internal workings leads to a convoluted attribution of blame, creating a responsibility gap where no single party can be clearly held liable:

2.5.2.1 The Lawyer

Given the lawyer's overarching duty of supervision, competence and ultimate responsibility for the advice provided to a client, is the lawyer solely accountable for any error originating from an AI tool they employ? This places a heavy burden on the lawyer to verify every AI output, regardless of its complexity or the time constraints of practice (Sharma, 2024). If a lawyer relies on an AI for legal research and the AI 'hallucinates' a non-existent case, leading to a malpractice claim, is the lawyer fully responsible for failing to catch the AI's error?

2.5.2.2 The AI Developer/Vendor

Is the software developer or vendor liable for defects in the AI system? This could fall under traditional product liability law. However, what if the error arises not from a coding flaw but from the AI's autonomous learning process, its interaction with novel data or from unforeseen emergent behavior? The traditional concept of a 'defect' becomes blurred when the system is designed to evolve and learn. Furthermore, developers often include disclaimers limiting their liability.

2.5.2.3 The Data Provider/Curator

If the AI's error stems from biased, inaccurate or incomplete training data, does responsibility extend to the entity that provided or curated that data? This could be a third-party data vendor or even the law firm itself if it used its own historical data.

2.5.2.4 The Client/User

Could the client bear some responsibility if they provided incomplete or flawed data to the AI tool or if they misused the AI tool in a manner inconsistent with its intended purpose like using a research AI for direct client advice without human review.

2.5.2.5 The AI Itself (Legal Personhood)

While currently a philosophical debate, some extreme views ponder whether advanced AI might eventually attain a form of legal personhood, allowing it to be held accountable. This is far from current reality but highlights the conceptual challenges.

2.5.3 Ethical Implications: Erosion of Trust and Justice

The absence of clear, robust accountability mechanisms could have profound and detrimental ethical implications for the entire legal system. It risks eroding public trust, as individuals who are harmed by algorithmic errors may perceive a lack of recourse or a system that shields powerful technology providers. It also challenges the fundamental principle of professional responsibility, where lawyers are traditionally held directly accountable for their actions and advice. If accountability is diffused or unassignable, it undermines the very notion of justice and the ability of individuals to seek redress for harm (Kumar & Sanjaya, 2025b). This accountability vacuum creates a moral hazard where AI developers and users might externalize the risks of their systems onto individuals.

2.5.4 Need for New Frameworks: Legal and Regulatory Innovation

There is an urgent and critical need for the development of innovative legal and ethical frameworks that clearly delineate liability and accountability for AI-driven decisions within the legal context. This will likely involve a multi-pronged approach:

2.5.4.1 New Forms of Insurance

Specialized professional liability insurance for lawyers using AI or novel product liability insurance for AI developers that specifically covers algorithmic errors or harms arising from AI's autonomous learning.

2.5.4.2 Regulatory Oversight Bodies and Standards

The establishment of new regulatory bodies or the expansion of existing ones, specifically tasked with setting technical standards for AI in legal contexts, auditing AI systems for fairness, accuracy and compliance with adjudicating disputes arising from AI errors. This could involve certification processes for legal AI tools (Kumar et al., 2025).

2.5.4.3 Revised Professional Conduct Rules

Further updates to professional conduct rules that provide more granular guidance on a lawyer's specific duties when using AI, including explicit requirements for due diligence on AI vendors, continuous validation of AI outputs, mandatory disclosure to clients about AI use and clear lines of responsibility for AI-assisted work.

2.5.4.4 Algorithmic Impact Assessments (AIAs)

Mandatory assessments prior to the deployment of AI systems in sensitive legal areas like criminal justice, family law, to identify potential risks, biases and assign responsibilities for mitigation. These assessments would be a prerequisite for deployment.

2.5.4.5 'Human-in-the-Loop' Requirements and Human Oversight

Mandating human oversight and final decision-making for critical legal processes, especially those involving significant rights or liberty interests. This ensures that AI remains an assistive tool rather than an autonomous decision-maker, allowing for human judgment and ethical intervention at crucial points. This could involve a double-check system where AI recommendations are always reviewed and approved by a human lawyer.

2.5.4.6 Strict Liability for High-Risk AI

Consideration of strict liability regimes for AI systems deployed in particularly high-stakes legal contexts, where the potential for harm is significant, shifting the burden of proof away from the harmed individual.

The challenge of accountability is not merely about assigning blame but about ensuring that victims of AI errors have a clear path to redress and that the integrity and trustworthiness of the legal process are maintained in an increasingly automated world.

3. AI IN LEGAL EDUCATION: PREPARING FOR THE AI-POWERED FUTURE

The ethical and efficient use of AI in law is intertwined and, largely dependent on, how legal education adjusts to train future legal professionals. Law schools, where the bulk of the lawyerly sausage is made, have a profound responsibility to prepare their students for life not just with options and futures in hand, judgment and legal reasoning, but with the technological literacy, critical thinking and ethical imagination to navigate, shape and lead in the emerging, AI-driven legal landscape. This necessitates a re-envisioning of the curriculum and of pedagogy and for faculty development, beyond models of yore.

3.1. Curriculum Reform: Beyond Traditional Legal Doctrine

In the past, traditional legal education has been oriented toward teaching substantive law, sound legal reasoning like issue spotting, rule statement, application, conclusion), and the art of advocacy. Although these elements will always provide the foundation of any legal education, AI forces a complete revamp in the curriculum if you are to graduate lawyers who are genuinely future-proofed. In addition to adding AI literacy, we need systemic standards reform. Accrediting organizations like bar associations and regulators should require minimum standards for technology and ethics training at law schools. Faculty development is no less vital; faculty must themselves be knowledgeable fluent in AI's technical fundamentals and ethical dimensions to effectively dispense with these reforms. Without systematized criteria and well-prepared teachers, curricular initiatives will continue to be fragmented.

3.1.1 AI Literacy and Data Science Fundamentals for Lawyers

Future lawyers do not need to be experts in programming or data science, but they absolutely must have a basic grasp of how AI operates in the abstract. That includes fundamentals anyone new to the field should understand, like machine learning (supervised, unsupervised, reinforcement, deep learning) and natural language processing (NLP) and the role NLP plays in legal text analysis, as well as predictive analytics and the building blocks of data analytics and statistical reasoning. Courses or units should take AI out of the black box and describe the algorithms, data input, training of the model and what the output means. The goal is to foster informed consumers and scrutinizers of AI tools so that they can pose the right questions regarding an AI system's design, its training data material, its underlying presumptions and its potential biases. This background will equip lawyers to intelligently interact with technologists and critically evaluate the reliability and ethical implications of AI tools (Eboigbe, 2024). Knowing how moments of NLP will misunderstand a legalese or how a predictive model can be biassed based on historical scenario is very important.

3.1.2 Ethical AI Principles and Law

There should also be explicit undergraduate or module courses on the Ethics of AI in Law that are a curriculum centric. They should involve in-depth discussions of algorithmic bias and fairness, data privacy and confidentiality in AI settings and accountability and liability frameworks for AI failures, including AI's effect on access to justice and the changing obligations of technological competence. Such courses would ideally provoke students to engage in vigorous ethical reasoning, where pre-existing principles of legal ethics such as zealous advocacy, loyalty are applied to never-before-seen AI situations, and inspire an attitude of proactivity about developing and deploying AI responsibly. Case studies of concrete AI failures in the world should be standard in such discussions.

3.1.3 Interdisciplinary Studies and Collaboration

Recognizing that AI is an exceedingly interdisciplinary area, law schools should actively promote and make possible cross-disciplinary research and work. That entails building strong partnerships and collaborative projects with CS departments, data science programs, ethics centers and social science faculties. Joint programs like JD/MS in Data Science, cross-listed courses, hackathons or guest speakers by citizens from these disciplines can help law students gain insight into AI's impact on society and technical foundation, enabling a more well-rounded view of the problems and solutions (Abbonato et al., 2024). This will prepare students to operate in multidisciplinary groups, something that will become more and more frequent in the practice of the law.

3.1.4 Future-Proofing Skills: Emphasizing the Uniquely Human and Strategic

As AI automates more rote and analytically-based duties, the focus of the curriculum must be on growing skills that AI cannot mimic or that demand human characteristics. These include:

i. Creativity/Innovation: Being able to come up with creative legal arguments, structure novel deals, create new types of legal services or develop new ways of addressing complex unstructured problems.
ii. Emotional Intelligence & Empathy: Needed to properly counsel clients, to gain rapport, to interpret nonverbal communications, to be successful in negotiation and to persuade judges in the courtroom.
iii. Complex Problem-Solving: Addressing complex legal problems that are not answerable by standard linear reasoning; synthesizing overlapping, conflicting data both legal data and non-legal information, parsing through ambiguity.
iv. Sales and Persuasion: The psychology, strategies and contributing guide to human negotiation and interaction.
v. Responsibility to Clients and Third Parties: Ethical leadership, judgment ethical and moral implications for the future regarding the development and implementation of these new technologies What is the moral and ethical role in determining what is right and wrong in the advent of new technologies that challenge the

boundaries of what is known? That includes the courage to question biased AI results.

vi. Strategic Advisory and Big Picture Thinking: Not just legal review, we add value through top level strategic advice, always mindful of the wider business, societal and political implications of your legal issues.
vii. Collaboration with AI/Human Teams: The skill to appropriately interact with, monitor, and make use of AI tools, to know when AI can be used and when not, and to integrate their outcomes into a wider human-driven legal process, to collaborate with diverse human teams.

This redefinition of core competencies is central, not just for individual lawyers who need to sustain their employing firms to stay relevant in an age of AI, but for the profession as a whole if it is to remain true to its social role as the heirs of justice and the custodians of the rule of law.

3.2. Pedagogical Approaches: Leveraging AI for Learning

AI should not just be learned as a subject; it should be integrated in pedagogy to cultivate critical interaction with the world. Customized learning platforms and adaptive assessment can enable differentiated instruction, and thoughtful policies can help protect integrity in a world with generative AI. Evaluations must stress ethical reasoning, algorithmic skepticism, and critique of AI outputs rather than imitation of them. Oral exams, project work and open documentation of use of AI, can help maintain the focus on academic rigor, but may introduce new tools.

3.2.1 AI-Powered Learning Tools for Personalized Education

AI can transform legal education through personalized learning that adapts to individual students based on their specific needs and learning methods. That will mean everything from adaptive quizzes that get harder or easier based on student performance, AI tutors that give instant feedback regarding a difficult legal concept or complex case brief and advanced legal research platforms that resemble the tools used in practice, benefiting students with the ability to more efficiently and accurately enhance their skills. AI can also automatically provide feedback on legal writing assignments, such as spotting grammatical errors, structural flaws, logical inconsistencies or opportunities for missing arguments in a paper, which could allow faculty to focus more of their time on providing commentary on higher-order aspects of the argument or strategy (Allen & Kendeou, 2023). This makes it possible for differentiated instruction and focused help.

3.2.2 Ethical Use in Assessment and Academic Integrity in the Age of Generative AI

The emergence of generative AI tools like large language models such as ChatGPT, poses grave challenges to academic integrity, plagiarism and student participation in genuinely authoring their work. Law schools need to create policies that are clear, comprehensive and subject to revision that will guide what is and is not appropriate when it comes to the use of AI on assignments, exams and research papers. Instead of blunt prohibition, which is typically impossible and backlashes, attention is directed to guiding responsible AI use and accentuating the instrumentality of AI over imitation of original thinking. Assessments need to be reimagined to assess critical thinking and ethical reasoning, the capacity to judge and improve AI outputs, not only to reproduce them. This could include students having to gather evidence of their use of AI or include their reasoning for their prompts, explain their selections and show their understanding on the limitations of the AI (Ekaterina et al., 2025). Open-book tests, oral examinations and project-based exams which require novel application of knowledge may also reduce risks.

3.2.3 Simulations and Experiential Learning with AI

AI could produce more accurate and engaging simulations of complicated legal scenarios, offering precious instances of experiential learning. They can practice client interviewing (using AI-driven virtual clients), witness examination (using AI-generated witness responses), trial advocacy (in simulated AI courtrooms) or contract drafting (with AI-based drafting tools) in a safe, repeatable and feedback-rich environment. These simulations can be customized to confront students with ethical dilemmas related to artificial intelligence in the real world, such as bias, privacy, responsibility or the human touch, in a low-stakes, hands-on environment. The practical learning students gain from this type of hands-on experiential engagement is invaluable in developing competency, ethical awareness and comfort-levels with the use of legal tech.

3.2.4 Fostering Critical Thinking and Algorithmic Skepticism

Teachers need to develop assignments and discussion prompts that call specifically for students to think critically about AI outputs, discern bias, and understand the limitations of algorithmic decision making. We should motivate students to reason critically about the data, the assumptions, and the conclusions of AI systems, and not to receive AI output passively. This cultivates a critical 'algorithmic skepticism' essential for applying AI responsibly in practice (Moustaghfir & Brigui, 2024). For example, a student might receive an AI-generated legal brief and be asked to how it is deficient or biased, or where human judgment is necessary. This is more than rote learning, but critical analysis at the higher order.

3.3 Access and Equity in Legal Education: Bridging the Digital Divide

Just as access to legal services is an ethical obligation for law practice, access to AI tools and education is an ethical duty in legal education (Li, 2023). Not doing so could result in a new kind of educational injustice, leaving students with socio-economic challenges at a disadvantage.

i. Providing Universal Access to Tools and Training: Law schools need to be proactive in ensuring that all students have equal access to the AI tools, software licenses and support and training that they need, regardless of socioeconomic status, prior familiarity with technology or existing digital proficiency. This could mean issuing institutional licenses for cutting edge legal AI platforms, maintaining strong campus Wi-Fi and computing infrastructure like computer labs with high processing laptops/desktops and scheduling introductory workshops on basic digital literacy for students who lack the same. The point is to level the field.
ii. Addressing the Foundational Digital Divide: Steps should be taken to assist students who may not have foundational digital literacy, reliable access to internet and computing resources at home, outside of the university. That could look like remedial courses or workshops on fundamental computer skills, loaner laptops or tablets, mentorship programs with tech-savvy peers or faculty or working with community organizations to provide off-campus access points and assistance. Neglecting this division will only intensify the inequalities in the education system.
iii. Curriculum Design and Pedagogy: The curriculum must be developed with a focus on inclusive pedagogy that takes into account different styles of learning and backgrounds when introducing AI literacy. Inclusive teaching methods also should not make assumptions about prior tech knowledge, and offer scaffolding for students encountering such concepts for the first time. For instance, instead of giving only readings on AI, instructors might include interactive demonstrations, hands-on exercises, or group projects so that students can learn by doing. This ensures accessible and engaging instruction in AI literacy for all and avoids the creation of a two-tier educational system of AI- literate and AI illiterate alumni.
iv. Grants/Scholarships and Financial Support for Tech Integration: There are some grants, scholarships and financial assistance that are focused on technology

tools that are needed for use in education, or training for AI and/or high-speed internet connectivity would all work to break down some of these economic barriers to access. Law schools should also tap into legal tech companies for potential partnership to get discounts or even free access for students on their platforms.

4. NAVIGATING THE ETHICAL LANDSCAPE: TOWARDS RESPONSIBLE AI INTEGRATION

The ethical issues raised by AI in law are not stagnant, but rather complex, fluid and organically changing. To respond efficiently to such intricate challenges, a pro-active, participative and extremely adaptive solution has to be elaborated, integrating all the different key players of the legal ecosystem and beyond. That means moving from being a reactive problem solver to an ethical forecaster and steward.

4.1. Developing Robust Ethical Guidelines and Regulations

The legal profession together with regulatory bodies and governmental authorities need to work together to promptly develop and promulgate unambiguous, comprehensive ethical standards, guidelines and where appropriate laws relating to AI, its ethical use in the law and its regulation (Shukla, 2024). It is not something for any one entity to do, but it is something which will need a combined, cross-industry approach to create a meaningful, enforceable structure.

4.1.1 Updating Professional Codes of Conduct with Granular Detail

Bar associations and professional organizations around the world should continue to revise their rules of professional conduct to explicitly address in detail the complexities of the integration of AI. That includes being specific about the changing obligations of tech competence like what is required due diligence in retaining AI vendors and monitoring its outputs, making explicit what it means to protect client confidences in the context of AI like data minimization and secure data transfer protocols, providing examples of what bias spotting and remediation looks like including, when necessary, mandating bias audits for certain AI applications, and defining potential liability when bad things happen as a result of the use of AI like, who has responsibility for the advice an AI generates. These updates would be living, regularly reviewed and updated documents as AI technology continues to develop, possibly every year or year-and-a-half.

4.1.2 Adopting a Principles-Based Approach for Longevity

Instead of bringing out too-specific, prescriptive rules which would likely be hopelessly outdated in no time due to fast evolving technology, a durable evergreen structure can be a principles-based approach. This would center on preserving fundamental ethical principles such as fairness, transparency, accountability, human oversight, privacy, beneficence and non-maleficence as principles in AI development and use in the law. Through history, such principles can help make decisions long after the technologies have shifted, a moral beacon that extends beyond the details of the technology. For example, she suggested, we could be guided by a principle of human flourishing in designing AI tools that do not so much replace human abilities as supercharge them.

4.1.3 Fostering International Cooperation and Harmonization for Global Challenges

AI development is inherently global, as is the flow of data and legal practice to a growing extent, international cooperation is critical. Ensuring that ethical standards and regulatory approaches are aligned across jurisdictions can help to avoid regulatory arbitrage, the practice wherein companies search for less regulated environments and foster consistency in ethical expectations and responsible cross-border deployment of legal AI applications. International organizations like UN and OECD, legal bodies like International Bar Association and intergovernmental organizations could have an important role to play in encouraging this discussion, sharing best practices, and encouraging agreement on global AI ethics in law (Bostancı & Yıldırım, 2025).

4.1.4 Implementing Regulatory Sandboxes and Innovation Hubs for Controlled Experimentation

To reconcile the tension between the need for innovation and responsible oversight, governments and regulators might well want to introduce specialised regulatory sandboxes or innovation hubs for legal AI. These controlled environments offer the opportunity to experiment with new AI legal technologies under regulatory oversight, such that developers can innovate and accumulate real-world insights, while regulators can diagnose and address emerging ethical risks, map the practical effects of the technology, and promulgate best practices ahead of unpiloted implementation. This process of trial and error supports learning and adaptation for the emergence of 'fit-for-purpose' regulations.

4.2. Promoting Transparency and Explainability (XAI)

The black box problem, where the inner working of many leading AI systems are not transparent is a real ethical hurdle, in a field like law especially where due process, a right to understand decisions in the law and to question adverse outcomes is so crucial. Justice must not only be right; it must be intelligible (Blinova et al., 2023).

4.2.1 Developing Explainable AI (XAI) for Legal Contexts as a Necessity

There are critical needs to advance and reify XAI competencies. XAI is intended to give human-interpretable explanations of the innards of an AI system, how it formulated a decision, prediction or recommendation. In the legal field, that may mean that lawyers have to be able to explain to clients, judges, juries and regulatory entities not just what the AI tool decided, but how it came to that decision, identifying the most important data points, features and algorithmic logic that played into the result. This transparency is necessary to foster the trust, detect biases, allow AI-informed decisions to be properly challenged and ultimately help maintain the accountability of legal reasoning. For instance, an XAI system could point out the particular clauses in a contract that resulted in a risk assessment or the specific precedents that informed a prediction.

4.2.2 Mandatory Auditing and Validation by Independent Bodies

There should be routine, mandatory independent audits of AI systems used in sensitive legal contexts and not alternatives. Such audits would certify the fairness, accuracy, robustness and alignment with agreed-on moral standards and established laws of the AI. Audits should look into the quality and representativeness of the training data, the model and methodology used and performance in the field, including disparities among different demographic groups. Frequent, unbiased validation supports continuous integrity and identifies concept drift or decay of the model. They should be conducted by independent, competent third parties.

4.2.3 Ethical Disclosure to Clients as a Professional Duty

It is incumbent on lawyers to be transparent with clients about when and how AI tools are being used in their case. This disclosure should be clear and complete, made in plain language and should also explain the specific benefits of using AI and risks like data security implications, potential for bias, limitations of the technology. Explicit and informed client consent for use of AI especially when sensitive data is utilized or new implementations are launched, is an essential element of this obligation. This provides transparency in the law-client relationship and gives clients some control over how they are represented.

4.3. Fostering Interdisciplinary Collaboration

The inherent complexity of AI's ethical implications, spanning technology, law, ethics and social science, unequivocally demands robust and sustained collaboration across disciplines. No single field possesses all the necessary expertise to address these challenges effectively; siloed approaches will inevitably fail.

4.3.1 Bridging the Gap Between Lawyers and Technologists for 'Ethics-by-Design'

It is absolutely crucial that we develop effective means of communication and cooperation between lawyers and developers of artificial intelligence. counsel must articulate their ethical principles, their legal obligations and their real-world needs in AI tools, expressing legal concepts through implementable technical properties. On the other hand, technologists have to know enough about the particular legal and ethical constraints, the intricate logic of the law, and the social implications of what they build. Work in partnership can result in ethics-by-design tools for the legal industry, in which the machine is born with consideration for the ethical issues within it rather than that being an afterthought (Primlani et al., 2025). This is where joint workshops, hackathons, and combined research projects can allow such a dialogue to take place.

4.3.2 Integrating Ethicists and Social Scientists for Holistic Understanding

Incorporating the invaluable perspectives of ethicists, philosophical, sociological and other social science analyses, can led to a richer and more nuanced understanding of the broader societal impact of AI, its potential to violate human rights and its implications for the social structure. Their knowledge can contribute to the development of stronger human-centered ethical foundations that will support more than principles of compliance with more fundamental concerns of justice, human welfare/power and social good. They can provide much needed critical views on fairness, autonomy and dignity considering algorithmic decision-making.

4.4. Continuous Learning and Adaptation

The field of AI is characterized by its exponential pace of evolution. Consequently, ethical frameworks, professional practices and educational methodologies must be inherently dynamic, adaptable and committed to continuous learning (Liu et al., 2023). Stagnation is not an option.

4.4.1 Embracing Lifelong Learning as a Professional Imperative

Lawyers, from green graduates to greybeard practitioners, need to embrace lifelong learning as a professional constant. This means to keep up on advances in AI, learn new use cases and to continually be thinking about their ethical implications. That could mean formal CLE on AI and specialization certifications in legal tech or AI ethics or it could be informal learning through legal industry publications, conferences, webinars, or peer networks. These resources are made available through bar associations.

4.4.2 Cultivating Ethical Reflection and Dialogue within Institutions

An open conversation and regular discussion of professional responsibility issues within law firms, corporate legal departments, bar associations and law schools are needed to identify emerging ethical issues, discuss best practices and help collectively craft solutions. Providing safe places for attorneys to discuss AI-related ethical challenges without judgment is vital to developing a culture of responsible innovation and shared problem-solving. This could be something along the lines of periodic AI ethics roundtables or formal committees.

4.4.3 Proactive Engagement and Shaping the Future of AI in Law

The legal profession must do more than just respond to the challenges posed by AI. Rather than remain on the side line, it will have to take a proactive stance in AI development, which includes participating in policy debates, supporting relevant research and shaping the design and implementation of AI. The legal profession must shape AI's path by ensuring that these powerful tools are developed and used consistent with the basic values of justice, fairness and human dignity rather than simply adapting legal norms to technology (Kashefi et al., 2024).

5. CONCLUSION: TOWARDS A JUST AND ETHICAL AI-POWERED LEGAL FUTURE

Looking at the ethical applications of AI for legal professionals brings about significant opportunities and challenges. So, whilst the above has set out some of the-professional, regulatory, and ethical issues that arise from AI use in legal-services plenty more positions can be held on each of these matters – the pedagogic aspect has featured less prominently in this title, in contrast. Because, the lawyers of tomorrow will necessarily inherit an AI-augmented profession, and so legal education should figure much more prominently as a theme—in this formulation, not so much as an ancillary concern as one of the central pillars of the conversation.

Currently, the medicine of education is calling for curriculum revolution, cross-cutting cooperation, and building up AI muscles. But that could be taken to further elements in some crucial aspects. First, the discussion should emphasize that law schools ought to integrate ethical foresight into their curriculum, so that students not only learn how to use AI tools, but also learn how to critically question their assumptions, outputs, and societal effects. Second, there is potential for further inquiry into how faculty development, accreditation standards, and continuing legal education can systematically inculcate technological competence and algorithmic skepticism throughout an attorney's life. Third the equity dimension – addressing digital divides between students – deserves further explication as a matter for reflection on professional ethics, so as to guard against access to AI-enabled education reproducing the very inequalities the profession is mandated to address.

Finally, an increased educational remit would bring the work into closer alignment with its stated aspiration to engage with both practice and pedagogy. But AI is also changing the nature of the work lawyers do, and reshaping what it means to educate, evaluate and employ them in a time of rapid technological change. By further situating the educational analysis in relation to practical concerns, the conversation can better map out a path to an AI-enabled legal future that is both just and responsibly taught.

REFERENCES

Abbonato, D., Bianchini, S., Gargiulo, F., & Venturini, T. (2024). Interdisciplinary Research in Artificial Intelligence: Lessons from COVID-19. *Quantitative Science Studies*, *5*(4), 1–20. DOI: 10.1162/qss_a_00329

Allen, L. K., & Kendeou, P. (2023). ED-AI Lit: An Interdisciplinary Framework for AI Literacy in Education. *Policy Insights from the Behavioral and Brain Sciences*, *11*(1), 3–10. Advance online publication. DOI: 10.1177/23727322231220339

Blinova, U., Rozhkova, N., & Rozhkova, D. (2023). NFT (Non-Fungible Tokens) as an Object of Accounting. *Journal of Digital Art & Humanities*, *4*(1), 3–9. DOI: 10.33847/2712-8148.4.1_1

Bostancı, S. H., & Yıldırım, S. (2025). Role of Government and International Institutions in Fostering Social Responsibility and Environmental Harmony. In *World Sustainability Series* (pp. 225–243). Springer Nature Switzerland., DOI: 10.1007/978-3-031-81469-3_10

Budhkar, A., Song, Q., Su, J., & Zhang, X. (2025). Demystifying the black box: A survey on explainable artificial intelligence (XAI) in bioinformatics. *Computational and Structural Biotechnology Journal*, *27*(1), 346–359. DOI: 10.1016/j.csbj.2024.12.027 PMID: 39897059

Chinnaraju, A. (2025). Explainable AI (XAI) for Trustworthy and Transparent decision-making: A Theoretical Framework for AI Interpretability. *World Journal of Advanced Engineering Technology and Sciences*, *14*(3), 170–207. DOI: 10.30574/wjaets.2025.14.3.0106

Dhabliya, D., Dari, S. S., Dhablia, A. N. A., Kachhoria, R., & Khetani, V. (2024). Addressing Bias in Machine Learning Algorithms: Promoting Fairness and Ethical Design. *E3S Web of Conferences, 491*(E3S Web Conf), 02040–02040. Web of Conferences. DOI: 10.1051/e3sconf/202449102040

Eboigbe, E. O. (2024). AI in Legal Analytics: Balancing Efficiency, Accuracy, and Ethics in Contract and Predictive Analysis. *Journal of Legal Education*, *72*(3 & 4). Advance online publication. DOI: 10.2139/ssrn.4997519

Ekaterina, K., Ana, M., & Maia, Z. (2025). Academic Integrity Within the Medical Curriculum in the Age of Generative Artificial Intelligence. *Health Science Reports*, *8*(2), e70489. Advance online publication. DOI: 10.1002/hsr2.70489 PMID: 39980818

Kashefi, P., Kashefi, Y., & Mirsaraei, A. G. (2024). Shaping the future of AI: Balancing innovation and ethics in global regulation. *Uniform Law Review*, *29*(3), 524–548. Advance online publication. DOI: 10.1093/ulr/unae040

Kumar, A. B., & Sanjaya, K. (2025a). AI Renaissance in Renewable Energy. In *Advances in environmental engineering and green technologies book series* (pp. 15–32). IGI Global., DOI: 10.4018/979-8-3373-0045-0.ch002

Kumar, A. B., & Sanjaya, K. (2025b). Ethics, Algorithms, and the Rules of Evidence. In *Forensic Intelligence and Deep Learning Solutions in Crime Investigation* (pp. 103–124). IGI Global., DOI: 10.4018/979-8-3693-9405-2.ch006

Kumar, A. B., Sanjaya, K., & Saleem, M. (2025). Justice in the Age of Algorithms. In *Advances in Computational Intelligence and Robotics* (pp. 191–210). IGI Global. DOI: 10.4018/979-8-3693-9395-6.ch009

Li, H. (2023). AI in Education: Bridging the Divide or Widening the Gap? Exploring Equity, Opportunities, and Challenges in the Digital Age. *Advances in Education. Humanities and Social Science Research*, *8*(1), 355–355. DOI: 10.56028/aehssr.8.1.355.2023

Liu, B., Mazumder, S., Robertson, E., & Grigsby, S. (2023). AI Autonomy: Self-initiated Open-world Continual Learning and Adaptation. *AI Magazine*, *44*(2), 185–199. Advance online publication. DOI: 10.1002/aaai.12087

Marwala, T. (2024). Avoidable and Unavoidable AI Algorithmic Bias. In *The Balancing Problem in the Governance of Artificial Intelligence* (pp. 121–136). Springer Singapore., DOI: 10.1007/978-981-97-9251-1_8

Mikeladze, T., Meijer, P. C., & Verhoeff, R. P. (2024). A comprehensive exploration of artificial intelligence competence frameworks for educators: A critical review. *European Journal of Education*, *59*(3), e12663. Advance online publication. DOI: 10.1111/ejed.12663

Moustaghfir, S., & Brigui, H. (2024). Navigating Critical Thinking in the Digital Era: An Informative Exploration. *International Journal of Linguistics. Literature and Translation*, *7*(1), 137–143. DOI: 10.32996/ijllt.2024.7.1.11x

Nabirye, K. (2025). *E-Discovery and the Language of Digital Evidence*. EURASIAN EXPERIMENT JOURNAL OF HUMANITIES AND SOCIAL SCIENCES (EE-JHSS). https://kiu.ac.ug/assets/publications/3441_e-discovery-and-the-language-of-digital-evidence.pdf

Ojha, N. K., & Thakur, S. (2025). Privacy Laws and Leak of Financial Data in the Era of Generative AI. In *Generative Artificial Intelligence in Finance: Large Language Models, Interfaces, and Industry Use Cases to Transform Accounting and Finance Processes* (pp. 265–281). Wiley Online Library. DOI: 10.1002/9781394271078.ch14

Primlani, N., Blythe, M., & Marshall, J. (2025). Design Courts: Workshops for Exploring Emerging Technology Ethics. *Sage Journals*, *9*(2), 1–12. DOI: 10.1145/3706598.3713774

Shah, A. (2025, March 8). *Artificial Intelligence In Legal Education And Practice: Global Opportunities, Ethical Dilemmas, And The Path*. IJLLR Journal; IJLLR Journal. https://www.ijllr.com/post/artificial-intelligence-in-legal-education-and-practice-global-opportunities-ethical-dilemmas-and

Sharma, S. (2024). Benefits or Concerns of AI: A Multistakeholder Responsibility. *Futures*, *157*(103328), 103328. DOI: 10.1016/j.futures.2024.103328

Shukla, S. (2024). Principles Governing Ethical Development and Deployment of AI. *International Journal of Engineering Business Management*, *8*(2), 26–46. DOI: 10.22161/ijebm.8.2.5

Thomas, P., Dzemidzic Kristiansen, S., & Von Hof, J. (2025). The Network Society: A Double-Edged Sword. In *Education and Cultural Evolution in Norway's Multiethnic Society* (pp. 119–130). Springer Nature Switzerland. DOI: 10.1007/978-3-031-89018-5_12

Zafar, A. (2024). Balancing the scale: Navigating ethical and practical challenges of artificial intelligence (AI) integration in legal practices. *Discover Artificial Intelligence*, *4*(1), 27. Advance online publication. DOI: 10.1007/s44163-024-00121-8

Zaid, T., & Garai, S. (2024). Emerging Trends in Cybersecurity: A Holistic View on Current Threats, Assessing Solutions, and Pioneering New Frontiers. *Blockchain in Healthcare Today*, *7*(1). Advance online publication. DOI: 10.30953/bhty.v7.302 PMID: 38715765

Chapter 9
Transforming Legal Education in the Age of AI:
Towards a Critical and Experiential Pedagogy

Tawney Bennett
https://orcid.org/0000-0001-9664-844X
Truman Bodden Law School, Cayman Islands

ABSTRACT

This chapter critically explores the integration of artificial intelligence (AI) into legal education through the lenses of critical pedagogy, experiential learning theory, and human-computer interaction. It argues that AI must not be treated as a neutral tool for enhancing efficiency but instead aligned with values of justice, equity, and democratic participation. Drawing on Freire's critical pedagogy and Kolb's experiential learning cycle, this chapter examines how AI can support interactive and student-centered legal education through simulations, intelligent tutoring systems, and adaptive assessment. It also highlights risks, such as algorithmic bias, epistemic injustice, and over-reliance on opaque systems developed without educator oversight. This chapter advocates participatory design, algorithmic transparency, and inclusive implementation strategies. It concludes by advancing practical recommendations for educators, curriculum designers, and policymakers to ensure that AI is deployed in ways that foster experiential, equitable, and justice-oriented legal education.

DOI: 10.4018/979-8-3373-3451-6.ch009

INTRODUCTION

The Changing Landscape of Legal Education

Undoubtedly, university-level education has undergone dramatic transformation in recent years, affected by a number of key phenomena such as mass expansion (Moser, 1988), the introduction of, and increase in tuition fees (Palfreyman & Tapper, 2016), the rise of marketization and consumerism(Bennett, 2020), and underfunding(Watson & Taylor, 1998). One of the most pressing issues in modern education is the advent of Artificial Intelligence (AI). Legal education, in particular, is witnessing a paradigm shift as it attempts to keep pace with rapid technological advancements in the legal profession (Dolidze, 2025). AI has introduced powerful new tools that supplement and enhance human capabilities, potentially revolutionizing the way that legal professionals and educators alike work(Susskind, 2019).

As the legal landscape continues to evolve, legal education must adapt. It is no longer adequate for law schools to train students solely in the interpretation and application of legal principles; they must also equip future lawyers to navigate and engage critically with emerging technologies. Tools such as AI-driven legal research platforms, intelligent tutoring systems, and automated contract analysis software are becoming increasingly standard practices within leading law firms and legal departments (Ashley, 2017). Implementing these technologies in legal education enables students to build technological proficiency and strengthen their analytical capabilities, which is essential for succeeding in an AI-equipped legal environment.

Simultaneously, the integration of AI into legal practice presents multifaceted ethical, regulatory, and educational challenges. Concerns about algorithmic bias, data privacy, the transparency of AI systems, and the shifting boundaries of legal professional roles demand thoughtful and critical examinations (Dolidze, 2025). Thus, any use of AI in legal education must be thoughtfully deployed to ensure that such ethical challenges are judiciously navigated.

Current Pedagogical Challenges

The literature highlights a growing recognition of the disparity between legal education and the practical needs of the legal profession, emphasizing the need for curriculum reform to prepare law students for real-world practice (James, 2008; Miller, 2014; O'Leary, 2021). Legal education has traditionally relied on methods such as the Socratic method and case-law analysis. However, these approaches face challenges in addressing the diverse needs of contemporary students and the evolving demands of the legal profession (Shugan 2006; Stoddard and O'Dell 2016)(Spencer, 2022). In basic terms, the Socratic method involves the student stating a position, with the teacher then asking a series of questions to expose weaknesses in their arguments and encourage deeper, more critical thinking. This assists students and educators in determining the extent of their knowledge of a particular matter(Paul & Elder, 2007). Although it can be a valuable way of developing learning and critical thinking when applied appropriately, this method has also been criticized for disadvantaging and even alienating some students, particularly women (Tsaoussi, 2020). Spencer (2022) argues that the Socratic method risks alienating introverted students and perpetuating a culture of aggression in the legal profession. She challenges the assumption that successful lawyers must be loud and aggressive, arguing instead of a shift towards more contemplative and relationally focused approaches in legal practice(Spencer, 2022). Thus, there is a need for a less confrontational and equitable approach to instilling these important legal skills in law students, one that recognizes and accommodates a range of personality types and avoids alienating students who could help diversify the profession. Furthermore, while there are some examples of the Socratic method being built into experiential learning experiences(Abenoza & Arjona, 2017), its scope to bridge the gap between the classroom and preparing students for real-world practice is limited.

Furthermore, ongoing advancements in legal technology, automation, and artificial intelligence necessitate a shift in legal education to equip students with the digital skills needed for a rapidly evolving landscape (Weinberg & Hyams, 2023). Although traditional legal skills such as professionalism, problem solving, and client relationship management are still highly valued, some studies have found that experience with legal technology is not a prerequisite for entry into today's legal profession (Alexander, Mcconnell, Mitchell, & Mcgrane, 2024). Alexander et al. (2024) found that understanding the nature and potential of legal technology is more important in the legal profession than in hands-on experience. However, it must be noted that their research rested on the distribution of a questionnaire to legal professionals in early 2021, which was prior to a number of significant innovations in AI, such as large language model (LLM) generative AI tools such as ChatGPT. Research conducted by (Ajevski, Barker, Gilbert, Hardie, & Ryan, 2023) highlighted the dual challenge faced by law schools in responding to ChatGPT and similar AI technologies. On the one hand, there is a need to develop strategies to make assessments more challenging for AI to prevent cheating, but on the other hand, AI technology must be incorporated into legal education to prepare students for an evolving legal workplace. The authors suggest that rather than trying to ban or ignore these technologies, law schools should embrace them as an opportunity to rethink assessment methods and teach students about the ethical use of AI in their future careers (Ajevski, Barker, Gilbert, Hardie, & Ryan, 2023). Although an in-depth analysis of the particular impact of AI on student assessment lies outside the scope of this chapter, this balanced approach to AI use goes some way to recognize both the risks and benefits of AI in legal education and practice, highlighting the need for adaptability in the face of rapid technological change.

Overview of AI's Increasing Influence on Legal Education

The advent of artificial intelligence (AI) emerged in the mid-20th century. Turing first speculated on the possibility of machines replicating human reasoning in 1950, which laid the philosophical foundations for AI. This field formally emerged in 1956 at the Dartmouth Conference, which is often identified as the foundational event for AI research. Early progress in this area was much less advanced than the AI systems we know today, and earlier progress focused on symbolic reasoning and rule-based systems owing to limited computational power and availability.

The 1980s saw the rise of 'expert systems' which were designed based on user-defined rules were used in generative tasks that required specialized knowledge, such as medical diagnosis (He, Cao and Tan, 2025). Subsequently, a new wave of progress arrived in the 1990s and the 2000s with advances in machine learning, where algorithms could be improved through data exposure rather than explicit programming. Increasing the computational power during this period led to breakthroughs in natural language processing and pattern recognition.

In the 2010s, a more sophisticated type of AI, called 'deep learning, ' transformed the field. These systems learned by processing large amounts of data instead of relying on human programming, which led to marked improvements in image recognition, speech processing, and language translation (He, Cao and Tan, 2025). These techniques underpin modern AI applications that are ubiquitous in everyday life such as search engines, recommendation systems, and autonomous vehicles.

More recently, generative AI tools powered by LLMs, such as ChatGPT, have gained popularity owing to their transformative ability to generate humanistic text, images, and even code. Unlike previous iterations, such models are not confined to narrow tasks and can instead engage in adaptive dialogue, draft documents, or even simulate complex scenarios. This shift in capability, accessibility, and scalability has brought AI into the mainstream, and it is now widely used in education and the legal profession.

For legal education in particular, AI technologies offer novel opportunities to enhance legal pedagogy by introducing interactive and personalized learning experiences (Farahani and Ghasmi, 2024). Integrating AI into legal education can help bridge gaps in accessibility, provide real-time feedback, and simulate practical legal scenarios, thereby preparing students more effectively for their professional careers (Onesi-Ozigagun et al., 2024).

AI-driven adaptive learning systems can analyze student performance data to create customized learning paths, ensuring that legal students receive content at their own pace and level of understanding. This personalized approach has been shown to improve student engagement and academic performance in legal studies (Onesi-Ozigagun et al., 2024). Furthermore, AI can facilitate the development of intelligent tutoring systems that simulate human tutors and deliver personalized and adaptive educational experiences in legal education without excessive resource expenditure (Tang, 2024).

Importantly, whilst artificial intelligence offers considerable benefits for legal education, its transformative potential risks are undermined if it is employed merely to replicate and automate traditional pedagogical methods, rather than reimagining them. Particular concerns include issues with data privacy, algorithmic bias, and the need for teacher training specific to legal pedagogy (Onesi-Ozigagun et al., 2024). Additionally, the integration of AI into legal education must address issues of inclusion and equity, ensuring that all law students have equal access to these advanced learning tools (Tang, 2024). This chapter offers a nuanced exploration of both the affordances and limitations of AI in the legal education context. Furthermore, it is crucial to address the challenges and ethical considerations associated with AI integration to maximize its positive impact on legal education (Farahani & Ghasmi, 2024). While not offering an in-depth analysis of the ethical issues associated with AI integration, this chapter situates the discussion within the broader context of advancements in educational technology and the specific imperatives of modern legal training.

Rationale for Focusing on Experiential Learning

To address the pedagogical challenges discussed earlier in this chapter, legal education could benefit from adopting more inclusive and experiential teaching approaches. Inclusive curriculum design, which prioritizes the creation of learning environments that accommodate varied backgrounds, abilities, and learning styles, has the potential to significantly enhance educational equity (Akintayo et al., 2024). This is particularly imperative in legal education where broadening access to the profession remains a pressing priority. The introduction of the Solicitor's Qualifying Examination (SQE) demonstrates a shift towards standardizing entry into the profession and potentially broadening access by removing some of the financial and structural barriers associated with traditional pathways, although its impact in achieving such ends is disputed (see for example Guth & Dutton, 2018). A comprehensive meta-analysis of the relationship between experiential learning and learning outcomes found that experiential learning pedagogies significantly enhanced educational outcomes compared with traditional learning environments (Burch, et al., 2019). Burch et al. 's research highlights the applicability of experiential learning across various fields, providing substantive evidence that supports the integration of experiential learning into teaching practices. Additionally, experiential learning has emerged as a powerful transformative approach in legal education, equipping students with practical skills and providing them with real-world experiences that are crucial for their development as competent legal practitioners (Miller, 2014). The integration of experiential learning into legal curricula addresses the need for students to engage more deeply with the practice of law, bridging the gap between theoretical knowledge and practical application (Miller, 2014; Schepard, 2022; Sossin, 2014; Voskobitova, 2021). It may also comprise a combination of academic instruction with meaningful community services, which allows students to apply their legal knowledge to real-world scenarios while addressing the needs of the community. Such programs allow for the amalgamation of important educational components, such as reflection, practice, and research, which together aim to drive social change and encourage sensitization to social justice issues(Derreth, Levin, & Jones, 2021). By embracing experiential teaching methods and focusing on inclusive design, legal education can better prepare students for the complexities of the modern legal profession while fostering a more equitable, engaging, and, in some cases, socially responsible learning environment.

THEORETICAL FRAMEWORK

Kolb's Experiential Learning Cycle

This chapter is grounded in David Kolb's (1984) Experiential Learning Cycle (ELC), originally founded by John Dewey, which emphasizes learning through experience and reflection. It offers an enriched version of the ELC that integrates emerging pedagogical practices that effectively complement its framework. This chapter will also incorporate principles from critical pedagogy, expanding upon Freire's (1970) seminal work, but with a focus on empowering students and addressing the issues of equity and inclusion. The application of AI in education is examined through the lens of human-computer interaction and participatory design approaches (such as Gross (2014)) considering how technology mediates learning experiences. This chapter argues that AI systems that support adaptive learning and legal simulations offer new modalities, through which Kolb's experiential cycle can unfold in digital contexts.

While Kolb's Experiential Learning Theory provides the core pedagogical structure for this chapter, its application is significantly enriched when interpreted through the critical and interactive lenses of Freire's pedagogy and human–computer interaction theory. Together, these frameworks offer not only a blueprint for experiential design, but also the ethical and interactional principles that must guide how AI mediates legal learning experiences. Unlike prior studies that explore AI or experiential learning in isolation, this chapter brings them together under a coherent pedagogical framework, offering practical guidance on designing transformative legal education for the digital age.

Kolb's experiential learning theory conceptualizes learning as a cyclical process that involves four key stages: concrete experience, reflective observation, abstract conceptualization, and active experimentation (Kolb, 1984). This model underpins many contemporary approaches to professional and legal education, in which learning is viewed as iterative, relational, and context-sensitive.

Concrete experience refers to direct, hands-on engagement with real or simulated new experiences and the crux of experiential learning. In traditional legal education, this might involve participating in moots, legal clinics, or role-plays that replicate professional challenges. The emphasis here is on situational learning, being immersed in a scenario in which learners can act, respond, and observe real-time outcomes. AI-driven simulations in engineering or medical training are known to offer learners the chance to participate in situations that would be impractical or unsafe in the real world (Botelho et al., 2016). In legal education, these technologies can simulate courtroom environments or legal scenarios, allowing students to engage in practical tasks that replicate real-world experiences in psychologically safe spaces (Fromm et al., 2021).

Reflective observation requires learners to step back and critically analyze their experience. This stage encouraged questioning: What happened? Why did this happen in this manner? What legal or ethical framework are involved? Reflection facilitates deeper understanding by connecting the experience to prior knowledge and broader contexts, helping students make sense of their experiences. Educational platforms utilizing AI-powered analytical and personalized feedback on tasks have the potential to help students compare their experiences with theoretical knowledge, thus bridging practical experiences with observational learning (Matsuo, 2015). This stage emphasizes the need for AI tools to support critical thinking and reflection, drawing insights from students' actions and decisions (Chalkiadakis et al., 2024).

Abstract Conceptualization involves drawing generalized insights from experiences. In the context of traditional legal education, learners may develop or revise legal theories, mental models, or conceptual frameworks based on their observations and reflections. This is an important stage that promotes higher-order thinking and supports the integration of doctrinal knowledge with practical judgement. AI has the potential to support the cognitive process of abstracting legal principles and theories from experiential learning. Fromm et al. (2021) found that the use of intelligent agents in providing textual explanations of concepts and recommending further study to improve individual weaknesses afforded abstract conceptualization. Similarly, AI-driven intelligent tutoring systems and virtual assistants may be deployed to achieve this aim.

The active experimentation completes the cycle. At this stage, learners test their new understanding by applying it to novel situations. This could involve revisiting a scenario with a new strategy, engaging with a different legal issue, or contributing to collaborative problem solving in a dynamic setting. At this stage, AI can facilitate experimentation by allowing learners to test their hypotheses in a controlled, simulated environment. This experimentation may assist in reinforcing learning by allowing students to actively engage with legal content and adapt their approaches based on AI-provided insights and predictions (Fromm et al., 2021; Chalkiadakis et al., 2024).

Integrating AI into each stage of Kolb's cycle enhances legal education by providing dynamic, interactive, and personalized learning experiences. While AI offers significant promise, challenges such as cost, technical barriers, and teacher readiness must also be addressed to fully realize its potential in legal education settings (Chalkiadakis et al., 2024). Moreover, Kolb's (1984) framework offers a structured pathway for designing immersive AI experiences, but it must be enacted in tandem with the ethical and political sensibilities of Freire's pedagogy and the design-focused responsiveness of human–computer interaction principles. Only through this combined lens can AI be deployed not just to enhance skill acquisition, but to promote equitable, student-centered, and justice-oriented legal learning.

Freire's Critical Pedagogy

Freire's critical pedagogy provides a valuable lens through which AI can be used for legal education practices. Freire (1970) critiques the traditional 'banking model' of education, where teachers deposit information into passive students, arguing that learning should foster dialogue, critical consciousness (conscientização), and liberation. In practice, this means that educators should engage in collaborative exchanges with their students, co-creating knowledge through questions, reflection, and action, rather than repetition and memory recall. Thus, the Freirean approach supports the notion that AI should be used to empower learners as active, critical participants in education rather than simply passive recipients. It further supports the development of critical consciousness and awareness of social, political, and legal structures that enable students to challenge injustice and support sensitization to social justice issues, which is a common benefit associated with certain experiential learning activities.

In legal education, the Freirean perspective implies that teaching law should go beyond rote learning of statutes and cases. Instead, it should encourage students to critically examine how laws function in society, their interests, and how legal systems might perpetuate or alleviate injustice. This aligns with movements in critical legal education and criminology, which view law through the lens of social justice and power relations. For example, clinical legal education programs often explicitly aim to instill social justice values and an ethics of service in students(Kee, 2024). Rather than treating law students as passive recipients of legal doctrine, a freire-inspired approach treats them as agents capable of understanding and transforming the legal system to better serve equity and justice. Any use of technology in this context must support empowerment and liberation, helping students experience the law in action, reflect on it, and develop a commitment to justice. Many specific AI applications can be used to manifest these ideals and create experiential and equitable learning environments, particularly legal simulations, chatbots, and adaptive learning systems. The particular AI-powered applications that may help create interactive, immersive, and student-centered learning experiences will be discussed later in this chapter.

Human Computer Interaction Theory

Adopting AI in legal education poses design challenges in addition to the pedagogical implications discussed earlier in this chapter. Human–computer interaction (HCI) originally evolved as a subfield of computer science, but has transformed into its own interdisciplinary field over the last decades focused on the design, evaluation, and implementation of interactive computing systems for human use (Gross, 2014). HCI explores how people interact with computers and technology with the aim of making those interactions more effective, intuitive, and accessible(Nancholas, 2023). Research on HCI education provides a useful framework for understanding how technology mediates learning experiences and how it can be designed to uphold pedagogical values such as experiential and equitable learning. HCI highlights the need for AI simulation, as with any use of technology, to be dynamic and responsive to human interaction(Gross, 2014). Gross (2014) posited that complex learning experiences arise from meaningful engagement, not just automated content delivery, which is a danger of implementing AI technologies without pedagogical grounding. One fundamental insight HCI provides is that technology is *not neutral*; the design of an AI tool shapes how students interact with knowledge, peers, and instructors. Thus, the medium of learning through AI tools may either reinforce a banking model (designed for passive consumption and one-way content delivery) or facilitate a dialogical model (designed for interactivity, exploration, and user agency). Furthermore, any implementation of such tools should be guided by a strong pedagogical understanding of how students learn and what they need to enrich their learning processes.

AI-DRIVEN EXPERIENTIAL METHODS IN LEGAL EDUCATION

Simulation

Experiential learning in law often relies on simulations, such as mock cases, moot courts, and client role-plays, and AI is elevating these simulations to new levels of realism and interactivity. (Mollick, et al., 2024) explored the potential of generative artificial intelligence (AI) for creating adaptive educational simulations. Simulation, where learners practice skills in appropriately realistic low-stakes settings, is increasingly being recognized as an effective tool for learning, generally(Vlachopoulos & Makri, 2017)(Chernikova, Heitzmann, Holzberger, Seidel, & Fischer, 2020), and more specifically in legal education(Waters, 2016). AI-driven simulation platforms can immerse students in virtual legal scenarios where they must apply doctrine and skills in real time and learn by doing. For example, AI-powered systems (sometimes using virtual reality (VR) or augmented reality (AR)) now allow law students to step into simulated courtrooms or law office environments(Aderonke & Salami, 2025). (Mollick, et al., 2024) advocated the use of AI-powered simulations to provide personalized learning experiences, offering students the opportunity to practice skills in scenarios with AI-generated mentors, role-players, and instructor-facing evaluators. In these simulations, students might conduct a mock trial, cross-examine a virtual witness, negotiate a contract with an AI-driven client avatar, or practice law-firm tasks, all within a safe, controlled setting. Despite the effectiveness of simulation in legal education, (Mollick, et al., 2024) its widespread adoption remains challenging owing to its difficulty and expense in creation. Simulations require detailed scripting, design, and customized software, making them costly and time consuming to develop. Thus, it is proposed that generative AI has the potential to expand the creation and accessibility of educational simulations by significantly lowering the barrier to entry and providing instant feedback on performance, which may not necessarily be available when relying on human resources. This immediate feedback loop offers students the ability to immediately reflect upon and improve their advocacy, negotiation, and problem-solving skills through practice and repetition. Mollick et. al. (2024) particularly highlighted the educational potential of Pitchquest, a prototype venture capital pitching simulator that showcases the capabilities of AI in delivering instruction, facilitating practice, providing tailored feedback, and how it can be used to create adaptive educational simulations.

Another popular and accessible tool for legal simulation is ChatGPT, which is informally adopted by educators and students to replicate a range of legal roles and scenarios. Students and/or educators can input prompts into ChatGPT to simulate client interviews, courtroom cross-examinations, negotiation exercises, or legal problem-solving based on the IRAC method. Recent studies have evaluated ChatGPT's ability to perform legal reasoning using this method and have found that its responses often align closely with the analytical patterns used by legal professionals (Kang et al., 2023). For example, a student may instruct ChatGPT's LegalSimulator to role-play as a client in a tenancy dispute, receiving varied responses based on the clarity, empathy, or accuracy of their questioning, thus enabling real-time feedback, reflection, and iteration. This offers a clear alignment with Kolb's experiential learning cycle in that students gain concrete experience through simulated legal tasks, reflect on the interaction with the simulated client, abstract key legal principles, and improve their knowledge of such concepts before experimenting with improved approaches. From a Freirean perspective, such simulations also offer opportunities to democratize access to legal practice environments, particularly for students in under-resourced settings, by enabling dialogic, self-paced, and exploratory learning without the pressure or gatekeeping of live courtrooms or clinical settings. However, the quality of such simulations depends heavily on how prompts are constructed and interpreted, and educators must be cautious about AI hallucinations (Magesh et. Al., 2025), inaccurate legal content (Kang et al., 2023), and the risk of uncritical reliance on AI outputs (Yang, 2025). Although reflexively and in combination with peer or tutor debriefs, ChatGPT can serve as a scalable, low-barrier entry point for experiential legal learning.

Chatbots and Virtual Assistants

AI-driven chatbots or virtual assistants may also be employed to engage students in experiential learning through legal education. Chatbots and virtual assistants have the power to engage students in dialogue on the subject matter, simulating critical legal discussion while providing immediate feedback (Fromm et al., 2021) (Farber, 2024). These systems function as on-demand tutors for law students, available 24/7 to answer questions, clarify complex legal concepts, or even engage in Socratic dialogue(Aderonke & Salami, 2025). This means that a well-designed law tutor chatbot does not just spoon-feed answers; it pushes students to analyze hypotheticals, identify issues, and refine their arguments through iterative Q&A, much like an experienced professor would in class. However, using AI-facilitated Socratic questioning allows the benefits of scaling that experience to every student, while supporting experiential learning by immersing students in active, dialogue-based inquiry that mirrors the intellectual engagement of a classroom. This digital interaction offers a psychologically safe environment for students to challenge assumptions, reflect on their reasoning, and construct knowledge through iterative dialogue, aligning closely with the various stages of Kolb's (1984) experiential learning cycle (Fromm et al., 2021). Moreover, by allowing students to engage in dialogic learning without fear of embarrassment or performance anxiety, AI-mediated Socratic dialogue can promote more equitable participation, aligning with Freirean's emphasis on student voice, critical reflection, and empowerment.

The University of Oklahoma College of Law has developed and implemented a ChatGPT-integrated quiz system called Quizbot to help students learn legal concepts in a contemporary, customizable, and interactive manner(University of Oklahoma, 2025). The system employs a Socratic method-inspired chatbot to engage students in substantive conversations about course materials, thus providing a novel method for evaluating student learning and engagement. The key benefits offered include enhanced student engagement with course materials, practical experience in AI interaction for future legal practice, immediate feedback and assessment, and alignment with the Socratic tradition in law schools(Harrington, 2024). Furthermore, it engages students in experiential learning by requiring them to interact with the AI system, mirroring the skills required for future-ready legal practice. Harrington (2024) discussed the structure and implementation of this system, including its grading methodology and rubric, and addressed challenges, particularly in ensuring fairness and consistency in AI-generated questions, maintaining academic integrity, and balancing AI assistance with human oversight in grading. The pedagogical implications of this innovation include a shift from memorization to conceptual understanding, encouragement of critical thinking through AI interaction, and preparation of students for AI-integrated legal practice. This feedback loop reflects the 'active experimentation' and 'reflective observation' stages of Kolb's (1984) cycle, allowing students to trial arguments, receive critiques, and refine their approach iteratively.

One of the most intriguing aspects of this AI-assisted quiz system is its potential for broader application and future development. Harrington (2024) suggests that this system could be integrated into other more advanced law school courses, used for the longitudinal assessment of student progress, and even applied to bar exam preparation and continuing legal education. The author calls for further research and broader implementation of AI-assisted assessment in law schools to fully understand its impact and potential for preparing the next generation of legal professionals for an AI-integrated legal landscape. This innovative approach not only addresses current challenges in legal education, but also anticipates and prepares for the evolving needs of the legal profession in an increasingly AI-driven world.

Personalized and Adaptive Learning Pathways

AI-driven personalized and adaptive learning systems also have the potential to facilitate experiential learning in legal education. Instead of a one-size-fits-all curriculum, these platforms dynamically adjust the content and difficulty based on individual performance. Such systems can pinpoint weaknesses and provide targeted resources or exercises to bolster our understanding(Aderonke & Salami,

2025). Conversely, students who master the material quickly are challenged with more complex problems, ensuring continual growth and skill development. This personalized approach keeps learners optimally stimulated and supported, improving outcomes by tailoring help to each student's needs, thus creating a student-centered environment where each learner can advance at their own pace. By shifting away from passive lectures toward individualized learning paths, these AI systems foster more active learning and critical thinking than the traditional "stand and lecture" model advocated by Freire. Law schools worldwide are beginning to use such adaptive platforms to cater to students' strengths and weaknesses, thereby boosting their engagement and comprehension. For example, BPP University's use of Adapt creates tests and quizzes that are personalized to the students, their strengths, and weaknesses. Adapt also shares data with tutors so that they can identify problem areas and step in with personalized support, where needed (BPP, 2023). These systems combine AI use with human oversight, illustrating in line with HCI and Freire's critical pedagogy, that when thoughtfully deployed, this collaboration can democratize access to interactive learning and one-on-one feedback in legal education. It also clearly assists students with the reflective observation stage of Kolb's ELC and, depending on the scope and level of support offered, has the potential to assist students in revisiting concepts to enhance abstract conceptualization.

In addition to bespoke platforms such as Quizbot or institutional systems such as BPP's Adapt, more accessible tools such as Kahoot! and Quizlet are also evolving to include an AI-driven functionality that can support experiential and equitable learning. Kahoot! Traditionally known for its gamified quizzes is now integrating AI to help generate adaptive questions and provide instant feedback tailored to individual student responses (Kahoot!, 2025). Similarly, Quizlet introduced AI-powered Q-Chat, a virtual tutor that engages students in Socratic-style dialogue around flashcards and problem sets, simulating interactive learning through natural language processing and Magic Notes that summarize and generate study aids (Quizlet, 2023). These tools embody several stages of Kolb's (1984) experiential cycle, particularly concrete experience, active experimentation, and reflective observation, by encouraging learners to interact with quizzes and trial responses, receive instant feedback, and iterate their understanding in real time. Moreover, their mobile compatibility and widespread adoption across educational levels make them particularly valuable for promoting digital equity (Mhlanga, 2024). Freirean pedagogy emphasizes that learners must have agency and voice in the learning process and platforms such as Kahoot! and Quizlet, when used intentionally, can foster that agency by making active, student-led engagement possible, even in large or resource-constrained legal education settings (Freire, 1970).

How They Enhance Skill Development, Feedback Loops, and Experiential Learning

As outlined in the examples above, the hallmark of AI-driven learning tools is their capacity to provide continuous feedback and thereby accelerate skill development, helping bridge the gap between theory and practice. In conventional legal education, students may receive limited feedback, often only formal, written feedback once or twice per module in the form of a formative and summative assessment (Nicol & Macfarlane-Dick, 2006). AI tools, by contrast, AI tools can provide real-time, individualized, and iterative feedback at scale. For example, an intelligent tutoring system such as Quizbot can immediately tell a student if their legal analysis misses a key issue or suggests how to strengthen an argument, instead of the student waiting weeks for professor comments (Aderonke & Salami, 2025) (Harrington, 2024). These rapid feedback loops create a more responsive learning process, allowing students to safely trial different approaches, receive instant critique, and adjust their thinking in minutes, embodying the learning-by-doing cycle crucial to experiential education (Kolb, 1984).

Research indicates that AI-powered learning environments can be effective catalysts for developing critical skills such as critical thinking, legal reasoning, and problem solving (see, for example, (Essien, Bukoye, O'Dea, & Kremantzis, 2025);(Gonsalves, 2024)(Aderonke & Salami, 2025). Through the presentation of complex and authentic legal scenarios, AI platforms prompt students to critically analyze information, identify pertinent legal issues, and formulate reasoned solutions, offering a level of interactivity and applied learning that surpasses the capabilities of conventional textbook instruction. Importantly, these systems often monitor how students arrive at an answer, and not just whether it is correct. For instance, programs such as BPP's Adapt can track the steps in a student's legal research strategy or the arguments they consider in a negotiation exercise. Based on this, the system can provide targeted feedback on students' thought process. Such granular, data-driven feedback helps students refine their substantive knowledge and cognitive strategies, guiding them toward more sophisticated legal thinking. In other words, AI does not replace the professor's guidance but augments it with personalized coaching at a scale in line with HCI(Gross, 2014).

Another key advantage of AI-driven legal education is its capacity to support early intervention and continuous skill development through learning analytics and adaptive feedback mechanisms. AI platforms can systematically analyze student performance across diverse exercises, assessments, and interactions, identifying patterns that may indicate conceptual misunderstandings or skill deficiencies. This capacity for real-time monitoring enables educators to intervene early and more effectively, providing targeted support before gaps in understanding become entrenched. In line with formative pedagogical approaches, such interventions can be tailored to individual needs, whether through additional practice activities, scaffolded tasks, or tailored explanations, allowing for incremental skill building over time rather than relying solely on summative assessments(Nicol & Macfarlane-Dick, 2006).

Recent empirical studies further support the value of this approach. A recent experiment conducted at the University of Minnesota Law School found that when GPT-4 was integrated into coursework, students with initially lower performance significantly improved in subsequent assessments compared with their peers, suggesting that generative AI can provide meaningful support to those who may be at risk of falling behind(Choi, Hickman, Monahan, & Schwarcz, 2022). This aligns with wider research in educational technology, which highlights how adaptive AI systems can serve as "intelligent tutors," offering feedback loops and iterative learning opportunities that enhance engagement and retention (Fromm et al., 2021) (Luckin, Holmes, Griffiths, & Forcier, 2016);(Gligorea, et al., 2023). Such systems exemplify Kolb's (1984) experiential learning cycle, particularly the stages of active experimentation and reflective observation, by allowing learners to engage with materials, receive timely feedback, and adjust their strategies accordingly.

Importantly, this functionality not only enhances academic performance, but also supports equity in legal education. By providing additional scaffolding and individualized learning pathways, AI platforms can help level the playing field for students who lack prior academic capital, legal familiarity, or confidence in traditional classroom settings (Choi, Hickman, Monahan, & Schwarcz, 2022). This aligns with Freire's vision of education as a liberatory process, one that recognizes learners' diverse starting points and seeks to empower them through dialogue, reflection, and praxis. When integrated thoughtfully, AI enables a more inclusive model of legal education, in which each student is supported to develop the complex reasoning, communication, and ethical judgement necessary for professional practice. Thus, AI-driven experiential learning platforms transform each interaction from quizzes to simulations into an opportunity for diagnostic insights and skill refinement. Rather than reserving feedback for high-stakes assessments, these technologies foster a proactive, student-centered learning environment in which legal competencies are developed through sustained engagement, adaptive support, and personalized feedback and better prepare students for the iterative nature of real-world legal problem solving.

Table 1. Summary of educational AI tools and their uses in legal education

Educational AI Tool	Use in Legal Education
Kahoot!	A gamified quiz platform with AI-enhanced adaptive questions. Supports interactive classroom engagement, formative assessment and instant feedback on self-test questions.
Quizlet	AI powered flashcards and tutor facilitates Socratic dialogue, self-testing and study support whilst encouraging reflection and knowledge reinforcement.
Adapt (BPP University)	Creates customised quizzes based on student performance; provides tutors with data to target support.
ChatGPT/ Large Language Models (LLMs)	Used to simulate client interviews, cross-examinations, and problem-solving exercises; helps students practise advocacy, reasoning and drafting.
Quizbot (University of Oklahoma)	Engages students in dialogue-based Q&A on course materials, supports assessment, and provides immediate feedback.
BodySwaps	Enables experiential learning in professional ethics and client interactions through simulated AI and VR scenarios.

DESIGNING AI-ENHANCED LEGAL LEARNING ENVIRONMENTS

As discussed in this chapter, to realize the transformative potential of AI in legal education, its design must be grounded in pedagogical principles that prioritize active participation, critical reflection, and empowerment. Freire's critical pedagogy (1970), human–computer interaction (HCI) (Gross, 2014), and Kolb's ELC (1984) provide a powerful framework for developing AI tools that humanize the learning process and align with the broader mission of legal education to foster justice-oriented professionals.

First, AI-enhanced legal learning environments must be designed to support dialogue in the Freirean sense: not merely the exchange of information, but also a collaborative, inquiry-based engagement between learner and system. From an HCI perspective, interaction design should prioritize usability, responsiveness, and learner agency(Norman, 2014). Chatbots, conversational agents, and virtual legal simulations offer meaningful opportunities to support dialogic interaction. When students pose questions to an AI legal tutor or engage in role-play through a virtual courtroom, AI must be capable of prompting, questioning, and responding in ways that simulate the dynamics of human dialogue. This aligns with Kolb's reflective observation stage, in which learners consider different perspectives, and HCI's emphasis on designing interfaces that afford meaningful feedback loops to enhance human activity and experience(Carroll, 2014). The goal is to shift learners from passive recipients to active interlocutors, ensuring that technology scaffolds critical engagement rather than the automation of rote learning.

Second, AI must be leveraged to promote critical consciousness, which is a core aim of Freire's pedagogy. Legal education involves equipping students to interrogate systemic inequalities, power structures, and the social impact of law. AI-based tools should be deliberately constructed to present complex ethically challenging scenarios that require interpretation and judgement. For example, simulations can model sentencing outcomes that differ based on the defendant's socioeconomic background, prompting students to reflect on fairness and justice. This design aligns with Kolb's abstract conceptualization and active experimentation stages, as students theorize and test their responses to complex stimuli. It also draws upon HCI theories that highlight how technology can shape cognition and social understanding (Gross, 2014). Furthermore, AI systems can embed links to contextual materials such as case data, critical scholarship, or real-world statistics, thereby encouraging learners to connect doctrinal issues with broader societal narratives. This multimodal, interdisciplinary exposure is essential for developing legal professionals capable of systemic critiques and reforms.

A Freirean-aligned AI system must also foster liberation and empowerment, ensuring that learners develop a sense of agency and social responsibility. This requires AI design to go beyond knowledge delivery and support experiential, value-driven learning. Adaptive systems should personalize learning paths while preserving learner autonomy, helping students see themselves as problem-solvers rather than merely test-takers. AI simulations can be designed to support community lawyering, for example, by modelling client interviews in which students must address both legal and non-legal needs. These experiences mirror Kolb's concrete experience stage and elucidate the importance of learning-by-doing, an approach that is both experiential and humanizing. Moreover, when students are invited to co-create or customize AI tools, such as contributing to legal information chatbots used in clinics, they not only learn the law but also experience its real-world impact, consistent with both Freirean empowerment and participatory HCI design.

Finally, effective AI design in legal education must reject the "banking model" of learning, which treats students as passive vessels to be filled with information. Instead, AI must be used to support co-creation and shared authority during the learning process. Tools such as AI-generated notes or summaries are convenient, risk-reinforcing passivity if not paired with tasks that require synthesis, explanation, and reflection. By contrast, AI can be designed to prompt students to explain legal principles in their own words, evaluate arguments, or make decisions within a branching case scenario. This approach resonates with Freire's call for learners to be treated as co-authors of knowledge and Kolb's emphasis on cycling through experience, reflection, and conceptualization. It also reflects HCI's shift of HCI toward learner-centered systems that adapt to user input and promote deep engagement(Luckin, 2018).

In summary, the design of AI tools in legal education must be deeply informed by pedagogical theory if they are to fulfil their transformative potential. Freirean dialogics, critical consciousness, and empowerment provide an ethical foundation; HCI contributes a focus on interactional quality and learner agency; and Kolb's ELC offers a structured pathway for developing, testing, and refining legal understanding. When these frameworks are meaningfully integrated, AI becomes not just a technological enhancement, but a liberatory tool for equitable, critical, and experiential legal education.

Practical Examples of implementation

The integration of AI into legal education offers practical opportunities to embody Freirean pedagogy, HCI, and experiential learning principles across different stages of legal training. These principles are best understood through a series of contextualized implementations that illustrate how AI can facilitate active, dialogic, and reflective learning without replacing the essential human elements of education.

At the undergraduate level, for instance, a foundational and introductory law module may incorporate an AI-powered adaptive learning platform to support weekly case analysis activities. Students may engage with the system by working through a scenario-based prompt, accompanied by tailored questions reviewed by the tutor. AI dynamically responds to each student's input by providing Socratic prompts, explanatory videos, or micro-tutorials when it detects misconceptions about foundational concepts such as jurisdiction or justiciability. In addition, students may consult an AI chatbot tutor to clarify legal terminology or request examples from doctrinal applications. This model does not supplement the instructor, but instead allows faculty to shift from reiterating foundational content to facilitating higher-order critical discussions during class time. Drawing on the HCI principles of responsive design and learner agency (Carroll, 2014), the platform generates analytical insights that help educators identify common conceptual challenges. These are then used to structure dialogic Freirean-style classroom debates in which students collectively interrogate the meaning and implications of the law. Such hybrid models blend personalized support with communal reflection, and have been shown to enhance both accessibility and inclusivity in large-group legal education settings (Luckin et al., 2016).

More advanced experiential learning occurs in clinical-legal-education-based modules, where AI-based simulations can prepare students for real-world interactions with clients. In the context of criminal law and justice-based modules, this may involve exposing the students to the complexities of identifying and analyzing potential miscarriages of justice for an innocence project. Innocence projects are well recognized as a form of innovative and applied work-integrated learning, having positive effects on law students' job prospects and career trajectories (Stratton et, al., 2023). A simulated version may involve an AI-powered case file assistant that presents students with a digitized dossier from a historical conviction, including transcripts, appellate judgements, and police interview summaries. The AI system, trained on legal reasoning patterns, can respond to students' questions about the case or generate plausible responses as though "interviewed" by a law student re-investigating the conviction. For example, AI might simulate the voice of a wrongfully convicted individual or generate alternate procedural timelines based on overlooked evidence. As students interrogate the case, the system flags inconsistencies in witness testimony or reveals potential forensic failures, encouraging them to critically evaluate the reliability of the original trial process. This approach draws upon the HCI principles of interactive narrative (Gross, 2014) and mirrors Freire's call for dialogic learning and critical consciousness, which requires learners not only to understand legal rules but also to interrogate power, error, and injustice within the legal system. Post-simulation, AI-generated feedback can help identify gaps in students' investigative strategies or ethical reasoning, which are then explored in reflective, tutor-led seminars. This stage, identified in Kolb's (1984) ELC as reflective observation, supports the transition from procedural legal analysis to deep critical inquiry, transforming a law student's role from a passive observer into a proactive agent of justice.

At the continuing professional development level, AI offers innovative approaches to legal ethics and lifelong learning. For example, continuing legal education (CLE) online modules or micro-credentials might employ AI simulations where practising lawyers navigate ethical dilemmas, such as potential conflicts of interest, and experience the consequences of their decisions in real time. Instead of passively reading through a regulatory code or clicking through an e-learning module, the learner is immersed in a scenario in which a client's trust erodes or a disciplinary inquiry is triggered based on their choices. The adaptation of existing AI-powered immersive simulations, such as Bodyswaps, could facilitate the combination of AI and augmented reality, offering an immersive experience that mirrors real-world experience in an emotionally safe space (see St Georges University London, n.,d; WhatWorked Education, 2023; Bodyswaps 2023a, 2023b). Moreover, AI-driven chatbots can serve as reflective interlocutors for lawyers navigating complex situations, proposing guiding questions, and identifying key ethical considerations without offering prescriptive answers. This use of AI as a dialogic aid rather than an authoritative solution mirrors Freire's rejection of the banking model and encourages reflective, contextualized decision-making. Indeed, recent studies have explored how immersive AI-enhanced training can bridge the gap between theoretical instruction and professional judgement (Choi et al., 2022).

Across these diverse applications, AI functions as a catalyst for deeper learning and not as a replacement for human teaching. It generates scenarios, poses questions, and offers feedback but crucially leaves interpretive and ethical work to the learner. Such systems, when designed with pedagogical intentionality, support the "humanization, conscientization, and radical engagement with the world" advocated by Freire (1970). In essence, AI becomes a facilitator of enriched, experiential, legal education, and an extension of the skilled teacher's role, rather than a mechanical content dispenser.

POWER, DESIGN, AND THE POLITICS OF AI IN LEGAL EDUCATION

Although AI offers considerable potential to enhance legal education, it must not be considered a politically neutral tool. As Freire (1970) reminds us, all education is inherently political, and so are the technologies that shape its delivery. The design, deployment, and regulation of AI systems are shaped by the assumptions, values, and power structures of their creators, who are often large technology firms or elite academic institutions whose priorities may not align with social justice or educational equity (Simon, Wong, & Rieder, 2020). Other academics have documented how computational power dynamics, such as concentrated resources in elite universities and corporations, may skew AI development towards priorities that reinforce dominance rather than democratic or justice-oriented outcomes (Ahmed & Wahed, 2020; Birhane et al., 2021). This dynamic raises concerns about the ideological and epistemological foundations of these technologies. Without deliberate scrutiny, AI systems may uncritically encode dominant worldviews and institutional biases under the guise of neutrality, efficiency, or innovation (Luckin, 2018). In the legal sphere, natural language processing tools trained on historical case law may perpetuate systemic inequities by reproducing the biases embedded in legal data. This concern is well documented in the justice system, for example, in research into the COMPAS risk assessment tool, which is not only more accurate than untrained humans (Dressel & Farid, 2018) but also biases decisions against Black and younger defendants (Engel, Linhardt, & Schubert, 2024). These authors further demonstrated how algorithmic adjustments can remove bias or exacerbate normative trade-offs, demonstrating that such compromises should be explicit and transparent and not concealed within opaque systems. Meanwhile, Rudin et al. (2018) argue that COMPAS's secretive nature of COMPAS violates procedural fairness, calling for interpretable models that can be properly scrutinized. When such tools are deployed in legal education without critical reflection and scrutiny, they risk passing on these systemic biases to students, reinforcing dominant legal narratives, and shaping understanding of justice in ways that may undermine educational equity. Freire's notion of critical consciousness (conscientização) demands that learners and educators interrogate the systems that shape their learning. In an AI-mediated legal classroom, this means cultivating awareness of the social, legal, and political implications of the algorithmic systems. Legal education should not only use AI to simulate practice, but also teach students how to critically appraise the power relations embedded in legal data, decision-making tools, and digital pedagogy itself (Kee, 2024). Rather than simply teaching how to use AI, law schools must teach students how to understand and question its logic, limitations, and latent injustices.

Moreover, the adoption of AI tools in legal education risks deepens existing inequalities unless these technologies are explicitly designed to redress structural disparities. Commercial AI platforms are often developed and priced for institutions with significant financial and technical resources, potentially marginalizing underfunded law schools and students in lower socioeconomic regions (Williamson & Eynon, 2020; Knox, 2020). Students without reliable Internet access, prior exposure to digital platforms, or fluency in dominant linguistic and cultural norms may also face barriers to participation, further entrenching digital and epistemic divides (Kuhn et., al, 2023). This dynamic mirrors longstanding critiques of legal education as a "reproducing" institution that privileges elite forms of cultural capital and excludes alternative ways of knowing (Wintersteiger, 2020; Thornton, 2001). A Freirean approach to AI integration in legal education demands that equity and social justice be embedded from the outset and not applied with retrospective afterthought. This requires participatory and inclusive design processes that meaningfully involve students and educators, particularly those from marginalized backgrounds, in the co-creation of tools that reflect their legal realities (Costanza-Chock, 2020; Williamson & Eynon, 2020). It also calls for algorithmic transparency and explainability so that users can interrogate how AI-generated outcomes are produced and their terms. Finally, a critical legal pedagogy must resist the uncritical imposition of globalized, standardized legal logic by promoting decolonial and localized approaches to AI-in-law, particularly in postcolonial jurisdictions, to avoid erasing plural legal traditions and compounding epistemic injustice (Mohamed et., al, 2020).

The increasing adoption of third-party AI platforms by law schools also poses the challenge of institutional dependency, whereby control over curriculum design, data ownership, and pedagogical autonomy shifts toward commercial providers. This dynamic threatens academic freedom and fosters creeping commodification of education. Analyses of ed-tech platforms have shown that, when managed by external vendors, data analytics and AI tools can constrain faculty oversight and influence teaching practices (Komljenovic & Williamson, 2024). Concurrently, systematic reviews highlight how an overreliance on AI dialogue systems risks diminishing critical thinking, as learning becomes shaped by corporate-designed "solutions" rather than pedagogical choices made by educators (Zhai et al., 2024). On a broader scale, the concentration of AI development power among elite tech companies and top universities, referred to as the "compute divide," further reinforces dependence, as lesser-resourced institutions lack both access and leverage to shape AI tools to their contextual needs (Ahmed & Wahed, 2020). These developments reflect a form of educational imperialism, where standardized proprietary AI systems are imposed on institutions with little voice, potentially erasing local pedagogical traditions and compounding epistemic injustice. Faculty across disciplines, particularly in law, must therefore resist not only the "banking model" of education but also this subtle commodification of knowledge via proprietary AI systems (Couldry & Mejias, 2019; Komljenovic & Williamson, 2024).

CHALLENGES AND CONSIDERATIONS

While the integration of AI into legal education offers transformative potential, it also raises a number of challenges, ranging from pedagogical to practical and ethical, which must be critically examined. These concerns are not ancillary, but central to ensuring that AI is harnessed in ways that are equitable, empowering, and pedagogically sound. If deployed uncritically, AI tools may reinforce the educational inequalities and hierarchies Freire (1970) sought to dismantle.

Access and Equity Gaps

The promise of personalized, adaptive, and immersive legal education through AI is contingent on equitable access to required resources and infrastructure. However, significant disparities exist across institutions and student populations in terms of access to reliable Internet, compatible devices, digital literacy, and supportive learning environments. These gaps risk creating a digital divide that mirrors and exacerbates existing inequalities in legal education, particularly in under-resourced or post-colonial jurisdictions (Beckles and Richards-Kennedy, 2021). Freire's critical pedagogy compels us to ask not only who benefits from AI tools, but also those who are excluded from their full use. As discussed throughout this chapter, students from lower socioeconomic backgrounds may find themselves disadvantaged in AI-rich learning environments, particularly when these tools become central to teaching, assessment, or progression (Williamson & Eynon, 2020; Knox, 2020; Kuhn et., al, 2023). If AI platforms are deployed without deliberate strategies to promote digital inclusion, such as mobile-friendly design, offline accessibility, or scaffolded digital skill development, they may deepen existing inequalities, rather than mitigate them.

Over-Reliance and Dehumanization

A second challenge lies in the propensity of AI platforms to inadvertently reify the "banking model" of education that Freire (1970) critiques, where learners are positioned as passive recipients of pre-packaged knowledge. Although these tools often claim to offer adaptive and personalized learning, many still rely heavily on reductive assessment methods such as multiple-choice questions, keyword matching, and quantifiable metrics, which fail to capture the nuances of legal reasoning, ethical judgement, or lived experience (Luckin, 2018). Digital pedagogy research warns that such approaches can fragment complex learning processes, privileging surface-level recall over deep critical engagement (Bjork et al., 2013). Freire's emancipatory pedagogy emphasizes critical dialogue, whereas HCI research highlights the value of relational and co-constructive learning environments (Wang et al., 2025). However, investigations into AI-mediated tutoring have shown that the presence of AI can reduce meaningful dialogue. In a study on one-on-one math tutoring, it was found that automated systems often default on didactic patterns, limiting student reflection and bidirectional inquiry (Wang et al., 2025). This shift echoes the concern of an "illusion of competence," where surface-level fluency supplements real understanding, meaning that students feel they know more than they actually do (Bjork et al., 2013).

Furthermore, controlled studies have revealed that over-reliance on AI dialogue systems may degrade critical thinking. A study found that 75% of university undergraduates reported reduced engagement and diminished critical reasoning when routinely using AI for writing or study prompts compared to when they used peer or tutor feedback (Zhai et al., 2024). The outcome may be termed a "technological mask," where the system offers the appearance of feedback or Socratic questioning but lacks the ethical, emotional, and interpersonal dimensions essential to legal education (Zhai et al., 2024). Without purposeful design and critical reflection built into the curriculum, AI risks reducing legal education to mechanical drills rather than fostering reflective judgement, empathy, and justice orientations that define transformative learning.

Bias, Transparency, and Algorithmic Justice

As previously discussed, AI systems are only fair and accurate, as the data and assumptions underpin them. In the context of legal education, this raises critical concerns about the risk of algorithmic bias, especially when systems are trained on historical legal data embedded with racial, gendered, or class-based injustices (Engel, Linhardt, & Schubert, 2024). Freire's notion of critical consciousness (conscientização) reminds us that learners must be empowered not only to use AI, but also to understand and question the power structures embedded in its design. Many current AI systems are opaque by design, and their decision-making processes are shielded by proprietary algorithms or unexplainable codes. This lack of transparency undermines both academic integrity and ethical learning, preventing students from developing the critical digital literacy they will need in an AI-integrated legal profession. To counter this, legal educators must advocate explainable AI (XAI) systems that make their processes visible and challenging to facilitate learning (Miller, 2019). Moreover, institutions should seek participatory design models in which students, educators, and technologists collaboratively shape the values, features, and evaluation mechanisms of legal education technologies (Constanza-Chock, 2020; Williamson & Eynon, 2020).

Capacity, Training, and Institutional Readiness

Finally, even the most ethically designed AI system cannot fulfil its pedagogical promise without thoughtful implementation. Many educational establishments lack internal, technical, financial, or cultural capacity to integrate AI and other digital transformations in a meaningful way (Selwyn, 2019; Williamson & Eynon, 2020; Knox, 2020). Faculty members may feel unprepared to adopt AI tools or uncertain how to align them with established pedagogical goals (Bliss, 2024). Without adequate training and support, there is a risk that AI adoption will become superficial, driven more by novelty or institutional branding than by educational efficacy. To prevent this, professional development must focus not only on how to operate AI tools but also on how to teach them, embedding them into the learning design in ways that reinforce active, reflective, and student-centered learning. Interdisciplinary collaboration among legal academics, learning designers, and technologists is crucial for building capacity and developing AI applications that reflect the unique demands of legal education.

LIMITATIONS

In addition to the challenges discussed above, this study had several limitations. First, as the study is largely conceptual and theoretical in nature, it relies heavily on drawing from existing literature and pedagogical frameworks rather than original empirical research. Therefore, many of the arguments put forward in this chapter are illustrative and require empirical testing to demonstrate their practical effectiveness.

It must also be acknowledged that the field of AI in legal education is constantly evolving at a pace; thus, the specific examples illustrated in this chapter may be quickly outdated. Therefore, although this chapter aims to capture current trends and developments in the field, the dynamic nature of technological advancement limits the longevity of its claims. Furthermore, much of the discussion is shaped by sources from well-resourced Western academic contexts. This has the potential to obscure perspectives from under-resourced, post-colonial, or small islands, developing dominions, where the challenges may be more acute or substantially different. Additionally, although the chapter highlights the importance of equity and inclusion, it cannot fully account for infrastructural barriers, such as digital access, institutional readiness, or costs, that may inhibit effective implementation. In addition, although this chapter broadly applies the theoretical frameworks across legal education, they may not translate seamlessly into all educational contexts or regulatory environments due to the idiosyncrasies of the particular environment. Finally, while this chapter has provided a conceptual analysis of both the opportunities and risks of the use of AI in legal education, many of the tools discussed remain under-researched in the context of legal education; therefore, further empirical investigation is needed to fully understand the pedagogical impact, ethical implications, and ultimately their role in shaping the future of legal education.

CONCLUSION

As discussed throughout this chapter, the integration of artificial intelligence into legal education presents a pivotal opportunity to reimagine legal pedagogy, go beyond merely digitizing traditional practices, and towards transform them. The adoption of AI in legal education must not be a race to keep up with technological trends but a reflective, inclusive, and justice-driven process. Rather than solely focusing on how AI can increase the efficiency of legal education, it is essential to consider how these technologies can be leveraged to enhance reflective learning, foster critical thinking, and expand access to transformative legal education. When framed as pedagogical imperatives rather than merely technical challenges, these goals illuminate the responsibility of legal educators to shape AI-integrated futures that remain rooted in the principles of human dignity, equity, and democratic participation.

This chapter has argued that AI, when grounded in experiential learning theory, critical pedagogy, and human-computer interaction design, can be harnessed to support legal education that is more equitable, interactive, and socially responsive. Drawing on Kolb's (1984) Experiential Learning Cycle, this study has demonstrated how AI tools such as simulations, chatbots, and adaptive platforms can enhance each stage of learning, from concrete experience to active experimentation. Freire's (1970) critical pedagogy provides a vital ethical lens, reminding us that AI must empower students as agents of change rather than reinforcing top-down models of passive learning that follow the traditional banking model. Finally, human–computer interaction theory emphasizes the importance of intentional design in shaping learning interactions that are dialogic, intuitive, and learner-centered (Gross, 2014). However, this vision cannot be realized without careful attention to the challenges of access, algorithmic bias, pedagogical integrity, and institutional capacity. AI is not a neutral or inevitable force; it must be actively shaped by educators, students, and communities seeking to make legal education more just, inclusive, and transformative. To this end, the chapter concludes with a series of practical recommendations for key stakeholders.

RECOMMENDATIONS

For Legal Educators

Legal educators should ensure that AI tools are designed and integrated with pedagogy at the forefront of their minds. This ensures that such tools provide clear learning outcomes based on experiential and inclusive principles, avoiding the danger of integrating AI solely for novelty purposes.

Legal educators should ensure that any implementation of AI is used to foster AI literacy. This means equipping students with the skills needed to understand, critique, and ethically engage with AI tools, not just using them as opaque "black boxes" whose internal processes remain unexamined. This requires legal educators to help students interrogate how AI tools work, ask questions about what legal data they are trained on, reflect on why an answer is generated, and develop skills to verify, challenge, or improve AI outputs.

Legal educators should ensure that any use of AI is blended with human interactions. Thus, educators should use AI to enhance and not replace the relational and dialogic dimensions of legal teaching. For example, AI feedback is paired with peer or instructor dialogue.

Finally, legal educators should incorporate ethical reflections into legal technology use by ensuring that students reflect on how AI tools might replicate or resist injustice in law and education.

For Curriculum Designers and Law Schools

Curriculum designers should embed AI-enhanced experiential learning in the curriculum. All stages of education, from first-year courses to clinical modules, simulations, and adaptive platforms, can scaffold skill development if aligned with coherent pedagogy. Free or low-cost AI powered tools, such as Kahoot! Quizlet offers scalable entry points for experiential learning in under-resourced or remote learning contexts.

Curriculum designers should invest in staff development. The faculty needs time and training to experiment with and critically reflect on AI tools and how they work, but also how they can be designed and deployed effectively in their teaching delivery.

Curriculum designers must also support inclusive design and access. This means prioritizing low-bandwidth, mobile-friendly, and multilingual tools and offering offline alternatives where needed to mitigate accessibility concerns.

Finally, curriculum designers should adopt transparent procurement policy. This means evaluating AI platforms not only on functionality but also on their alignment with educational values, such as data ethics, accessibility, explainability, and openness.

For Policymakers and Regulatory Bodies

Policymakers and regulatory bodies should develop robust AI teaching standards in legal education. As part of this, they should encourage frameworks that promote responsible, equitable, and pedagogically grounded AI. This guidance can also be implemented in existing policies, such as online learning and academic integrity.

Policymakers and regulatory bodies should also fund pilot programmes and research. Sufficient investment should support innovation in AI-enhanced experiential learning through funded trials, particularly in underresourced institutions or small jurisdictions.

Finally, policymakers and regulatory bodies should monitor the legal edtech market to ensure sufficient competition, interoperability, and transparency in AI learning platforms to prevent monopolization and protect institutional autonomy.

Figure 1. Summary of recommendations

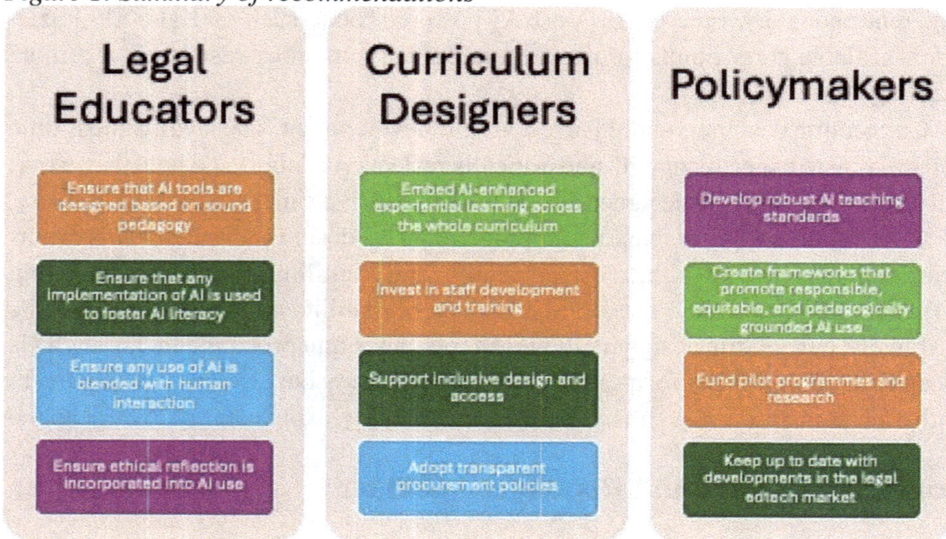

FUTURE DIRECTIONS

The evolving intersection of artificial intelligence and legal education presents both a pressing challenge and a transformative opportunity. This chapter argues that AI holds significant potential to enrich legal pedagogy through experiential, dialogic, and ethically responsive applications. Simultaneously, it has warned against the risks posed by uncritical, technocratic, or inequitable deployments of these technologies, particularly where they reproduce existing hierarchies or reinforce dominant epistemologies.

Future research must engage more directly with the lived experiences of students interacting with AI-enhanced legal learning environments. There is an urgent need for empirical studies that examine whether AI tools genuinely foster critical thinking, legal reasoning, and reflective judgement across diverse learner populations within the legal and justice milieu. Such research should focus on issues of access, inclusion, and digital fluency, and explore how these variables intersect with socioeconomic status, race, gender, and geographic location.

In addition to assessing outcomes, researchers should study the design and development processes behind AI applications in legal education. Participatory design approaches remain underexplored in the legal scholarship. Future research might examine whether such co-creation practices lead to more equitable, explainable, and contextually relevant AI systems, and how these collaborative processes might be scaled or institutionalized.

Further research is needed to investigate the extent to which AI-powered legal simulators, particularly those relying on historical case law and natural language processing, risk embedding, and perpetuating structural biases. Legal education must not become a site where racialized sentencing patterns, gendered assumptions about credibility, or class-based exclusions are transmitted to the next generation of lawyers, under the guise of digital neutrality. Instead, AI tools should be designed to surface these biases and enable the critical interrogation of legal authority and precedence.

Finally, future scholarship should contribute to the development of normative frameworks for ethical and unk-tice-oriented AI pedagogy in legal education. Such frameworks must draw on interdisciplinary insights from law, education, computer science, and critical theory and be attuned to the specific needs of the educational and legal jurisdiction in which they operate. The aim should not be to retrofit existing systems with ethical considerations as an afterthought but to embed justice, transparency, and human dignity at the heart of design and implementation from the outset.

Thus, artificial intelligence in legal education should not be treated as an inevitable technological advance to be passively managed, but as a contested and negotiable terrain. The task before legal educators is not only to understand and adopt emerging tools but also to shape their development in ways that expand, rather than constrain, the emancipatory possibilities of legal learning.

REFERENCES

Abenoza, S., & Arjona, C. (2017). Socrates behind bars: A report on an experimental course on justice and philosophy. *The Law Teacher, 51*(3), 327–348. DOI: 10.1080/03069400.2016.1272041

Aderonke, A., & Salami, S. (2025). AI-powered personalized learning in legal education: A tool for developing future ready lawyers. International Journal of Law. *Justice and Jurisprudence, 5*(1), 323–327. DOI: 10.22271/2790-0673.2025.v5.i1d.192

Ahmed, N., & Wahed, M. (2020). The de democratization of AI: Deep learning and the compute divide in artificial intelligence research. arXiv. https://doi.org//arXiv.2010.15581DOI: 10.48550

Ajevski, M., Barker, K., Gilbert, A., Hardie, L., & Ryan, F. (2023). ChatGPT and the future of legal education and. *The Law Teacher, 57*(3), 352–364. DOI: 10.1080/03069400.2023.2207426

Akintayo, O. T., Eden, C. A., Ayeni, O. O., & Onyebuchi, N. C. (2024). Integrating AI with emotional and social learning in primary education: Developing a holistic adaptive learning ecosystem. *Open Access Research Journal of Multidisciplinary Studies, 7*(2), 42–51. DOI: 10.53022/oarjms.2024.7.2.0025

Alexander, J., Mcconnell, S., Mitchell, R., & Mcgrane, A. (2024). Technological challenges for modern law schoolpedagogy: Preparing graduates for the modern legalworkplace. *The Law Teacher, 58*(1), 32–57. DOI: 10.1080/03069400.2023.2287393

Ashley, K. D. (2017). *Artificial Intelligence and Legal Analytics: New Tools for Law Practice in the Digital Age*. Cambridge University Press. DOI: 10.1017/9781316761380

Beckles, H., & Richards Kennedy, S. (2021). Accelerating the future into the present: Re-imagining higher education in the Caribbean. In van't Land, H., Corcoran, A., & Iancu, D.-C. (Eds.), *The Promise of Higher Education* (pp. 363–369). Springer., DOI: 10.1007/978-3-030-67245-4_54

Bennett, T. (2020). The effects of student-consumerism on discipline specific teaching practices: a comparison of education and law. Journal of Further and Higher Education, 45(3), 417-432. doi:https://doi-org.liverpool.idm.oclc.org/10.1080/0309877X.2020.1774050

Birhane, A., Kalluri, P., Card, D., Agnew, W., Dotan, R., & Bao, M. (2021). The values encoded in machine learning research. arXiv. https://doi.org//arXiv.2106.15590DOI: 10.48550

Bjork, R. A., Dunlosky, J., & Kornell, N. (2013). Self-regulated learning: Beliefs, techniques, and illusions. *Annual Review of Psychology*, *64*(1), 417–444. DOI: 10.1146/annurev-psych-113011-143823 PMID: 23020639

Bliss, J. (2024). Teaching Law in the Age of Generative AI. *Jurimetrics Journal*, *64*, 111–161.

Bodyswaps. (2023a). Brighton and Sussex Medical School pilot: Navigating angry conversations. https://bodyswaps.co/resources/research

Bodyswaps. (2023b). Case study: Sheffield Hallam University—Training health-care students at scale with immersive learning. https://bodyswaps.co/resources/case-studies

Botelho, W. T., Marietto, M. G. B., Ferreira, J. C. M., & Pimentel, E. P. (2016). Kolb's experiential learning theory and Belhot's learning cycle guiding the use of computer simulation in engineering education: A pedagogical proposal to shift toward an experiential pedagogy. *Computer Applications in Engineering Education*, *24*(1), 79–88. DOI: 10.1002/cae.21674

BPP. (2023, October 30). AI in Law: technology in legal education and the profession. Retrieved from BPP: https://www.bpp.com/insights/ai-in-law

Burch, G. F., Hoover, J. D., Batchelor, J. H., Heller, N. A., Burch, J. J., & Giambattista, R. (2019). A Meta-Analysis of the Relationship Between Experiential Learning and Learning Outcomes. *Decision Sciences Journal of Innovative Education*, *17*(3), 239–273. DOI: 10.1111/dsji.12188

Carroll, J. (2014, January 1). Human Computer Interaction - A Brief Intro. Retrieved from Interaction Design Foundation: https://www.interaction-design.org/literature/book/the-encyclopedia-of-human-computer-interaction-2nd-ed/human-computer-interaction-brief-intro?srsltid=AfmBOornFGhtXHb9Q5n1VAdP8ye3DFvs0FtL8jJkEFkaefQVL1zR-EYI

Chalkiadakis, A., Seremetaki, A., Kanellou, A., Kallishi, M., Morfopoulou, A., Moraitaki, M., & Mastrokoukou, S. (2024). Impact of Artificial Intelligence and Virtual Reality on Educational Inclusion: A Systematic Review of Technologies Supporting Students with Disabilities. *Education Sciences*, *14*(11), 1223. Advance online publication. DOI: 10.3390/educsci14111223

Chernikova, O., Heitzmann, N., Holzberger, D., Seidel, T., & Fischer, F. (2020). Simulation-based learning in higher education: A meta-analysis. *Review of Educational Research, 90*(4), 499–541. DOI: 10.3102/0034654320933544

Choi, J., Hickman, K., Monahan, A., & Schwarcz, D. (2022). ChatGPT Goes to Law School. *Journal of Legal Education, 71*(3), 387–400.

Costanza-Chock, S. (2020). *Design justice: Community-led practices to build the worlds we need.* MIT Press. DOI: 10.7551/mitpress/12255.001.0001

Couldry, N., & Mejias, U. A. (2019). *The costs of connection: How data is colonizing human life and appropriating it for capitalism.* Stanford University Press.

Derreth, R. T., Levin, M. B., & Jones, V. C. (2021). Preparing Public Health Professionals to Address Social Injustices Through Critical Service-Learning. *Pedagogy in Health Promotion, 7*(4), 354–357. DOI: 10.1177/23733799211007183

Dolidze, T. (2025). The Evolving Role of Artificial Intelligence in Legal Education and Research. *Law and World, 11*(33), 92–105.

Dressel, J., & Farid, H. (2018). The accuracy, fairness, and limits of predicting recidivism. *Science Advances, 4*(1), eaao5580. Advance online publication. DOI: 10.1126/sciadv.aao5580 PMID: 29376122

Engel, C., Linhardt, L., & Schubert, M. (2024). Code is law: How COMPAS affects the way the judiciary handles the risk of recidivism. *Artificial Intelligence and Law.* Advance online publication. DOI: 10.1007/s10506-024-09389-8

Essien, A., Bukoye, O., O'Dea, X., & Kremantzis, M. (2025). The influence of AI text generators on critical thinking skills in UK business schools. *Studies in Higher Education, 49*(5), 865–882. DOI: 10.1080/03075079.2024.2316881

Farahani, M. S., & Ghasmi, G. (2024). Artificial Intelligence in education: A comprehensive study. *Forum for Education Studies, 2*(3), 1379. DOI: 10.59400/fes.v2i3.1379

Farber, S. (2024). Harmonizing AI and human instruction in legal education: A case study from Israel on training future legal professionals. *International Journal of the Legal Profession, 31*(3), 349–363. DOI: 10.1080/09695958.2024.2430018

Freire, P. (1970). Pedagogy of the Oppressed. *Continuum : an Interdisciplinary Journal on Continuity of Care.*

Fromm, J., Radianti, J., Wehking, C., Stieglitz, S., Majchrzak, T. A., & vom Brocke, J. (2021). More than experience? – On the unique opportunities of virtual reality to afford a holistic experiential learning cycle. *The Internet and Higher Education, 50*, 100804. Advance online publication. DOI: 10.1016/j.iheduc.2021.100804

Gligorea, I., Cioca, M., Oancea, R., Gorski, A.-T., Gorski, H., & Tudorache, P. (2023). Adaptive Learning Using Artificial Intelligence in e-Learning: A Literature Review. *Education Sciences, 13*(12), 1216. DOI: 10.3390/educsci13121216

Gonsalves, C. (2024). Generative AI's Impact on Critical Thinking: Revisiting Bloom's Taxonomy. *Journal of Marketing Education*, •••, 16. DOI: 10.1177/02734753241305980

Gross, T. (2014). Human-computer interaction education and diversity. *Lecture Notes in Computer Science, 8510*, 187–198. DOI: 10.1007/978-3-319-07233-3_18

Gross, T. (2014). Human-Computer Interaction Education and Diversity. In Kuroso, M. (Ed.), *Human-Computer Interaction, Part I* (pp. 187–198). Springer.

Guth, J., & Dutton, K. (2018). SQE-ezed out: SRA, status and stasis. *The Law Teacher, 52*(4), 425–438. DOI: 10.1080/03069400.2018.1534341

Harrington, S. (2024, October 3). Introducing QuizBot an Innovative AI-Assisted Assessment in Legal Education. Retrieved from *SSRN*: https://papers.ssrn.com/sol3/papers.cfm?abstract_id=4975804 DOI: 10.2139/ssrn.4975804

He, R., Cao, J., & Tan, T. (2025). Generative artificial intelligence: A historical perspective. *National Science Review, 12*(5), nwaf050. Advance online publication. DOI: 10.1093/nsr/nwaf050 PMID: 40191253

James, C. (2008). Lawyer Dissatisfaction, Emotional Intelligence and Clinical Legal Education. *Legal Education Review, 18*(1). Advance online publication. DOI: 10.53300/001c.6208

Kahoot! (2025, July). Kahoot! AI Tools. Retrieved from Kahoot: https://kahoot.com/ai-tools/#What-is-the-most-useful-AI-tool-for-teachers

Kang, X., Qu, L., Soon, L.-K., Trakic, A., Zhuo, T., Emerton, P., & Grant, G. (2023). Can ChatGPT Perform Reasoning Using the IRAC Method in Analyzing Legal Scenarios Like a Lawyer? In *Findings of the Association for Computational Linguistics: EMNLP 2023* (pp. 13900–13923). Association for Computational Linguistics. DOI: 10.18653/v1/2023.findings-emnlp.929

Kee, S. (2024). Legal Clinic Under The Lens of Paulo Freire: A Theoretical Interpretation of Clinical Legal Education at Australian University Law Schools. Murdoch University. Retrieved from https://researchportal.murdoch.edu.au/view/pdfCoverPage? instCode=61MUN_INST&filePid=13176902410007891&download=true

Knox, J. (2020). Artificial intelligence and education in China. *Learning, Media and Technology*, *45*(3), 298–311. DOI: 10.1080/17439884.2020.1754236

Kolb, D. A. (1984). *Experiential Learning: Experience as the Source of Learning and Development*. Prentice Hall.

Komljenovic, J., & Williamson, B. (2024). Behind the platforms: ed tech platform adoption and its impact on academic freedom. University of Edinburgh Research Explorer. PDF retrieved from research repository. arxiv.orgresearch.ed.ac.uk

Kuhn, C., Khoo, S. M., Czerniewicz, L., Lilley, W., Bute, S., Crean, A., Abegglen, S., Burns, T., Sinfield, S., Jandrić, P., Knox, J., & MacKenzie, A. (2023). Understanding Digital Inequality: A Theoretical Kaleidoscope. *Postdigit Sci Educ*, *5*(3), 894–932. DOI: 10.1007/s42438-023-00395-8 PMID: 40479087

Luckin, R. (2018). *Machine Learning and Human Intelligence: The future of education for the 21st Century*. UCL IOE Press.

Luckin, R., Holmes, W., Griffiths, M., & Forcier, L. (2016). Intelligence Unleashed: An Argument for AI in Education. London: Open Ideas: Pearson Education. Retrieved from https://oro.open.ac.uk/50104/1/Luckin%20et%20al.%20-%202016%20-%20Intelligence%20Unleashed.%20An%20argument%20for%20AI%20in%20Educ.pdf

Magesh, V., Surani, F., Dahl, M., Suzgun, M., Manning, C. D., & Ho, D. E. (2025). Hallucination-free? assessing the reliability of leading ai legal research tools. *Journal of Empirical Legal Studies*, *22*(2), 216–242. DOI: 10.1111/jels.12413

Matsuo, M. (2015). A Framework for Facilitating Experiential Learning. *Human Resource Development Review*, *14*(4), 442–461. Advance online publication. DOI: 10.1177/1534484315598087

Mhlanga, D. (2024). Digital transformation of education, the limitations and prospects of introducing the fourth industrial revolution asynchronous online learning in emerging markets. *Discover Education*, *3*(32), 32. DOI: 10.1007/s44217-024-00115-9

Miller, J. B. (2014). Bridging the Gap: The Role of Legal Clinics in Legal Education. *Clinical Law Review*, *21*(1), 1–34.

Miller, T. (2019). Explanation in artificial intelligence: Insights from the social sciences. *Artificial Intelligence*, *267*, 1–38. DOI: 10.1016/j.artint.2018.07.007

Mohamed, S., Png, M. T., Isaac, W., & Decolonial, A. I. (2020). Decolonial Theory as Sociotechnical Foresight in Artificial Intelligence. *Philosophy & Technology*, *33*(4), 659–684. DOI: 10.1007/s13347-020-00405-8

Mollick, E., Mollick, L., Bach, N., Ciccarelli, L., Przystanski, B., & Ravipinto, D. (2024). AI Agents and Education: Simulated Practice at Scale. ArXiv. /arXiv.2407.12796DOI: 10.2139/ssrn.4871171

Moser, C. (1988). The Robbins Report 25 Years After-and the Future of the Universities. *Oxford Review of Education*, *14*(1), 5–20. DOI: 10.1080/0305498880140102

Nancholas, B. (2023, November 10). What is Human-Computer Interaction? Retrieved from Keele University: https://online.keele.ac.uk/what-is-human-computer-interaction/

Nicol, D., & Macfarlane-Dick, D. (2006). Formative assessment and self-regulated learning: A model and seven principles of good feedback practice. *Studies in Higher Education*, *31*(2), 199–218. DOI: 10.1080/03075070600572090

Norman, D. (2014). *The Design of Everyday Things*. The MIT Press.

O'Leary. Dyane, 'Smart' Lawyering: Integrating Technology Competence into the Legal Practice Curriculum (2021). University of New Hampshire Law Review, Vol. 9, No. 2, 2021, Available at SSRN: https://ssrn.com/abstract=3671632 or http://dx.doi.org/DOI: 10.2139/ssrn.3671632

Onesi-Ozigagun, O., Ololade, Y., Ogundipe, D., & Eyo-Udo, N. (2024). Revolutionizing Education through AI: A Comprehensive Review of Enhancing Learning Experiences. *International Journal of Applied Research in Social Sciences*, *6*(4), 589–607. DOI: 10.51594/ijarss.v6i4.1011

Palfreyman, D., & Tapper, T. (2016). The Marketization of English Higher Education and the Financing of Tuition Fees. *London Review of Education*, *14*(1), 47–55. DOI: 10.18546/LRE.14.1.06

Paul, R., & Elder, L. (2007). The Art of Socratic Questioning. *Journal of Developmental Education*, *31*(1), 36–37.

Quizlet. (2023, August 8). Welcome to Quizlet's AI Study Era: Studying will never be the same. Retrieved from Quizlet: https://quizlet.com/blog/ai-study-era

Rudin, C., Wang, C., & Coker, B. (2018). The age of secrecy and unfairness in recidivism prediction. Harvard Data Science Review. Advance online publication. https://hdsr.mitpress.mit.edu/pub/7z10o269/release/7

Schepard, A. (2022). Family Law with Skills Ten Years Later: Experiential Education in the Introductory Family Law Course. *Family Court Review*, *60*(2), 276–289. DOI: 10.1111/fcre.12678

Shugan, S. M. (2006). Editorial: Save Research: Abandon the Case Method of Teaching. *Marketing Science*, *25*(2), 109–115. https://www.jstor.org/stable/40056994. DOI: 10.1287/mksc.1060.0202

Simon, J., Wong, P.-H., & Rieder, G. (2020). Algorithmic bias and the Value Sensitive Design approach. *Internet Policy Review*, *9*(4). Advance online publication. DOI: 10.14763/2020.4.1534

Sossin, L. (2014). Experience the Future of Legal Education. *Alberta Law Review*, *41*(2), 466–498.

Spencer, R. (2022). "Hell is other people": Rethinking the Socratic method for quiet law students. *The Law Teacher*, *56*(1), 90–104. DOI: 10.1080/03069400.2021.2005305

Stoddard, H. A., & O'Dell, D. V. (2016). Would Socrates Have Actually Used the "Socratic Method" for Clinical Teaching? *Journal of General Internal Medicine*, *31*(9), 1092–1096. DOI: 10.1007/s11606-016-3722-2 PMID: 27130623

Stratton, G., Moffa, M., Sigamoney, A., & Ruyters, M. (2023). Innocence projects, work-integrated learning, and student career pathways. *Journal of Criminal Justice Education*, *35*(3), 1–17. DOI: 10.1080/10511253.2023.2231050

Susskind, R. (2019). *Online Courts and the Future of Justice*. Oxford University Press. DOI: 10.1093/oso/9780198838364.001.0001

Susskind, R. (2019). Online courts and the future of justice.. DOI: 10.1093/oso/9780198838364.001.0001

Tang, K. H. D. (2024). Implications of Artificial Intelligence for Teaching and Learning. *Acta Pedagogia Asiana*, *3*(2), 65–79. DOI: 10.53623/apga.v3i2.404

Thornton, M. (2001). *Privatising the public university: The case of law*. Routledge.

Tsaoussi, A. (2020). Using Soft Skills Courses to Inspire Law Teachers: A New Methodology for a More Humanistic Legal Education. *The Law Teacher*, *54*(1), 1–30. DOI: 10.1080/03069400.2018.1563396

University of Oklahoma. (2025, February 13). OU Law Launches AI QuizBot to Improve Student Engagement, Outcomes. Retrieved from The University of Oklahoma College of Law: https://law.ou.edu/about/news/ou-law-launches-ai-quizbot-improve-student-engagement-outcomes#:~:text=has%20launched%20a%20ChatGPT,in%20a%20modern%2C%20interactive%20way

Vlachopoulos, D., & Makri, A. (2017). The effect of games and simulations on higher education: A systematic literature review. *International Journal of Educational Technology in Higher Education, 14*(1), 1–33. DOI: 10.1186/s41239-017-0062-1

Voskobitova, E. (2021). Online Simulations for Teaching Professional Legal Skills. *Kutafin Law Review, 2021*(2), 36–56. DOI: 10.17803/2313-5395.2021.4.18.519-545

Waters, A. (2016). A Part to Play: The Value of Role-Play Simulation in Undergraduate Legal Education. *The Law Teacher, 50*(2), 148–166. DOI: 10.1080/03069400.2016.1162404

Waters, B. (2016). A Part to Play: The Value of Role-Play Simulation in Undergraduate Legal Education. *The Law Teacher, 50*(2), 172–194. DOI: 10.1080/03069400.2016.1162404

Watson, D., & Taylor, D. (1998). *Lifelong Learning and the University: A Post-Dearing Agenda*. Falmer.

Weinberg, J., & Hyams, R. (2023). *The Law Tech Clinic: Leading the way in entrepreneurial law clinics* (Special Edition). International Journal of Clinical Legal Education., DOI: 10.19164/ijcle.2023.1349

WhatWorked Education. (2023). Bodyswaps public speaking pilot: RCT final report. https://bodyswaps.co/resources/research

Williamson, B., & Eynon, R. (2020). Historical threads, missing links, and future directions in AI in education. *Learning, Media and Technology, 45*(3), 223–235. DOI: 10.1080/17439884.2020.1798995

Wintersteiger, L. (2020) Pedagogies of justice: critical approaches to public legal education. [Thesis] (Unpublished)

Yang, M. (2025, May 31). US lawyer sanctioned after being caught using ChatGPT for court brief. The Guardian. Retrieved from https://www.theguardian.com/us-news/2025/may/31/utah-lawyer-chatgpt-ai-court-brief

Zhai, C., Wibowo, S. W., & Li, L. D. (2024). The effects of over reliance on AI dialogue systems on students' cognitive abilities: A systematic review. *Smart Learning Environments, 11*(1), 28. DOI: 10.1186/s40561-024-00316-7

Zhong, Z., Chen, X., & Chen, D. (2022). Towards measuring bias in legal language models. arXiv preprint arXiv:2203.13369.https://doi.org//arXiv.2203.13369DOI: 10.48550

KEY TERMS AND DEFINITIONS

Adaptive Learning Systems: Educational technologies that personalize the learning experience by dynamically adjusting individual students' needs, preferences, and progress.

Algorithmic Bias: Systematic errors or unfair outcomes in AI decision making arise from biased training data, design assumptions, or implementation contexts.

Artificial Intelligence (AI): Computer systems that perform tasks normally require human intelligence.

Banking Model: A teaching model in which students are treated as passive recipients of knowledge without dialogue or critical engagement.

Case Law Analysis: The process of examining past judicial decisions to understand how laws have been interpreted and applied in specific situations and to determine how those decisions might influence future rulings.

Clinical Legal Education: Education involves students providing supervised legal assistance to real clients by combining academic studies with practical services.

Conscientizacao: Paulo Freire's term for the process of developing critical consciousness; an appreciation of social, political, and legal structures; and the ability to challenge injustice.

Digital Divide: The gap between those with reliable access to digital technology and skills and those without may exacerbate educational inequity.

Experiential Learning: Learning through experience. A pedagogical approach in which individuals learn by actively engaging in experiences and then reflecting on those experiences to extract knowledge and develop skills.

Explainable AI: AI systems are designed to make their outputs and decision-making processes transparent and understandable to the users.

Generative AI: A subtype of AI that produces new content such as text, images, or simulations (e.g., ChatGPT).

Human-Computer-Interaction: an interdisciplinary field studying the interaction of people and technology, focusing on the design of systems that are intuitive, responsive, and user-centered.

Innocence Project: A type of legal clinic, often university-based, where students investigate claims of wrongful conviction, with a view to overturn the conviction if a miscarriage of justice has occurred.

Institutional Dependency: In educational technology, this refers to the condition in which institutions (such as universities) become reliant on external providers for digital learning platforms, AI tools, or data infrastructure.

Large Language Model (LLM): An advanced AI system is trained on vast datasets of text to predict and generate human-like languages (e.g., ChatGPT).

Socratic Method: A form of dialogue in which the educator guides students through a series of questions to help them discover knowledge for themselves rather than directly providing information.

Chapter 10
Redesigning Legal Pedagogy in the Age of Artificial Intelligence: Insights From Educational Psychology

Swatee Yogessh
ILS Law College, Savitribai Phule Pune University, India

Hrucha Milind Dhamdhere
https://orcid.org/0009-0006-6264-7207
ILS Law College, Savitribai Phule Pune University, India

ABSTRACT

Legal pedagogy is at a turning point in the 21st century, particularly with the rise of Artificial Intelligence (AI). In professional fields like law, pedagogy is central to shaping the institution of justice. Traditionally grounded in disciplines like political science, sociology, and law, legal pedagogy must now draw from educational psychology to meet evolving needs. As AI enters the law classroom both as content and as a tool it enhances learning while also posing cognitive and ethical challenges. This chapter offers a psychological and technological framework for redesigning legal pedagogy. It emphasizes the distinctive nature of legal education, the critical role of pedagogy in developing legal professionals, and the implications of AI in teaching and learning. The chapter also addresses concerns surrounding AI integration and proposes a model that balances its potential benefits and risks with foundational pedagogical goals.

DOI: 10.4018/979-8-3373-3451-6.ch010

INTRODUCTION

Legal pedagogy stands at a pivotal crossroads in the 21st century, spurred by both the rapid integration of Artificial Intelligence (AI) technologies and the persistent demand for reform within law schools worldwide (Bar Council of India, 2024; Rajya Sabha Secretariat, 2024; Twining, 1994). Historically, legal pedagogy has drawn on traditions from political science, sociology, and law itself to shape not only the professional identities of lawyers but also the broader social institution of justice (Justice Krishna Iyer, Maneka Gandhi v. Union of India, 1978). This foundational role is inseparable from law's mission to uphold justice, social order, and ethical governance, demonstrating how pedagogical choices directly influence the legal consciousness of successive generations (Lord Neuberger, 2016; Chandrachud, 2024).

The swift adoption of AI in educational environments now challenges these established approaches. AI's capabilities to process vast legal information, personalize learning, and simulate court experiences are transforming how law is taught and learnt globally (Digital Education Council, 2024; Susskind, 2019). While AI enhances access to knowledge and supports individualized learning trajectories, it simultaneously raises concerns about its impact on cognitive development, ethical decision-making, and the cultivation of critical thinking which are core competencies essential to legal training (UNESCO, 2024). These developments compel urgent reconceptualization of legal pedagogy that integrates the insights of educational psychology with AI-driven tools, recognizing law's unique focus on complex problem-solving, advocacy, and ethical judgment in a technologically mediated world (Prensky, 2001; Stuckey et al., 2007).

This chapter explores how legal pedagogy can be redesigned to harness AI's potential without compromising the profession's foundational values. It interrogates critical questions including: How can psychological principles guide effective integration of AI in law teaching? What are the cognitive and ethical challenges arising from AI adoption? And what frameworks and assessment strategies can support the development of a future-ready, ethically grounded legal pedagogy? By centering these concerns, the chapter offers evidence-based recommendations and models for educators, learners, and institutions navigating this transformative era (Bar Council of India, 2024; Digital Education Council, 2024).

Building on this foundation, the chapter undertakes an extensive review of the literature across three interconnected domains: educational theories, psychology of education and learning critiques of contemporary legal pedagogy (including calls for interdisciplinarity and practical relevance and role of technology/ AI) (Rajya Sabha Secretariat, 2024; Legal Education and Training Review [LETR], 2013; Sullivan et al., 2007), research on AI's cognitive and ethical impacts in educational settings (UNESCO, 2024; Williamson & Eynon, 2020), and international policy developments and educational reforms responding to AI integration (Chandrachud, 2024; NYU Law, n.d., Columbia Law School, n.d.).

Methodologically, the chapter employs a mixed-method approach combining comparative policy analysis, empirical data synthesis from global student surveys (Digital Education Council, 2024). This methodology grounds the chapter's conceptual claims, proposing a practical "Learning Theory Framework for AI-Enhanced Legal Pedagogy" laying down the roadmap for educators and learners in light of developments in AI.

WHY LEGAL EDUCATION WORLD OVER MUST EVOLVE

The dynamic interplay of globalization, technological advances, and rapidly changing societal expectations has exposed critical limitations in traditional legal education systems worldwide (Twining, 1994). As legal practice becomes increasingly complex and intertwined with socio-technological transformations, the conventional focus on doctrinal instruction and rote learning now proves inadequate for preparing future lawyers to navigate multifaceted legal landscapes. The ongoing digital revolution, most prominently signified by artificial intelligence (AI), has brought forth unprecedented challenges and opportunities that legal pedagogy can no longer afford to ignore (UNESCO, 2024).

Legal education has historically enabled students to connect legal theory with the intricate realities of practice serving not only as technical training but as a foundation for cultivating values of justice, social responsibility, and essential human skills (Twining, 1994, p. 58). Pedagogical methods have long shaped how emerging lawyers understand law, justice, power, and their own roles within legal systems. The choices educators make what to teach, how to foster understanding, and which competencies to prioritize actively construct the collective legal consciousness of each generation, thereby influencing the practice of law and the principles underpinning justice itself (Lord Neuberger, 2016; Chandrachud, 2024; Maneka Gandhi v. Union of India, 1978).

Across jurisdictions, mounting evidence points to legal education's growing disconnection from the realities of practice. In India, critiques are focused on its overly theoretical and insular nature, leading to graduates who often struggle with essential professional skills (Bar Council of India, 2024; Rajya Sabha Secretariat, 2024). The legal academy has displayed marked resistance to interdisciplinarity despite the fact that today's legal issues intersect economics, sociology, technology, psychology, and environmental science. This disciplinary isolation restricts students' ability to engage with the true complexity of justice in modern society.

Internationally, the United Kingdom's Legal Education and Training Review (LETR, 2013) acknowledged that legal education was ill-suited to instill commercial and ethical judgment, adaptability, and practical skills appropriate for contemporary legal work. Similarly, the Carnegie Report in the United States identified that while American law schools excelled at teaching legal analysis, they often neglected experiential learning and the development of professional identity, resulting in a skills mismatch for new graduates a shortfall now being addressed through mandated experiential learning components and expanded clinical opportunities (Sullivan et al., 2007; NYU Law, n.d.; Columbia Law School, n.d.).

At the same time, the arrival of AI has presented both potential and peril. Law students, most of whom are digital natives and are accustomed to interactive and technologically rich environments, demand more dynamic, flexible, and engaging modes of learning (Prensky, 2001). Yet, a significant gap remains in legal education's ability to adapt, with many institutions persisting in passive, text-centric teaching that inadequately harnesses digital tools and AI-driven personalization (Digital Education Council, 2024). The risk of exacerbating inequalities also looms large, as students must not only master technology usage but also critically assess its ethical, legal, and social impact on justice delivery and legal practice (UNESCO, 2024).

Legal pedagogy thus faces a dual imperative i.e. it must reform not just to keep pace with a changing profession and broader global context, but also to fulfill its essential function in shaping fair and effective systems of justice for society. Evolution is no longer a matter of choice or convenience; it is fundamental to ensuring law schools remain relevant, equitable, and capable of empowering graduates for the present and future demands of the legal profession (Chandrachud, 2024; Lord Neuberger, 2016; Rajya Sabha Secretariat, 2024).

In summary, the urgency for evolution in legal education arises from the convergence of technological disruption, growing demand for interdisciplinarity, the inadequacy of traditional approaches, and the unique role of pedagogy in sustaining the ideals and practicalities of justice across diverse societies. This also necessitates identifying the peculiarities and uniqueness of Legal Pedagogy to accelerate evolution of Legal education in the Age of AI.

UNIQUENESS OF LEGAL PEDAGOGY IN THE AGE OF AI

Legal pedagogy possesses a distinctive character that arises not only from the complexity of law itself but from its enduring function in shaping legal reasoning, critical consciousness, and the social values underpinning justice (Twining, 1994). Traditionally, legal pedagogy has integrated doctrinal instruction with case analysis and skill-building exercises, preparing graduates to connect theoretical frameworks with real-world legal problems. However, what further sets legal pedagogy apart is its dual mandate: cultivating both the technical expertise required for legal practice and the moral-ethical capacities central to the rule of law (Sullivan et al., 2007).

In the era of artificial intelligence, this distinctiveness assumes new dimensions. First, AI and law now constitute an essential interdisciplinary subject within legal education. The integration of AI transforms the curriculum students must not only understand the substantive and procedural aspects of law, but also engage with the ethical, regulatory, and societal implications of data analytics, automation, and algorithmic governance (UNESCO, 2024; Digital Education Council, 2024). This demands that pedagogical approaches move beyond siloed knowledge, equipping students to interpret, critique, and ethically navigate the evolving interface of law and technology (Bar Council of India, 2024).

Second, there is a growing imperative to impart skills that prepare future lawyers for AI-driven governance. The expanding use of AI in courts, regulatory agencies, and dispute resolution requires graduates who can utilize digital tools for legal research, e-discovery, and predictive analytics while maintaining their professional judgment and ethical standards (Centre for Research and Planning, 2024). Legal pedagogy, therefore, must foster digital literacy, critical thinking, and adaptability skills that go beyond the mechanics of law to encompass the responsible stewardship of AI in justice delivery (Rajya Sabha Secretariat, 2024; LETR, 2013).

Third, AI is enhancing legal teaching itself through innovative, adaptive, and experiential tools. AI-driven platforms can generate tailored case hypotheticals, simulate courtrooms, or automate feedback in writing and research, facilitating active learning and reflection (Chandrachud, 2024). These technologies allow pedagogical practices to be more personalized, collaborative, and responsive to diverse student needs and the realities of practice (Columbia Law School, n.d.; NYU Law, n.d.). Importantly, the use of AI in pedagogy must be critical and reflective, ensuring equitable access and fostering a nuanced understanding of both the capacities and limitations of these technologies (UNESCO, 2024).

Finally, the uniqueness of legal pedagogy in the age of AI lies in its persistent commitment to bridging knowledge, values, and practice, while dynamically incorporating new technological realities. It is this adaptability that ensures legal education remains vital, relevant, and ethically grounded even as it evolves to meet the needs of an AI-mediated legal order (Twining, 1994; Sullivan et al., 2007; Prensky, 2001; Lord Neuberger, 2016).

The identified uniqueness of legal pedagogy needs a re-invention to deliver to the challenges posed by the AI advent in all walks of life generally and in the legal world specifically.

The changing cognitive abilities and needs of learners in the AI-driven legal profession necessitates an exploration of ways to integrate the foundational tenets of educational psychology in re-designing and catering to the uniqueness of legal pedagogies.

PSYCHOLOGY INFORMED LEGAL PEDAGOGY

Legal education, like medicine and engineering, can be grounded in educational psychology principles, which explore how individuals learn and apply knowledge (Eggen & Kauchak, 2010). Pedagogical frameworks of pedagogy (traditionally for children) and andragogy (adult learning), (Knowles, 1980; Knowles, Holton, & Swanson, 2015) have evolved into learner-centered strategies now used for learners of all ages. Foundational theories such as Behaviorism (Skinner, 1974), Constructivism (Piaget, 1969-2000), Experiential (Kolb, 1984), and Transformative Learning (Mezirow, 1997) can shape legal teaching by explaining how learners develop critical skills. Bloom's Taxonomy (Bloom, 1956; Anderson & Krathwohl, 2001) remains central in structuring curricula and assessment, ensuring that legal education adapts to a rapidly changing, AI-influenced world. The following section explores the use and relevance of these psychological educational theories in enhancing legal pedagogy with the help of AI.

Information Processing Theory (Atkinson & Shiffrin, 1968) likens learning to how computers process information via sensory, short-term, and long-term memory. Legal teaching can benefit from this by ensuring students process and retain complex material through discussion and repeated applied practice. AI can support this cycle by capturing attention, breaking concepts into parts, enabling spaced repetition, and helping track mastery and metacognition.

The Humanistic Approach (Rogers, 1969) prioritizes learner-centered, supportive environments, helping law students navigate ethical dilemmas and develop empathy. AI can enhance this by personalizing content, supporting emotional expression, and freeing educators to focus more on mentorship and student welfare.

Constructivism (Piaget, 1969-2000; Vygotsky, 1978) sees learners actively building understanding through experience and problem-solving, making active legal engagement central. AI can simulate legal scenarios, provide adaptive feedback, and scaffold learning, helping students personally construct legal knowledge.

Behaviorism (Skinner, 1974) focuses on learning via reinforcement, valuable for mastering routine legal skills. AI-driven drills and feedback foster effective habits, though these strategies should be integrated with approaches that encourage critical thinking and judgment.

Social Learning Theory (Bandura, 1977) emphasizes learning through observation and imitation. In law, students internalize values by watching peers and professionals in modelling environments-an experience that AI simulations, virtual mentors, and collaborative tools can enhance, fostering professional and ethical behavior.

Kolb's Experiential Learning Theory (1984) frames learning as a cycle: experience, reflection, conceptualization, and active experimentation. AI can create immersive simulations, structured reflection tools, theory-building supports, and practice scenarios that reinforce this cycle in legal training.

Knowles' Andragogy (1984) underlines that adults learn best when education is relevant, self-directed, and based on experience. AI tools can individualize learning, offer real-world simulations, and analyze reflective practices, supporting adult learners' needs for autonomy and practical engagement.

Cognitive Load Theory (Sweller, 1988) points to the limits of working memory and the need for well-structured materials. AI can organize dense legal content, generate summaries, highlight essential points, and administer adaptive quizzes, reducing cognitive overload.

Fleming's VARK model (Fleming & Mills, 1992) identifies visual, aural, read/write, and kinesthetic learning preferences. AI can deliver content in formats suited to each style, making legal education more inclusive and engaging.

Teachers' diverse instructional styles must intersect meaningfully with different student learning modes. In the era of AI, educators must intentionally cultivate habits like ethical reasoning and empathy which technology cannot replicate.

Jack Mezirow's (1997) Transformative Learning Theory highlights the need for law students to question assumptions, reflect on biases, and reconsider their perspectives about law and society. AI tools can introduce new viewpoints, stimulate critical reflection, and trace conceptual growth through journaling and simulations.

Bloom's Taxonomy (Anderson & Krathwohl, 2001) structures legal learning from memorization to creation and analysis. AI can support each stage-from knowledge recall to drafting legal documents-encouraging critical thinking at all levels.

Dual-Process Theory (Evans & Stanovich, 2013) distinguishes between intuitive ("System 1") and analytical ("System 2") thinking. Legal pedagogy trains students to shift from intuition to reasoned analysis, and AI can aid by prompting structured engagement with legal materials.

In sum, legal pedagogy, informed by psychological theory and aided by AI, enables learners to engage critically, build their professional identities, and respond to continuous change. Using these frameworks, educators can create inclusive, reflective, and adaptive learning environments essential for ethical and impactful lawyering. By aligning psychological theories with practical, AI-driven applications, legal pedagogy can meaningfully personalize, deepen, and humanize learning, turning abstract knowledge into real-world, reflective practice. Such integration ensures that future lawyers are not only tech-savvy and doctrinally sound but also ethical, empathetic, and ready to innovate within rapidly evolving legal landscapes. These theories not only guide legal educators in designing the legal pedagogy but also aid in identifying the perils of AI and its impact on human cognition. This facilitates mapping the scope, use and limitations of AI in redesigning the legal pedagogy. The next section elaborates on how a balanced approach can be adopted in redesigning the legal pedagogies while being mindful of the risks and challenges that AI may pose.

REDESIGNING CORE LEGAL PEDAGOGIES IN THE AGE OF AI - METHODS AND RISKS

Worldwide, legal education is gearing up to redesign its existing core legal pedagogies to match up with the evolution of AI. This section elaborates how the traditional legal pedagogies can be modified to leverage benefits and risks associated with such redesigning it in the age of AI.

Socratic Discussion

This method is a foundational approach in legal education, relies on probing questions and guided dialogue to foster analytic rigor and clarity in legal reasoning (Williamson & Eynon, 2020). In an AI-driven legal profession, the Socratic method can be meaningfully redesigned through interactive tools like the Socratic Quizbot (Quizbot, n.d.) and Socratic Mind (Socratic Mind, n.d.), which simulate iterative, question-based learning. Legal-technology scholars note that LLM-powered tools especially those specialized for legal contexts support deeper engagement with legal texts and enhance legal research through prompting and transparency techniques (Harrington, 2023). These platforms, powered by large language models (LLMs), may allow educators to automate follow-up questioning, mimic courtroom-style interrogation, and personalize critical reasoning practice. These tools may help the neurodiverse learners to focus (Global Online Academy, n.d.). However, such tools often require robust digital infrastructure, data security protocols, and subscription-based access, which may limit their immediate applicability in developing countries where institutional bandwidth, funding, and tech training remain uneven. In such contexts, open-source alternatives like custom GPT deployments via Google Colab or lightweight LMS plugins (e.g., Moodle Socratic AI scripts) offer more accessible entry points. Nonetheless, caution is essential: excessive reliance on AI risks undermining the unpredictability and ethical subtlety inherent in live Socratic dialogue. AI-generated prompts can become formulaic, favoring memorization over deeper normative inquiry. Legal educators must therefore co-design AI prompts, monitor AI-student interactions, and ensure these tools are rooted in pedagogical intentions rather than novelty (Fakour & Imani, 2025). Ultimately, while AI can scale and enrich Socratic learning, it must be used critically and contextually, especially in resource-constrained legal systems.

Langdellian Case Study

This pedagogy centers on close reading and dissection of judicial opinions, grounding students in precedent and doctrinal analysis (LexisNexis, n.d.). Adapting the Langdellian case-study method for the AI-era could involve tools like Lexis+ AI (LexisNexis, n.d.), Casetext CARA (Casetext, n.d.), and the AI4Chat Legal Case Study Creator (AI4Chat, n.d.). Students would analyze a judicial opinion, then use Lexis+ AI's conversation-style search to explore underlying legal principles (powered by NLP and predictive analytics) (Wow Labz, n.d.). Casetext's CARA feature helps surface relevant precedents and context-specific hypotheses based on the case facts. For a hands-on generator, AI4Chat creates full case studies around key fact patterns, enabling richer iterative exploration AI4Chat. Yet, these advanced platforms Lexis+ AI and Casetext primarily serve users in North America or institutions with paid subscriptions, limiting access in many developing countries. One of such AI tools available in India is Jurisphere (Jurisphere, n.d.). For broader reach, open-source systems like Stanford's STORM (Stanford Open Virtual Assistant Lab, n.d.) can generate structured case outlines and dialectical prompts via any web connection. Still, educators must carefully moderate, as the AI-generated prompts may become overly formulaic or biased and can risk oversimplifying normative complexity. However, the risk, is that AI can produce fabricated, hallucinated or misapplied precedents, potentially eroding students' understanding of authoritative legal sources if unchecked hence, regular faculty validation and robust citation checking remain indispensable (LexisNexis, n.d.; Williamson & Eynon, 2020). Teachers should co-design scenarios, validate AI answers, and emphasize ethical reasoning. Moreover, in low-resource settings, hybrid approaches combining SMS-based AI bots or offline downloads with in-person Socratic feedback ensure the method remains inclusive and pedagogically sound.

Legal Writing Assignments

This is a common pedagogy that has been used for evaluation and assessments of the law learners across legal institutions. The legal writing assignments are a pedagogical tool as well as an evaluation tool. These assignments may range from basic law essays to legal research papers to legislative comments to the research thesis. Legal writing assignments impart the learner with the hands-on skill of organizing the law, facts, legal reasoning, deductions, inductions and conclusion in a structured manner. A skill which is quintessential for any avenue of the legal profession.

AI-powered platforms like Grammarly (Grammarly, n.d.), BriefCatch (BriefCatch, n.d.), and Lexis+ AI (LexisNexis, n.d.) are transforming legal writing pedagogy by offering real-time enhancement of grammar, style, citation accuracy, and analytical flow. Tools such as Grammarly, now widely integrated across Word, Google Docs, and browser platforms, offer support for grammar correction, tone adjustment, spelling, and even plagiarism detection, alongside generative writing suggestions (Ravaglia, 2023; LawRank, 2021). These features make it particularly useful for drafting legal briefs or memos. However, law students have reported that while Grammarly enhances surface-level clarity, it often struggles to interpret legal jargon or the deeper structural and contextual nuances specific to legal writing. As observed in peer discussions (Reddit law students, 2024), its outputs require critical review rather than passive acceptance.

In contrast, legal-specific tools such as BriefCatch have been developed with the unique demands of legal writing in mind. This tool supports students in improving flow, brevity, plain language, and legal accuracy especially in Word-based legal assignments (MemoCards, 2025). Similarly, Lexis+ AI offers more advanced functionalities including citation verification, logical coherence checks, and structural critiques that are particularly beneficial for research-based writing.

While many of these platforms are available globally on freemium or subscription models, their most advanced features remain institutionally locked and often limited to users in North America or Europe. This creates accessibility challenges for students and institutions in emerging regions. Open-source writing tools, such as those developed from the Effidit project (Shi et al., 2022), or multilingual AI models running on local servers, offer potential alternatives to bridge this digital divide.

Nonetheless, a critical concern persists in the risk of over-reliance. As students increasingly incorporate AI tools into their writing processes, there is a real possibility of undermining the development of their own analytical reasoning and drafting capabilities. Though the relevance of the legal writing assignments stays in the present AI-driven world, the existence of AI tools such as various LLMs pose a severe challenge in imparting this skill. As Dr. Amy Clukey aptly exclaimed "*I'm no longer a teacher. I'm just a human plagiarism detector. I used to spend my grading time giving comments for improving writing skills. Now most of that time is just checking to see if a student wrote their own paper. What a waste of life.*" (as cited in Harrington & Brice, 2024). To address this challenge, the pedagogy can be redesigned to require learners to generate legal writing assignments and subsequently identify errors or hallucinations produced by the LLMs. This approach ensures that students continue to engage with the AI, but through the modified pedagogy, they are also actively involved in the assignment process, thereby guaranteeing that the intended skill set is effectively imparted and acquired by the learners. Legal educators, therefore, must design writing pedagogies that do not simply account for AI use, but intentionally incorporate safeguards such as maintaining draft histories, enforcing attribution norms, and embedding human-led feedback loops. The task ahead is not to resist the use of AI but to reimagine the legal writing process in ways that preserve originality, enhance learning, and uphold professional integrity.

Moot Courts and Mock Trials

This pedagogy has long provided immersive experiences for advocacy and procedural skill-building. With the advent of AI the moot simulating apps have been generated and used by various institutions in developed nations. Conduct of moots and mocks is a rigorous time-consuming process and hence conducting it often may not be practically possible. Multiple attempts in moots or mocks make the learners learn the nuances of argument and drafting. To leverage the maximum benefits of moots and mocks within limited resources and time may be possible with the help of AI.

AI-driven platforms like Jurors.ai (Jurors.ai, n.d.), Heyeve.ai (Heyeve.ai, n.d.), and ImootCourt (ImootCourt, n.d.) are reshaping moot courts and mock trials by offering scalable, immersive environments that emulate real-world courtroom dynamics. Jurors.ai provides 24/7 access to AI juries, where law students can upload case materials and receive simulated verdicts and juror reasoning generated through ChatGPT powered chain-of-thought prompting. Heyeve.ai offers immersive, voice-driven mock trials and judicial interviews through VR or web interfaces, delivering real-time coaching and feedback to enhance students' advocacy and courtroom presence Heyeve - AI Chatbot Assistant.

Platforms such as ImootCourt are now enabling law students to participate in simulated moot court exercises using AI-generated judges, opposing counsel, and team collaboration tools. These simulations are particularly useful for fostering global engagement, as they offer analytics and progress tracking features that allow for comparative evaluation across diverse legal systems. While these platforms are generally accessible online, some of their advanced features, especially those that rely on virtual reality may require high-bandwidth internet and come with premium subscriptions, potentially limiting equitable access.

In such cases, lower-resource alternatives like text-based AI juries e.g., ScholarEd Mock Jury (ScholarEd Mock Jury, n.d.) and open-source court simulators e.g., AgentCourt (Chen et al., 2025) can be deployed via mobile or offline setups, ensuring inclusivity. However, educators must proceed with caution. The risk here is that, if these avatars utilize inaccurate legal standards or hallucinated case law in their scoring, students could internalize flawed concepts. Additionally, scenarios using sensitive trial data raise confidentiality concerns, a challenge acute in the legal context given the professional norms governing case privacy (ImootCourt, n.d.; Stuckey et al., 2007). AI interactions risk becoming formulaic, failing to capture the unpredictability of human judges or jurors. Instructors should validate AI feedback, co-author prompts, and pair digital simulations with live debriefings to preserve nuanced legal reasoning and professional judgment. Moreover, ethical safeguards are essential to prevent overreliance and maintain educational rigor.

Group Discussions and Debates

Such pedagogies are vital for cultivating collaborative reasoning and debate etiquette, and they are increasingly augmented by AI-powered forums that analyze logical structures and flag participation trends. AI-enhanced platforms like Kialo Edu, Parlay Ideas, and DebateBrawl are modernizing classroom discussions and debates through structured argument mapping, AI moderation, and real-time analytics (Kialo Edu, n.d.; Parlay Ideas, n.d.; Aryan, 2024). Kialo Edu offers hierarchical argument trees and pro/con voting for in-depth debate, while Parlay Ideas uses AI-driven prompts and participation tracking to engage students in reflective discussion. DebateBrawl applies advanced AI techniques to simulate adaptive opposition for competitive debate training (Aryan, 2024). Platforms like Kialo Edu (free), Parlay (freemium), and DebateBrawl (open access) enable wider participation, though teachers should monitor for bias and supplement digital sessions with live reflection to maintain fairness and interpersonal learning. Hybrid methods, like SMS-based debate summaries, can help ensure equitable access in low-connectivity regions. However, the risk remains that automated moderation and feedback may reproduce majority biases or algorithmically silence minority perspectives, undermining the tradition of critical challenge central to legal discourse (European Commission, 2024).

To address these risks continuous human oversight is essential to identify and correct algorithmic biases and prevent minority perspectives from being silenced. Transparent moderation and regular audits of AI tools further reduce bias. Educators should complement AI forums with live reflection sessions to maintain interpersonal learning. Hybrid approaches, like SMS summaries, help ensure equitable access in low-connectivity areas. These measures balance AI benefits with safeguards that uphold fairness and critical discourse consistent with broader AI risk management principles.

Legal Aid and Legal Literacy Clinics

This pedagogy represents law schools' primary point of contact with marginalized communities, offering real-world avenues for experiential justice. This plays a dual role offering access to justice to marginalized communities while imparting experiential learning to the law students.

AI-augmented clinics are transforming how legal aid and literacy services operate; tools like Juris chatbot, LawPal, Botler AI, and Jagrit empower frontline clinics to offer interactive guidance, document assistance, and multilingual support. The Juris legal research chatbot, developed by Lone Star Legal Aid, helps staff quickly locate case law and administrative documents, reducing turnaround for clients with structured AI support (Lone Star Legal Aid, n.d.). In India, LawPal (Panchal et al., 2025) uses a Retrieval-Augmented Generation (RAG) (Lewis et al., 2020) architecture to answer legal queries accurately using local statutes and the Constitution designed for offline and low-bandwidth environments. Canada's Botler AI (Botler AI, n.d.) provides intelligent legal screening for harassment claims, while India's Jagrit chatbot offers multilingual self-help for domestic violence survivors via WhatsApp or Telegram, with lawyer-verified content (i-Probono, 2024). These tools vary in access: Juris and Botler are available in North America; LawPal and Jagrit are designed for India. Open-source alternatives like Niyam SahaAI (LawGlance, n.d.) and other GitHub legal-aid chatbots offer customizable, globally accessible solutions, and document translation tools like Anuvaadbhashini facilitate multilingual outreach.

The risk here is twofold and particularly acute for the law. AI may carry forward and even amplify historical or jurisdictional biases in legal data, and an overemphasis on automated service can distance students from the empathy and ethical judgement nurtured by direct client engagement (Panchal et al., 2025; i-Probono, 2024).

To mitigate the risk, caution is essential that AI responses are verified to check if they are inaccurate or biased, and client confidentiality must be rigorously safeguarded. Clinics must include human oversight, integrate trained lawyer review, and ensure data protection. In regions with limited digital access, mobile-based chatbots or offline deployment via local servers can ensure inclusive, sustainable implementation.

Mediation, Negotiation, and Arbitration

This pedagogy forms the foundation of non-adversarial legal skills, crucial as dispute resolution increasingly occurs outside courts. Traditional methods use negotiation exercises, mediation simulations, and arbitration role-plays to build collaboration, active listening, and principled compromise. AI integration greatly enhances these methods: AI negotiation bots simulate varied behaviors for strategic practice; virtual mediation platforms let students engage with AI avatars employing different tactics; and arbitration simulators create scenarios reflecting current transnational trends (ImootCourt, n.d.; European Commission, 2024).

Mediation Simulators pair AI-driven parties and mediators with natural language processing, giving students immediate feedback on tone, empathy, proposal crafting, and even bias in their communication. These tools help learners recognize emotional cues, explore BATNA/WATNA (Best/Worst Alternative to Negotiated Agreement) analysis, and adjust strategies for consensus-building. In India and the UK, institutions have piloted AI mediation environments where trainees manage multilingual, cross-cultural disputes, an essential experience for the global legal market (European Commission, 2024; ImootCourt, n.d.). Yet, distinct risks accompany this transformation. If AI-generated adversaries or parties rely on limited archetypes or data, students may develop an unrealistic sense of negotiation dynamics or implicit cultural bias. Overuse of automated modules may also stunt real-world skills such as managing unpredictable human reactions or addressing emotions. Law schools therefore ensure balance by alternating between AI-controlled scenarios and supervised live exercises, and routinely auditing scenario diversity and fairness. Ensuring reflection where students analyze both their negotiation process and the underlying human dimensions remains central to the ethical and practical practice of non-adversarial law (European Commission, 2024; Stuckey et al., 2007).

This AI-enhanced redesign of mediation, negotiation, and arbitration pedagogy thus upholds the fundamental values of legal education: nurturing empathy, analytical flexibility, and the ability to foster consensus skills ever more vital in an evolving, globally interconnected legal order.

In sum, the redesign of legal pedagogies through AI comes with tremendous promise and precise, discipline-specific hazards. Vigilance grounded in intentional pedagogical design, ongoing faculty oversight, and digital literacy remains crucial to maintaining the doctrinal authority, critical independence, and justice orientation central to the legal tradition (Selwyn, 2019; Stuckey et al., 2007; European Commission, 2024).

The redesigned legal pedagogies informed by educational theories elaborated in this chapter shall guide the teachers and learners of the Law in deciding which skill set is to be imparted or learnt with the help of AI. The integration of psychological educational theories into the mapping of skills and learning goals gives a comprehensive functional matrix for the law teachers and learners in effectively using AI for achieving the goals of legal education.

LEARNING THEORY FRAMEWORK FOR AI-ENHANCED LEGAL PEDAGOGY

A framework is proposed here for identifying the uniqueness of legal pedagogy based on field-informed classification that links legal pedagogy to the specific skill sets required across varied legal roles and probable reinvention in light of developments in AI. See Table 1

The skills and roles that today's law students are expected to harness for tomorrow's professional world may be classified broadly into following types, viz. Judges who can be divided into further two types i.e. trial judges and appellate judges; Lawyers who can be further divided into Litigation Lawyers and Transaction Lawyers; the litigating lawyers can be further divided into trial lawyers and appellate lawyers; Pro-Bono Lawyers; Global/ International Lawyers who can be further divided into Conflict of Law/Private International Law Lawyers and International Lawyers, Alternate Dispute Resolution (ADR) Lawyers further classified into Commercial and Domestic ADR lawyers and lastly administrative lawyers who are either the consultants to the executives or administrators or they themselves are administrators in either public or private sectors. This classification, with little bit of differences, exists in all types of Legal Systems in the world.

The framework recognizes that while some core skills such as legal research, problem-solving, communication, ethics, and reflective judgment are common to all legal professionals (ABA, 1992; Sullivan et al., 2007), other skills are specific to particular roles. For example, trial lawyers must master oral advocacy and cross-examination, while transactional lawyers require proficiency in negotiation and regulatory drafting. Similarly, mediators and arbitrators must cultivate listening skills, neutrality, and emotional intelligence, while judges need clarity in reasoning, procedural rigor, and ethical restraint.

This approach is not isolated but complements the broader international discourse on legal education reform. Foundational reports such as the MacCrate Report (ABA, 1992) and the Carnegie Report (Sullivan et al., 2007) have long advocated for pedagogies that move beyond doctrinal instruction, urging the integration of practice-based and context-sensitive learning.

Across jurisdictions, many law schools have begun incorporating such models into their curriculum, recognizing the value of system-responsive and role-oriented education, one that prepares students not merely for exams, but for the dynamic demands of legal practice in a globalized, technologically evolving world. However, the effective implementation of these pedagogies often hinges on practical constraints including institutional resources, time availability, faculty training, and supportive academic policies.

It is here that Artificial Intelligence can play a catalytic role. AI-driven tools can help simulate elements of real-world practice to which the learners have limited physical access, thus mitigating locational or resource-based disadvantages. AI can also assist in designing structured, scalable, and customizable versions of these pedagogies from virtual courtrooms and guided legal observatories to adaptive internship management systems ensuring that the intended skill sets are cultivated even within resource-constrained environments.

In this way, the use of AI does not replace the value of lived, field-based experiences, but strategically enhances their accessibility, reach, and impact allowing legal education institutions across diverse geographies to deliver professional preparedness aligned with the needs of future lawyers, judges, and legal professionals.

Table 1. Learning Theory Framework for AI-Enhanced Legal Pedagogy

Skill to be imparted	Bloom's Level	Learning Theory	Traditional Pedagogy	AI-Assisted Pedagogy Reinvention	Peculiar Risks with AI Redesign	Safeguard/Good Practice	Legal Professional for whom the skill set is suitable
Socratic Discussion	Analyze, Evaluate	Humanistic Approach, Constructivism	Socratic Discussion	AI Socratic quizbots/ chatbots	AI-generated prompts can become formulaic, favoring memorization over deeper normative inquiry	Faculty-curated and co-designed AI prompts, analytics reviews, monitor AI-student interactions, ensure tools are rooted in pedagogical intentions rather than novelty.	All legal professionals, particularly Judges, Trial Lawyers
Legal Reasoning & Problem-Solving	Apply, Analyze, Evaluate	Constructivism, Information Processing Theory	Case Study Method	Lexis+ AI, CaseText CARA, AI4Chat Legal Case Study Creator, Jurisphere, STORM	Fabricated, hallucinated, or misapplied precedents	Faculty validation, citation checks, co-design of scenarios, validate AI answers, and emphasize ethical reasoning	All legal professionals, particularly Litigating Lawyers
Legal Writing & Research	Apply, Analyze, Create	Cognitive Load Theory	Legal Writing, Library-based research, guided legal memos	Grammarly, BriefCatch, Lexis+ AI, LawRank	Over-reliance. loss of reasoning, undermining analytical reasoning and drafting skills	Maintain draft histories, faculty feedback loops, design pedagogy incorporating attribution norms, and embed human-led feedback mechanisms	Transactional Lawyers, Litigating Lawyers, Academics
Advocacy & Trial Practice	Apply, Analyze, Evaluate	Kolb's Experiential Learning Theory	Moot Courts, Mock Trials	ImootCourt, Jurors.ai, Heyeve.ai, ScholarEd Mock Jury, AgentCourt	AI hallucinated judgments, loss of unpredictability, privacy risks, formulaic simulations	Faculty validation of AI feedback, co-authoring AI prompts, paired with live debriefings	Trial Lawyers, Appellate Lawyers, ADR Practitioners
Group Discussion & Debate	Analyze, Evaluate	Social Learning Theory, Constructivism	Group Discussions, Debates	Kialo Edu, Parlay Ideas, DebateBrawl	Reproduction of majority biases, algorithmical silencing of minorities, undermining critical challenge traditions	Continuous human oversight, detecting and correcting biases, transparent moderation, regular auditing of AI tools; pairing AI forums with live reflections. Hybrid methods to ensure equity in low-connectivity regions.	Litigating Lawyers, Lawyers in Training, ADR Lawyers

continued on following page

Table 1. Continued

Skill to be imparted	Bloom's Level	Learning Theory	Traditional Pedagogy	AI-Assisted Pedagogy Reinvention	Peculiar Risks with AI Redesign	Safeguard/Good Practice	Legal Professional for whom the skill set is suitable
Legal Aid & Literacy Clinics	Apply, Analyze, Evaluate	Social Learning Theory, Behaviorism	Clinical Legal Education, Legal Aid Clinics	Jagrit, LawPal, Botler, i-probono.in	Legal/ cultural bias, accuracy gaps, overemphasis on automation risking reduced empathy and ethical judgment arising from direct client engagement	Human oversight with trained lawyer reviews, robust data protection, ethical guidelines for chatbot usage, use offline/mobile modes in low-access areas to ensure inclusion	Pro Bono Lawyers, NGOs, Legal Consultants
Mediation, Negotiation & Arbitration	Apply, Analyze, Evaluate	Kolb's Experiential Learning Theory, Social Learning Theory	Role-plays, Simulations, Workshops	AI mediation/ negotiation bots, virtual arbitration platforms	Stereotyped scenarios, loss of authentic dialog, unrealistic negotiation dynamics	Hybrid AI-human role-plays, scenario audits for diversity, facilitator-led debriefing/reflections, regular updates to minimize bias	ADR Lawyers (Commercial & Domestic), Administrative Lawyers
Legal Ethics & Reflective Judgment	Evaluate, Create	Transformative Learning Theory, Dual Process Theory	Ethics Seminars, Reflection Journals	AI-facilitated reflective prompts and ethical dilemma simulations	AI prompts possibly formulaic or biased; risk of superficial engagement with ethical concepts	Faculty-facilitated discussions, critical assessment of AI outputs, integration with lived experiences and case studies, safeguards against over-reliance	All legal professionals, esp. Judges and Admin Lawyers

ROADMAP FOR EDUCATORS AND LEARNERS

To effectively redesign legal pedagogy in the era of artificial intelligence (AI), educators and learners need to adopt a systematic, reflective, and iterative approach that aligns educational objectives with suitable learning experiences, incorporate AI tools thoughtfully, evaluate outcomes rigorously, and adapt dynamically over time. This section elaborates a step wise roadmap as proposed by Roy Stuckey (2007), which is built over and modified to integrate it in redesigning the legal pedagogy in the age of AI. The roadmap presents a clear, practical sequence of steps for redesigning legal pedagogy. It draws on foundational educational theories while directly addressing the distinct challenges and opportunities introduced by AI integration in legal education. This structured approach will equip educators to thoughtfully align objectives, methods, and tools to ensure that legal instruction remains adaptive, relevant, and effective in the evolving technological landscape.

Roadmap for Educators

Step 1: Identifying Educational Objectives

Begin by clarifying what the course or unit intends to achieve. Use AI-powered curriculum mapping tools to connect the objectives with 21st-century legal skills. Few skills are identified in the framework above. Clearly define the Pedagogical Goal-such as critical thinking, collaboration, or persuasive advocacy and align it with Bloom's Taxonomy (e.g., Apply, Analyze, Create) for the desired cognitive level. Relate each goal to a foundational learning theory (e.g., Constructivism for building on prior knowledge, Experiential Learning for skills acquisition through practice).

'Learning Theory Framework for AI-Enhanced Legal Pedagogy' proposed above may be used for mapping the educational objective with expected skill set to be imparted while redesigning the pedagogical tools.

Step 2: Selecting Effective Learning Experiences

After setting clear objectives, select learning experiences most likely to help students achieve them. Consider psychological theories of learning to match student needs: for example, use case-based learning for critical reasoning (Constructivism) or simulation for skill-building (Experiential Learning). AI tools can facilitate this mapping by suggesting instructional methods based on the identified objectives and chosen theory, offering customized course schematics and activities that fit the learner profile.

Step 3: Organizing Learning Experiences for Instruction

Plan the delivery and sequencing of the selected experiences for maximum impact, factoring in resources and time constraints. Organize sessions to balance in-class and out-of-class activities. Start with Traditional Pedagogies (e.g., moot courts, Socratic dialogue, legal clinics) to build confidence in familiar formats. Leverage AI platforms as specified in Table 1, to schedule, structure, or supplement these pedagogies, ensuring smooth integration of digital and experiential learning opportunities.

Step 4: Designing Evaluation Methods

Develop robust, multi-method strategies for assessing the effectiveness of learning experiences. Adapt strategies according to subject matter and student level. Harness AI to create rapid feedback loops and adaptive quizzes, helping pinpoint whether intended objectives are being met and where instruction may need to be adapted. Use a combination of outcome-based rubrics, formative self-assessments, automated peer review, and AI-generated analytics to holistically assess progress and inform continuous improvement.

Step 5: Curate and Choose AI Tools

Choose AI Tool/Platform such as Lexis+ AI, ChatGPT for imparting Legal reasoning. Legal databases such as Westlaw Edge, ROSS etc. for Legal Research. Grammarly, BriefCatch, CoCounsel etc. for imparting writing skills. Use of Socratic VR or custom chatbot builders for simulating ethical dilemmas etc. Integrate AI Tools Gradually. Start with demonstrations and low-stakes tasks (e.g., AI-assisted summaries) and Encourage experimentation while providing guidance. Design Scaffolded Assignments by combining traditional + AI modes for e.g. draft a legal memo using library research and AI input.

Step 6: Provide Ethical Framing

Openly discuss the strengths, weaknesses, and ethical implications of AI in legal education. Explain potential biases, "hallucinations," and limitations of generative AI in legal practice and research. Refer students to sample policies such as those produced by The AI Pedagogy Project, metaLAB at Harvard (AI Pedagogy Project, metaLAB (at) Harvard, n.d.), to instill a responsible, reflective approach to AI use in legal studies and practice. Ensure students understand the importance of critical oversight, accuracy checks, and upholding academic integrity.

Step 7: Update & Reflect

Establish a routine of collecting and acting on student feedback, regarding both content and tool efficacy. Modify course material and AI tool selection regularly as the legal and technological landscape evolves. Use peer collaboration, rubrics, and reflection sessions to refine both instructional methods and tool integration each year, ensuring that the pedagogy remains current and impactful.

This roadmap equips teachers to thoughtfully integrate AI, learning theory, ethical awareness, and continuous improvement into legal education empowering students with the adaptive, evaluative, and reflective skills most needed in a rapidly evolving professional environment.

Roadmap for Learners

Step 1: Know the Skill Goal

Understand what skill set needs to be harnessed, e.g., critical reasoning, empathy, cross-border legal understanding. Depending on the skill sought to be learnt, decide which AI tool may assist in learning that respective skill. Be mindful of knowing whether the AI assistance will merely assist in the learning process or will substitute the skill. For example, if the learner is using LLM such as ChatGPT for generating submissions on critical essays, the learner should ensure that the critical reasoning skill is learnt by seeking assistance from LLM in providing information or facts like a learner would get from the library in the traditional mode, but the actual analysis of the text and information should be done by the learner.

Step 2: Use Traditional Methods First

To integrate the AI in learning mode, learners should start with the traditional method first such as Reading cases, engaging in role-plays, attempting manual legal drafting before seeking AI assistance. Unless the learner does it manually the learner will not be able to understand what is being generated by AI is relevant or not.

Step 3: Select the Right AI Tool

Choose AI tools based on the learning objectives and tasks. For example, for brainstorming use ChatGPT, for document analysis tools like Kira are better suited. Matching tools to specific purposes optimizes one's learning efficiency and effectiveness. The learners should familiarize themselves with the strengths and limitations of each AI resource so as to make informed choices that align with the skill goals.

Step 4: Practice AI-Led Tasks

Engage actively by using AI to generate ideas, explore scenarios, or simulate legal interactions. Approach AI outputs critically-do not accept them at face value; verify facts, refine outputs, and integrate them thoughtfully into the work. This iterative process strengthens the judgment and helps combine AI efficiency with personal insight.

Step 5: Collaborate & Peer Review

Share the AI-assisted work with peers to compare approaches, discuss best practices, and address ethical questions that emerge from AI use. Group discussions around AI's role encourage diverse perspectives and deeper understanding of its implications. Peer review also enforces accountability, helping in spotting the errors or biases in AI-generated content.

Step 6: Reflect Often

Maintain learning journals or use digital dashboards to record how AI tools impact progress and skill development. Self-assessment encourages mindfulness about what is learned and how AI has contributed to learning. Regular reflection enables identifying gaps, adjusting strategies, and consolidating the understanding, ensuring continuous improvement.

Step 7: Stay Updated

Actively follow new developments in legal technology, AI regulations, and scholarly debates on AI's role in law and education. Staying informed helps in adapting to changes and responsibly integrating emerging tools. Engage with communities, webinars, and publications to remain aware of innovations and ethical standards. Upgrading the faculty skills by training in new technology and AI tools would ensure readiness to face newer challenges posed by ever evolving AI.

Step 8: Follow AI Ethics Guidelines

Adhere strictly to ethical rules and policies outlined by the educational institution or department of affiliation, regarding AI use. Address and respect issues such as data privacy, transparency, and academic integrity. Being ethically responsible enhances trustworthiness and prepares the learners for professional standards in AI-augmented legal practice.

This elaborated roadmap guides learners to develop legal skills effectively by balancing traditional learning with AI integration, critical evaluation, ethical mindfulness, and continuous reflection.

By systematically foregrounding these principles, legal education can harness AI's benefits while ensuring that the advancement of pedagogy genuinely supports equity, diversity, and ethical responsibility across the legal profession. Adopting the proposed 'Learning Theory Framework for AI-Enhanced Legal Pedagogy' will facilitate both educators and learners to harness the power of AI to enrich legal education, enhance critical skills, and uphold the ethical responsibilities foundational to the profession.

CONCLUSION

In conclusion, redefining legal pedagogy in the age of AI is not a matter of technological adaptation alone, it is a profound reorientation of legal education toward relevance, inclusion, and reflective professionalism. This chapter has proposed a multidimensional framework grounded in educational psychology, skill mapping, and context-sensitive innovation. By weaving together traditional pedagogical strengths with AI-enabled tools, legal educators can create a future-ready learning environment that is adaptive, ethical, and learner-centric. As we navigate this evolving terrain, the challenge is not merely to teach law with AI, but to teach law about AI and to do so in ways that preserve human values at the heart of justice.

It is important to note, however, that the framework presented here is not intended to be exhaustive or prescriptive. It serves as an illustrative model, one possible roadmap among many for integrating AI meaningfully into legal education. Pedagogical approaches must be responsive to diverse institutional contexts, infrastructural realities, and individual teaching philosophies. Each institution, instructor, and learner must ultimately calibrate these tools and methods according to their goals, constraints, and evolving needs.

While AI-enhanced pedagogies present new possibilities, it is important to recognize the equity challenges that persist across and within jurisdictions. Digital infrastructure, faculty readiness, language barriers, and socioeconomic disparity continue to constrain the equitable adoption of AI in many developing nations. For example, legal education in South Asia or Sub-Saharan Africa may lack institutional bandwidth to deploy immersive AI tools. Therefore, it is crucial to develop AI-integrated solutions that are affordable, mobile-compatible, and language-diverse. Incorporating open-source tools, text-based chatbots, and hybrid offline-online learning systems can serve as bridges across the digital divide (UNESCO, 2023). Additionally, inclusive AI design must consider learners with disabilities, first-generation students, and those from marginalized communities to avoid further entrenching educational disparities (World Bank, 2022).

Transformation of legal pedagogy must align with national and institutional accreditation norms. Regulatory bodies such as the Bar Council of India, the American Bar Association, or the Solicitors Regulation Authority must evolve policies to encourage innovation without compromising core legal competencies. Institutions should pilot AI tools through sandbox models and collaborative research with edtech partners.

A final caveat: the only way to truly understand, interrogate, and ethically shape the future of AI in legal education is to actively engage with it. Avoidance or resistance may leave legal academia unprepared for the profound shifts AI will inevitably bring. Embracing AI critically, not uncritical, is the more responsible path forward. In doing so, we position ourselves not just as users of technology, but as co-authors of its legal, ethical, and pedagogical future.

REFERENCES

AI4Chat. (2024). *Legal Case Study Creator*. Retrieved July 12, 2025, from https://www.ai4chat.co/pages/legal-case-study-creator

AI Pedagogy Project. *metaLAB (at) Harvard. (n.d.). AI Pedagogy Project: Critical and creative engagement with AI.* https://aipedagogy.org/

American Bar Association. (1992). *Report of the Task Force on Law Schools and the Profession: Narrowing the Gap.* ABA Section of Legal Education and Admissions to the Bar. Retrieved from https://www.americanbar.org/content/dam/aba/publications/misc/legal_education/Standards/standardsarchive/1992_93_standards.pdf

Anderson, L. W., Krathwohl, D. R., Airasian, P. W., Cruikshank, K. A., Mayer, R. E., Pintrich, P. R., . . . Wittrock, M. C. (2001). *A taxonomy for learning, teaching, and assessing: A revision of Bloom's taxonomy of educational objectives*. Longman. *Retrieved* from https://cmapspublic2.ihmc.us/rid=1Q2PTM7HL-26LTFBX-9YN8/Krathwohl%202002.pdf

Aryan, P. (2024, December 9). LLMs as debate partners: Utilizing genetic algorithms and adversarial search for adaptive arguments. arXiv. https://doi.org//arXiv.2412.06229.DOI: 10.1109/ICEI64305.2024.10912343

Atkinson, R. C., & Shiffrin, R. M. (1968). Human memory: A proposed system and its control processes. In Spence, K. W., & Spence, J. T. (Eds.), *The* psychology *of learning and motivation* (Vol. 2, pp. 89-195). Academic Press. Retrieved from http://rca.ucsd.edu/selected_papers/2_Human_memory_A_proposed_system_and_its_control_processes.pdf

Bandura, A. (1977). *Social learning theory*. Prentice Hall. Retrieved from https://www.asecib.ase.ro/mps/Bandura_SocialLearningTheory.pdf

Bar Council of India. (2024, May 20). *BCID-0468-2024 (LE Circular-06/2024): Comprehensive implementation of legal education reforms, mandatory guidelines, norms & rules of legal education* [Circular]. Bar Council of India. https://www.barcouncilofindia.org/info/bcid-0468--g87cul

Bloom, B. (1956). *Taxonomy of Educational Objectives: The Classification of Educational Goals.* Retrieved from https://eclass.uoa.gr/modules/document/file.php/PPP242/Benjamin%20S.%20Bloom%20-%20Taxonomy%20of%20Educational%20Objectives%2C%20Handbook%201_%20Cognitive%20Domain-Addison%20Wesley%20Publishing%20Company%20%281956%29.pdf

Botler, A. I. (n.d.). *Your AI guide to laws, rights & justice.* Retrieved July 14, 2025, from https://botler.com/

BriefCatch. (n.d.). *BriefCatch: Your trusted legal writing assistant.* Retrieved July 14, 2025, from https://briefcatch.com/

Casetext. (n.d.). *CARA (Case Analysis Research Assistant) legal research tool.* Retrieved July 14, 2025, from https://www.legal.io/legal-software/198/Casetext legal.io.

Chandrachud, D. Y. (2024, April 10). *Integration of AI in modern processes raises complex ethical, legal, practical considerations:* CJI. Indian Express. https://indianexpress.com/article/india/integration-ai-modern-processes-ethical-legal-practical-considerations-cji-9267700/

Chen, G., Fan, L., Gong, Z., Xie, N., Li, Z., Liu, Z., Li, C., Qu, Q., Alinejad-Rokny, H., Ni, S., & Yang, M. (2025). *AgentCourt: Simulating court with adversarial evolvable lawyer agents.* In Proceedings of the 63rd Annual Meeting of the Association for Computational Linguistics (pp. 508-515). Association for Computational Linguistics. https://aclanthology.org/2025.findings-acl.304.pdf

Columbia Law School. (n.d.). *Experiential learning.* Columbia Law School. https://www.law.columbia.edu/academics/experiential

Digital Education Council. (2024, August 2). *Digital Education Council global AI student survey 2024.* Digital Education Council. https://www.digitaleducationcouncil.com/post/digital-education-council-global-ai-student-survey-2024

Eggen, P., & Kauchak, D. P. (2010). *Educational psychology: Windows on classrooms* (8th ed.). Merrill/Prentice Hall., Retrieved from https://sehthehfoundation.org/wp-content/uploads/2023/09/Paul-Eggen-Don-Kauchak-Educational-Psychology_-Windows-On-Classrooms.-8th-edition-Merrill-Pearson-2010.pdf

European Commission. (2024). *EU Artificial Intelligence Act.* Retrieved from https://digital-strategy.ec.europa.eu/en/policies/european-approach-artificial-intelligence

Evans, J. St. B. T., & Stanovich, K. E. (2013). Dual-process theories of higher cognition: Advancing the debate. *Perspectives on Psychological Science, 8*(3), 223–241. DOI: 10.1177/1745691612460685 PMID: 26172965

Fakour, H., & Imani, M. (2025). Socratic wisdom in the age of AI: A comparative study of ChatGPT and human tutors in enhancing critical thinking skills. *Frontiers in Education, 10,* 1528603. Advance online publication. DOI: 10.3389/feduc.2025.1528603

Fleming, N. D., & Mills, C. (1992). Not another inventory, rather a catalyst for reflection. *To Improve the Academy*, *11*(1), 137–155. https://digitalcommons.unl.edu/cgi/viewcontent.cgi?article=1245&context=podimproveacad. DOI: 10.1002/j.2334-4822.1992.tb00213.x

Global Online Academy. (n.d.). *Student perspective: Reflecting on the role of AI in education*. Retrieved July 12, 2025, from https://globalonlineacademy.org/insights/articles/student-perspective-reflecting-on-the-role-of-ai-in-education

Grammarly. (n.d.). *Grammarly: Free AI writing assistance*. Retrieved July 14, 2025, from https://www.grammarly.com/

Harrington, S., & Brice, K. (2024, December). *Revolutionizing legal education with AI: The Socratic Quizbot*. AI Law Librarians. https://www.ailawlibrarians.com/2024/12/10/socratic-quizbot/

Harrington, S. A. (2023, June 26). *The case for large language model optimism in legal research from a law & technology librarian. SSRN.* https://ssrn.com/abstract=4492121 DOI: 10.2139/ssrn.4492121

Heyeve.ai. (n.d.). *AI Chatbot Assistant for legal training & consultation.* Retrieved July 12, 2025, from https://heyeve.ai/

i-Probono. (2024). *AI for legal empowerment: Collaborative effort behind Jagrit Chatbot*. Retrieved July 14, 2025, from https://i-probono.in/ipb_casestudy/ai-for-legal-empowerment-collaborative-effort-behind-jagrit-chatbot/

Jurisphere. (n.d.). *AI-powered legal assistant*. Retrieved July 14, 2025, from https://jurisphere.ai/

Jurors.ai. (n.d.). *Mock trials using AI*. Retrieved July 12, 2025, from https://jurors.ai/

Justice Connect. (n.d.). *Our AI Model – Justice Connect.* https://justiceconnect.org.au/about/innovation/legal-help-experience/ai-project/

Kialo Inc. (n.d.). Kialo: Structured debate platform. Retrieved July 12, 2025, from https://www.kialo.com/

Knowles, M. S. (1980). *The modern practice of adult education: From pedagogy to andragogy*. Cambridge Adult Education. Retrieved from https://www.umsl.edu/~henschkej/articles/a_The_%20Modern_Practice_of_Adult_Education.pdf

Knowles, M. S., Holton, E. F.III, & Swanson, R. A. (2015). *The adult learner: The definitive classic in adult education and human resource development* (8th ed.). Routledge., Retrieved from https://api.pageplace.de/preview/DT0400.9781000072891_A39784180/preview-9781000072891_A39784180.pdf

Kolb, D. (1984). *Experiential Learning: Experience as the Source of Learning and Development.* Fullerton.edu. Retrieved from https://www.fullerton.edu/cice/_resources/pdfs/sl_documents/Experiential%20Learning%20-%20Experience%20As%20The%20Source%20Of%20Learning%20and%20Development.pdf

LawGlance. (n.d.). *LawGlance.* Retrieved July 15, 2025, from https://lawglance.com/

LawRank. (2021, May 4). *Grammarly: A top writing tool for lawyers.* https://lawrank.com/grammarly-a-top-writing-tool-for-lawyers/

Legal Education and Training Review (LETR). (2013). *Setting standards: The future of legal services education and training regulation in England and Wales – Main report.* https://letr.org.uk/the-report/

Lewis, P., Perez, E., Piktus, A., Petroni, F., Karpukhin, V., Goyal, N., Küttler, H., Lewis, M., Yih, W.-t., Rocktäschel, T., Riedel, S., & Kiela, D. (2020). *Retrieval-augmented generation for knowledge-intensive NLP tasks. Advances in Neural Information Processing Systems, 33.* arXiv. https://doi.org/DOI: 10.48550/arXiv.2005.11401

LexisNexis. (n.d.). *Lexis+ AI: Legal research platform & AI assistant.* Retrieved July 14, 2025, from https://www.lexisnexis.com/en-us/products/lexis-plus-ai.page.

Lone Star Legal Aid. (n.d.). *TIG AI Chatbot Project.* Retrieved July 14, 2025, from https://www.lonestarlegal.org/tig-ai-chatbot-project

Memo.Cards. (2025). *Top 7 AI tools for legal writing feedback.* Retrieved July 12, 2025, from https://www.memo.cards/blog/top-7-ai-tools-for-legal-writing-feedback

Mezirow, J. (1997). Transformative learning: Theory to practice. *New Directions for Adult and Continuing Education, 1997*(74), 5–12. DOI: 10.1002/ace.7401

Neuberger, D. (2016, June 15). *Ethics and advocacy in the twenty-first century* (The Lord Slynn Memorial Lecture). Supreme Court of the United Kingdom. https://supremecourt.uk/uploads/speech_160615_78f4e3d8a0.pdf

New York University School of Law. (n.d.). *Experiential Learning Lab.* NYU School of Law. https://www.law.nyu.edu/experientiallearninglab

Panchal, D., Gole, A., Narute, V., & Joshi, R. (2025). *LawPal: A Retrieval Augmented Generation based system for enhanced legal accessibility in India* (arXiv preprint, arXiv:2502.16573). arXiv. https://doi.org//arXiv.2502.16573.DOI: 10.48550

Parlay Ideas. (n.d.). *Parlay: AI-powered class discussions.* Retrieved July 12, 2025, from https://parlayideas.com/

Piaget, J. (1972). *The psychology of the child*. Basic Books. Retrieved from https://www.alohabdonline.com/wp-content/uploads/2020/05/The-Psychology-Of-The-Child.pdf

Quizbot. (n.d.). *Quizbot: AI-powered quiz and assessment platform*. https://quizbot.ai/

Rajya Sabha Secretariat. (2024, February). *Report No. 142: Strengthening legal* education *in view of emerging challenges before the legal profession* (Department-related Parliamentary Standing Committee on Personnel, Public Grievances, Law and Justice). Parliament of India. https://sansad.in/getFile/rsnew/Committee_site/Committee_File/ReportFile/18/191/142_2024_2_12.pdf?source=rajyasabha

Ravaglia, R. (2023, August 28). *Generative AI makes Grammarly an essential student learning tool*. Forbes. Retrieved from https://www.forbes.com/sites/rayravaglia/2023/08/28/generative-ai-makes-grammarly-an-essential-student-learning-tool/

Reddit law students. (2024, July 19). *Grammarly for LRW? [Discussion thread]. r/LawSchool.* https://www.reddit.com/r/LawSchool/comments/1e74hac

Rogers, C. R. (1969). *Freedom to* learn. Merrill. Retrieved from https://www.scribd.com/document/609262438/Freedom-to-Learn-by-Carl-R-Rogers-H-Jerome-Freiberg-Z-lib-org

ScholarEd. (n.d.). *Mock Jury - AI-powered jury simulation*. Retrieved July 12, 2025, from https://www.yeschat.ai/gpts-9t557feQ6Lr-ScholarEd-Mock-Jury

Selwyn, N. (2019). *Should Robots Replace Teachers? AI and the Future of Education*. Polity. Retrieved from https://www.scribd.com/document/808141299/Neil-Selwyn-Should-Robots-Replace-Teachers-AI-and-the-Future-of-Education-2019-convertido-1

Shi, S., Zhao, E., Tang, D., Wang, Y., Li, P., Bi, W., & Ma, D. (2022). Effidit: Your AI writing assistant *[Technical report]*. arXiv. https://arxiv.org/abs/2208.01815

Skinner, B. F. (1974). *About behaviorism*. Knopf.

Socratic Mind. (n.d.). *Socratic Mind: AI-powered oral assessment platform*. https://socraticmind.com/

Stanford Open Virtual Assistant Lab. (n.d.). *STORM (Synthesis of Topic Outlines through Retrieval and Multi-Perspective Question Asking)* [AI writing research preview]. Stanford University. Retrieved July 14, 2025, from https://storm.genie.stanford.edu/

Stuckey, R.. (2007). *Best Practices for Legal Education: A Vision and a Road Map*. Clinical Legal Education Association.

Suffolk University Law School. (2025). *Dispute resolution.* https://www.suffolk.edu/law/academics-clinics/what-can-i-study/dispute-resolution

Sullivan, W. M., Colby, A., Wegner, J. W., Bond, L., & Shulman, L. S. (2007). *Educating lawyers: Preparation for the profession of law* (The Carnegie Foundation report). Jossey-Bass. Retrieved from_http://archive.carnegiefoundation.org/publications/pdfs/elibrary/elibrary_pdf_632.pdf

Supreme Court of India. *Centre for Research and Planning. (n.d.). Publications.* https://www.sci.gov.in/centre-for-research-and-planning/#Publications

Supreme Court of India. (1978). *Maneka Gandhi v. Union of India*, AIR 1978 SC 597.

Susskind, R. (2019). *Tomorrow's lawyers: An introduction to your future* (2nd ed.). Oxford University Press.

Sweller, J. (1988). Cognitive load during problem solving: Effects on learning. *Cognitive Science, 12*(2), 257–285. https://onlinelibrary.wiley.com/doi/epdf/10.1207/s15516709cog1202_4. DOI: 10.1207/s15516709cog1202_4

Twining, W. (1994). *Blackstone's tower: The English law school* (Hamlyn Lectures No. 46). Stevens & Sons. Retrieved from_https://karnatakajudiciary.kar.nic.in/hcklibrary/pdf/HamylanLectures/46%20Blackstone's_Tower.pdf

UNESCO. (2023). *AI and the right to education: Global perspectives on challenges and opportunities.*_https://unesdoc.unesco.org

UNESCO. (2024, September 3). *What you need to know about UNESCO's new AI competency frameworks for students and teachers.* Retrieved July 12, 2025, from https://www.unesco.org/en/articles/what-you-need-know-about-unescos-new-ai-competency-frameworks-students-and-teachers

University of California. Berkeley, School of Law. (n.d.). *Samuelson Law, Technology & Public Policy Clinic.* https://www.law.berkeley.edu/experiential/clinics/samuelson-law-technology-public-policy-clinic/

Vygotsky, L. S. (1978). *Mind in Society: The Development of Higher Psychological Processes.* Harvard University Press. Retrieved from_https://home.fau.edu/musgrove/web/vygotsky1978.pdf

Williamson, B., & Eynon, R. (2020). Historical Threads, Missing Links, and Future Directions in AI and Education. *Learning, Media and Technology, 45*(3), 223–235. DOI: 10.1080/17439884.2020.1798995

Williamson, B., & Eynon, R. (2020). Historical Threads, Missing Links, and Future Directions in AI and Education. *Learning, Media and Technology*, *45*(3), 223–235. DOI: 10.1080/17439884.2020.1798995

World Bank. (2022). *Digital divide in education: Policy recommendations for inclusive AI.* https://worldbank.org/education/ai-divide

WOWLabz. (2023, August 28). *How AI is transforming legal research.* Retrieved from https://wowlabz.com/ai-for-legal-research

KEY TERMS AND DEFINITIONS

Andragogy: The approach to adult learning, focusing on self-direction, real-life relevance, and experience-based, collaborative learning. In this chapter, pedagogy and andragogy are used interchangeably since most law students are adults.

Artificial Intelligence (AI): Technology that mimics human intelligence in machines. In legal education, AI enhances teaching and learning, is a subject for legal regulation, and is an essential skill for future lawyers.

Artificial Intelligence Tools (AI Tools): Digital applications using AI for tasks like analysis, writing, prediction, and automation. In law, general AI tools (e.g., ChatGPT) aid communication, while legal-specific tools (e.g., CaseMine) help with research and case analysis.

Educational Psychology: The study of how people learn, focusing on mental, emotional, and social processes. Here, it guides the design of effective legal teaching methods aligned with how learners absorb knowledge.

Ethical AI in Legal Education: Using AI in law teaching responsibly, upholding values like fairness and justice. Law students must learn with and about AI, and be able to address its ethical challenges.

Law Educators: People who teach law, such as classroom teachers, professional trainers, and legal experts educating students, lawyers, other professionals, or the public.

Law: A system of rules, principles, and norms used to regulate conduct and resolve disputes, enforced by institutions. Law includes statutes, judicial decisions, customs, and regulations across traditions.

Legal System: The framework for making, interpreting, and applying laws, differing by country and tradition (common, civil, religious, etc.). The chapter uses an inclusive view to discuss legal education reforms.

Law Learners: Anyone acquiring legal knowledge, including students, practicing lawyers, professionals from other fields, and the public attending legal awareness programs.

Learning Theory: Frameworks that explain how knowledge is acquired and retained. They shape legal teaching by aligning methods with learning outcomes.

Legal Education Reform: Revising legal teaching methods to be more relevant, inclusive, and skill-focused, especially through AI integration and fostering critical thinking.

Legal Pedagogy: Methods and strategies for teaching law. Used here generally to mean law teaching approaches, regardless of learners' age or stage.

LegalTech Integration (LawEdTech Integration): Adding legal tech tools, like AI research engines and automation, into legal teaching. This prepares students for real-world tech use and critical evaluation.

Reinvention / Redesigning: Reinvention refers to the overall shift in legal teaching in the AI era; redesigning is the practical process of updating teaching methods and curriculum.

Learning Management System (LMS) Plugins: Add-ons for platforms such as Moodle or Canvas that support teaching via features like video calls, plagiarism checks, quizzes, analytics, and integration with legal research databases.

STORM: An AI tool from Stanford that creates structured, source-based articles using simulated expert questioning and web searches.

Retrieval-Augmented Generation (RAG): An AI method that improves outputs by retrieving and using external information alongside model knowledge, enabling more accurate and current responses, useful in law and education.

Socratic Method: A teaching approach using probing questions to foster critical thinking and reveal assumptions. Common in law, it encourages students to reflect on and defend their ideas.

Chapter 11

AI-Driven Legal Writing and Drafting:

Skills for the Next Generation of Lawyers

Mohit Yadav
https://orcid.org/0000-0002-9341-2527
JGBS, O.P. Jindal Global University, India

Ali Najeeb
https://orcid.org/0000-0003-4663-9347
Qasim Ibrahim School of Business, Villa College, Maldives

ABSTRACT

The integration of artificial intelligence (AI) is transforming legal writing and drafting, redefining the skills required for contemporary legal practice. AI tools, including natural language processing and generative systems, enhance efficiency, accuracy, and consistency in document creation, while also supporting legal research, contract analysis, and quality control. These technological advancements present opportunities for improved client service, greater access to justice, and innovative practice models. However, they also raise challenges related to ethical responsibility, data privacy, algorithmic bias, and regulatory compliance. This chapter examines the evolution of legal drafting, highlights AI applications and their benefits, and identifies the hybrid skill set necessary for the next generation of lawyers, including digital literacy, critical oversight, and ethical judgment. Finally, it explores the implications for legal education, professional training, and future practice, emphasizing a collaborative model where human expertise complements AI capabilities.

DOI: 10.4018/979-8-3373-3451-6.ch011

INTRODUCTION

The AI boom has transformed various professional fields at an exponential rate, and the legal world is no exception. Writing and drafting, which have historically been regarded as the height of an attorney's craft, are increasingly being impacted by AI tools that leverage natural language processing (NLP), machine learning, and generative AI to automate drafting to a higher speed, precision, and viability. Legal practitioners are increasingly relying on AI programs to not just search and read precedents but also draft contracts, pleadings, and legal memoranda in ways unimaginable previously (Ashley, 2017; Katz et al., 2021). This transformation reflects more profound shifts in the legal profession as technological competence is becoming as much a part of being a practitioner as having an understanding of law (American Bar Association, 2020).

Utilization of AI in legal drafting has far-reaching consequences for the next-gen lawyer's skills set. While traditional skills such as critical thinking, persuasive writing, and reasoning continue to be essential skills, lawyers also have to learn proficiency in working with AI tools, data interpretation, and ethical oversight (Surden, 2019). The growing application of AI-powered drafting raises questions about the adequate alignment of law school and professional training program curricula to prepare lawyers to practice technology-facilitated law. Moreover, issues of dependability, transparency, and accountability in AI systems must be carefully addressed to ensure that technology complements and not supplants legal reasoning and professional judgment (Remus & Levy, 2016).

Against this backdrop, the chapter addresses the emerging role of AI in legal drafting and writing, the benefits, drawbacks, and emerging skillsets needed for future legal professionals. With a view to looking at the convergence of the technological, pedagogical, and ethical challenges, it aims to determine a way forward to equip the future generation of lawyers to face an emerging legal world in which technology becomes ever more dominant and pervasive.

EVOLUTION OF LEGAL DRAFTING AND WRITING

Drafting and legal writing have remained at the center of the legal practice for centuries as the central way in which lawyers present arguments, interpret statutes, and establish formal contracts. Legal documents were historically written out by hand, often with complicated sentence structure, archaic words, and formalism necessitated by centuries of common law traditions (Mellinkoff, 1963). Before the age of the computer, lawyers relied nearly exclusively on typed or written-out drafts, large stores of case law materials, and administrative support to produce legal documents.

It was laborious, time-consuming, and prone to error, but it encouraged precision, reason, and rhetorical flair as traits of professional excellence (Garner, 2013).

Word processing technology that emerged at the close of the twentieth century transformed all that. Lawyers gained the ability to edit, revise, and standardize documents more easily, providing room for wholesale use of templates, style guides, and computerized formatting software (Susskind, 2010). At the same time, the computerization of legal research on electronic databases such as LexisNexis and Westlaw revolutionized how lawyers accessed precedents, statutes, and learned commentary, further embedding technology into the drafting process (Haapio & Passera, 2013). These developments not only facilitated the preparation of documents, but they also began to shape expectations about speed and productivity within the profession.

The newest phase in this cycle is the integration of artificial intelligence into legal drafting and writing. Artificial intelligence systems with natural language processing can review great collections of legal documents, generate contract clauses, and even suggest arguments or tactics tailored to particular cases (Ashley, 2017). As opposed to previous tools, which simply allowed for formatting and research, AI brings a generative and interpretive component to the table, allowing attorneys to work with technology in creating meaningful legal content. This change is a profound revolution in the nature of legal practice, where the role of the lawyer is increasingly determined not only by his or her proficiency at writing but also by the capacity to control, edit, and ethically direct AI-generated content (Katz, Bommarito, & Blackman, 2021).

AI APPLICATIONS IN LEGAL WRITING AND DRAFTING

The application of artificial intelligence to legal practice has ushered legal writing and drafting into a new era where technology is no longer relegated to the field of only formatting but is applied to assistively aid in the generation of content, analysis, and review. Legal research and analysis of precedents is likely to be one of the most significant applications of AI. AI systems employ NLP and machine learning to scan gigantic databases of case law, statutes, and regulations and point out suitable authorities instantly that inform drafting tasks. AI products even make patterns in judicial thinking apparent, allowing lawyers to construct arguments that reflect mainstream jurisprudence (Ashley, 2017).

AI also brings about a revolutionary effect on contract drafting and proofreading. Smart drafting tools can perform boilerplate clause proposal on automation, highlight risk areas, and detect inconsistencies within documents. Other software, such as automated contract analysis applications, screen drafts against industry standards and regulation, reducing due diligence and negotiation time by several times

(Surden, 2019). By embedding compliance checks during drafting, AI minimizes human errors while ensuring consistency and accuracy.

Another substantial application is the automated generation of documents, where AI software programs create initial drafts of standard legal documents such as contracts, wills, pleadings, and non-disclosure agreements. Such generative applications utilize templates and training data to create documents specifically tailored to a client's specific needs, which attorneys can review and modify (Katz, Bommarito, & Blackman, 2021; Trivedi et al., 2023). Similarly, AI-facilitated brief-writing software can recommend case citations, write persuasive arguments, and recommend edits for clarity and conciseness.

Finally, AI facilitates quality control and linguistic refinement of legal drafting. Intelligence systems such as style checkers and grammar checkers analyze readability, consistency, and conformity to rules of plain language, now even emphasized in modern legal drafting (Garner, 2013). With these tools embedded, AI enables lawyers to work more efficiently, spend more time on challenging analytical tasks, and enhance overall quality of legal communication. But these advances also raise issues about what the appropriate balance between technological assistance and human discretion is, an issue addressed later in this chapter.

BENEFITS AND OPPORTUNITIES

Adoption of artificial intelligence in legal drafting and writing provides numerous benefits beyond strict efficiency gain, creating possibilities for innovation, accessibility, and better client service. Perhaps one of the most valuable benefits is enhanced efficiency and less time usage. Artificial intelligence programs can rapidly create draft documents, conduct legal research, and review contracts faster than a human lawyer, allowing legal professionals to concentrate on higher-level analytical and strategic work (Susskind, 2019). Not only does this greater productivity reduce the cost of operation of law firms, but it also allows clients to receive services more effectively, creating a competitive edge in increasingly globalized legal markets.

A second major benefit is in precision and uniformity. By having access to big databases as well as predefined norms, AI programs minimize human errors, encourage similarity in documents, and warn for potential inconsistencies or gaps (Remus & Levy, 2016). This is very convenient in complex transactions, where slight drafting errors can be of significant legal or financial importance (Tayal et al., 2021). AI systems also enable improved knowledge management, allowing attorneys to use best practices, precedents, and industry vocabulary when drafting documents in order to improve quality and reliability.

AI also helps enhance access to justice as well as legal service democratization. Automated document creation and cheap legal drafting websites allow people and small companies who cannot afford traditional legal services to access basic legal documents and guidance (Surden, 2019). This expands the availability of legal services and is aligned with greater goals of justice and equity in the justice system. Further, the application of plain-language and readability elements enhances readability of legal documents to make them accessible and understandable by clients and the public, which enhances trust and transparency in legal processes (Garner, 2013).

Finally, AI brings the promise of new jobs and specialties to the legal profession. Lawyers who acquire expertise in AI-assisted drafting, compliance monitoring, and data analytics for law will be well-positioned to deal with technology-enabled practice environments (Trivedi, V., Banerji, D., & Yadav, M., 2023). Such a shift is nudging cross-disciplinary collaboration between law, computer science, and business and spurring innovation and redesigning the delivery of legal services. In capitalizing on them, the next generation of lawyers can transform their function as document drafters into that of strategic advisers and technology implementers while retaining human judgment and ethical accountability at the center of an AI-enhanced profession (Katz, Bommarito, & Blackman, 2021).

SKILLS FOR THE NEXT GENERATION OF LAWYERS

With legal writing and drafting transformed through artificial intelligence, the skill set required of future lawyers far exceeds the traditional strong points of research, logical analysis, and persuasive writing. Most critically among the new abilities is digital literacy, which encompasses not only familiarity with legal databases but also understanding how to utilize AI-based drafting platforms, automated contract analysis systems, and generative writing platforms (McGinnis & Pearce, 2014). Lawyers who are skilled in these technologies will be more efficient, generate better outputs, and remain competitive in an evolving legal marketplace.

No less important is cultivating the critical thinking and oversight skills. While AI might help generate drafts and identifying relevant legal authority, it lacks the nuanced judgment, sensitivity to context, and ethical reasoning that define professional legal practice (Remus & Levy, 2016). Attorneys must then develop the ability to critically analyze AI-produced content, revise it for accuracy and appropriateness, and adapt it to client objectives as well as legal boundaries. This delicate balance demands human attorneys to function as anything but passive consumers but rather as active regulators of AI-enhanced work.

The moral use of AI in law writing also requires professional responsibility and technology responsibility abilities. Legal practitioners must understand issues such as information privacy, algorithmic bias, and the limits of automatization as a means of preventing misuse and protecting clients' interests (Surden, 2019). This means integrating ethical reasoning in regular practice and adopting a careful and reflective technology-facilitated drafting approach. Second, while more clients increasingly insist that lawyers demonstrate efficiency through technology, the professional duty of transparency entails describing the use of AI tools and justifying their reliability (Yadav et al., 2019).

In addition to technical and ethical skills, the next generation of lawyers will value interdisciplinary collaboration skills. Working with data scientists, software engineers, and compliance experts will become more common, especially in large firms and in-house law firms (Susskind, 2019). This requires being able to shift, work together, and turn legal requirements into technical specifications and vice versa. Finally, focus on lifelong learning is required. Because of how fast technology evolves, lawyers are under obligation to continue learning, try new technologies, and be agile in accepting innovations (Yadav & Rangnekar, 2016). By the combination of traditional legal expertise with digital, ethical, and collaborative competencies, the next-generation lawyer can thrive in an AI-driven legal sector without compromising the human judgment that still underpins the business (Katz, Bommarito, & Blackman, 2021).

REIMAGINING LEGAL EDUCATION AND TRAINING

Growing adoption of AI-driven legal writing and drafting calls for a reimagination of lawyer training and education at its very core. The traditional model of legal education has been centered on doctrinal understanding, reading cases, and argumentative writing, but these alone are insufficient in an age when considerable drafting is technology-mediated. Professional societies and law schools must incorporate technological literacy and familiarity with AI as part of their curriculum to provide their graduates with the ability to practice in the digitally transformed legal system (McGinnis & Pearce, 2014). This does not just refer to exposure to drafting and research tools based on AI but also instruction on how their employment is professionally and legally required.

A key part of this transformation is simulation- and experience-based education. Rather than focusing on theory exercises, legal education can integrate AI-assisted drafting tools with clinical courses, mooting courts, and drafting workshops to allow students to learn to supervise and edit AI-drafted documents (Susskind, 2019). Through this manner, students are taught critical oversight skills to ensure quality and reliability as well as learn the knowledge of how to utilize technology as a supporting co-partner rather than a replacement for professional expertise (Choudhary et al. 2024).

Also, the interdisciplinary nature of AI in law practice addresses cross-disciplinary education as a necessity. Law students can benefit from studies in fields such as data science, coding, and business analytics because they help understand how AI systems function and effectively communicate with technology experts (Ashley, 2017). Hybrid courses or joint degree programs that connect law and technology can promote innovation and equip graduates with cross-disciplinary skill sets in increasing demand by employers.

In addition, continuing legal education and lifelong learning must adapt to support practicing lawyers in keeping up with rapid technological development. Professional bodies can be the hub of this activity through workshops, certification, and microlearning modules for uses of AI in legal practice (Surden, 2019). Both new and old practitioners can adapt to new tools without compromising on ethical standards or client trust.

Ultimately, reforming legal education is not an issue of replacing traditional skills but one of enriching the lawyer's arsenal with digital competence, responsible AI governance, and cross-disciplinary collaboration. By incorporating these skills into law school education and ongoing training programs, the legal profession is able to equip future attorneys with the ability not just to be skilled drafters but also skilled managers of AI uses, and combine technological effectiveness with human judgment and professional responsibility (Katz, Bommarito, & Blackman, 2021).

ETHICAL AND REGULATORY ISSUES

The application of artificial intelligence to the drafting and writing of law is fraught with grave ethical and regulatory concerns to be addressed if professional integrity and public faith in the judiciary are to be upheld. Accountability is one of the important concerns. When legal documents are created or suggested by AI technologies, the ultimate onus of correctness and appropriateness rests with the lawyer. Granting AI too much authority without proper oversight risks errors, blunders, or misinterpretations that could harm clients and erode professional obligations (Remus & Levy, 2016). Keeping lawyers in control as the final decision-makers is crucial to maintain the integrity of the profession.

Another concern which arises with great immediacy is data confidentiality and privacy. Artificial intelligence software used in legal drafting are often grounded in big data and cloud computing, which raise concerns over protecting confidential client information. Lawyers must evaluate security protocols implemented by these tools in an effort to comply with confidentiality under professional conduct codes

(American Bar Association, 2020). There is also the concern of algorithmic bias, which raises ethical considerations. AI algorithms that are trained on biased data can be used to perpetuate or even reinforce disparities, creating discriminatory or unfair draft outputs, particularly in areas like employment contracts or compliance documents (Citron, 2019).

Regulatorially, bar associations and legal regulatory bodies are beginning to emphasize technological competency as part of professional requirements. For example, the American Bar Association Model Rules of Professional Conduct currently require lawyers to have an understanding of relevant technology to be competent in representation (ABA, 2020). Globally, jurisdictions such as the European Union are considering regulation encompassing transparency, explainability, and accountability in AI-backed decision-making (European Commission, 2021). These advances highlight the growing expectation that lawyers not only use AI effectively but also acknowledge its limitations and risks.

At the end of the day, the ethical application of AI in document drafting calls for openness to clients. Lawyers should disclose when AI technology is used in document preparation and set forth the benefits, dangers, and safeguards in place. Disclosure builds trust and adheres to the duty of candor. In the longer term, standards of industry, certification schemes for AI tools, and open regulatory regimes will be vital to ensuring that the deployment of AI reinforces, not undermines, values of justice, fairness, and accountability. By engaging with these ethical and regulatory challenges, the legal profession can advance safely on the possibilities of AI without threatening its core duties to clients and society.

FUTURE OUTLOOK

The future of legal drafting and writing will be influenced to a large extent by the continued development of artificial intelligence, with tendencies set to shift in the direction of increased embedding of generative systems, additional automation, and novel models of cooperation between lawyers and machines. One of the trends that is likely to gain broad acceptance is the utilization of generative AI to generate sophisticated legal documents. While current software is primarily used to generate boilerplate contracts or preliminary drafts, future systems will handle more advanced pleadings, multi-state contracts, and regulatory filings with greater sophistication and precision (Ashley, 2017). This capability would revolutionize drafting into a process where AI generates full first drafts that attorneys review and refine, changing the role of the lawyer from writer to caretaker and strategist.

There is also the possibility of increased development of specialized, client-oriented drafting solutions. AI programs can become increasingly dependent on client data, preferences, and risk profiles to tailor documents with a degree of precision never before imagined (Susskind, 2019). This level of tailoring improves client satisfaction and efficiency and reduces conflict through more precise compliance with unique requirements. At the same time, natural language generation improvements can facilitate easier legal writing, bridging technical legal jargon and everyday language expression.

Regulatory reforms worldwide are also expected to shape the future of legal drafting based on AI. The European Union's Artificial Intelligence Act and similar programs around the world suggest a transition towards standardized rules of transparency, accountability, and trustfulness of AI in legal proceedings (European Commission, 2021). These regulations could encourage the development of certified, trustworthy AI tools, build confidence for lawyers and clients alike, but they will also involve compliance expenses, and law firms will have to invest in monitoring and governance software.

Finally, there will be new professional identities and models of practice. AI-drafting-capable lawyers are able to craft hybrid roles that combine legal expertise with technology management, and certain law firms may establish distinct legal technology departments. Such shifts can make legal services accessible globally and increase access to justice in remote locations using low-cost AI-powered drafting platforms (Remus & Levy, 2016). Yet, the profession must remain vigilant against risks such as overreliance on automation, loss of critical drafting skills, and erosion of ethical standards. Ultimately, the outlook suggests not a replacement of lawyers by machines but a reconfiguration of legal work, where human judgment, creativity, and ethics are complemented by AI's efficiency and scalability.

CONCLUSION

The integration of artificial intelligence into legal writing and drafting is reshaping the foundations of legal practice. With its original definition founded mainly on hand accuracy, cogent reasoning, and mastery of legal terminology, drafting has arrived at a point where technology facilitates, streamlines, and even generates substantive legal papers. This evolution is characterized by glaring benefits—efficiency, precision, standardization, and enhanced access to justice—but also significant challenges in the areas of dependability, ethical accountability, and compliance with regulations. As the technology of AI becomes ever stronger, the legal profession is evolving from sole drafter to manager of technology-driven outputs, and this will require new attitudes and new skills (Remus & Levy, 2016; Susskind, 2019).

To adapt to these developments, successive generations of lawyers must acquire a hybrid skill set combining traditional legal reasoning with technical expertise, critical oversight, and moral discernment. Law schools, continuing education centers, and bar organizations can take a crucial role in incorporating AI literacy and ethical AI use into their teaching modules and training programs. At the same time, regulatory bodies have to provide clear guidance and frameworks that make AI applications adhere to essential legal principles like fairness, accountability, and protection of clients (European Commission, 2021).

Looking forward, the future for AI application in legal drafting is not one of replacement, but of reorganization—a blend of human imagination and machine efficiency. Lawyers who adapt to this shift will not only become more professionally effective, but also expand the reach and availability of legal services. Lastly, the opportunity and challenge are ensuring that AI augments instead of diminishing human judgment, creativity, and ethical accountability critical to practicing law (Ashley, 2017; Katz, Bommarito, & Blackman, 2021).

REFERENCES

American Bar Association. (2020). *Formal Opinion 477R: Securing communication of protected client information*. ABA. https://www.americanbar.org

Ashley, K. D. (2017). *Artificial intelligence and legal analytics: New tools for law practice in the digital age*. Cambridge University Press. DOI: 10.1017/9781316761380

Choudhary, S., Yadav, M., & Srivastava, A. P. (2024). Cognitive biases among millennial Indian investors: Do personality and demographic factors matter? *FIIB Business Review*, *13*(1), 106–117. DOI: 10.1177/23197145211057343

Citron, D. K. (2019). A new compact for sexual privacy. *William and Mary Law Review*, *62*(7), 1769–1798.

. European Commission. (2021). *Proposal for a regulation laying down harmonised rules on artificial intelligence (Artificial Intelligence Act)*. COM(2021) 206 final.

Garner, B. A. (2013). *Legal writing in plain English: A text with exercises* (2nd ed.). University of Chicago Press.

Haapio, H., & Passera, S. (2013). Contracts as interfaces: Exploring visual representation patterns in contract design. In Biasiotti, M. A., Sartor, G., & Tiscornia, P. (Eds.), *Proceedings of the International Conference on Electronic Government and the Information Systems Perspective* (pp. 1–12). Springer.

Katz, D. M., Bommarito, M. J., & Blackman, J. (2021). *The law of artificial intelligence and smart machines*. Wolters Kluwer.

McGinnis, J. O., & Pearce, R. G. (2014). The great disruption: How machine intelligence will transform the role of lawyers in the delivery of legal services. *Fordham Law Review*, *82*(6), 3041–3066.

Mellinkoff, D. (1963). *The language of the law*. Little, Brown and Company.

Remus, D., & Levy, F. (2016). Can robots be lawyers? Computers, lawyers, and the practice of law. SSRN *Electronic Journal*. DOI: 10.2139/ssrn.2701092

Surden, H. (2019). Artificial intelligence and law: An overview. *Georgia State University Law Review*, *35*(4), 1305–1338.

Susskind, R. (2010). *The end of lawyers? Rethinking the nature of legal services*. Oxford University Press.

Susskind, R. (2019). *Tomorrow's lawyers: An introduction to your future* (2nd ed.). Oxford University Press.

Tayal, R., Upadhyay, R. K., Yadav, M., & Singh, R. (2021). The development and validation of the organizational effectiveness scale using confirmatory factor analysis. *Global Business Review*, *22*(3), 821–843. DOI: 10.1177/0972150918811720

Trivedi, S. K., Vishnu, S., Singh, A., & Yadav, M. (2023). Research trends in sustainable E-payment systems: A study using topic modeling approach. *IEEE Transactions on Engineering Management*, *71*, 7511–7525. DOI: 10.1109/TEM.2023.3280216

Trivedi, V., Banerji, D., & Yadav, M. (2023). Expecting the surprises: Role of hope in consumer repurchase intentions in an online shopping environment. *Journal of Strategic Marketing*, *31*(4), 794–816. DOI: 10.1080/0965254X.2021.1996449

Yadav, M., & Rangnekar, S. (2016). Role clarity and organizational citizenship behaviour: Does tenure matter? A study on Indian power sector. *Global Business Review*, *17*(3, suppl), 207S–224S. DOI: 10.1177/0972150916631216

Yadav, M., Rangnekar, S., & Srivastava, A. P. (2019). Demographic variables as moderators between QWL and OCB. *Industrial and Commercial Training*, *51*(7/8), 396–408. DOI: 10.1108/ICT-04-2018-0040

Compilation of References

Aammou, S., Zakaria, T., & Tarik, T. (2024). *Enhancing socio-pedagogical engagement in Moodle through AI-driven personalized learning*. Cadernos de Educação Tecnologia e Sociedade.

ABA. (2009). Rule 1.1 Competence — Comment. https://www.americanbar.org/groups/professional_responsibility/publications/model_rules_of_professional_conduct/rule_1_1_competence/comment_on_rule_1_1/

Abbonato, D., Bianchini, S., Gargiulo, F., & Venturini, T. (2024). Interdisciplinary Research in Artificial Intelligence: Lessons from COVID-19. *Quantitative Science Studies*, *5*(4), 1–20. DOI: 10.1162/qss_a_00329

Abenoza, S., & Arjona, C. (2017). Socrates behind bars: A report on an experimental course on justice and philosophy. *The Law Teacher*, *51*(3), 327–348. DOI: 10.1080/03069400.2016.1272041

Abu-Lughod, L. (2013). *Do Muslim women need saving?* Harvard University Press. DOI: 10.4159/9780674726338

Abu-Zayd, N. (2013). The status of women between the Qur'an and *Fiqh*. In Mir-Hosseini, Z., Vogt, K., Larsen, L., & Moe, C. (Eds.), *Gender and equality in Muslim family law: Justice and ethics in the Islamic legal tradition* (pp. 153–168). I. B. Tauris. DOI: 10.5040/9780755609277.ch-007

Aderonke, A., & Salami, S. (2025). AI-powered personalized learning in legal education: A tool for developing future ready lawyers. International Journal of Law. *Justice and Jurisprudence*, *5*(1), 323–327. DOI: 10.22271/2790-0673.2025.v5.i1d.192

Ahmed, N., & Wahed, M. (2020). The de democratization of AI: Deep learning and the compute divide in artificial intelligence research. arXiv. https://doi.org//arXiv.2010.15581DOI: 10.48550

Ahmed, L. (1991). Early Islam and the position of women: The problem of interpretation. In Keddie, N., & Baron, B. (Eds.), *Women in Middle Eastern history: Shifting boundaries in sex and gender* (pp. 58–73). Yale University Press.

AI Pedagogy Project. *metaLAB (at) Harvard. (n.d.). AI Pedagogy Project: Critical and creative engagement with AI.* https://aipedagogy.org/

AI4Chat. (2024). *Legal Case Study Creator.* Retrieved July 12, 2025, from https://www.ai4chat.co/pages/legal-case-study-creator

Ait Elfqih, K., & Monti, J. (2024). Large language models as legal translators of Arabic legislatives: Does ChatGPT and Gemini care for context and terminology? In *Proceedings of the Second Arabic Natural Language Processing Conference* (pp. 111–122). Association for Computational Linguistics. DOI: 10.18653/v1/2024.arabicnlp-1.10

Ajevski, M., Barker, K., Gilbert, A., Hardie, L., & Ryan, F. (2023). ChatGPT and the future of legal education and. *The Law Teacher*, *57*(3), 352–364. DOI: 10.1080/03069400.2023.2207426

Akila, V., Prabhu, G., Akila, R., & Swadhi, R. (2025). Performance Metrics in Blockchain-Enabled AIML for Cognitive IoT in Large-Scale Networks: Optimizing Data Analytics for Enhanced Network Performance. In AI for Large Scale Communication Networks (pp. 265-288). IGI Global.

Akintayo, O. T., Eden, C. A., Ayeni, O. O., & Onyebuchi, N. C. (2024). Integrating AI with emotional and social learning in primary education: Developing a holistic adaptive learning ecosystem. *Open Access Research Journal of Multidisciplinary Studies*, *7*(2), 42–51. DOI: 10.53022/oarjms.2024.7.2.0025

Al Kuwaiti, A., Nazer, L., Al-Reedy, A., Al Shehri, S., Al-Muhanna, A., Subbarayalu, A. V., Al Muhanna, D., & Al-Muhanna, F. A. (2023). A Review of the Role of Artificial Intelligence in Healthcare. *Journal of Personalized Medicine*, *13*(6), 951. https://www.mdpi.com/2075-4426/13/6/951. DOI: 10.3390/jpm13060951 PMID: 37373940

Alarie, B., Niblett, A., & Yoon, A. H. (2018). How Artificial Intelligence Will Affect the Practice of Law. *University of Toronto Law Journal*, *68*(1, supplement 1), 106–124. https://utppublishing.com/doi/10.3138/utlj.2017-0052. DOI: 10.3138/utlj.2017-0052

Albudairat, M. (2023). *Mabadi' alqanun* [Introduction to Law]. Maktabat Almutanabi.

Alexander, J., Mcconnell, S., Mitchell, R., & Mcgrane, A. (2024). Technological challenges for modern law schoolpedagogy: Preparing graduates for the modern legal-workplace. *The Law Teacher*, *58*(1), 32–57. DOI: 10.1080/03069400.2023.2287393

Alexander, R. J. (2008). Towards dialogic teaching: Rethinking classroom talk. *Diálogos (San José).*

Al-Harz, M. (2021). *Jaafari judiciary in Al-Ahsa.* Al-Ahsa Heritage. https://www.alhasa-turath.org

Ali, M.Enas Mohamed Ali Quteishat. (2024). Exploring the role of ai in modern legal practice: Opportunities, challenges, and ethical implications. J. *Electrical Systems*, *20*(6s), 3040–3050. DOI: 10.52783/jes.3320

Allen, L. K., & Kendeou, P. (2023). ED-AI Lit: An Interdisciplinary Framework for AI Literacy in Education. *Policy Insights from the Behavioral and Brain Sciences*, *11*(1), 3–10. Advance online publication. DOI: 10.1177/23727322231220339

Altamimi, D. H. F. (2025). Unlocking potential: Saudi EFL male students' perspectives on AI tools for enhancing English writing proficiency. *Arab World English Journal*, 40–58. DOI: 10.24093/awej/AI.3

American Bar Association. (1992). *Report of the Task Force on Law Schools and the Profession: Narrowing the Gap.* ABA Section of Legal Education and Admissions to the Bar. Retrieved from https://www.americanbar.org/content/dam/aba/publications/misc/legal_education/Standards/standardsarchive/1992_93_standards.pdf

American Bar Association. (2020). *Formal Opinion 477R: Securing communication of protected client information.* ABA. https://www.americanbar.org

American Bar Association. (2020). Model rules of professional conduct: Rule 1.1 competence. https://www.americanbar.org/groups/professional_responsibility/publications/model_rules_of_professional_conduct/rule_1_1_competence/comment_on_rule_1_1/

American Bar Association. (2023). 2023--2024 ABA standards and rules for the approval of law schools. Standard 303. https://www.americanbar.org/groups/legal_education/resources/standards/High Educ 21, 4 (2024). DOI: 10.1186/s41239-023-00436-z

American Bar Association. (n.d.). *AI and legal education.* https://www.americanbar.org/groups/centers_commissions/center-for-innovation/artificial-intelligence/ai-in-legal-education/

Anderson, J., Rainee, L., & Luchsinger, A. (2018). Artificial Intelligence and the Future of Humans. *Pew Research Center*, 10(12), 1. https://www.pewresearch.org/internet/wp-content/uploads/sites/9/2018/12/PI_2018.12.10_future-of-ai_FINAL1.pdf

Anderson, L. W., Krathwohl, D. R., Airasian, P. W., Cruikshank, K. A., Mayer, R. E., Pintrich, P. R., . . . Wittrock, M. C. (2001). *A taxonomy for learning, teaching, and assessing: A revision of Bloom's taxonomy of educational objectives*. Longman. *Retrieved* from https://cmapspublic2.ihmc.us/rid=1Q2PTM7HL-26LTFBX-9YN8/Krathwohl%202002.pdf

Angom, S. (2015). Private higher education in India. *Higher Education for the Future, 2*(1), 92–111. DOI: 10.1177/2347631114558192

Anuyah, O., Wan, R., Adejoro, C., Yeh, T., Metoyer, R., & Badillo-Urquiola, K. (2023). Cultural considerations in AI systems for the Global South: A systematic review. In *Proceedings of the 4th African Human Computer Interaction Conference* (pp. 125–134). Association for Computing Machinery. DOI: 10.1145/3628096.3629046

Armour, J., & Sako, M. (2020). AI-Enabled Business Models in Legal Services: From Traditional Law Firms to Next-Generation Law Companies? *Journal of Professions and Organization*, 7(1), 27–46. DOI: 10.1093/jpo/joaa001

Arockia, V. J., Vettriselvan, R., Rajesh, D., Velmurugan, P. R. R., & Cheelo, C. (2025). Leveraging AI and Learning Analytics for Enhanced Distance Learning: Transformation in Education. In AI and Learning Analytics in Distance Learning (pp. 179-206). IGI Global Scientific Publishing.

Aryan, P. (2024, December 9). LLMs as debate partners: Utilizing genetic algorithms and adversarial search for adaptive arguments. arXiv. https://doi.org//arXiv.2412.06229.DOI: 10.1109/ICEI64305.2024.10912343

Ashley, K. D. (2017). *Artificial Intelligence and Legal Analytics: New Tools for Law Practice in the Digital Age*. Cambridge University Press. DOI: 10.1017/9781316761380

Atkinson, R. C., & Shiffrin, R. M. (1968). Human memory: A proposed system and its control processes. In Spence, K. W., & Spence, J. T. (Eds.), *The* psychology *of learning and motivation* (Vol. 2, pp. 89-195). Academic Press. Retrieved from http://rca.ucsd.edu/selected_papers/2_Human_memory_A_proposed_system_and_its_control_processes.pdf

Atkinson, K., Bench-Capon, T., & Bollegala, D. (2020). Explanation in AI and law: Past, present and future. *Artificial Intelligence, 289*, 103387. DOI: 10.1016/j.artint.2020.103387

Babic, M. M., & Dowling, M. (2015). Social support, the presence of barriers and ideas for the future from students with disabilities in the higher education system in Croatia. *Disability & Society, 30*(4), 614–629. DOI: 10.1080/09687599.2015.1037949

Baker, R. S., & Siemens, G. (2014). Educational data mining and learning analytics. In Sawyer, R. K. (Ed.), *The Cambridge handbook of the learning sciences* (2nd ed., pp. 253–274). Cambridge University Press. DOI: 10.1017/CBO9781139519526.016

Balan, A. (2024). Examining the ethical and sustainability challenges of legal education's AI revolution. *International Journal of the Legal Profession, 31*(3), 323–348. DOI: 10.1080/09695958.2024.2421179

Balan, A. (2025). *AI and Legal Education: Ethical and Sustainable Approaches*. Taylor & Francis. DOI: 10.4324/9781003607397

Baldassarre, M. T., Caivano, D., Nieto, B. F., Gigante, D., & Ragone, A. (2024). Fostering human rights in responsible AI: A systematic review for best practices in industry. *IEEE Transactions on Artificial Intelligence, 6*(2), 416–431. DOI: 10.1109/TAI.2024.3394389

Bandura, A. (1977). *Social learning theory*. Prentice Hall. Retrieved from https://www.asecib.ase.ro/mps/Bandura_SocialLearningTheory.pdf

Bandyopadhyay, M. (2006). Education of marginalised groups in India: From the perspective of social justice. *Social Change, 36*(2), 98–113. DOI: 10.1177/004908570603600207

Banks, C. P. (2023). *The American legal profession: The myths and realities of practicing law*. Routledge. DOI: 10.4324/9781003122074

Bar Council of India. (2024, May 20). *BCID-0468-2024 (LE Circular-06/2024): Comprehensive implementation of legal education reforms, mandatory guidelines, norms & rules of legal education* [Circular]. Bar Council of India. https://www.barcouncilofindia.org/info/bcid-0468--g87cul

Barnes, C., & Mercer, G. (1999). *Exploring Disability: A Sociological Introduction*. https://ci.nii.ac.jp/ncid/BA41776188

Barton, L., Barnes, C., & Oliver, M. (2002). Disability studies today. In *Polity Press eBooks*. http://ci.nii.ac.jp/ncid/BA58891420

Basic Law of Governance, Royal Decree No. A/90 (1992).

Beck, J., Stern, M., & Haugsjaa, E. (n.d.). *Applications of AI in Education*. https://dl.acm.org/doi/fullHtml/10.1145/332148.332153

Beckles, H., & Richards Kennedy, S. (2021). Accelerating the future into the present: Re-imagining higher education in the Caribbean. In van't Land, H., Corcoran, A., & Iancu, D.-C. (Eds.), *The Promise of Higher Education* (pp. 363–369). Springer., DOI: 10.1007/978-3-030-67245-4_54

Bennett, T. (2020). The effects of student-consumerism on discipline specific teaching practices: a comparison of education and law. Journal of Further and Higher Education, 45(3), 417-432. doi:https://doi-org.liverpool.idm.oclc.org/10.1080/0309877X.2020.1774050

Bhatty, K. (1998). Educational deprivation in India-A Survey of Field Investigations. *Economic and Political Weekly/Economic & Political Weekly, 33*(27). https://www.jstor.org/stable/4406962

Biddle, B. (2014). Social class, poverty and education. In *Routledge eBooks*. DOI: 10.4324/9780203951040

Bjork, R. A., Dunlosky, J., & Kornell, N. (2013). Self-regulated learning: Beliefs, techniques, and illusions. *Annual Review of Psychology*, *64*(1), 417–444. DOI: 10.1146/annurev-psych-113011-143823 PMID: 23020639

Blinova, U., Rozhkova, N., & Rozhkova, D. (2023). NFT (Non-Fungible Tokens) as an Object of Accounting. *Journal of Digital Art & Humanities*, *4*(1), 3–9. DOI: 10.33847/2712-8148.4.1_1

Bliss, J. (2024). Teaching Law in the Age of Generative AI. *Jurimetrics Journal*, *64*, 111–161.

Bloom, B. (1956). *Taxonomy of Educational Objectives: The Classification of Educational Goals*. Retrieved from https://eclass.uoa.gr/modules/document/file.php/PPP242/Benjamin%20S.%20Bloom%20-%20Taxonomy%20of%20Educational%20Objectives%2C%20Handbook%201_%20Cognitive%20Domain-Addison%20Wesley%20Publishing%20Company%20%281956%29.pdf

Bloomberg Law. (n.d.). *AI tools for lawyers: A practical guide*. https://pro.bloomberglaw.com/insights/technology/ai-in-legal-practice-explained/

Bodyswaps. (2023a). Brighton and Sussex Medical School pilot: Navigating angry conversations. https://bodyswaps.co/resources/research

Bodyswaps. (2023b). Case study: Sheffield Hallam University—Training health-care students at scale with immersive learning. https://bodyswaps.co/resources/case-studies

Bostancı, S. H., & Yıldırım, S. (2025). Role of Government and International Institutions in Fostering Social Responsibility and Environmental Harmony. In *World Sustainability Series* (pp. 225–243). Springer Nature Switzerland., DOI: 10.1007/978-3-031-81469-3_10

Bostrom, N. (2017). Ethical Issues in Advanced Artificial Intelligence. In Wallach, W., & Asaro, P. (Eds.), *Machine Ethics and Robot Ethics*. Routledge., https://www.taylorfrancis.com/chapters/edit/10.4324/9781003074991-7/ethical-issues-advanced-artificial-intelligence-nick-bostrom

Bostrom, N., & Yudkowsky, E. (2018). The Ethics of Artificial Intelligence. In Yampolskiy, R. V. (Ed.), *Artificial Intelligence Safety and Security*. Routledge., https://www.taylorfrancis.com/chapters/edit/10.1201/9781351251389-4/ethics-artificial-intelligence-nick-bostrom-eliezer-yudkowsky DOI: 10.1201/9781351251389-4

Botelho, W. T., Marietto, M. G. B., Ferreira, J. C. M., & Pimentel, E. P. (2016). Kolb's experiential learning theory and Belhot's learning cycle guiding the use of computer simulation in engineering education: A pedagogical proposal to shift toward an experiential pedagogy. *Computer Applications in Engineering Education*, *24*(1), 79–88. DOI: 10.1002/cae.21674

Botler, A. I. (n.d.). *Your AI guide to laws, rights & justice*. Retrieved July 14, 2025, from https://botler.com/

BPP. (2023, October 30). AI in Law: technology in legal education and the profession. Retrieved from BPP: https://www.bpp.com/insights/ai-in-law

Brand, P. (1992). *The Origins of the English Legal Profession*. Blackwell.

Brescia, R. H. (2020). Lessons from the present: Three crises and their potential impact on the legal profession. *Hofstra Law Review*, *49*, 607.

BriefCatch. (n.d.). *BriefCatch: Your trusted legal writing assistant*. Retrieved July 14, 2025, from https://briefcatch.com/

Brom, M. (2022). Legal Representation and the Metaverse: The Ethics of Practicing in Multiple Realities. DePaul Bus. &. *Comm. LJ*, *21*, 125.

Brooks, C., Gherhes, C., & Voley, T. (2020). Artificial Intelligence in the Legal Sector: Pressures and Challenges of Transformation. *Cambridge Journal of Regions, Economy and Society*, *13*(1), 135–152. https://academic.oup.com/cjres/article/13/1/135/5716343. DOI: 10.1093/cjres/rsz026

Brunette, A. (2024). Humanizing Justice: The Transformational Impact of AI in Courts, From Filing to Sentencing. *Thomson Reuters*. https://www.thomsonreuters.com/en-us/posts/ai-in-courts/humanizing-justice/

Budhia, N., & Behera, S. (2023). Challenges and oppourtunities of digital education in India. *Asian Journal of Education and Social Studies*, *45*(3), 1–7. DOI: 10.9734/ajess/2023/v45i3982

Budhkar, A., Song, Q., Su, J., & Zhang, X. (2025). Demystifying the black box: A survey on explainable artificial intelligence (XAI) in bioinformatics. *Computational and Structural Biotechnology Journal*, *27*(1), 346–359. DOI: 10.1016/j.csbj.2024.12.027 PMID: 39897059

Burch, G. F., Hoover, J. D., Batchelor, J. H., Heller, N. A., Burch, J. J., & Giambattista, R. (2019). A Meta-Analysis of the Relationship Between Experiential Learning and Learning Outcomes. *Decision Sciences Journal of Innovative Education*, *17*(3), 239–273. DOI: 10.1111/dsji.12188

Camelo, A. P., & Lucena, C. (2021). Elements of a strategic roadmap to legal education and accreditation in the digital environment. Technology, Innovation and Access to Justice, 229.

Carella, G., & Colombo, F. (2024). Teaching design and actively applying it through projectbased learning format: A practical case study of a collaboration between a university course and a company. *INTED Proceedings*, •••, 2391–2398. DOI: 10.21125/inted.2024.0664

Carroll, J. (2014, January 1). Human Computer Interaction - A Brief Intro. Retrieved from Interaction Design Foundation: https://www.interaction-design.org/literature/book/the-encyclopedia-of-human-computer-interaction-2nd-ed/human-computer-interaction-brief-intro?srsltid=AfmBOornFGhtXHb9Q5n1VAdP8ye3DFvs0FtL8jJkEFkaefQVL1zR-EYI

Casetext. (n.d.). *CARA (Case Analysis Research Assistant) legal research tool*. Retrieved July 14, 2025, from https://www.legal.io/legal-software/198/Casetext legal.io.

Chalkiadakis, A., Seremetaki, A., Kanellou, A., Kallishi, M., Morfopoulou, A., Moraitaki, M., & Mastrokoukou, S. (2024). Impact of Artificial Intelligence and Virtual Reality on Educational Inclusion: A Systematic Review of Technologies Supporting Students with Disabilities. *Education Sciences, 14*(11), 1223. Advance online publication. DOI: 10.3390/educsci14111223

Chan, C. K. Y., & Hu, W. (2023). Students' voices on generative AI: Perceptions, benefits, and challenges in higher education. *International Journal of Educational Technology in Higher Education, 20*(1), 43. Advance online publication. DOI: 10.1186/s41239-023-00411-8

Chandarin, C. (2024, May 29). Ethical use of artificial intelligence in Cambodian education. Cambodianess. https://cambodianess.com/article/ethical-use-of-artificial-intelligence-in-cambodian-education

Chandrachud, D. Y. (2024, April 10). *Integration of AI in modern processes raises complex ethical, legal, practical considerations:* CJI. Indian Express. https://indianexpress.com/article/india/integration-ai-modern-processes-ethical-legal-practical-considerations-cji-9267700/

Chen, G., Fan, L., Gong, Z., Xie, N., Li, Z., Liu, Z., Li, C., Qu, Q., Alinejad-Rokny, H., Ni, S., & Yang, M. (2025). *AgentCourt: Simulating court with adversarial evolvable lawyer agents.* In Proceedings of the 63rd Annual Meeting of the Association for Computational Linguistics (pp. 508-515). Association for Computational Linguistics. https://aclanthology.org/2025.findings-acl.304.pdf

Chernikova, O., Heitzmann, N., Holzberger, D., Seidel, T., & Fischer, F. (2020). Simulation-based learning in higher education: A meta-analysis. *Review of Educational Research, 90*(4), 499–541. DOI: 10.3102/0034654320933544

Child Protection Law, Royal Decree No. M/14 (2014), as amended by Royal Decree No. M/72 (2023).

Chinnaraju, A. (2025). Explainable AI (XAI) for Trustworthy and Transparent decision-making: A Theoretical Framework for AI Interpretability. *World Journal of Advanced Engineering Technology and Sciences, 14*(3), 170–207. DOI: 10.30574/wjaets.2025.14.3.0106

Choi, J., Hickman, K., Monahan, A., & Schwarcz, D. (2022). ChatGPT Goes to Law School. *Journal of Legal Education, 71*(3), 387–400.

Chopra, T. (2013). Expanding the Horizons of Disability Law in India: A Study from a Human Rights Perspective. *The Journal of Law, Medicine & Ethics, 41*(4), 807–820. DOI: 10.1111/jlme.12091 PMID: 24446939

Choudhary, S., Yadav, M., & Srivastava, A. P. (2024). Cognitive biases among millennial Indian investors: Do personality and demographic factors matter? *FIIB Business Review, 13*(1), 106–117. DOI: 10.1177/23197145211057343

Choudhury, P. K., Kumar, A., & Gill, A. S. (2021). Who all access private coaching in higher education and how much do they spend? Evidence from India. *Journal of the Asia Pacific Economy, 28*(4), 1433–1455. DOI: 10.1080/13547860.2021.1954302

Chu, Z., Wang, S., Xie, J., Zhu, T., Yan, Y., Ye, J., Zhong, A., Hu, X., Liang, J., Yu, P. S., & Wen, Q. (2025). *LLM agents for education: Advances and applications.* arXiv preprint. /arXiv.2503.11733DOI: 10.18653/v1/2025.findings-emnlp.743

Citron, D. K. (2019). A new compact for sexual privacy. *William and Mary Law Review, 62*(7), 1769–1798.

Code of Law Practice, Royal Decree No. M/38 (2001).

Columbia Law School. (n.d.). *Experiential learning.* Columbia Law School. https://www.law.columbia.edu/academics/experiential

Cornell University. (n.d.). *Ethical AI for teaching and learning.* https://teaching.cornell.edu/generative-artificial-intelligence/ethical-ai-teaching-and-learning

Costanza-Chock, S. (2020). *Design justice: Community-led practices to build the worlds we need.* MIT Press. DOI: 10.7551/mitpress/12255.001.0001

Couldry, N., & Mejias, U. A. (2019). *The costs of connection: How data is colonizing human life and appropriating it for capitalism.* Stanford University Press.

Darder, A. (2014). *Freire and Education.* Routledge. DOI: 10.4324/9780203109021

Dar, W. A., & Najar, I. A. (2018). Educational anthropology, tribal education and responsible citizenship in India. *South Asia Research, 38*(3), 327–346. DOI: 10.1177/0262728018800759

Degen, D. (2025). Resurrecting Socrates in the Age of AI: A Study Protocol for Evaluating a Socratic Tutor in Research Question Generation. *arXiv.* https://arxiv.org/abs/2504.06294

Derreth, R. T., Levin, M. B., & Jones, V. C. (2021). Preparing Public Health Professionals to Address Social Injustices Through Critical Service-Learning. *Pedagogy in Health Promotion, 7*(4), 354–357. DOI: 10.1177/23733799211007183

Dhabliya, D., Dari, S. S., Dhablia, A. N. A., Kachhoria, R., & Khetani, V. (2024). Addressing Bias in Machine Learning Algorithms: Promoting Fairness and Ethical Design. *E3S Web of Conferences, 491*(E3S Web Conf), 02040–02040. Web of Conferences. DOI: 10.1051/e3sconf/202449102040

Digital Education Council. (2024, August 2). *Digital Education Council global AI student survey 2024*. Digital Education Council. https://www.digitaleducationcouncil.com/post/digital-education-council-global-ai-student-survey-2024

Dimitropoulos, G. (2023). Artificial Intelligence and International Adjudication. Oxford Public International Law. https://opil.ouplaw.com/display/10.1093/law-mpeipro/e3888.013.3888/law-mpeipro-e3888?d=%

Doleck, T., Lemay, D. J., Basnet, R. B., & Bazelais, P. (2019). Predictive analytics in education: A comparison of deep learning frameworks. *Education and Information Technologies*, *25*(3), 1951–1963. DOI: 10.1007/s10639-019-10068-4

Dolidze, T. (2025). The Evolving Role of Artificial Intelligence in Legal Education and Research. *Law and World*, *11*(33), 92–105.

Donahue, J. (2018). A Primer on Using Artificial Intelligence in the Legal Profession. *JOLT Digest*, https://jolt.law.harvard.edu/digest/a-primer-on-using-artificial-intelligence-in-the-legal-profession

Dressel, J., & Farid, H. (2018). The accuracy, fairness, and limits of predicting recidivism. *Science Advances*, *4*(1), eaao5580. Advance online publication. DOI: 10.1126/sciadv.aao5580 PMID: 29376122

Dykstra, J. G. (2018). Beyond the" Practice Ready" Buzz: Sifting Through the Disruption of the Legal Industry to Divine the Skills Needed by New Attorneys. *Drexel L. Rev.*, *11*, 149.

Eager, B., & Brunton, R. (2023). Prompting higher education towards AI-Augmented Teaching and Learning practice. *Journal of University Teaching & Learning Practice*, *20*(5). Advance online publication. DOI: 10.53761/1.20.5.02

Eboigbe, E. O. (2024). AI in Legal Analytics: Balancing Efficiency, Accuracy, and Ethics in Contract and Predictive Analysis. *Journal of Legal Education*, *72*(3 & 4). Advance online publication. DOI: 10.2139/ssrn.4997519

Educause. (2024, December 5). *Striking a balance: Navigating the ethical dilemmas of AI in higher education*, by Katalin Wargo and Brier Anderson. https://er.educause.edu/articles/2024/12/striking-a-balance-navigating-the-ethical-dilemmas-of-ai-in-higher-education

Eggen, P., & Kauchak, D. P. (2010). *Educational psychology: Windows on classrooms* (8th ed.). Merrill/Prentice Hall., Retrieved from https://sehthehfoundation.org/wp-content/uploads/2023/09/Paul-Eggen-Don-Kauchak-Educational-Psychology_-Windows-On-Classrooms.-8th-edition-Merrill-Pearson-2010.pdf

Ekaterina, K., Ana, M., & Maia, Z. (2025). Academic Integrity Within the Medical Curriculum in the Age of Generative Artificial Intelligence. *Health Science Reports*, *8*(2), e70489. Advance online publication. DOI: 10.1002/hsr2.70489 PMID: 39980818

Eltahir, M., & Babiker, F. M. E. (2024). The influence of artificial intelligence tools on student performance in e-learning environments: Case study. *Electronic Journal of e-Learning*, *22*(9), 91–110. DOI: 10.34190/ejel.22.9.3639

Emejuo, C. C., Joseph, O. C., Odeyemi, E., & Igwe, A. O. (2025). The Impact of Artificial Intelligence on Legal Practice: Enhancing Legal Research, Contract Analysis, and Predictive Justice. *International Journal of Science and Research Archive*, *14*(1), 603–611. https://journalijsra.com/node/336. DOI: 10.30574/ijsra.2025.14.1.0124

Engel, C., Linhardt, L., & Schubert, M. (2024). Code is law: How COMPAS affects the way the judiciary handles the risk of recidivism. *Artificial Intelligence and Law*. Advance online publication. DOI: 10.1007/s10506-024-09389-8

Enrollify. (2024, November 26). *Ethical considerations for AI use in education*, by Shelby Moquin. https://www.enrollify.org/blog/ethical-considerations-for-ai-use-in-education

Erevelles, N. (2005). (Dis)Embodied form: Issues of disabled women. *Disability Studies Quarterly*, *25*(2). Advance online publication. DOI: 10.18061/dsq.v25i2.567

Essien, A., Bukoye, O., O'Dea, X., & Kremantzis, M. (2025). The influence of AI text generators on critical thinking skills in UK business schools. *Studies in Higher Education*, *49*(5), 865–882. DOI: 10.1080/03075079.2024.2316881

Esteban-Escaño, J., Esteban-Sánchez, A., & Sein-Echaluce, M. (2017). Engineering final project supervised in an adaptive way with Moodle support. *IEEE Revista Iberoamericana de Technologias del Aprendizaje*, *12*(1), 10–16. DOI: 10.1109/RITA.2017.2655178

European Commission. (2021). Ethics guidelines for trustworthy AI. Publications Office of the EU. https://www.europarl.europa.eu/cmsdata/196377/AI%20HLEG_Ethics%20Guidelines%20for%20Trustworthy%20AI.pdf

European Commission. (2024). *EU Artificial Intelligence Act*. Retrieved from https://digital-strategy.ec.europa.eu/en/policies/european-approach-artificial-intelligence

Evans, J. St. B. T., & Stanovich, K. E. (2013). Dual-process theories of higher cognition: Advancing the debate. *Perspectives on Psychological Science*, *8*(3), 223–241. DOI: 10.1177/1745691612460685 PMID: 26172965

Ewick, P., & Silbey, S. (1998). *The common place of law: Stories from everyday life*. The University of Chicago Press. DOI: 10.7208/chicago/9780226212708.001.0001

Ezzaim, A., Dahbi, A., Haidine, A., & Aqqal, A. (2024). The impact of implementing a Moodle plug-in as an AI-based adaptive learning solution on learning effectiveness: Case of Morocco. *International Journal of Interactive Mobile Technologies*, *18*(1), 133–149. DOI: 10.3991/ijim.v18i01.46309

Fadieieva, L. O. (2021). *Enhancing adaptive learning with Moodle's machine learning*. Educational Dimension.

Fakour, H., & Imani, M. (2025). Socratic wisdom in the age of AI: A comparative study of ChatGPT and human tutors in enhancing critical thinking skills. *Frontiers in Education*, *10*, 1528603. Advance online publication. DOI: 10.3389/feduc.2025.1528603

Farahani, M. S., & Ghasmi, G. (2024). Artificial Intelligence in education: A comprehensive study. *Forum for Education Studies*, *2*(3), 1379. DOI: 10.59400/fes.v2i3.1379

Farber, S. (2024). Harmonizing AI and human instruction in legal education: A case study from Israel on training future legal professionals. *International Journal of the Legal Profession*, *31*(3), 349–363. DOI: 10.1080/09695958.2024.2430018

Favero, C., Pérez-Ortiz, J. A., Käse, T., & Oliver, N. (2024). Enhancing critical thinking in education by means of a Socratic chatbot. *arXiv*. https://arxiv.org/abs/2409.05511

Fernsel, L., Kalff, Y., & Simbeck, K. (2024). Where is the evidence? A plugin for auditing Moodle's learning analytics. In *Proceedings of the 2024 Learning Analytics and Knowledge Conference* (pp. 262–269). DOI: 10.5220/0012689800003693

Fleming, N. D., & Mills, C. (1992). Not another inventory, rather a catalyst for reflection. *To Improve the Academy*, *11*(1), 137–155. https://digitalcommons.unl.edu/cgi/viewcontent.cgi?article=1245&context=podimproveacad. DOI: 10.1002/j.2334-4822.1992.tb00213.x

Floridi, L. (2023). On Good and Evil, the Mistaken Idea that Technology is Ever Neutral, and the Importance of the Double-Charge Thesis. *Philosophy & Technology*, 36(60). https://link.springer.com/article/10.1007/s13347-023-00661-4

Floridi, L., & Cowls, J. (2019). A Unified Framework of Five Principles for AI in Society. *Harvard Data Science Review, 1*(1). https://hdsr.mitpress.mit.edu/pub/l0jsh9d1/release/8

Flynn, S. (2021, June 9). How natural language processing (NLP) AI is used in law. Law Technology Today. American Bar Association. https://www.americanbar.org/groups/law_practice/resources/law-technology-today/2021/how-natural-language-processing-nlp-ai-is-used-in-law/

Formpl.us. (2023, April 24). Desk research: Definition, types, application, pros & cons. https://www.formpl.us/blog/desk-research-definition-types-application-pros-cons

Fornasier, M. O. (2021). The Impact of the Introduction of Artificial Intelligence in Advocacy: Skills and Professional Ethics Necessary for the Future Lawyer. *Revista Da Faculdade De Direito UFPR*, 66(2), 69-94. https://revistas.ufpr.br/direito/article/view/73458

Freire, P. (1970). Pedagogy of the Oppressed. *Continuum : an Interdisciplinary Journal on Continuity of Care.*

Freire, P. (1970). *Pedagogy of the Oppressed.* Herder and Herder.

Fromm, J., Radianti, J., Wehking, C., Stieglitz, S., Majchrzak, T. A., & vom Brocke, J. (2021). More than experience? – On the unique opportunities of virtual reality to afford a holistic experiential learning cycle. *The Internet and Higher Education, 50,* 100804. Advance online publication. DOI: 10.1016/j.iheduc.2021.100804

Gale, L., Bhushan, P., Eidnani, S., Graham, L., Harrison, M., McKay-Brown, L., Pande, R., Shreeraman, S., & Sivashunmugamb, C. (2021). Overcoming barriers to inclusion in education in India. SSRN *Electronic Journal.* DOI: 10.2139/ssrn.3786018

Garner, B. A. (2013). *Legal writing in plain English: A text with exercises* (2nd ed.). University of Chicago Press.

General Authority for Statistics. (2025). https://www.stats.gov.sa

Glasser, N. M., Green, F. M., Zumwalt, G., & Wold, I. (2025). AI and Ethics in the Legal Profession. *Epstein Becker Green.* https://www.ebglaw.com/assets/htmldocuments/eltw/eltw385/AI-and-Ethics-in-the-Legal-Profession-Epstein-Becker-Green.pdf

Glendon, M. A., & Alford, W. P. (2025). Legal Profession. *Britannica.* https://www.britannica.com/topic/legal-profession

Glendon, M. A., & Alford, W. P. (2025a). Legal Education. *Britannica.* https://www.britannica.com/topic/legal-education

Gligorea, I., Cioca, M., Oancea, R., Gorski, A.-T., Gorski, H., & Tudorache, P. (2023). Adaptive Learning Using Artificial Intelligence in e-Learning: A Literature Review. *Education Sciences*, *13*(12), 1216. DOI: 10.3390/educsci13121216

Global Online Academy. (n.d.). *Student perspective: Reflecting on the role of AI in education*. Retrieved July 12, 2025, from https://globalonlineacademy.org/insights/articles/student-perspective-reflecting-on-the-role-of-ai-in-education

Goel, R., Ashok, N., & Rani, S. (2024). AI IN RURAL INDIA: NAVIGATING CHALLENGES, EMBRACING OPPORTUNITIES. *International Journal of Engineering Science & Humanities.*, *14*(Special Issue 1), 195–205. DOI: 10.62904/rkr2dk52

Gökçearslan, Ş., Tosun, C., & Erdemir, Z. G. (2024). Benefits, Challenges, and Methods of Artificial intelligence (AI) chatbots in Education: A Systematic Literature review. *International Journal of Technology in Education*, *7*(1), 19–39. DOI: 10.46328/ijte.600

Gonsalves, C. (2024). Generative AI's Impact on Critical Thinking: Revisiting Bloom's Taxonomy. *Journal of Marketing Education*, •••, 16. DOI: 10.1177/02734753241305980

Gordon, J. S. (2021). AI and law: Ethical, legal, and socio-political implications. *AI & Society*, *36*(2), 403–404. DOI: 10.1007/s00146-021-01194-0

Grammarly. (n.d.). *Grammarly: Free AI writing assistance*. Retrieved July 14, 2025, from https://www.grammarly.com/

Gross, T. (2014). Human-Computer Interaction Education and Diversity. In Kuroso, M. (Ed.), *Human-Computer Interaction, Part I* (pp. 187–198). Springer.

Gross, T. (2014). Human-computer interaction education and diversity. *Lecture Notes in Computer Science*, *8510*, 187–198. DOI: 10.1007/978-3-319-07233-3_18

Gupta, A. (2008). International trends and private higher education in India. *International Journal of Educational Management*, *22*(6), 565–594. DOI: 10.1108/09513540810895462

Guth, J., & Dutton, K. (2018). SQE-ezed out: SRA, status and stasis. *The Law Teacher*, *52*(4), 425–438. DOI: 10.1080/03069400.2018.1534341

Haapio, H., & Passera, S. (2013). Contracts as interfaces: Exploring visual representation patterns in contract design. In Biasiotti, M. A., Sartor, G., & Tiscornia, P. (Eds.), *Proceedings of the International Conference on Electronic Government and the Information Systems Perspective* (pp. 1–12). Springer.

Habrusiev, V., Tereshchuk, H., Panchenko, V., Martyniuk, S., Sysoiev, O., & Henseruk, H. (2023). Enhancing online learning in LCM Moodle through interactive adaptive learning. *13th International Conference on Advanced Computer Information Technologies (ACIT)*, 650–655. DOI: 10.1109/ACIT58437.2023.10275436

Hammond, C. (1999). Teaching practical legal problem solving skills: Preparing law students for the realities of legal life. *Legal Educ. Rev.*, *10*(2), 191. DOI: 10.53300/001c.6122

Hans, V. B. PP, S., & KS, Y. (2025). *Education sector in India - ailment and treatment*. Pen and Paper Academy.

Harankaha, M., & Thilakarathna, K. A. A. N. (2024). AI in Legal Education: Balancing Opportunities and Challenges in the Sri Lankan Context. Issue 6 Int'l JL Mgmt. &. *Human.*, *7*, 137.

Harrington, S., & Brice, K. (2024, December). *Revolutionizing legal education with AI: The Socratic Quizbot*. AI Law Librarians. https://www.ailawlibrarians.com/2024/12/10/socratic-quizbot/

Harrington, S. (2024, October 3). Introducing QuizBot an Innovative AI-Assisted Assessment in Legal Education. Retrieved from *SSRN*: https://papers.ssrn.com/sol3/papers.cfm?abstract_id=4975804 DOI: 10.2139/ssrn.4975804

Harrington, S. A. (2023, June 26). *The case for large language model optimism in legal research from a law & technology librarian. SSRN.* https://ssrn.com/abstract=4492121 DOI: 10.2139/ssrn.4492121

Hazard, G. C.Jr. (1998). The Legal Profession: The Impact of Law and Legal Theory. *Fordham Law Review*, *67*, 239–248. https://ir.lawnet.fordham.edu/cgi/viewcontent.cgi?article=3503&context=flr

Heap, T., Hudson, C., & Archibald, A. (2020). Investigating the impact of an AI-driven discussion platform on educator perceptions and feedback. *EDEN Conference Proceedings*. DOI: 10.38069/edenconf-2020-ac0010

Hebbar, C. (2020). Impact of digital India on education system. *International Journal of Case Studies in Business IT and Education*, 65–70. DOI: 10.47992/IJCSBE.2581.6942.0079

Heng, S., Tsilionis, K., Scharff, C., & Wautelet, Y. (2022). Understanding AI ecosystems in the Global South: The cases of Senegal and Cambodia. *International Journal of Information Management*, *64*, 1–15. DOI: 10.1016/j.ijinfomgt.2021.102454

He, R., Cao, J., & Tan, T. (2025). Generative artificial intelligence: A historical perspective. *National Science Review*, *12*(5), nwaf050. Advance online publication. DOI: 10.1093/nsr/nwaf050 PMID: 40191253

Herrington, A. (2019). How AI Can Make Legal Services More Affordable. *Smart-Lawyer*. https://nationaljurist.com/smartlawyer/how-ai-can-make-legal-services-more-affordable/

Heyeve.ai. (n.d.). *AI Chatbot Assistant for legal training & consultation*. Retrieved July 12, 2025, from https://heyeve.ai/

Holmes, W., Bialik, M., & Fadel, C. (2022). *Artificial intelligence in education: Promises and implications for teaching and learning* (2nd ed.). Center for Curriculum Redesign., https://discovery.ucl.ac.uk/id/eprint/10139722/

Holmes, W., Porayska-Pomsta, K., Holstein, K., Sutherland, E., Baker, T., Shum, S. B., Santos, O. C., Rodrigo, M. T., Cukurova, M., Bittencourt, I. I., & Koedinger, K. R. (2022). Ethics of AI in Education: Towards a Community-Wide Framework. *International Journal of Artificial Intelligence in Education*, *32*(3), 504–526. https://link.springer.com/article/10.1007/s40593-021-00239-1. DOI: 10.1007/s40593-021-00239-1

Hull, H. G. (2013). Diversity in the legal profession: Moving from the rhetoric to reality. *Colum. J. Race & L.*, *4*, 1.

Hu, X., Xu, S., Tong, R., & Graesser, A. (2025). Generative AI in Education: From Foundational Insights to the Socratic Playground for Learning. *arXiv*. https://arxiv.org/abs/2501.06682

Ibn Qudama, M. (1997). *Al-Mughni fi fiqh al-Imam Ahmad ibn Hanbal* [The Sufficient in the Jurisprudence of Imam Ahmad ibn Hanbal]. Dar Alam Alkutub.

India. Dept of Elementary Education and Literacy. (2006). *Education for all: India marches ahead*. National Insitute of Education Planning and Administration.

Ioannidi, V., & Malafantis, K. D. (2023). Inclusive education and creative learning styles. International opportunities and challenges. *European Journal of Literature. Language and Linguistics Studies*, *7*(1), 77–86. DOI: 10.46827/ejlll.v7i1.445

i-Probono. (2024). *AI for legal empowerment: Collaborative effort behind Jagrit Chatbot*. Retrieved July 14, 2025, from https://i-probono.in/ipb_casestudy/ai-for-legal-empowerment-collaborative-effort-behind-jagrit-chatbot/

Iqbal, J., Asgarova, V., Hashmi, Z. F., Ngajie, B. N., Asghar, M. Z., Arslan, M. M., Hassan, E., & Järvenoja, H. (2025). Exploring faculty experiences with generative AI tool integration in second language curricula in Chinese higher education. Discover Computing, 28(1), 1–29. https://link.springer.com/article/10.1007/s10791-025-09655-6

Jabbour, J., Kleinbard, K., Miller, O., Haussman, R., & Reddi, V. J. (2025). SocratiQ: A Generative AI-Powered Learning Companion for Personalized Education and Broader Accessibility. *arXiv*. https://arxiv.org/abs/2502.00341 DOI: 10.1145/3743646.3750010

Jacobowitz, J. L. (2018). Happy Birthday, Siri! Dialing in Legal Ethics for Artificial Intelligence, Smart Phones, and Real Time Lawyers. *Texas A&M Journal of Property Law*, 4(5), 407-442. https://scholarship.law.tamu.edu/cgi/viewcontent.cgi?article=1078&context=journal-of-property-law

James, C. (2008). Lawyer Dissatisfaction, Emotional Intelligence and Clinical Legal Education. *Legal Education Review*, *18*(1). Advance online publication. DOI: 10.53300/001c.6208

Jurisphere. (n.d.). *AI-powered legal assistant*. Retrieved July 14, 2025, from https://jurisphere.ai/

Jurors.ai. (n.d.). *Mock trials using AI*. Retrieved July 12, 2025, from https://jurors.ai/

Justice Connect. (n.d.). *Our AI Model – Justice Connect*. https://justiceconnect.org.au/about/innovation/legal-help-experience/ai-project/

Kahoot! (2025, July). Kahoot! AI Tools. Retrieved from Kahoot: https://kahoot.com/ai-tools/#What-is-the-most-useful-AI-tool-for-teachers

Kaiss, W., Mansouri, K., & Poirier, F. (2023). Effectiveness of an adaptive learning chatbot on students' learning outcomes based on learning styles. [iJET]. *International Journal of Emerging Technologies in Learning*, *18*(13), 250–261. DOI: 10.3991/ijet.v18i13.39329

Kang, X., Qu, L., Soon, L.-K., Trakic, A., Zhuo, T., Emerton, P., & Grant, G. (2023). Can ChatGPT Perform Reasoning Using the IRAC Method in Analyzing Legal Scenarios Like a Lawyer? In *Findings of the Association for Computational Linguistics: EMNLP 2023* (pp. 13900–13923). Association for Computational Linguistics. DOI: 10.18653/v1/2023.findings-emnlp.929

Karagiannis, I. E., & Satratzemi, M. (2018). An adaptive mechanism for Moodle based on automatic detection of learning styles. *Education and Information Technologies*, *23*(3), 1331–1357. DOI: 10.1007/s10639-017-9663-5

Kashefi, P., Kashefi, Y., & Mirsaraei, A. G. (2024). Shaping the future of AI: Balancing innovation and ethics in global regulation. *Uniform Law Review, 29*(3), 524–548. Advance online publication. DOI: 10.1093/ulr/unae040

Kashyap, A. K. (2016). Professional legal education in India: challenges and the way forward. *Educational Quest- an International Journal of Education and Applied Social Sciences, 7*(3), 141. DOI: 10.5958/2230-7311.2016.00035.0

Katz, D. M., Bommarito, M. J., & Blackman, J. (2021). *The law of artificial intelligence and smart machines*. Wolters Kluwer.

Kaur, S., & Choudhury, P. K. (2025). *COVID-19 and education in India: Impact on Access, Inclusion and Learning*. Taylor & Francis. DOI: 10.4324/9781003461371

Kay, J. (2012). AI and Education: Grand Challenges. *IEEE Intelligent Systems, 27*(5), 66–69. DOI: 10.1109/MIS.2012.92

Kearns, M., & Roth, A. (2020). *The Ethical Algorithm: The Science of Socially Aware Algorithm Design*. Oxford University Press.

Kee, S. (2024). Legal Clinic Under The Lens of Paulo Freire: A Theoretical Interpretation of Clinical Legal Education at Australian University Law Schools. Murdoch University. Retrieved from https://researchportal.murdoch.edu.au/view/pdfCoverPage? instCode=61MUN_INST&filePid=13176902410007891&download=true

Keo, V., Sam, R., Lan, B., & Wen, R. (2024). Challenges and opportunities of educational technology integration in Cambodian higher education institutions: A literature review. International Journal of Education, Psychology and Counseling, 9(54). https://gaexcellence.com/ijepc/article/view/285

Khan, S. R. (2017). Problems and challenges for the first generation learners. *International Journal of Applied Linguistics and English Literature, 6*(7), 318. DOI: 10.7575/aiac.ijalel.v.6n.7p.317

Khoalenyane, N. B., & Ajani, O. A. (2024). A systematic review of artificial intelligence in higher education-South Africa. *Social Sciences and Education Research Review, 11*(1), 17–26. DOI: 10.5281/zenodo.15258127

Kialo Inc. (n.d.). Kialo: Structured debate platform. Retrieved July 12, 2025, from https://www.kialo.com/

Kim, E. (2024). The Limited Potential for AI Implementation in US Courts. *Research Association for Interdisciplinary Studies: Conference Proceedings*, 65-74. https://rais.education/wp-content/uploads/2024/07/0394.pdf.

Kim, M.-Y., & Wilkinson, I. A. G. (2019). *What is dialogic teaching? Constructing, deconstructing, and reconstructing a pedagogy of classroom talk.* https://www.sciencedirect.com/science/article/abs/pii/S2210656118301764

King Abdulaziz University. (2024). *College of Law.* https://law.kau.edu.sa

King Saud University. (2025). *College of Law and Political Sciences.* https://clps.ksu.edu.sa

Kirschner, P., & Hendrick, C. (2020). *How Learning Happens. Seminal Works in Educational Psychology and What They Mean in Practice.* Routledge. DOI: 10.4324/9780429061523

Knowles, M. S. (1980). *The modern practice of adult education: From pedagogy to andragogy.* Cambridge Adult Education. Retrieved from https://www.umsl.edu/~henschkej/articles/a_The_%20Modern_Practice_of_Adult_Education.pdf

Knowles, M. S., Holton, E. F.III, & Swanson, R. A. (2015). *The adult learner: The definitive classic in adult education and human resource development* (8th ed.). Routledge., Retrieved from https://api.pageplace.de/preview/DT0400.9781000072891_A39784180/preview-9781000072891_A39784180.pdf

Knox, J. (2020). Artificial intelligence and education in China. *Learning, Media and Technology, 45*(3), 298–311. DOI: 10.1080/17439884.2020.1754236

Koch, I. E. (2009). From Invisibility to Indivisibility: The International Convention on the Rights of Persons with Disabilities. In *Brill | Nijhoff eBooks* (pp. 67–79). DOI: 10.1163/ej.9789004169715.i-320.24

Köchling, A., & Wehner, M. C. (2022). Better explaining the benefits why AI? Analyzing the impact of explaining the benefits of AI-supported selection on applicant responses. *International Journal of Selection and Assessment, 31*(1), 45–62. DOI: 10.1111/ijsa.12412

Kolb, D. (1984). *Experiential Learning: Experience as the Source of Learning and Development.* Fullerton.edu. Retrieved from https://www.fullerton.edu/cice/_resources/pdfs/sl_documents/Experiential%20Learning%20-%20Experience%20As%20The%20Source%20Of%20Learning%20and%20Development.pdf

Kolb, D. A. (1984). *Experiential Learning: Experience as the Source of Learning and Development.* Prentice Hall.

Komljenovic, J., & Williamson, B. (2024). Behind the platforms: ed tech platform adoption and its impact on academic freedom. University of Edinburgh Research Explorer. PDF retrieved from research repository. arxiv.orgresearch.ed.ac.uk

Kritzer, H. M. (1999). The professions are dead, long live the professions: Legal practice in a postprofessional world. *Law & Society Review*, *33*(3), 713–759. DOI: 10.2307/3115110

Kuhn, C., Khoo, S. M., Czerniewicz, L., Lilley, W., Bute, S., Crean, A., Abegglen, S., Burns, T., Sinfield, S., Jandrić, P., Knox, J., & MacKenzie, A. (2023). Understanding Digital Inequality: A Theoretical Kaleidoscope. *Postdigit Sci Educ*, *5*(3), 894–932. DOI: 10.1007/s42438-023-00395-8 PMID: 40479087

Kumar, A. B., Sanjaya, K., & Saleem, M. (2025). Justice in the Age of Algorithms. In *Advances in Computational Intelligence and Robotics* (pp. 191–210). IGI Global. DOI: 10.4018/979-8-3693-9395-6.ch009

Kumar, A. B., & Sanjaya, K. (2025a). AI Renaissance in Renewable Energy. In *Advances in environmental engineering and green technologies book series* (pp. 15–32). IGI Global., DOI: 10.4018/979-8-3373-0045-0.ch002

Kumar, A. B., & Sanjaya, K. (2025b). Ethics, Algorithms, and the Rules of Evidence. In *Forensic Intelligence and Deep Learning Solutions in Crime Investigation* (pp. 103–124). IGI Global., DOI: 10.4018/979-8-3693-9405-2.ch006

Kumar, N. (2017). Private coaching factories: Widening educational divide and exclusion in India. *International Journal of Higher Education and Sustainability*, *1*(4), 275. DOI: 10.1504/IJHES.2017.090190

Kumar, N. D., & Singh, N. D. M. (2022). India's New Education Policy (NEP) 2020 Creating Children with Disability. *International Journal of Advanced Research in Science Communication and Technology*, *70–74*, 70–74. Advance online publication. DOI: 10.48175/IJARSCT-2505

Kunnath, S. K., & Mathew, S. N. (2019). Higher Education for Students with Disabilities in India: Insights from a Focus Group Study. *Higher Education for the Future*, *6*(2), 171–187. DOI: 10.1177/2347631119840540

Labadze, L., Grigolia, M., & Machaidze, L. (2023). Role of AI chatbots in education: Systematic literature review. *International Journal of Educational Technology in Higher Education*, *20*(1), 56. Advance online publication. DOI: 10.1186/s41239-023-00426-1

Lai, M. K. (2025). AI-personalized learning in higher education: A study on learning outcomes and motivation among university students. *International Journal of Research and Innovation in Social Science*, *9*(6), 6075–6085. https://rsisinternational.org/journals/ijriss/articles/ai-personalised-learning-in-higher-education-a-study-on-learning-outcomes-and-motivation-among-university-students/

Lampou, R. (2023). The integration of artificial intelligence in education: Opportunities and challenges. *Review of Artificial Intelligence in Education*, *4*(00), e15. DOI: 10.37497/rev.artif.intell.educ.v4i00.15

Law of the Judiciary, Royal Decree No. M/78 (2007).

Law, Civil Procedures, & No, Royal Decree. M/1 (2013).

Law, Enforcement, & No, Royal Decree. M/43 (2012).

Law, Evidence, & No, Royal Decree. M/53 (2021).

LawGlance. (n.d.). *LawGlance*. Retrieved July 15, 2025, from https://lawglance.com/

Law, Personal Status, & No, Royal Decree. M/73 (2022).

LawRank. (2021, May 4*). Grammarly: A top writing tool for lawyers.* https://lawrank.com/grammarly-a-top-writing-tool-for-lawyers/

Law, Social Security, & No, Royal Decree. M/32 (2020).

Legal Education and Training Review (LETR). (2013). *Setting standards: The future of legal services education and training regulation in England and Wales – Main report.* https://letr.org.uk/the-report/

Leng, P., & Srun, M. (2025). Liberal arts for ethical and critical AI adoption in Cambodia. Science Technology and Sustainability Review, STS002/25, 1–15. https://camtech.edu.kh/wp-content/uploads/2025/08/CC_001_25_Liberal-Arts-Education.pdf

Lewis, P., Perez, E., Piktus, A., Petroni, F., Karpukhin, V., Goyal, N., Küttler, H., Lewis, M., Yih, W.-t., Rocktäschel, T., Riedel, S., & Kiela, D. (2020). *Retrieval-augmented generation for knowledge-intensive NLP tasks. Advances in Neural Information Processing Systems, 33.* arXiv. https://doi.org/DOI: 10.48550/arXiv.2005.11401

LexisNexis. (n.d.). *AI is preparing the next generation of lawyers*, by Ray Collitt. https://www.lexisnexis.com/html/ai-is-preparing-the-next-generation-of-lawyers/

LexisNexis. (n.d.). *Lexis+ AI: Legal research platform & AI assistant*. Retrieved July 14, 2025, from https://www.lexisnexis.com/en-us/products/lexis-plus-ai.page

Libraries, J. M. U. (2025, May 2). *Research guides: Artificial intelligence (AI) in education: AI and ethics*. https://guides.lib.jmu.edu/AI-in-education/ethics

Li, H. (2023). AI in Education: Bridging the Divide or Widening the Gap? Exploring Equity, Opportunities, and Challenges in the Digital Age. *Advances in Education. Humanities and Social Science Research*, *8*(1), 355–355. DOI: 10.56028/aehssr.8.1.355.2023

Linawati, W., N., Sukadarmika, G., Suyadnya, I. M. A., & Krishne, D. C. (2016). Adaptive online learning design using Moodle. 2016 International Conference on Smart Green Technology in Electrical and Information Systems, 98–101.

Liu, B., Mazumder, S., Robertson, E., & Grigsby, S. (2023). AI Autonomy: Self-initiated Open-world Continual Learning and Adaptation. *AI Magazine*, *44*(2), 185–199. Advance online publication. DOI: 10.1002/aaai.12087

Lone Star Legal Aid. (n.d.). *TIG AI Chatbot Project*. Retrieved July 14, 2025, from https://www.lonestarlegal.org/tig-ai-chatbot-project

Luckin, R., Holmes, W., Griffiths, M., & Forcier, L. (2016). Intelligence Unleashed: An Argument for AI in Education. London: Open Ideas: Pearson Education. Retrieved from https://oro.open.ac.uk/50104/1/Luckin%20et%20al.%20-%202016%20-%20Intelligence%20Unleashed.%20An%20argument%20for%20AI%20in%20Educ.pdf

Luckin, R. (2018). *Machine Learning and Human Intelligence: The future of education for the 21st Century*. UCL IOE Press.

Ma, B., & Hou, Y. (2021). Artificial Intelligence Empowers the Integrated Development of Legal Education: Challenges and Responses. *Future Human Image*, 16, 43-54. https://www.fhijournal.org/16-4/

Maas, M. M. (2019). International Law Does Not Compute: Artificial Intelligence and the Development, Displacement, or Destruction of the Global Legal Order. *Melbourne Journal of International Law*, *20*(1). https://classic.austlii.edu.au/au/journals/MelbJIL/2019/3.html

Madaan, H., & Gupta, S. (2021). AI improving the lives of physically disabled. In *Advances in intelligent systems and computing* (pp. 103–112). DOI: 10.1007/978-3-030-73689-7_11

Magesh, V., Surani, F., Dahl, M., Suzgun, M., Manning, C. D., & Ho, D. E. (2025). Hallucination-free? assessing the reliability of leading ai legal research tools. *Journal of Empirical Legal Studies*, *22*(2), 216–242. DOI: 10.1111/jels.12413

Mali, N. V. (2019). *Leveraging digital innovation for governance, public administration, and citizen services: Emerging Research and Opportunities*. Information Science Reference.

Margolis, E., & Murray, K. (2016). Using Information Literacy to Prepare Practice-Ready Graduates. *U. Haw. L. Rev., 39*, 1.

Marwala, T. (2024). Avoidable and Unavoidable AI Algorithmic Bias. In *The Balancing Problem in the Governance of Artificial Intelligence* (pp. 121–136). Springer Singapore., DOI: 10.1007/978-981-97-9251-1_8

Matsuo, M. (2015). A Framework for Facilitating Experiential Learning. *Human Resource Development Review, 14*(4), 442–461. Advance online publication. DOI: 10.1177/1534484315598087

Maute, J. L. (2013). Facing 21st Century Realities. *Miss. CL Rev., 32*, 345.

McGinnis, J. O., & Pearce, R. G. (2014). The great disruption: How machine intelligence will transform the role of lawyers in the delivery of legal services. *Fordham Law Review, 82*(6), 3041–3066.

Mellinkoff, D. (1963). *The language of the law*. Little, Brown and Company.

Memarian, B., & Doleck, T. (2024). Teaching and learning artificial intelligence: Insights from the literature. *Education and Information Technologies, 29*(16), 21523–21546. DOI: 10.1007/s10639-024-12679-y

Memo.Cards. (2025). *Top 7 AI tools for legal writing feedback.* Retrieved July 12, 2025, from https://www.memo.cards/blog/top-7-ai-tools-for-legal-writing-feedback

Menon, R. (2012). Book review: Who goes to school? Exploring exclusion in Indian education. *Contemporary Education Dialogue, 9*(1), 125–130. DOI: 10.1177/097318491100900110

Merry, S. E. (1990). *Getting justice and getting even: Legal consciousness among working-class Americans*. University of Chicago Press.

Mezey, N. (2003). Law as culture. In Sarat, A., & Simon, J. (Eds.), *Cultural analysis, cultural studies, and the law: Moving beyond legal realism* (pp. 37–72). Duke University Press. DOI: 10.1215/9780822384755-002

Mezirow, J. (1997). Transformative learning: Theory to practice. *New Directions for Adult and Continuing Education, 1997*(74), 5–12. DOI: 10.1002/ace.7401

Mhlanga, D. (2024). Digital transformation of education, the limitations and prospects of introducing the fourth industrial revolution asynchronous online learning in emerging markets. *Discover Education, 3*(32), 32. DOI: 10.1007/s44217-024-00115-9

Michel-Villarreal, R., Vilalta-Perdomo, E., Salinas-Navarro, D. E., Thierry-Aguilera, R., & Gerardou, F. S. (2023). Challenges and opportunities of Generative AI for higher Education as explained by ChatGPT. *Education Sciences*, *13*(9), 856. DOI: 10.3390/educsci13090856

Migliorini, S., & Moreira, J. I. (2025). The case for nurturing AI literacy in law schools. *Asian Journal of Legal Education*, *12*(1), 1–15. DOI: 10.1177/23220058241265613

Mikeladze, T., Meijer, P. C., & Verhoeff, R. P. (2024). A comprehensive exploration of artificial intelligence competence frameworks for educators: A critical review. *European Journal of Education*, *59*(3), e12663. Advance online publication. DOI: 10.1111/ejed.12663

Miller, J. B. (2014). Bridging the Gap: The Role of Legal Clinics in Legal Education. *Clinical Law Review*, *21*(1), 1–34.

Miller, T. (2019). Explanation in artificial intelligence: Insights from the social sciences. *Artificial Intelligence*, *267*, 1–38. DOI: 10.1016/j.artint.2018.07.007

Min, H. (2010). Artificial Intelligence in Supply Chain Management: Theory and Applications. *International Journal of Logistics*, *13*(1), 13–39. DOI: 10.1080/13675560902736537

Ministry of Higher Education. Malaysia. (2022). Standards and criteria for law programmes (2nd ed.). Malaysian Qualifications Agency. https://www.mqa.gov.my/new/mqf.cfm?utm_source=chatgpt.com#gsc.tab=0

Ministry of Justice. (2013). *A collection of judicial rulings*. Ministry of Justice.

Ministry of Law and Justice. (2023). Action Plan for Simple, Accessible, Affordable, and Speedy Justice. https://www.pib.gov.in/PressReleasePage.aspx?PRID=1947490

Ministry of Law and Justice. (2025). Use of AI in Supreme Court Case Management. https://www.pib.gov.in/PressReleasePage.aspx?PRID=2113224

Ministry of Post and Telecommunications (MPTC). Cambodia. (2025). Press release on process of artificial intelligence governance. https://mptc.gov.kh/en/2025/04/press-release-on-process-of-artificial-intelligence-governance/?utm_source=chatgpt.com

Mittelstadt, B. D., Allo, P., Taddeo, M., Wachter, S., & Floridi, L. (2016). The Ethics of Algorithms: Mapping the Debate. *Big Data & Society*, *3*(2), 2053951716679679. https://journals.sagepub.com/doi/10.1177/2053951716679679. DOI: 10.1177/2053951716679679

MoEYS. (2021). Private education statistics and indicators 2020-2021. https://moeys.gov.kh/index.php/en/emis/4205.html#.YSy6MtOA63I

MoEYS. (2025). Education Congress: The Education, Youth and Sport Performance in the Academic Year 2023-2024.

Mohamed, S., Png, M. T., Isaac, W., & Decolonial, A. I. (2020). Decolonial Theory as Sociotechnical Foresight in Artificial Intelligence. *Philosophy & Technology*, *33*(4), 659–684. DOI: 10.1007/s13347-020-00405-8

Mollick, E., Mollick, L., Bach, N., Ciccarelli, L., Przystanski, B., & Ravipinto, D. (2024). AI Agents and Education: Simulated Practice at Scale. ArXiv. /arXiv.2407. 12796DOI: 10.2139/ssrn.4871171

Morze, N., Varchenko-Trotsenko, L., & Terletska, T. (2021). Stages of adaptive learning implementation by means of Moodle LMS. Myroslav I. Zhaldak Symposium on Advances in Educational Technology. DOI: 10.5220/0012065500003431

Moser, C. (1988). The Robbins Report 25 Years After-and the Future of the Universities. *Oxford Review of Education*, *14*(1), 5–20. DOI: 10.1080/0305498880140102

Moustaghfir, S., & Brigui, H. (2024). Navigating Critical Thinking in the Digital Era: An Informative Exploration. *International Journal of Linguistics. Literature and Translation*, *7*(1), 137–143. DOI: 10.32996/ijllt.2024.7.1.11x

Muhidin, E., Suparman, E., Perwira, I., & Hamzah, M. G. (2023). Digital Acceleration During Covid-19 Pandemic: How the Indonesian Constitutional Court Brings the Citizens Justice. DOI: 10.36745/ijca.512

Na'im, A. A. A. (1996). *Toward an Islamic reformation: Civil liberties, human rights, and international law*. Syracuse University Press.

Nabirye, K. (2025). *E-Discovery and the Language of Digital Evidence*. EURASIAN EXPERIMENT JOURNAL OF HUMANITIES AND SOCIAL SCIENCES (EE-JHSS). https://kiu.ac.ug/assets/publications/3441_e-discovery-and-the-language-of-digital-evidence.pdf

Nadjia, M. (2024). The impact of artificial intelligence on legal systems: challenges and opportunities. Проблеми законності, (164), 285-303.

Nancholas, B. (2023, November 10). What is Human-Computer Interaction? Retrieved from Keele University: https://online.keele.ac.uk/what-is-human-computer-interaction/

National Law Review. (2025, January 28). *The Growth of AI Law: Exploring legal challenges in artificial intelligence*, by Shari Davidson of The National Law Review's Guest Contributors - NLR. https://natlawreview.com/article/growth-ai-law-exploring-legal-challenges-artificial-intelligence

Neuberger, D. (2016, June 15). *Ethics and advocacy in the twenty-first century* (The Lord Slynn Memorial Lecture). Supreme Court of the United Kingdom. https://supremecourt.uk/uploads/speech_160615_78f4e3d8a0.pdf

Neufeldt, A., & Mathieson, R. (1995). Empirical Dimensions of Discrimination against Disabled People. *Health and Human Rights*, *1*(2), 174. DOI: 10.2307/4065213 PMID: 10395720

New York University School of Law. (n.d.). *Experiential Learning Lab*. NYU School of Law. https://www.law.nyu.edu/experientiallearninglab

Ng, D. T. K., Lee, M., Tan, R. J. Y., Hu, X., Downie, J. S., & Chu, S. K. W. (2023). A review of AI teaching and learning from 2000 to 2020. *Education and Information Technologies*, *28*(7), 8445–8501. DOI: 10.1007/s10639-022-11491-w

Nicol, D., & Macfarlane-Dick, D. (2006). Formative assessment and self-regulated learning: A model and seven principles of good feedback practice. *Studies in Higher Education*, *31*(2), 199–218. DOI: 10.1080/03075070600572090

Norman, D. (2014). *The Design of Everyday Things*. The MIT Press.

Nurata, Z. C. (2022). The Concept of Professional Ethics and Debates on Professional Ethics in the Legal Profession: The Case of Ankara. *SİYASAL: Journal of Political Science*, 31(1), 173-193. https://dergipark.org.tr/en/download/article-file/2064936

O'Keefe, P. B. (2007). People with disabilities in India: from commitments to outcomes. *World Bank*, 1–186. https://documents.worldbank.org/curated/pt/358151468268839622/People-with-disabilities-in-India-from-commitments-to-outcomes

O'Leary. Dyane, 'Smart' Lawyering: Integrating Technology Competence into the Legal Practice Curriculum (2021). University of New Hampshire Law Review, Vol. 9, No. 2, 2021, Available at SSRN: https://ssrn.com/abstract=3671632 or http://dx.doi.org/DOI: 10.2139/ssrn.3671632

Ocen, S., Elasu, J., Aarakit, S. M., & Olupot, C. (2025). Artificial intelligence in higher education institutions: Review of innovations, opportunities and challenges. *Frontiers in Education*, *10*, 1530247. DOI: 10.3389/feduc.2025.1530247

Offit Kurman. (2025, May 12). *AI in law: Ethical risks & limits of legal tech*, by Louis Tambaro. https://www.offitkurman.com/offit-kurman-blogs/ai-legal-ethics-risks-law-firms

Ojha, N. K., & Thakur, S. (2025). Privacy Laws and Leak of Financial Data in the Era of Generative AI. In *Generative Artificial Intelligence in Finance: Large Language Models, Interfaces, and Industry Use Cases to Transform Accounting and Finance Processes* (pp. 265–281). Wiley Online Library. DOI: 10.1002/9781394271078.ch14

Oliver, M. (1996). *Understanding disability*. DOI: 10.1007/978-1-349-24269-6

Onesi-Ozigagun, O., Ololade, Y., Ogundipe, D., & Eyo-Udo, N. (2024). Revolutionizing Education through AI: A Comprehensive Review of Enhancing Learning Experiences. *International Journal of Applied Research in Social Sciences, 6*(4), 589–607. DOI: 10.51594/ijarss.v6i4.1011

Ørberg, J. W. (2017). Uncomfortable encounters between elite and "shadow education" in India—Indian Institutes of Technology and the Joint Entrance Examination coaching industry. *Higher Education, 76*(1), 129–144. DOI: 10.1007/s10734-017-0202-5

Padilla Flores, E., & Mean, U. (2024). Digital Transformation in Cambodian Higher Education and Its Impact on Teaching and Learning Outcomes. *Journal of Accounting, Finance, Economics, and Social Sciences, 9*(1), 23–34. DOI: 10.62458/jafess9(1)3

Palfreyman, D., & Tapper, T. (2016). The Marketization of English Higher Education and the Financing of Tuition Fees. *London Review of Education, 14*(1), 47–55. DOI: 10.18546/LRE.14.1.06

Pandya, R. (2011). Education, training and skill development in India : first Five Year Plan (1951-56) to eleventh Five Year Plan (2007-12). In *New Century Publications eBooks*. https://ci.nii.ac.jp/ncid/BB12139541

Parlay Ideas. (n.d.). *Parlay: AI-powered class discussions.* Retrieved July 12, 2025, from https://parlayideas.com/

Paul, R., & Elder, L. (2007). The Art of Socratic Questioning. *Journal of Developmental Education, 31*(1), 36–37.

Paustian, T., & Slinger, B. (2024). Students are using large language models and AI detectors can often detect their use. *Frontiers in Education, 9*, Article 1374889. Media SA. DOI: 10.3389/feduc.2024.1374889

Personal, Status Law Regulations, & No, Royal Order. 59641 (2025).

Piaget, J. (1972). *The psychology of the child.* Basic Books. Retrieved from https://www.alohabdonline.com/wp-content/uploads/2020/05/The-Psychology-Of-The-Child.pdf

Prakash, G. A., & Nair, V. (2024). Integrating generative AI into legal education: From casebooks to code, opportunities and challenges. Law. *Technology and Humans*, *6*(3), 60–79. DOI: 10.5204/lthj.3640

Primlani, N., Blythe, M., & Marshall, J. (2025). Design Courts: Workshops for Exploring Emerging Technology Ethics. *Sage Journals*, *9*(2), 1–12. DOI: 10.1145/3706598.3713774

Prince Sultan University. (2025). *College of Law*. https://www.psu.edu.sa/ar/CL/llb-plan

Protection from Abuse Law, Royal Decree No. M/52 (2013), as amended by Royal Decree No. M/72 (2023).

Qamar, Y., Agarwal, R. K., & Samad, T. A. (2020). When Technology Meets People: The Interplay of Artificial Intelligence and Human Resource Management. *Journal of Enterprise Information Management*, *34*(5), 1339–1370. DOI: 10.1108/JEIM-11-2020-0436

Qanoniah. (2024). *The annual report of laws in the Kingdom of Saudi Arabia*. Qanoniah.

Quizbot. (n.d.). *Quizbot: AI-powered quiz and assessment platform*. https://quizbot.ai/

Quizlet. (2023, August 8). Welcome to Quizlet's AI Study Era: Studying will never be the same. Retrieved from Quizlet: https://quizlet.com/blog/ai-study-era

Rahman, F. (2002). *Islam*. University of Chicago Press.

Rajya Sabha Secretariat. (2024, February). *Report No. 142: Strengthening legal* education *in view of emerging challenges before the legal profession* (Department-related Parliamentary Standing Committee on Personnel, Public Grievances, Law and Justice). Parliament of India. https://sansad.in/getFile/rsnew/Committee_site/Committee_File/ReportFile/18/191/142_2024_2_12.pdf?source=rajyasabha

Ramachandran, V. (2004). Gender and social equity in primary education : hierarchies of access. In *SAGE Publications eBooks*. http://ci.nii.ac.jp/ncid/BA70505038

Ramaswamy, M. P.M.P.Ramaswamy. (2024). Evolving Norms Governing AI Engagement in Legal Practice and the Prospective Alignment of Law School Curriculum. *UCP Journal of Law & Legal Education*, *2*(2), 28–53. DOI: 10.24312/ucp-jlle.02.02.349

Ravaglia, R. (2023, August 28). *Generative AI makes Grammarly an essential student learning tool*. Forbes. Retrieved from https://www.forbes.com/sites/rayravaglia/2023/08/28/generative-ai-makes-grammarly-an-essential-student-learning-tool/

Ray, R. (2000). Poverty, household size and child welfare in India. *Economic and Political Weekly/Economic & Political Weekly, 35*(39), 3511–3520. https://www.cabdirect.org/abstracts/20013029257.html

Reddit law students. (2024, July 19). *Grammarly for LRW? [Discussion thread]. r/LawSchool.* https://www.reddit.com/r/LawSchool/comments/1e74hac

Remus, D., & Levy, F. (2016). Can robots be lawyers? Computers, lawyers, and the practice of law. SSRN *Electronic Journal*. DOI: 10.2139/ssrn.2701092

Remus, D., & Levy, F. (2017). Can robots be lawyers: Computers, lawyers, and the practice of law. *The Georgetown Journal of Legal Ethics*, *30*, 501.

Remus, D., & Levy, F. (2017). Can robots be lawyers? Computers, lawyers, and the practice of law. *The Georgetown Journal of Legal Ethics*, *30*(3), 501–558. https://www.iadclaw.org/assets/1/7/10.1-_Remus_Levy.pdf?utm_source=chatgpt.com

Renfrew, (2014). *Mikhail Bakhtin*. Routledge.

Rhode, D. L. (2003). *In the interests of justice: Reforming the legal profession*. Oxford University Press.

Rights of Persons with Disabilities Law, Royal Decree No. M/27 (2023).

Rights, Elderly, Law, Care, & No, Royal Decree. M/47 (2022).

Roba, G. B., & Maric, P. (2023). AI in Customer Relationship Management. In Kryvinska, N., Greguš, M., & Fedushko, S. (Eds.), *Developments in Information and Knowledge Management Systems for Business Applications*. Springer., https://link.springer.com/chapter/10.1007/978-3-031-25695-0_21 DOI: 10.1007/978-3-031-25695-0_21

Rogers, C. R. (1969). *Freedom to* learn. Merrill. Retrieved from https://www.scribd.com/document/609262438/Freedom-to-Learn-by-Carl-R-Rogers-H-Jerome-Freiberg-Z-lib-org

Rogers, E. M. (2003). *Diffusion of Innovations* (5th ed.). Free Press., https://www.simonandschuster.co.uk/books/Diffusion-of-Innovations-5th-Edition/Everett-M-Rogers/9780743222099?utm_source=chatgpt.com

Roll, I., & Wylie, R. (2016). Evolution and revolution in artificial intelligence in education. *International Journal of Artificial Intelligence in Education*, *26*(2), 582–599. DOI: 10.1007/s40593-016-0110-3

Rose, J. (1998). The Legal Profession in Medieval England: A History of Regulation. *Syracus Law Review*, 48(1). https://papers.ssrn.com/sol3/papers.cfm?abstract_id=1422764

Rose, L., Holmes, W., Griffiths, M., & Forcier, L. B. (2016). Intelligence Unleashed: An Argument for AI in Education. https://oro.open.ac.uk/50104/

Roy, A. K., Singh, P., & Roy, U. N. (2015). Impact of Rural-urban Labour Migration on Education of Children: A Case Study of Left behind and Accompanied Migrant Children in India. *Space and Culture India*, *2*(4), 17–34. DOI: 10.20896/saci.v2i4.74

Rudin, C., Wang, C., & Coker, B. (2018). The age of secrecy and unfairness in recidivism prediction. Harvard Data Science Review. Advance online publication. https://hdsr.mitpress.mit.edu/pub/7z10o269/release/7

Ryan, F., & Hardie, L. (2024). ChatGPT, I have a legal question? The impact of Gen AI tools on law clinics and access to justice. *International Journal of Clinical Legal Education*, *31*(1), 166–205. DOI: 10.19164/ijcle.v31i1.1401

Sadiku, M. N. O., Ajayi, S. A., & Sadiku, J. O. (2025). Artificial Intelligence in Legal Practice: Opportunities, Challenges, and Future Directions. *Journal of Engineering Research and Reports*, *27*(4), 68–80. https://journaljerr.com/index.php/JERR/article/view/1456. DOI: 10.9734/jerr/2025/v27i41456

Saikia, N., Bora, J. K., Jasilionis, D., & Shkolnikov, V. M. (2016). Disability Divides in India: Evidence from the 2011 Census. *PLoS One*, *11*(8), e0159809. DOI: 10.1371/journal.pone.0159809 PMID: 27490469

Sam, R., Lan, B., Keo, V., Kheuy, S., & Em, S. (2025a). Emerging Trends in Educational Leadership Research: A Systematic Literature Review. In Musundire, A. (Ed.), *Research Methods for Educational Leadership and Management* (pp. 31–66). IGI Global Scientific Publishing., DOI: 10.4018/979-8-3693-9425-0.ch002

Sam, R., Li, X., Sok, K., Tieng, M., & Yoeng, H. (2025d). Effective Turnaround Leadership Practices in Cambodia: Perspectives from School Principals. In Liu, P., & Thien, L. M. (Eds.), *Turnaround Leadership in Southeast Asian Countries*. Springer., DOI: 10.1007/978-981-96-7894-5_5

Sam, R., Serey, M., Ry, H., Sarith, C., Tieng, M., & Yoeng, H. (2025c). Academic Accreditation and Evaluation in Cambodian Higher Education Institutions: Development, Challenges, and Opportunities. In Lytras, M., & erban, A. (Eds.), *Academic Accreditation and Evaluation in Higher Education: Practices, Experiences, and Quality Assurance* (pp. 241–262). IGI Global Scientific Publishing., DOI: 10.4018/979-8-3693-5608-1.ch010

Sam, R., Souriyavongsa, T., Md Zain, A. N., Jamil, H., Wu, X., & Sovath, S. (2013). Conceptualizing institutional policies for students' academic success in Cambodian universities: What matters for policy? *Asian Social Science*, *9*(10), 283–293. DOI: 10.5539/ass.v9n10p283

Sam, R., Tieng, M., Yoeng, H., Sarith, C., Serey, M., & Sam, S. (2025b). Enhancing Research for Academicians in Cambodian Higher Education Institutions: A Policy Perspective. In Mdikana, A. (Ed.), *Enhancing Research for Academicians in Higher Education* (pp. 225–248). IGI Global Scientific Publishing., DOI: 10.4018/979-8-3693-4496-5.ch012

Sanmartin, A. V., & Niemi, J. (2023). Virtual reality in legal education. Challenges and possibilities to transform normative knowledge. In *The European Digital Economy* (pp. 120–140). Routledge. DOI: 10.4324/9781003450160-10

Saqr, R., Al-Somali, S., & Sarhan, M. Y. (2023). Exploring the acceptance and user satisfaction of AI-driven e-learning platforms (Blackboard, Moodle, Edmodo, Coursera and edX): An integrated technology model. *Sustainability (Basel)*, *16*(1), 204. DOI: 10.3390/su16010204

Sarker, S. P., & Sharma, P. (2020). Bridging the Gap: Understanding the Trends in Indian Legal Education from Recent Developments. *Asian Journal of Legal Education*, *7*(1), 57–72. DOI: 10.1177/2322005819881100

Saudi Data and AI Authority. (2025). SDAIA. https://sdaia.gov.sa/en/Services/Pages/FreeServicesAndPrograms.aspx

Saudi Press Agency. (2021, Feb 9). Saudi press: HRH Crown Prince announces 4 new laws to reform the Kingdom's judicial institutions. https://www.spa.gov.sa/2187851

Schepard, A. (2022). Family Law with Skills Ten Years Later: Experiential Education in the Introductory Family Law Course. *Family Court Review*, *60*(2), 276–289. DOI: 10.1111/fcre.12678

ScholarEd. (n.d.). *Mock Jury - AI-powered jury simulation*. Retrieved July 12, 2025, from https://www.yeschat.ai/gpts-9t557feQ6Lr-ScholarEd-Mock-Jury

Schukoske, J. E. (2009). Legal Education Reform in India: Dialogue among Indian law teachers. SSRN *Electronic Journal*. DOI: 10.2139/ssrn.1452888

Scott, C. (2012). Collaborating with the real world: Opportunities for developing skills and values in law teaching. *Ind. Health L. Rev.*, *9*(2), 411. DOI: 10.18060/16614

Seabrooke, T., Schneiders, E., Dowthwaite, L., Krook, J., Leesakul, N., Clos, J., Maior, H., & Fischer, J. (2024). A survey of lay people's willingness to generate legal advice using large language models (LLMs). In *Proceedings of the Second International Symposium on Trustworthy Autonomous Systems* (pp. 1–5). Association for Computing Machinery. DOI: 10.1145/3686038.3686043

Sebastian, G. (2023). Privacy and data protection in ChatGPT and other AI chatbots. *International Journal of Security and Privacy in Pervasive Computing, 15*(1), 1–14. DOI: 10.4018/IJSPPC.325475

Secretariat, A. S. E. A. N. (2023, December). Tech for Good Institute; ASEAN Digital Economy Framework Agreement (DEFA) Report. Tech for Good Institute. https://techforgoodinstitute.org/wp-content/uploads/2023/12/TFGI_DEFA-Report.pdf?utm_source=chatgpt.com#page=26.26

Selbst, A. D., Boyd, D., Friedler, S. A., Venkatasubramanian, S., & Vertesi, J. (2019). Fairness and Abstraction in Sociotechnical Systems. *Proceedings of the Conference on Fairness, Accountability, and Transparency*, 59-68. https://dl.acm.org/doi/10.1145/3287560.3287598

Selwyn, N. (2019). Should robots replace teachers? AI and the Future of Education. (1st ed.) Polity Press. https://www.wiley.com/en-gb/Should+Robots+Replace+Teachers%3F%3 A+AI+and +the+Future+of+Education-p-9781509528967

Selwyn, N. (2019). *Should Robots Replace Teachers? AI and the Future of Education*. Polity. Retrieved from https://www.scribd.com/document/808141299/Neil-Selwyn-Should-Robots-Replace-Teachers-AI-and-the-Future-of-Education-2019-convertido-1

Shah, A. (2025, March 8). *Artificial Intelligence In Legal Education And Practice: Global Opportunities, Ethical Dilemmas, And The Path*. IJLLR Journal; IJLLR Journal. https://www.ijllr.com/post/artificial-intelligence-in-legal-education-and-practice-global-opportunities-ethical-dilemmas-and

Shanthi, H. J., Gokulakrishnan, A., Sharma, S., Deepika, R., & Swadhi, R. (2025). Leveraging Artificial Intelligence for Enhancing Urban Health: Applications, Challenges, and Innovations. In Nexus of AI, Climatology, and Urbanism for Smart Cities (pp. 275-306). IGI Global Scientific Publishing.

Sharma, A., Lin, I. W., Miner, A. S., Atkins, D. C., & Althoff, T. (2023). Human–AI collaboration enables more empathic conversations in text-based peer-to-peer mental health support. *Nature Machine Intelligence, 5*(1), 46–57. DOI: 10.1038/s42256-022-00593-2

Sharma, D., & Kumari, S. (2024). Role of Legal Education in Advancement of Access to Justice: A panormic insight. *Asian Journal of Legal Education, 11*(2), 141–149. DOI: 10.1177/23220058241253403

Sharma, S. (2024). Benefits or Concerns of AI: A Multistakeholder Responsibility. *Futures, 157*(103328), 103328. DOI: 10.1016/j.futures.2024.103328

Sheldon, K. M., & Krieger, L. S. (2004). Does Legal Education Have Undermining Effects on Law Students? Evaluating Changes in Motivation, Values, and Well-being. *Behavioral Sciences & the Law, 22*(2), 261–286. https://onlinelibrary.wiley.com/doi/epdf/10.1002/bsl.582. DOI: 10.1002/bsl.582 PMID: 15048864

Shi, S. J., Li, J. W., & Zhang, R. (2023). A Study of the Impact of Generative Artificial Intelligence-Supported Situational Interactive Teaching on Students' 'Flow' Experience and Learning Effectiveness — A Case Study of Legal Education in China. *Asia Pacific Journal of Education, 44*(1), 112–138. https://www.tandfonline.com/doi/full/10.1080/02188791.2024.2305161. DOI: 10.1080/02188791.2024.2305161

Shi, S., Zhao, E., Tang, D., Wang, Y., Li, P., Bi, W., & Ma, D. (2022). Effidit: Your AI writing assistant *[Technical report]*. arXiv. https://arxiv.org/abs/2208.01815

Shugan, S. M. (2006). Editorial: Save Research: Abandon the Case Method of Teaching. *Marketing Science, 25*(2), 109–115. https://www.jstor.org/stable/40056994. DOI: 10.1287/mksc.1060.0202

Shukla, S. (2024). Principles Governing Ethical Development and Deployment of AI. *International Journal of Engineering Business Management, 8*(2), 26–46. DOI: 10.22161/ijebm.8.2.5

Silviu, G. A. (2025). The Use of Artificial Intelligence in Industrial Management. In Rackov, M., Miltenović, A., & Banić, M. (Eds.), *Machine and Industrial Design in Mechanical Engineering. KOD 2024. Mechanisms and Machine Science* (Vol. 174). Springer., DOI: 10.1007/978-3-031-80512-7_80

Simon, J., Wong, P.-H., & Rieder, G. (2020). Algorithmic bias and the Value Sensitive Design approach. *Internet Policy Review, 9*(4). Advance online publication. DOI: 10.14763/2020.4.1534

Singal, N. (2006). Inclusive Education in India: International concept, national interpretation. *International Journal of Disability Development and Education, 53*(3), 351–369. DOI: 10.1080/10349120600847797

Sinha, S. (2013). Child labour and education. *Indian Journal of Human Development, 7*(2), 377–379. DOI: 10.1177/0973703020130224

Sisinternational. (2025, August 27). Secondary desk research. https://www.sisinternational.com/solutions/qualitative-quantitative-research-solutions/desk-research/

Skinner, B. F. (1974). *About behaviorism*. Knopf.

Socratic Mind. (n.d.). *Socratic Mind: AI-powered oral assessment platform*. https://socraticmind.com/

Sok, S., Heng, K., & Pum, M. (2025). Investigating High School Students' Attitudes Toward the Use of AI in Education: Evidence from Cambodia. *SAGE Open*, *15*(3), 21582440251353575. Advance online publication. DOI: 10.1177/21582440251353575

Solanki, S. C. (2021). Artificial Intelligence and Legal Profession. *International Journal of Law*, *7*(5), 173–175. https://www.lawjournals.org/assets/archives/2021/vol7issue5/7-5-45-715.pdf

Sossin, L. (2014). Experience the Future of Legal Education. *Alberta Law Review*, *41*(2), 466–498.

Souali, K., Rahmaoui, O., Ouzzif, M., & El Haddioui, I. (2019). Recommending Moodle resources using chatbots. *15th International Conference on Signal-Image Technology & Internet-Based Systems (SITIS)*.

Spencer, R. (2022). "Hell is other people": Rethinking the Socratic method for quiet law students. *The Law Teacher*, *56*(1), 90–104. DOI: 10.1080/03069400.2021.2005305

Srivastava, P. (2010). Public–private partnerships or privatisation? Questioning the state's role in education in India. *Development in Practice*, *20*(4–5), 540–553. DOI: 10.1080/09614521003763079

Stagg-Taylor, J. (2011). Lawyers' Business: Conflicts of Duties Arising from Lawyers' Business Models. *Legal Ethics (Oxford, England)*, *14*(2), 173–192. https://philpapers.org/rec/STALBC. DOI: 10.5235/146072811798828558

Stanford Open Virtual Assistant Lab. (n.d.). *STORM (Synthesis of Topic Outlines through Retrieval and Multi-Perspective Question Asking)* [AI writing research preview]. Stanford University. Retrieved July 14, 2025, from https://storm.genie.stanford.edu/

Stoddard, H. A., & O'Dell, D. V. (2016). Would Socrates Have Actually Used the "Socratic Method" for Clinical Teaching? *Journal of General Internal Medicine*, *31*(9), 1092–1096. DOI: 10.1007/s11606-016-3722-2 PMID: 27130623

Stratton, G., Moffa, M., Sigamoney, A., & Ruyters, M. (2023). Innocence projects, work-integrated learning, and student career pathways. *Journal of Criminal Justice Education, 35*(3), 1–17. DOI: 10.1080/10511253.2023.2231050

Stuckey, R.. (2007). *Best Practices for Legal Education: A Vision and a Road Map*. Clinical Legal Education Association.

Suffolk University Law School. (2025). *Dispute resolution.* https://www.suffolk.edu/law/academics-clinics/what-can-i-study/dispute-resolution

Sujatha, R., Aarthy, S. L., & Vettriselvan, R. (2021). *Integrating Deep Learning Algorithms to Overcome Challenges in Big Data Analytics*. CRC Press. DOI: 10.1201/9781003038450

Sullivan, W. M., Colby, A., Wegner, J. W., Bond, L., & Shulman, L. S. (2007). *Educating lawyers: Preparation for the profession of law* (The Carnegie Foundation report). Jossey-Bass. Retrieved from_http://archive.carnegiefoundation.org/publications/pdfs/elibrary/elibrary_pdf_632.pdf

Sullivan, M., Kelly, A., & McLaughlan, P. (2022). ChatGPT in higher education: Considerations for academic integrity and student learning. *Journal of Applied Learning & Teaching*, *6*(1), 12–25. DOI: 10.37074/jalt.2023.6.1.17

Sullivan, W. M., Colby, A., Wegner, J. W., Bond, L., & Shulman, L. S. (2007). *Educating lawyers: Preparation for the profession of law* (Vol. 2). John Wiley & Sons.

Supreme Court of India. (1978). *Maneka Gandhi v. Union of India*, AIR 1978 SC 597.

Supreme Court of India. *Centre for Research and Planning. (n.d.). Publications.* https://www.sci.gov.in/centre-for-research-and-planning/#Publications

Surden, H. (2019). Artificial intelligence and law: An overview. Georgia State University Law Review, 35(4), 1305–1345. https://readingroom.law.gsu.edu/gsulr/vol35/iss4/8/?utm_ source=chatgpt.com

Surden, H. (2019). Artificial intelligence and law: An overview. *Georgia State University Law Review*, *35*(4), 1305–1338.

Susskind, R. (2010). *The end of lawyers? Rethinking the nature of legal services.* Oxford University Press.

Susskind, R. (2019). *Online Courts and the Future of Justice.* Oxford University Press. DOI: 10.1093/oso/9780198838364.001.0001

Susskind, R. (2023). *Tomorrow's lawyers: An introduction to your future* (3rd ed.). Oxford University Press., https://global.oup.com/academic/product/tomorrows-lawyers-9780192864727?utm_source=chatgpt.com DOI: 10.1093/9780192864727.001.0001

Susskind, R. E., & Susskind, D. (2015). *The Future of the Professions: How Technology Will Transform the Work of Human Experts*. Oxford University Press. DOI: 10.1093/oso/9780198713395.001.0001

Sweller, J. (1988). Cognitive load during problem solving: Effects on learning. *Cognitive Science*, *12*(2), 257–285. https://onlinelibrary.wiley.com/doi/epdf/10.1207/s15516709cog1202_4. DOI: 10.1207/s15516709cog1202_4

Tahiru, F. (2020). AI in Education. *Journal of Cases on Information Technology*, *23*(1), 1–20. DOI: 10.4018/JCIT.2021010101

Tang, K. H. D. (2024). Implications of Artificial Intelligence for Teaching and Learning. *Acta Pedagogia Asiana*, *3*(2), 65–79. DOI: 10.53623/apga.v3i2.404

Tan, J., Westermann, H., & Benyekhlef, K. (2023). ChatGPT as an artificial lawyer? In *Proceedings of the Workshop on Artificial Intelligence for Access to Justice*. CEUR.

Tayal, R., Upadhyay, R. K., Yadav, M., & Singh, R. (2021). The development and validation of the organizational effectiveness scale using confirmatory factor analysis. *Global Business Review*, *22*(3), 821–843. DOI: 10.1177/0972150918811720

Tewathia, N., Kamath, A., & Ilavarasan, P. V. (2020). Social inequalities, fundamental inequities, and recurring of the digital divide: Insights from India. *Technology in Society*, *61*, 101251. DOI: 10.1016/j.techsoc.2020.101251

Thanaraj, A., De Freitas, S., Chaplin, D., Gledhill, K., Unger, A., & Kennedy, R. (2022). Introduction: Exploring becoming future ready. In Teaching Legal Education in the Digital Age (pp. 1-15). Routledge.

The Executive Regulations of the Law of Civil Proceedings, Minister of Justice Decision No. 39933 (2014).

The National Artificial Intelligence Initiative Act of 2020. https://aip.brightspotcdn.com/37/63/f3a3682c6afce34c0d28f3d8e37e/national-ai-initiative-act-final.pdf

Thomas, P., Dzemidzic Kristiansen, S., & Von Hof, J. (2025). The Network Society: A Double-Edged Sword. In *Education and Cultural Evolution in Norway's Multiethnic Society* (pp. 119–130). Springer Nature Switzerland. DOI: 10.1007/978-3-031-89018-5_12

Thomas, C., McElhattan, L., & Carlo, S. (2023). Legal literacy and generative artificial intelligence: Comparing the education law knowledge of practicing educators and large language models like ChatGPT. *Education Law Reporter*, *414*, 783–798. DOI: 10/2139/ssrn.4967373

Thornton, M. (2001). *Privatising the public university: The case of law*. Routledge.

Tilak, J. B. G. (2018). Private higher education in India. In *Springer eBooks* (pp. 535–551). DOI: 10.1007/978-981-13-0250-3_18

Tlili, A., Huang, R., Shehata, B., Liu, D., Zhao, J., Metwally, A. H. S., Wang, H., Denden, M., Bozkurt, A., Lee, L., Beyoglu, D., Altinay, F., Sharma, R. C., Altinay, Z., Li, Z., Liu, J., Ahmad, F., Hu, Y., Salha, S., & Burgos, D. (2022). Is Metaverse in education a blessing or a curse: A combined content and bibliometric analysis. *Smart Learning Environments*, *9*(1), 24. Advance online publication. DOI: 10.1186/s40561-022-00205-x

Trani, J., & Loeb, M. (2010). Poverty and disability: A vicious circle? Evidence from Afghanistan and Zambia. *Journal of International Development*, *24*(S1). Advance online publication. DOI: 10.1002/jid.1709

Tripathy, B., Singha, K. M. K., & Dubey, L. K. (2025). *Indian Education Policy: with special reference to past & present*. SGSH Publications.

Trivedi, S. K., Vishnu, S., Singh, A., & Yadav, M. (2023). Research trends in sustainable E-payment systems: A study using topic modeling approach. *IEEE Transactions on Engineering Management*, *71*, 7511–7525. DOI: 10.1109/TEM.2023.3280216

Trivedi, V., Banerji, D., & Yadav, M. (2023). Expecting the surprises: Role of hope in consumer repurchase intentions in an online shopping environment. *Journal of Strategic Marketing*, *31*(4), 794–816. DOI: 10.1080/0965254X.2021.1996449

Tsaoussi, A. (2020). Using Soft Skills Courses to Inspire Law Teachers: A New Methodology for a More Humanistic Legal Education. *The Law Teacher*, *54*(1), 1–30. DOI: 10.1080/03069400.2018.1563396

Twining, W. (1994). *Blackstone's tower: The English law school* (Hamlyn Lectures No. 46). Stevens & Sons. Retrieved from_https://karnatakajudiciary.kar.nic.in/hcklibrary/pdf/HamylanLectures/46%20Blackstone's_Tower.pdf

Ubanyionwu, J. (2024). Ethical and cultural considerations in artificial intelligence (AI) application to customary law. *African Journal of Law. Ethics and Education*, *7*(2), 142–159.

Ueda, H., Furukawa, M., Yamaji, K., & Nakamura, M. (2018). SCORMAdaptiveQuiz: Implementation of adaptive e-learning for Moodle. *Procedia Computer Science, 126*, 2261–2270. DOI: 10.1016/j.procs.2018.07.223

UNESCO. (2021). *AI and education: Guidance for policy-makers*. UNESCO Publishing., DOI: 10.54675/PCSP7350

UNESCO. (2021). *Recommendation on the ethics of artificial intelligence*. https://www.unesco.org/en/artificial-intelligence/recommendation-ethics

UNESCO. (2023). *AI and the right to education: Global perspectives on challenges and opportunities*. https://unesdoc.unesco.org

UNESCO. (2024, September 3). *What you need to know about UNESCO's new AI competency frameworks for students and teachers*. Retrieved July 12, 2025, from https://www.unesco.org/en/articles/what-you-need-know-about-unescos-new-ai-competency-frameworks-students-and-teachers

UNESCO. (2025a). Artificial intelligence readiness assessment: Cambodia. United Nations Educational, Scientific and Cultural Organization. https://www.unesco.org/en/articles/cambodia-artificial-intelligence-readiness-assessment-report

UNESCO. (2025b, July 29). UNESCO's AI and the rule of law toolkit transforming legal education. https://www.unesco.org/en/articles/unescos-ai-and-rule-law-toolkit-transforming-legal-education

University of California. Berkeley, School of Law. (n.d.). *Samuelson Law, Technology & Public Policy Clinic*. https://www.law.berkeley.edu/experiential/clinics/samuelson-law-technology-public-policy-clinic/

University of Oklahoma. (2025, February 13). OU Law Launches AI QuizBot to Improve Student Engagement, Outcomes. Retrieved from The University of Oklahoma College of Law: https://law.ou.edu/about/news/ou-law-launches-ai-quizbot-improve-student-engagement-outcomes#:~:text=has%20launched%20a%20ChatGPT,in%20a%20modern%2C%20interactive%20way

Varghese, N., & Panigrahi, J. (2022). *India Higher Education Report 2021: Private Higher Education*. Taylor & Francis. DOI: 10.4324/9781003298724

Veasey, E. N. (2002). Ethics 2000 Chair's Introduction. *ABA*. https://www.americanbar.org/groups/professional_responsibility/publications/model_rules_of_professional_conduct/model_rules_of_professional_conduct_preface/ethics_2000_chair_introduction/

Venice, J. A., Arivazhagan, D., Suman, N., Shanthi, H. J., & Swadhi, R. (2025). Recommendation Systems and Content Personalization: Algorithms, Applications, and Adaptive Learning. In AI for Large Scale Communication Networks (pp. 323-348). IGI Global.

Venkatesh, V., Morris, M. G., Davis, G. B., & Davis, F. D. (2003). User acceptance of information technology: Toward a unified view. *Management Information Systems Quarterly*, *27*(3), 425–478. DOI: 10.2307/30036540

Vettriselvan, R., Deepan, A., Garg, P. K., Suresh, N. V., & Velmurugan, P. R. (2025). Advanced Text Analysis, Simplification, Classification, and Synthesis Techniques: Leveraging AI for Enhanced Medical Education. In Using AI Tools in Text Analysis, Simplification, Classification, and Synthesis (pp. 37-66). IGI Global Scientific Publishing.

Vlachopoulos, D., & Makri, A. (2017). The effect of games and simulations on higher education: A systematic literature review. *International Journal of Educational Technology in Higher Education*, *14*(1), 1–33. DOI: 10.1186/s41239-017-0062-1

Voskobitova, E. (2021). Online Simulations for Teaching Professional Legal Skills. *Kutafin Law Review*, *2021*(2), 36–56. DOI: 10.17803/2313-5395.2021.4.18.519-545

Vučić, F. (2023). Changes in Legal Education in the Digital Society of Artificial Intelligence. In Vasić, D., & Vasić, M. K. (Eds.), *Digital Transformation in Education and Artificial Intelligence Application* (pp. 159–176). Springer., https://link.springer.com/chapter/10.1007/978-3-031-36833-2_12

Vygotsky, L. S. (1978). *Mind in Society: The Development of Higher Psychological Processes*. Harvard University Press. Retrieved from https://home.fau.edu/musgrove/web/vygotsky1978.pdf

Wang, J., & Fan, W. (2025). The effect of ChatGPT on students' learning performance, learning perception, and higher-order thinking: Insights from a meta-analysis. *Humanities & Social Sciences Communications*, *12*(1), 1–21. DOI: 10.1057/s41599-025-04787-y

Wankhede, G. (2008). Accessing higher education: Affirmative action and structured inequality – The Indian experience. *Social Change*, *38*(1), 31–51. DOI: 10.1177/004908570803800102

Waters, A. (2016). A Part to Play: The Value of Role-Play Simulation in Undergraduate Legal Education. *The Law Teacher*, *50*(2), 148–166. DOI: 10.1080/03069400.2016.1162404

Watson, D., & Taylor, D. (1998). *Lifelong Learning and the University: A Post-Dearing Agenda*. Falmer.

Weber-Lewerenz, B. (2021). Corporate digital responsibility (CDR) in construction engineering ethical guidelines for the application of digital transformation and artificial intelligence (AI) in user practice. *SN Applied Sciences*, *3*(10), 1–25. DOI: 10.1007/s42452-021-04776-1

Weinberg, J., & Hyams, R. (2023). *The Law Tech Clinic: Leading the way in entrepreneurial law clinics* (Special Edition). International Journal of Clinical Legal Education., DOI: 10.19164/ijcle.2023.1349

WhatWorked Education. (2023). Bodyswaps public speaking pilot: RCT final report. https://bodyswaps.co/resources/research

Williams, A. (2018). Academic ableism: Disability and higher education. *Disability & Society*, *33*(4), 651–653. DOI: 10.1080/09687599.2018.1438052

Williamson, B., & Eynon, R. (2020). Historical threads, missing links, and future directions in AI in education. *Learning, Media and Technology*, *45*(3), 223–235. DOI: 10.1080/17439884.2020.1798995

Wilton, L., Ip, S., Sharma, M., & Fan, F. (2022). Where Is the AI? AI Literacy for Educators. In: Rodrigo, M.M., Matsuda, N., Cristea, A.I., Dimitrova, V. (eds) *Artificial Intelligence in Education. Posters and Late Breaking Results, Workshops and Tutorials, Industry and Innovation Tracks, Practitioners' and Doctoral Consortium.* AIED 2022. Lecture Notes in Computer Science, vol 13356. Springer, Cham. https://doi.org/DOI: 10.1007/978-3-031-11647-6_31

Wintersteiger, L. (2020) Pedagogies of justice: critical approaches to public legal education. [Thesis] (Unpublished)

Wirtz, B. W., Weyerer, J. C., & Geyer, C. (2018). Artificial Intelligence and the Public Sector — Applications and Challenges. *International Journal of Public Administration*, *42*(7), 596–615. DOI: 10.1080/01900692.2018.1498103

Wischmeyer, T., & Rademacher, T. (Eds.). (2020). *Regulating artificial intelligence*. Springer., DOI: 10.1007/978-3-030-32361-5

Wood, D., Bruner, J. S., & Ross, G. (1976). The role of tutoring in problem solving. *Journal of Child Psychology and Psychiatry, and Allied Disciplines*, *17*(2), 89–100. https://acamh.onlinelibrary.wiley.com/doi/10.1111/j.1469-7610.1976.tb00381.x. DOI: 10.1111/j.1469-7610.1976.tb00381.x PMID: 932126

World Bank. (2022). *Digital divide in education: Policy recommendations for inclusive AI.* https://worldbank.org/education/ai-divide

WOWLabz. (2023, August 28). *How AI is transforming legal research.* Retrieved from https://wowlabz.com/ai-for-legal-research

Wu, D., Li, H., & Chen, X. (2023). Analysis on the Influence of General Large Model of Artificial Intelligence on Education Application. *Open Education Research*, *2*, 19–25.

Yadav, M., Singh, S. K., Sharma, P., & Hung, T. H. (2024). AI and Lifelong Learning in Developing Countries. In *Advances in educational technologies and instructional design book series* (pp. 49–72). DOI: 10.4018/979-8-3693-0884-4.ch003

Yadav, M., & Rangnekar, S. (2016). Role clarity and organizational citizenship behaviour: Does tenure matter? A study on Indian power sector. *Global Business Review*, *17*(3, suppl), 207S–224S. DOI: 10.1177/0972150916631216

Yadav, M., Rangnekar, S., & Srivastava, A. P. (2019). Demographic variables as moderators between QWL and OCB. *Industrial and Commercial Training*, *51*(7/8), 396–408. DOI: 10.1108/ICT-04-2018-0040

Yamane, N. (2020). Artificial Intelligence in the Legal Field and the Indispensable Human Element: Legal Ethics Demands. *The Georgetown Journal of Legal Ethics*, *33*, 877–890. https://www.law.georgetown.edu/legal-ethics-journal/wp-content/uploads/sites/24/2020/09/GT-GJLE200038.pdf

Yang, M. (2025, May 31). US lawyer sanctioned after being caught using ChatGPT for court brief. The Guardian. Retrieved from https://www.theguardian.com/us-news/2025/may/31/utah-lawyer-chatgpt-ai-court-brief

Yenugu, S. (2022). The new National Education Policy (NEP) of India: Will it be a paradigm shift in Indian higher education? *Perspectives*, *26*(4), 121–129. DOI: 10.1080/13603108.2022.2078901

Yoon, A. H. (2016). The Post-Modern Lawyer: Technology and the Democratization of Legal Representation. *University of Toronto Law Journal*, *66*(4), 456–471. https://utppublishing.com/doi/10.3138/UTLJ.4007. DOI: 10.3138/UTLJ.4007

Zafar, A. (2024). Balancing the scale: Navigating ethical and practical challenges of artificial intelligence (AI) integration in legal practices. *Discover Artificial Intelligence*, *4*(1), 27. DOI: 10.1007/s44163-024-00121-8

Zaid, T., & Garai, S. (2024). Emerging Trends in Cybersecurity: A Holistic View on Current Threats, Assessing Solutions, and Pioneering New Frontiers. *Blockchain in Healthcare Today*, *7*(1). Advance online publication. DOI: 10.30953/bhty.v7.302 PMID: 38715765

Zawacki-Richter, O., Marín, V. I., Bond, M., & Gouverneur, F. (2019). Systematic review of research on artificial intelligence applications in higher education – Where are the educators? *International Journal of Educational Technology in Higher Education*, *16*(1), 1–27. DOI: 10.1186/s41239-019-0171-0

Zedan, A. (1993). *Almufassal fi Ahkam Al imra'a wa Albait Almuslim* [Provisions of women and the Muslim home]. Moasasat Alrisalah.

Zhai, C., Wibowo, S. W., & Li, L. D. (2024). The effects of over reliance on AI dialogue systems on students' cognitive abilities: A systematic review. *Smart Learning Environments*, *11*(1), 28. DOI: 10.1186/s40561-024-00316-7

About the Contributors

Rany Sam has been a dedicated civil servant with the Cambodian Ministry of Education, Youth, and Sport since 2007. Since 2017, he has served as the Vice-Rector of the National University of Battambang (NUBB), a prominent public university in northwest Cambodia. In this capacity, he oversees the Graduate School, Faculty of Arts, Humanities, and Education, the Institute of Foreign Languages, and the Confucius Institute. Previously, he served as Director of the Institute of Foreign Languages from 2010 to 2017. He has served as the Director of the Confucius Institute at NUBB in Cambodia since 2019. Dr. Sam is an active member of several academic organizations, including the Southeast Asia Research Academy (SEARA), the Society of Transnational Academic Researchers (STAR) as a country director, and Responsible Borneo (REBORN). He earned his PhD in Education from the School of Educational Studies at the University of Science Malaysia in 2016. Additionally, he completed diplomas in public administration, leadership, and innovation programs at the Royal School of Administration in Cambodia in 2017 and 2022. He holds a Bachelor's and Master's degree in Law (LL.B. and LL.M.) from the Royal University of Law and Economics, completed in 2004 and 2007, respectively. Dr. Sam has authored approximately 100 academic papers and book chapters. He serves as project coordinator for multiple initiatives, including Erasmus+ Capacity Building in Higher Education, Korean ODA, USAID, and the World Bank-funded Higher Education Improvement Project (HEIP). His editorial roles include associate editor of Frontiers in Education (Higher Education) and Frontiers in Political Science, as well as editor for IGI Global book chapters. He has peer-reviewed over 100 manuscripts and book chapters published by leading academic publishers, including Springer Nature, Sage, Taylor & Francis, and Routledge. His research interests encompass legal studies, public policy and administration, educational history and cooperation, educational leadership and management, as well as various social research areas.

***

Loujayn Alhokail is an Assistant Professor at the College of Law and Political Science at King Saud University in Riyadh, Saudi Arabia. She earned her bachelor's degree in law from King Saud University in 2009, followed by an LL.M. from the Schulich School of Law at Dalhousie University, Canada, in 2014. She then completed her Ph.D. in Law at Osgoode Hall Law School, York University, Toronto, Canada, in 2021. Alongside her academic role, Dr. Alhokail has served as a consultant for a range of prominent organizations, including the King Salman Humanitarian Aid and Relief Center, the Family Affairs Council, and the National Observatory for Women.

Tawney Bennett is a Lecturer in Law at the Truman Bodden Law School where she delivers the University of Liverpool's LL.B degree and serves as a civil servant within the Cayman Islands Government. She holds an LL.B, a Master's degree in Education, and is a Senior Fellow of the Higher Education Academy. With a passion for teaching, Tawney has experience across undergraduate, postgraduate, and work-based learning programs, specializing in Criminal Law and Criminal Justice. Beyond Crime and Justice, Tawney's research focuses on the integration of technology in legal education, with a particular interest in artificial intelligence and experiential learning methodologies.

VichekaChhoeurm is a dedicated academic and administrative practitioner from Battambang, Cambodia. He is presently an Administrative Staff and Vice-Rector Assistant in the Office of Administration and Finance at the National University of Battambang (NUBB), where he is also a contract teacher in Business Management and Marketing. His commitment to higher education is also attested to by his involvement in numerous national and international projects, including Reco-ASIA, Digi-CHE-Asia, and the Higher Education Improvement Project (HEIP), as well as projects supporting the Sustainable Development Goals in Journalism Reporting (SDGsJR). Mr. Chhoeurm Vicheka holds Bachelor's and Master's degrees in Business Management from NUBB. His research interests include entrepreneurship and small business success, and he has publications on SME growth and critical success factors in Battambang City. He is well known for his good service and professionalism and has been awarded several certificates of appreciation by H.E. Dr. Hang Chuon Naron and H.E. Sok Khorn for his contribution to education development. Beyond the academic community, Mr. Chhoeurm Vicheka is a firm believer in lifelong learning, collaboration, and self-improvement. He has a mix of high analytical ability, creativity, and commitment to the growth of Cambodia's higher education sector.

Hrucha Dhamdhere is a legal academic and qualified Company Secretary with a multidisciplinary background in commerce, law, regulatory compliance and governance. She holds an LL.B. from ILS Law College, Pune, a Master of Business Laws (MBL) from NLSIU Bangalore, and is currently pursuing an LL.M. in Intellectual Property Rights at Bharati Vidyapeeth Deemed University's New Law College, Pune. She is a certified Arbitrator (D.Arb – ICSI), a registered Social Auditor (ICSI-ISA), and a certified POSH (Prevention of Sexual Harassment) Trainer. She also serves as the Student Representative on the Internal Complaints Committee (ICC) under POSH at BVDU's New Law College, contributing to institutional compliance and gender justice initiatives. Hrucha brings professional experience across corporate law, compliance, and regulatory research. She has worked with law firms and legal research organizations on assignments including legal reporting, contract drafting, due diligence, litigation support, and corporate advisory. Her work reflects a blend of legal precision and practical insight, and she continues to engage in POSH consulting, training and academic roles. Her teaching and research interests span legal theory, jurisprudence, corporate and commercial laws, compliance frameworks, intellectual property rights, and the intersection of law, culture, and tradition. Her scholarly contribution includes co-authored a monograph titled "Jewish Customary Law Affecting Family Relations: An Indian Perspective" published by ILS Law College [ISBN-978-81-942114-0-2], which explores the personal laws of the Bene-Israeli community, a smaller sect of the larger Jewish diaspora in India. A Visiting Faculty at ILS Law College, Pune, for over three years, Hrucha actively contributes to classroom teaching, curriculum design, student mentoring, and co-curricular initiatives. She is deeply passionate about legal education and strives to make the study of law accessible, engaging, and enriching. Her student-focused approach simplifies complex legal concepts through clarity, interaction, and real-world relevance. With a strong research orientation, she seeks to bridge theory and practice, using legal scholarship to inform policy and social impact.

RyHour is currently Dean of Faculty of Business Administration and Tourism at the National University of Battambang, Cambodia.

Vasiliki Ioannidi (Ph.D./Dr.phil.). PhD in Pedagogy, specialization: "Special Education". Post Doc in Inclusive Education. CPD in Educational Sciences & Digital Education. Adjunct Faculty Member, Hellenic Open University, Greece. Adjunct Faculty Member, Open University of Cyprus, Cyprus. Researcher Fellow, National and Kapodistrian University of Athens, Greece.

Jimmy Jose is serving as an Assistant Professor at Symbiosis Law School, Nagpur, a constituent of Symbiosis International (Deemed University), Pune, India. He has an experience of more than 7 years in academic teaching and research. He has completed his B.Sc. (H) Mathematics and LL.B. from University of Delhi and LL.M. in Access to Justice from School of Law, Rights and Constitutional Governance, Tata Institute of Social Sciences, Mumbai. He is keen in exploring the human rights dimensions and investigating rule of law in the other branches of legal studies.

Jipson Joseph has a PhD in Ethics from DVK Bangalore. Currently, he is a Research Scholar at School of Law, Christ University, Bangalore, India. His research interests are in the fields of ethics, gender studies, constitutional law, human rights, human security, environmental justice, SDGs, developmental policies, and global poverty. He has published 6 books, co-edited one book, and contributed scholarly articles to many international and national journals and edited volumes including IGI Global Scientific Publishing's edited books.

SelviK. serves as Associate Professor in MBA Department at Saveetha Engineering College, bringing 24 years of academic excellence to her role. With a Ph.D. in Finance from Sri Venkateswara University and multiple master's degrees including MBA (Gold Medalist), M.Com, M.Phil, and M.F.M, she has established herself as a distinguished educator and researcher. Dr. Selvi is a recognized research supervisor under University of Madras with 3 completed Ph.D. scholars and one in progress. Her research portfolio includes 70 publications in reputed journals, including 12 Scopus-indexed papers focusing on finance, management, and AI applications. Dr. Selvi has secured 5 patents, authored 3 books, and received numerous awards including "Senior Woman Educator and Scholar Award" and "Best Professor Award - Pride of Education" (2024). As NBA Coordinator, she successfully led the MBA program to achieve 3-year accreditation (2024-2027) while also serving as Chairperson for the Women Empowerment Cell, Served as Director for Business Incubation Centre.

Sovann Ly is a PhD student at the National Institute of Education, Cambodia. He currently is deputy director of the Institute of Foreign Languages at the National University of Battambang, Cambodia.

Deepa Manokaran with over 10 years of experience in education and industry, possess a strong foundation in research and analysis, complemented by expertise in statistical tools such as SPSS, LISREL, and SmartPLS. Her research has been published in top-tier journals, including Scopus-indexed publications in Inderscience. She have also coordinated several international conferences and published research papers in numerous national and international conferences, contributing to academic discourse and knowledge sharing.

Ali Najeeb is the Vice Rector and Chief Operating Officer (COO) of Villa College (VC), Maldives and CEO of Bristol Institute of Business Management (BIBM), Sri-Lanka. He is also an Adjunct Associate Professor at the School of Hospitality, Tourism and Events, Taylor's University, Malaysia. He holds a PhD in Management and HR strategy at the University of Wollongong, Australia, a Master's Degree in Human Resource Management at the University of Newcastle, Australia, and BA in Business Studies from the University of the South Pacific, Fiji. He is a Chartered Professional Member of Chartered Institute of Personnel and Development (CIPD) and a Certified Professional Member of Australian Human Resource Institute (AHRI). Besides his official roles, he also holds several advisory roles and membership in local and international NGOs and professional bodies. His research interests include higher education and leadership, governance and management, industrial relations, employment law and labour issues in small island states, migrant workers, HRM/ER in tourism and hospitality industry, AI in higher education and sustainability. He has published several research papers in refereed international journals, shared his experience in local and international panel discussions and presented his research work in international scholarly conferences. He is a recipient of the Emerald Literati Award for Excellence 2014 – the outstanding paper award.

VoithnaNhean has joined National University of Battambang (NUBB), which is a public university located in Northwest Cambodia, since 2008. Currently, he is the Director of the Institute of Foreign Languages of NUBB. In 2020 he completed his Master's Degree in the field of International Relations from Ritsumeikan University in Kyoto, Japan. In late 2015, he received Graduate Certificate in TESOL and Foreign Language Teaching from University of Canberra in Australia. in 2008, he finished Master of Business Administration from National University of Management (NUM) in Cambodia. He also completed Bachelor of Education in English in 2005 from Institute of Foreign Languages of Royal University of Phnom Penh and Bachelor of Economics in 2002 from Royal University of Law Economics in Cambodia.

Sinath No currently serves as the Head of the Civil Engineering Department in the Faculty of Science and Technology, (NUBB). Prior to higher education, completed an Intensive English Academic Purpose program at the Pannasastra Institute of Foreign Languages in Cambodia (2005-2006), which prepared for international academic pursuits. Have begun higher education journey in Russia, where earned a Bachelor of Technics and Technology in the field of Construction from Voronezh State University of Architecture and Civil Engineering in 2010. Following bachelor's degree, pursued a graduate master's degree in Civil and Industrial Engineering, specializing in “Effective and Economy Composite Structures” at the same university, which completed in late 2012.In 2018, has successfully defended Professional Engineer certification (No. 0005343PE/Bldg.) and was honored with the title and decoration of Gold Medal by the Asian Engineering Register (AER). The professional excellence was further recognized in 2019 when was conferred the honorary title of a member of the Asian Federation of Engineering Organizations. In the journey of civil engineering is marked by continuously pursuit of knowledge and professional growth has received a certificate of design from the Ministry of Land Management, Urban Planning, and Construction in Cambodia, underscoring of expertise in engineering design. With a career spanning over a decade, continues to inspire future engineers and contribute to the development of sustainable and effective construction practices in Cambodia through role at NUBB. This expertise, coupled with commitment to education and professional development, makes a prominent figure in the field of civil engineering in Cambodia. Tel: (+855) 12543334 E-Mail: no.sinath@nubb.edu.kh

Pich Mina is a passionate Cambodian educator and lifelong learner from Battambang Province. He holds a master’s degree in TESOL (2017–2019) and a bachelor’s degree in English from the University of Battambang, where he studied on scholarship. His academic excellence earned him several honors, including the “Merit Certificate of Outstanding Student” and first prize in the university’s Writing Contest. Mina has extensive experience in education and administration. He has served as a professor at NUBB, an English teacher at the Modern Communication School, and an administrative assistant at the National University of Battambang’s Institute of Foreign Languages and Faculty of Business Administration beyond teaching. Mina, who holds multiple professional training certificates in teaching, facilitation, and communication, is committed to promoting critical thinking and personal development. He is also an entrepreneur, owning a Khmer noodle shop in Battambang. His interests include reading, writing, and exploring new ideas that promote education and development in his community.

DivyaranjaniR. is currently working as Assistant Professor (SG) in Department of Management Studies, Saveetha Engineering College. I have 15 years of teaching experience. I hold my bachelor degree in Electronics and Communication Engineering and MBA with specialization of Human Resources Management and Doctoral Degree in Human Resources Management in AMET University. I had presented more than 15 papers in International and National Conference and has published more than 56 research articles in SCOPUS indexed Journals and other reputed International Journals. I was working member in AMET International Journal of Management (AIJM) and also reviewer in many International Journals.

Vettriselvan R., an Associate Professor, AMET University, specialized in HRM and Marketing. He is acting as Mentor, Saraswathi Institute of Medical Sciences, Hapur. He served as Review Board member, National Council for Higher Education, Malawi, Head of the Department, School of Commerce and Management Studies, St. Eugene University, Zambia, and Director, Research and Publication, St. John the Baptist University, Malawi. He has published 28 books and 86 articles in peer reviewed journals and edited book chapters. Under his guidance two have completed and five are pursuing their PhD.

Mohammad Saleem is currently serving as an Assistant Professor at the Faculty of Law, Marwadi University, Rajkot, Gujarat. He is pursuing his Ph.D. in Law from the Vellore Institute of Technology School of Law (VITSOL), Chennai, Tamil Nadu, and also holds a Post-Graduate Diploma in Cyber Laws from Bhartiya Vidyapeeth, Pune. Prior to joining Marwadi University, he worked as an Assistant Professor at the Faculty of Law, SRM University, Delhi-NCR, and also taught at the Aligarh Muslim University Centre, Murshidabad, West Bengal. An active scholar, he has authored the book Words of Hate: A Statutory Analysis of Hate Speech in India and has presented numerous research papers at national and international conferences and seminars. His works have been published in reputed national and international journals on diverse areas of law. His academic interests primarily lie in Constitutional Law, Comparative Constitutional Law, Human Rights, Civil Liberties, Legal Philosophy, and Legal Reforms, through which he seeks to contribute to the empowerment of marginalized and underprivileged sections of society. His research areas span a wide spectrum, including rights related to women and children, freedom of speech and expression, preventive detention laws, election laws, democracy, and contemporary political developments at both national and international levels.

Karun Sanjaya is an Assistant Professor at Symbiosis Law School, Nagpur, specializing in Cyber Laws, Intellectual Property Laws, Artificial Intelligence, and allied fields. A two-time recipient of the Justice Krishna Iyer Memorial Merit Award (2019, 2022), he has also been honoured with the Adv. P.F. Thomas Memorial Gold Medal (2019) and the Dr. K.N. Chandrashekharan Pillai Gold Medal (2022) for his academic excellence. With over sixty research publications to his credit across diverse areas of law, he has established himself as a prolific scholar. He qualified UGC NET with JRF (Law) and is presently pursuing his PhD at VIT School of Law, Vellore Institute of Technology, Chennai, India. Prof. Karun also contributes to the global research community as part of the review team for Scopus-indexed journals, underscoring his commitment to advancing legal scholarship.

Chiv Sarith is currently the Vice-Rector at National Meanchey University, Cambodia.

Ahmad G. Al-Shtayyat is a faculty member in the College of Arts and Sciences at the University of Petra. I have extensive experience in e-learning, LMS administration, and IT education. Since 2014, I have been working as an LMS administrator specializing in Moodle, where I provide training, system customization, and user support. Previously, I worked as a lab supervisor in the Faculty of Information Technology at the University of Petra for eight years. My expertise includes programming, web development, and e-learning system management. I hold a Master's in Business Administration (E-Business) from Mut'ah University and a B.Sc. in Computer Information Systems from the Arab Academy for Banking and Financial Sciences.

ChendaSoeurn heads the Department of Tourism, the Faculty of Business Administration and Tourism, and the National University of Battambang (NUBB), a public university in northwestern Cambodia. She has been with NUBB since 2021 and took on her current role in 2022. In 2016, Soeurn Chenda graduated with a bachelor's degree in English Literature from the Institution of Foreign Languages at the National University of Battambang, Cambodia. In 2017, she earned a Teacher of Higher Education Degree from the National Institute of Education (NIE), in Phnom Penh, Cambodia. She worked as a Teacher of Higher Education Degree at Koas Kror High School for over three years (1-10-2017-2-08-2021) before moving to NUBB. in 2019, he held two master's degrees: an MA in TESOL and an M.Ed. Education Specialization in English. In 2021, she earned both Master's degrees: A master's degree in TESOL from NUBB, Cambodia, and a Master's Degree in Education, specializing in English from the University of Bengkulu, Indonesia. Currently, she is the head of the Department of Tourism responsible for the Tourism and Marketing major, and she also involves NUBB project.

Morin Tieng is the vice-rector at the National University of Battambang (Cambodia), where he oversees units such as the Faculty of Business Administration and Tourism, Social & Rural Development, the Document Center, and Student Affairs. His research focuses on higher education, institutional integration, academic development, and policy challenges in Cambodia. He has co-authored studies on topics including institutional integration and student development, intellectual property challenges in Southeast Asia, English-speaking anxiety in Cambodian higher education, and research productivity in universities.

Mohit Yadav is an Professor in the area of Human Resource Management at Jindal Global Business School (JGBS). He has a rich blend of work experience from both Academics as well as Industry. Prof. Mohit holds a Ph.D. from Department of Management Studies, Indian Institute of Technology Roorkee (IIT Roorkee) and has completed Master of Human Resource and Organizational Development (MHROD) from prestigious Delhi School of Economics, University of Delhi. He also holds a B.Com (Hons.) degree from University of Delhi and UGC-JRF scholarship. He has published various research papers and book chapters with reputed publishers like Springer, Sage, Emerald, Elsevier, Inderscience etc. and presented research papers in national and International conferences both in India and abroad. He has many best paper awards on his credit too. He is reviewer of various international journals like Computers in Human Behavior, Policing etc. His areas of interest are Organizational Behavior, HRM, Recruitment and Selection, Organizational Citizenship Behavior, Quality of work life and role.

Swatee Yogessh is a passionate teacher with over 20 years of experience in teaching and academic administration, and a certified mediator and certified Instructional Designer. She is an alumna and currently a faculty member at ILS Law College, Pune. She is founder president of Pune Inclusive Education Society, (PIES). She is also a Member of Board of Advisors for LHSS Collective, MNLU Mumbai and Expert invitee for developing interdisciplinary curriculum for The Center for Multidisciplinary Curriculum and Pedagogy at Maharashtra State Faculty Development Academy, MSFDA She holds a doctorate in International Corporate Crimes. Her areas of interest are Jurisprudence, Interpretation of Statutes, Constitutional Law in action i.e. Administrative Law, International Law and Legal Education. She has joined her alma mater after serving in various institutions (MNLU Mumbai, School of Law, Christ University, Bangalore, Balaji Law College and Symbiosis Law School, Pune). She has served in various capacities like Head of Department, Principal- In Charge, and Vice Principal. She has been Awarded 'Erasmus Mundus' Scholarship Of European Commission As A Visiting Scholar To Leibniz University, Hannover Germany in 2009-10. She has been awarded a Certificate Of Appreciation For "Value Consciousness And Constructive Leadership" For Academic year 2010-11, by Symbiosis Law School, Pune. She has delivered guest lectures for students, and conducted faculty training programs in various institutions such as Yashwantrao Chavan Academy Of Development Administration (YASHADA); Christ University School of Law, Lavasa; Shankarrao Chavan Law College, Pune; Leibniz University Hannover, Germany; University of Le Havre, France. She has delivered training in law to around 1000 government officers of various departments such as Maharashtra Town Planning Dept, Maharashtra Land Revenue Dept., Central Pollution Control Board of India, IAS officers LBSNAA

Musoorie to name a few. She has authored two e-books titled - 'Concept of Domicile in Private International Law' and 'Legal Aspects of Intellectual Disabilities in Primary Education in India'. She has published research papers in various national and international journals, more than ten Reading Materials for Law Schools and Government Institutions, and has participated in various conferences, seminars and colloquiums in India and abroad.

Index

A

C

D

E

F

G

R

S

T

www.ingramcontent.com/pod-product-compliance
Lightning Source LLC
LaVergne TN
LVHW062322300926
849161LV00007B/1538